# Economic Transition in Central and Eastern Europe

## Planting the Seeds

Analysing the key problems facing the transition countries in Central and Eastern Europe, this accessible book describes the legacy of the central planners, the progress achieved so far and the need for further reforms. It documents the outstanding successes and failures, and analyses why certain approaches to transition have worked and others have not. It tests where transition is over and shows how some countries have graduated from 'transition' to 'integration' through their efforts to join the European Union (EU). It discusses the costs and benefits of the eastern enlargement of the EU. The specific experiences of German unification, the Soviet Union's disintegration and Russia's complex reforms are examined, as are the specific issues that need to be addressed in the Balkans. The book concludes by indicating how the expanding EU could help the poor performers through inclusion in a continent-wide integrated economic area.

DANIEL GROS is the Director of the Centre for European Policy Studies, Brussels, and is presently a member of the advisory council of the French Prime Minister and Finance Minister. His major publications include *Open Issues in European Central Banking* (2000), *EMU and Capital Markets* (2000), *European Monetary Integration, from the EMS to EMU* (1992, 1998) and *Winds of Change: Economic Transition in Central and Eastern Europe* (1995), which he co-authored.

PROFESSOR ALFRED STEINHERR is Chief Economist at the European Investment Bank. His previous positions include Rector at the Free University of Bolzano, Italy, Head of Research at the European Investment Bank, a professorship at the Catholic University of Lauvain, Economic Adviser to the European Commission and Adviser to the International Monetary Fund. He is author of *Derivatives: The Wild Beast of Finance* (2000) and is co-author of *Winds of Change: Economic Transition in Central and Eastern Europe* (1995).

# Economic Transition in Central and Eastern Europe

## Planting the Seeds

DANIEL GROS AND ALFRED STEINHERR

CAMBRIDGE
UNIVERSITY PRESS

PUBLISHED BY THE PRESS SYNDICATE OF THE UNIVERSITY OF CAMBRIDGE
The Pitt Building, Trumpington Street, Cambridge, United Kingdom

CAMBRIDGE UNIVERSITY PRESS
The Edinburgh Building, Cambridge, CB2 2RU, UK
40 West 20th Street, New York, NY 10011–4211, USA
477 Williamstown Road, Port Melbourne, VIC 3207, Australia
Ruiz de Alarcón 13, 28014 Madrid, Spain
Dock House, The Waterfront, Cape Town 8001, South Africa

http://www.cambridge.org

First published 2004
Reprinted 2005, 2006

Printed in the United Kingdom at the University Press, Cambridge

*Typeface* Times NR MT 10/13 pt.     *System* LATEX 2$_\varepsilon$   [TB]

*A catalogue record for this book is available from the British Library*

*Library of Congress cataloguing in publication data*
Gros, Daniel, 1955–
Economic transition in Central and Eastern Europe : planting the seeds / by Daniel Gros
and Alfred Steinherr. – 2nd, updated ed.
    p.    cm.
Updated ed. of: The first ten years of transition. Cambridge, Mass. : MIT Press, 2001.
Includes bibliographical references and index.
ISBN 0 521 82638 1 – ISBN 0 521 53379 1 (pbk.)
1. Europe, Eastern – Econimic policy – 1989–   2. Europe, Central – Economic policy.
3. Free enterprise – Europe, Eastern.   4. Free enterprise – Europe, Central.
5. Post-communism – Europe, Eastern.   6. Post-communism – Europe, Central.
I. Steinherr, Alfred.   II. Title.
HC244.G689   2003   338.947 – dc21   2003048471

ISBN 0 521 82638 1 hardback
ISBN 0 521 53379 1 paperback

To the memory of my father: in his life (1900–1994) he witnessed both the rise and the fall of communism in Europe.

Daniel Gros

For my parents, who lost their youth in the darkest chapter of European history, but have lived to see the prospect of a new Europe.

Alfred Steinherr

# Contents

# Figures

# Boxes

# Tables

# Acknowledgements

This revised version of our work on transition to market economies in Central and Eastern Europe has taken a long time to complete. We cannot do justice here to all those who have helped us in so many ways to complete this project. But we would like to acknowledge our gratitude to those most closely involved: Armin Riess from the European Investment Bank, who took the time to read the draft and comment extensively and constructively on it, Alexandr Hobza, Kadri Kuusk and Kalina Manova, for research assistance so necessary to complete this manuscript, and Maureen Thibaut and Irene Poli, for cleaning the draft.

# Introduction

In 1995 we published *Winds of Change* to treat the key question for transition countries: 'How to reform?' In the meantime we can look back on more than ten years of transition experience. No country was able to jump-start its economy on market-based principles and converge rapidly. In all transition countries production fell after opening up. In some countries this fall was short-lived, but in most it lasted several years. In some the level of production is, twelve years after opening up, still below the level of 1989. There is no simple explanation of the diversity in transition performance, but starting conditions did play a central role.

Today, therefore, the question is no longer 'How to design reforms?' Rather, it is 'Why have certain approaches worked and others not?' This will be a major theme of this book. By implication, in many countries a lot still needs to be done. This is another major theme.

In this book we resist the temptation to produce a complete record of transition experience. We rather select the most significant experiences that may become, over time, classical reference cases. Of course, the overall experience in all transition countries will be presented, but it will not be pursued in depth for each country.

The outline of the book is as follows. In part I we start with a bit of history, an overview of communist experience. Part II summarises the transition process in formerly socialist countries, tests whether or where transition is over and what remains to be done in the lagging transition countries. Part III turns to specific experiences: German unification, the Soviet Union's disintegration, and Russia's complex reforms. Part IV focuses on the institutional architecture of the European Union's eastern endorsement and the specific issues to be addressed for reforms in the Balkan states. The last chapter attempts to assess future possible paths.

## The rise and decline of communism

Although we are told that many students in the United States are not interested in learning why communism failed, because, in fact, they have never heard of communism, we still think this is an important question, to which part I is devoted.

Today, communism appears to many as a historic stupidity and, without a shadow of a doubt, capitalism has victoriously emerged as the dominant paradigm. However, such a view is too short-sighted and conditioned by the recent demise of communism. It neglects at least two points. First, the realisation of any theory always differs from the theoretic model, which, at any rate, captures only part of societal organisation. History and the distribution of social and political values interfere with the economic model. For example, only under very restrictive assumptions could it be claimed that, say, colonial capitalism was superior to Soviet communism. Second, because the working class suffered from unbearable misery during the take-off phase of the now successfully developed capitalist countries – a misery still prevalent throughout the developing world – the Marxist vision gave hope to large fractions of society of both developed and developing countries, a hope that capitalism was unable to provide. And, despite the current universal popularity of capitalism, we can be sure that the capitalist paradigm will again be challenged at some point in the future.

There were times (before the Second World War and during the Cold War) when the West did not feel totally assured about its superior economic and military force and when a communist brush fire in poor parts of the world was feared. Western Europe, for geographic reasons, was concerned about Soviet aggression and its democracy felt internally weakened by Moscow-supported communist parties.

The Soviet view of communism was the prescribed model everywhere in the Soviet bloc. The need for incentives was, however, sometimes recognised and temporary concessions were granted; for example, in Catholic Poland, where farming largely remained in private hands and dissidents met with more tolerance than in other East European countries. Hungary, too, was allowed, after its abortive revolution in 1956, to embark on a more relaxed economic policy, which included incentives for workers and greater powers for middle management in agriculture and industry. But when Czechoslovakia seemed to be heading towards the dismantling of single-party rule in 1968 and to be espousing other 'bourgeois democratic' heresies, Soviet and Warsaw Pact troops marched in and restored communist order.

In all countries where communist parties took over government, single-party 'democracy' with dictatorship by the proletariat was the final outcome. But even in Western countries with strong democratic traditions and mature economies, Moscow-sponsored communist parties played a role, although their influence has waned of late. Figure I.1 summarises the situation in Western Europe in the 1970s at the height of that influence. At that time there were about 60 million communist party members in some ninety countries across the globe. While the party was not allowed in all countries in the West, it nevertheless achieved a membership of 3 million and more. The largest Western communist parties were those in Italy (1.8 million) and France (0.6 million).

The main issue addressed in Part I is whether communism failed because it was based on a model, in some sense inappropriate, or whether the particular Soviet incarnation was at fault. We shall argue that the model serves not too badly in special circumstances, such as the economic take-off in the terminology of Rostow (1960), but fails hopelessly in a mature economy. Moreover, the Soviet brand of communism suffers from the weight of Russian history and particularities that would have dragged down any approach – as witnessed by the current difficulties in reforming the Russian economy and introducing capitalism.

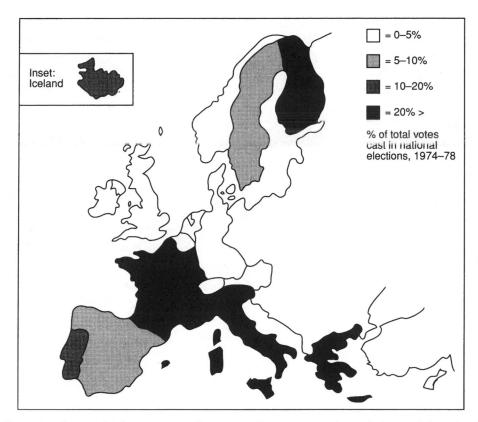

**Figure I.1** Communists in non-communist Europe: Western communist parties' strength in national elections, 1974–8
Note: *The lowest number of seats held by communists in national parliaments, 1974–8 was 0 (UK, Ireland, West Germany, Austria, Norway, Denmark). The highest, with 228 out of 630, was Italy.*

Chapter 1 elaborates those features of communist rule which were inherited from tsarist Russia: the centralisation of power and the need for ideology, the key role of the military and the imperial aspirations, the emphasis on heavy industry and the neglect of agriculture, and so on. In fact, according to Marxist theory, the socialist revolution should not even have occurred in Russia but instead in a more developed country such as Germany. The very start therefore contradicted theory, as did much in the later evolution. Chapter 1 shows, moreover, that the new regime was not equipped with a blueprint for running a communist society and instead had to proceed by trial and error, up to the very end.

What, then, was the basic equipment of the new regime? Marx provided both a critique of capitalism and a vision of a communist future in the 'long run', but not much for the interim period.

Marx taught the ultimate and inevitable collapse of the capitalist order and its replacement by a classless, communist one. Under communism, the state itself would be abolished and society would be governed by the principle 'from each according to his ability, to each according to his needs'. But there would be a transitional stage – Marx called it socialism[1] – that would be ruled by the principle 'from each according to his ability, to each according to his work'. Under socialism, the victorious workers, the proletariat, would exercise a form of dictatorship to ensure that socialism could be applied without obstruction from whatever 'capitalist attitudes' society might not yet have succeeded in getting rid of.

Marx had little concrete to say on how this proletarian revolution would come about. That job was left to Lenin – who is the major architect of pre-Stalinist communism (Marxist–Leninist) – and others.

One big controversy throughout most of the seventy years of communist rule in the Soviet Union centred on the 'party of the new type' that Lenin helped to build up. Lenin argued for the creation of a centralised, tightly disciplined revolutionary party. This was criticised by his rival in the Russian revolutionary movement, Leon Trotsky (1861–1940), until he eventually aligned himself with Lenin's ideas.

The Revolution of October 1917 was a watershed. All across Europe, during the late nineteenth century, reformists had been grouping themselves into a body whose direct descendant was the Socialist International. The revolutionaries joined the Communist International (Comintern), which Lenin had set up in Moscow in 1919. Lenin's principle of 'democratic centralism' – or compulsory adherence to central party policy – became the model for communist parties everywhere else. So did the one-party Soviet state established by Lenin and Trotsky and completed by Stalin. The key features of that state were:

- total control of the state by the ruling party, with complete power of political initiative and decisionmaking reserved for the inner leadership and ultimately the party leader alone;
- the absence of any real legal limitation on state power (despite a constitutional façade) with the state identified with the party;
- monopoly party control over all forms of social organisation;
- monopoly party control over all channels of communication, with the right to impose censorship and to mould public opinion.

One lesson of the Stalinistic period is that communism was able to rally forces not only against external threats but also to achieve internal targets (industrialisation), as long as belief in the system was sustained and as long as the target was a simple one (e.g. to double steel output). But this approach was doomed to fail over time. As the system did not allow a shift in supply to satisfy pent-up demands by citizens, support waned. And, equally important, whilst the command system can cope with standard industrial production (steel), it simply cannot evolve into a more modern economy serving complex consumer demands. This inherent contradiction on its own would be enough to explain the incapacity of fundamental reforms unsuccessfully attempted by all successors of Stalin up to and including Gorbachev. But there are also other barriers to reform. The most important is the difficulty of reconciling monoparty communist leadership with a more decentralised incentive and information system.

After this *tour d'horizon* of the history of the Soviet Union from an economic point of view in chapter 1, chapter 2 discusses two permanent policy priorities not dictated by socialism in itself which, perhaps curiously, turned out to be fatal in the end: the goal of autarkic development and the goal of catching up with the West. The first policy choice was dictated by political concerns (a strategy abandoned by China in 1978) and the second by the conviction that socialism could survive and dominate the world only if it could win the Darwinian race in terms of material production. Because it became clear in the 1980s that it had lost the race, a reverse that communists themselves singled out to be decisive,[2] Soviet communism disappeared – but left the sad inheritance of a highly polluted racetrack scattered with industrial junk, and with people so abused that the contest will not be forgotten for a long time. Was it the model? Was it the Soviet incarnation? Certainly, both joined hands to produce disaster. China proves that communism paired with economic reforms and foreign trade can perform remarkably well. But it does not prove that communism can and will survive.

## Transition: 1990–2000

When we wrote *Winds of Change*, between 1990 and 1995, the much debated questions concerning transition were what kind of policy and institutional choices were optimal and whether they should be implemented in a gradual way (and, if so, what should come first and what later), or all-at-once (that is, a 'big-bang' approach). After the triumph of capitalism over its main ideological opponent, communism, there was little doubt or debate about the final goals of transition. Only a fool would have questioned the merits of a capitalistic, market-based society.

In assessing the choices, economists took their inspiration from theory and concrete experiences in Western European post-war reconstruction, China's reforms after 1978, the emergence of Asian tigers, the instability problems in South America and many localised events. Of course, now, ten years later, the question is no longer how one should go about transition, but instead what has worked and why.

In chapter 3 we go over the key elements of a reform programme, as laid out, for example, in chapters 4–9 of *Winds of Change*. In the early 1990s most economists were fairly optimistic about the rapid reforms of transition economies. Taking these views as a benchmark, we can only be disappointed ten years later. Nobody would have expected that successor states of the former Soviet Union (FSU) would within a decade have an official GDP some 50 per cent of its 1989 level, with very unequal distributions of income and a rule of crime. Clearly, the reforms in these countries were not carried out as planned. But the real question is: Why?

Chapter 4 gives the answers. Some countries, in line with some academic recommendations, opted for a gradual reform process. At times gradual meant only very limited reforms. Hindsight confirmed our initial strong support for a 'big-bang' approach. Unsuccessful transformation is always the result of limited, partial reforms in the political, administrative and economic domains. Lack of democratic institutions, problems with law and order, corrupt and inefficient bureaucracies and poor economic performance all go together.

We then examine the question whether or where transition is over. It is not sufficient to look at economic performance because transition means moving from a socialist to a market-based economy; catching up with mature Western economies is a problem of economic development that takes a bit longer. We conclude that in Central Europe and the Baltic states the vestiges of socialist economies have been largely shed. In South-East Europe success has been only partial, and in the FSU even more efforts are required.

In chapter 5 we address some of the issues to be tackled to advance transformation in the laggardly transition countries. The major job consists in institution building. We analyse the need for more political reforms and for establishing a more reliable and efficient public administration. We show the possibility of two equilibria, a good one and a bad one, mainly depending on initial conditions. This analysis suggests that once a bad equilibrium is established, characterised by a high level of corruption and crime, it becomes very difficult to move to the good equilibrium. Even in the West we know these difficulties: once a mafia is powerfully established and connected, it is almost impossible to eliminate. Many weak reformers have experienced difficulties in maintaining a social safety net, in creating a monetised economy with financial intermediaries collecting the savings and financing enterprises. The result has been losses to the economic victims of transition (the retired and the unemployed), and therefore waning support for reforms, and a lack of normal finance for commerce and investment. Substitute mechanisms with low efficiency and little scope for improving the economic situation, such as barter trade and inter-enterprise credits, have developed. We discuss means to deal with such problems on the way to the establishment of a properly functioning financial market.

## Extreme cases for reform: scope for disagreements

Part III deals with the disappointments. With immediate EU membership and massive institutional and financial support, East Germany was thought to be a sure winner. Chapter 6 shows why it turned into a curse. Chapter 7 analyses the splitting up of the Soviet Union and chapter 8 the difficulties in reforming Russia. Much of what applies to Russia is also valid for the other successor states of the FSU.

East Germany is clearly apart from the rest because it has ceased to be an independent country, receives full financial and institutional support from former West Germany and has become a member of the European Community. This was expected to make the reconstruction of East Germany much easier and faster than that of neighbouring eastern countries. Yet, quite to the contrary, industrial production in East Germany has fallen more than in the Czech and Slovak Federal Republics, Hungary and Poland. What is the reason for this reversal of initial expectations? Is currency union the culprit? Or was wage convergence to the West German level unavoidable under any scenario and the main factor of the collapse of East German industry? Or could it be that, whilst collapse was more pronounced there than elsewhere, it is only a matter of speed of adjustment (massive Schumpeterian creative destruction, high speed of building up a market economy)?

Currency union spared East Germany from macroeconomic destabilisation and the need for a stabilisation policy. East Germany does not have macroeconomic problems, only microeconomic ones: how to attract private investors and generate jobs with unit labour costs above the US level.

Events since 1989 have shown that the reforms have been less successful the further one goes east. While the Central European countries have put the first phase of reforms behind them, most countries in the FSU still have to undertake some of the basic reform steps. The main reason for this difference in behaviour is that the Central Europeans had 'only' to return to Europe. And their populations and politicians decided that they would do whatever was required to achieve this goal. The newly independent states in the FSU area are in a different situation for obvious historical reasons. Each of these states would merit a separate analysis, but we concentrate on the most important one, namely Russia. Developments in Russia will affect all of Europe, for better or for worse, whereas the developments in other successor states of the FSU matter only to the extent that they provoke a reaction by Russia. Our focus on Russia is also justified by the fact that the problems in all successor states of the FSU are similar.

In relating events after the fall of the Soviet Union, we therefore concentrate on two aspects: the economic consequences of rapid disintegration and the lost decade for reforms in Russia.

The first basic fact of the FSU is its sudden disintegration, despite very intensive internal trade links. We do not pretend to offer any insights into why the political elites in most former Soviet republics (including Russia) suddenly chose to go for independence. The main factor behind this political development was certainly a reawakening of national feelings. On top of that came the unwillingness of the Union government under Gorbachev to consider radical economic reforms. We leave these political factors aside and concentrate on the economic aspects of the disintegration of this huge unified economic area that took place in 1991–2.

It is difficult to analyse the disintegration of the FSU dispassionately because opinions, inside and outside the FSU, about this issue tend to one of two extremes. One school of thought (prevalent among the radical reformers in Russia and some of their Western advisers) maintained that the economic links between the former Soviet republics were artificially created by central planners. The newly independent states should have introduced national currencies immediately in 1992 and terminated all preferential trade arrangements among themselves. The opposite extreme (prevalent among Western official institutions until the end of 1992) argued that the former Soviet republics were so tightly integrated that they should have stayed together in the economic sphere even after they became politically independent.

The analysis of this chapter suggests that both extremes were wrong and that serious policy mistakes were made during the transition. If the transition had been managed carefully, taking into account both the trade structures inherited and their likely future evolution, the economic costs of the collapse of the FSU could have been mitigated. The virtual breakdown of intra-CIS (Commonwealth of Independent States) trade could have been avoided, and even Russia's output decline could have been less severe.

We first show that, once reforms had started, it did not make sense to keep the former Soviet republics together in an economic and monetary union, as was often suggested in 1991–2. But we also do not agree that the FSU really had, during its last years of existence, 'the worst monetary constitution one can imagine'. In a similar vein, we also argue that the strange rouble zone that survived until late 1993 cannot be considered a cause of inflation in Russia and elsewhere, as has often been argued.

We argue that the transition to separate currencies should have been managed more carefully, with the aid of a multilateral clearing system. A treaty to that effect was actually signed, ratified and . . . never implemented. A missed opportunity!

While the disintegration of the FSU is a fait accompli and irreversible, despite the periodic attempts by some Russian policymakers to resurrect some imperial system through bilateral agreement, or through the CIS, the fate of reforms in Russia has not been totally decided yet. The experience of reforms in Russia is a sobering tale.

We do not pretend to give a complete picture of Russian reforms. This would be impossible, not only because the situation continues to change rapidly, but also (and mainly) because in Russia few things are really as they appear at first sight. For the first years of reform we concentrate on three specific issues that came up during the crucial initial reform efforts in 1992–3 to illustrate this general point. The three issues more closely examined are price liberalisation, trade liberalisation and the link between fiscal policy and macroeconomic stabilisation.

We argue that price liberalisation was unavoidable, but the most important part of it, namely the liberalisation of energy prices, never happened. Trade policy, the showpiece of the reformers, because of the liberalisation of imports, was a disaster area. Initially there were huge import subsidies and, all throughout the initial reform period, large export restrictions. This combination was deadly for Russian trade, which shrank, instead of expanding by 50 per cent as in the Central European countries. Inflation, which was brought partly under control only after two years, was probably due to a large fiscal deficit, but this cannot be proven because the official numbers are close to meaningless. Our analysis shows that the Russian government could have used the substantial foreign aid it received to stabilise the economy if it had conducted a completely different foreign trade policy. However, given the disastrous trade policy followed by Russia, most of the aid that was actually delivered in 1992–3 reduced welfare in Russia. Stabilisation could also have been achieved with a different kind of foreign assistance. Both sides thus contributed to this failure. But the major responsibility remains with Russia: the inability to generate a wide majority in favour of strong institutions that are the *sine qua non* of a well-functioning market economy.

We then analyse privatisation – arguably the most disastrous decision with long-lasting consequences – and the financial crash of 1998. We also answer the question 'Who lost Russia?' Where did the billions of dollars go?

The general lesson we draw from all this is that, in the case of Russia, most things are different from what they appear to be at first sight and a number of widespread preconceptions do not stand up to closer analysis. This also applies to the privatisation process. On paper, close to 100 per cent of Russian industry outside the military–industrial complex has been privatised. However, the behaviour of management has not changed noticeably for most enterprises. We suspect that this will continue to be the case and that the large swings in policy which are reported periodically in the Western press do not correspond to reality. Over the first few years there has been only very limited, but nevertheless tangible, progress towards a market economy. One should not expect much more from Russia, but also not much less.

## The new Europe from the Atlantic to the Urals

The map of Europe is in the process of being redesigned. In this book we make ample use of gravitational models and, once again, gravity suggests that the Western part of the former communist bloc fits better into the EU.

The EU has already engaged in a process of enlargement, although few people are at ease in assessing the wisdom, the costs and the benefits of enlargement to actual, or future, members of the EU. Chapter 9 deals with these questions. It also raises the issue of the optimal size of the EU and shows that the optimal size depends on the institutions in place and the goals adopted. The importance of goals is obvious: if the goal were simply free trade, the optimum size would be the world. If the goal were direct democracy for every decision, then a household may be the optimal size. This example also illustrates the critical roles of institutions.

Decisionmaking by majority increases the optimal size, as compared to unanimity rules. For these reasons we consider the EU reforms more crucial for successful enlargement than the convergence of applicant countries.

We also look at the costs and benefits of enlargement and find that the costs have been exaggerated.

Europe's catalytic role is not and should not be limited to future members of the EU. The EU must also be a partner of the FSU countries and must help those Eastern European countries not joining the EU (in the near future). These are the Balkan countries.

The EU already provides financial assistance for the Balkans. Chapter 10 argues that, as these countries are small and suffer from weak institutions, they should 'import' strong institutions. Some have already given up their monetary sovereignty by adopting currency boards or by operating on a euro basis. The whole of the Balkans could, and should, become a euro zone. They should also opt for free tade with the EU and any country of the EU free trade zone. They would then have free trade with each other, using the same currency and an optimal basis for creating more efficient and clearer public institutions, the necessary starting point for sustained growth.

In the concluding chapter 11 we assess the chances for future convergence and see three different destinies: Central Europe will soon be part of the European Union and its future is safe; the Balkan countries have much more reform work to do and will become members of the European Union in a second wave; the successor states of the Soviet Union have much more difficult starting conditions, are not favoured by history or geography, do not benefit from an obvious geopolitical future and could as easily end up in heaven as in hell.

## Notes

1. In this book we use the terms 'socialism' and 'communism' interchangeably, as has become the custom.
2. In fact, they fell victim to Marx's theory that for a *capitalist* society 'to accumulate is to conquer the world of social wealth . . .' (Marx 1933: 649).

# Part I

# The rise and decline of communism: an overview

'Every year humanity takes a step towards Communism. Maybe not you, but at all events your grandson will surely be a Communist.'

(N.S. Khrushchev, 1956)

# 1 From pre-war Russia to the fall of communism

***K. Marx:*** *'Sorry, guys! Gee, it was just one of my ideas . . .'*

Ever since the socialist takeover in Russia a debate has been raging about the profundity of the changes imposed on Russian society.[1] However, looking back on Russia's history since Peter the Great, we find that many features of Russian pre-revolutionary society survived, and indeed were sometimes reinforced, after the Revolution. The Soviet Union remained an empire with its border problems and nationality conflicts, and continued to police its population severely. Democracy was as absent and repression as regular after as before the Revolution. State organisation remained highly centralised and the problems of the periphery were, as always, ignored, misunderstood or repressed. Within the imperial borders the conflict between town and country was as acute in the 1930s as in the seventeenth century. The leadership remained divided between imperial expansion eastwards or westwards, and between opening up to or closing off foreign, mostly Western, influences. The empire invariably rooted its strength in strong ideological grounds: in pre-revolutionary days in absolute monarchy and religion and afterwards in the Marxist framework. Both regimes, each claiming to pursue a superior mission, had expansionary goals for which a strong and influential military was necessary. The need to equip the military, more than the desirability of improving the welfare of citizens, was in each case the driving force behind industrialisation.

A demonstration of these continuities scales down the historic importance of the communist revolt. Many features of developments in the Soviet Union that could be regarded as resulting from communist rule may well have emerged under a completely different regime. However, while we should not ignore these historic continuities, neither should we fatalistically assert that the communist regime was already dormant in the genes of Russian history.

To clarify these points we recall the salient features of Russian history in section 1 before outlining the socialist takeover in section 2. The new economic policy (NEP), which ended the search for a workable model of socialist economic management and then gave way to the Stalinist command economy, is discussed in section 3.

The end of the NEP was a turning point. From the First Five-Year Plan on, a system developed which the world has identified with the communist model: totalitarian in its political structure, and with a command economy as the economic complement. The Stalinist reorientation is discussed in section 4. When the regime was at its zenith, its totalitarian perfection basked in the flush of victory over the Nazi aggressor and served as a general model for export. However, towards the end of the Stalinist era, the country was left saddled with enormous unresolved problems arising from changes in the system to accommodate greater participation in decisionmaking, from the fading of the 'Stalingrad effect' of an invincible world power and, above all, from the need to reform the economy, in spite of a growth record never achieved before or since.

Section 5 then analyses the unsuccessful attempts by Khrushchev to push through these badly needed reforms. His failure to deliver precipitated a loss of credibility for the USSR as a world power, and reactionary forces rallied round Brezhnev to organise restoration (section 6).

Stationary conditions under Brezhnev bottled up what became an explosively pressing need for reform in all spheres of Soviet social, political and economic life. When Gorbachev lifted the lid off these repressed needs he was soon engulfed by a tidal wave of demands for reform. Section 7 demonstrates that partial reforms soon proved inadequate in light of the accumulated delays in dealing with complex and interdependent issues of economic reform, individual freedom and repressed nationalism. Section 8 then claims that the failure of Soviet-type communism was endogenous and had little to do with the men actually in charge. But it had a lot to do with the ingredients inherited from Russian history that contributed decisively to the Soviet realisation of communism.

## 1.1  Key features of Russian history up to the Socialist Revolution

Russia has always been something of an unknown quantity in Europe's western reaches. It has been considered as retarded and brutish, but also at times as a powerful and awe-inspiring foe. History and space produced a number of remarkable constraints for Russia, which survived even seventy-odd years of communist rule. This brief historical synopsis highlights some of these constraints.

A good starting point is Peter the Great, the founder of the pre-revolutionary Russian state, who brought the Middle Ages to a close during his reign from 1689 to 1725. It was he who provided the first impetus towards industrial revolution in Russia, chiefly in order to create a powerful navy and army.

In 1697 Peter set up the first foundry and cannon factory in the Urals with the aim of breaking his dependence on supplies from Sweden. At the time of his death there were twelve metallurgical factories in the Urals and the Russian metalworking industry had become the largest in Europe. Half of these factories belonged to the state, the other half to the ennobled bourgeoisie and the old aristocracy. A more efficient tax administration was set up to help finance his ventures; a head tax was implemented and domestic textile and steel production were heavily protected.

Peter's unsurpassed achievement (or act of folly) was, of course, the foundation of the new capital, St Petersburg. Construction commenced in 1703, draining resources in a way for which the poorly developed Russian economy was ill-prepared. He brought in large numbers of European experts (architects, engineers, scientists, officers and administrators) to westernise Russia. This demanded such a gigantic effort that the country was still reeling under its effects when Catherine the Great came to power in 1762.

Peter the Great had imperial ambitions that strangely resembled those of the Soviet Union 250 years later. He fought a long drawn-out war with Sweden for more than twenty years in a bid to extend his influence over the Baltics. By securing access to the Baltic Sea and the Black Sea, Peter the Great helped to elevate Russia to the position of first continental European power. He failed, however, in his quest to modernise Russia sufficiently to set it on a sustainable path of modernisation and growth – as did the communists.

A second attempt at modernisation was made by Catherine the Great. In 1766 she set up a commission to prepare a code fixing the rights and obligations of the nobility and of ordinary citizens. The result was hailed as the most liberal work of eighteenth-century Russia and was applauded by Diderot and Voltaire alike. Catherine herself had contributed personal writings inspired by Montesquieu and Beccaria. However, the project was put on ice and then finally discarded. After failing to implement changes, and after facing open rebellion, she turned much more traditionalist and set to completing Peter's work in embellishing St Petersburg and expanding the empire, aided and abetted by an endless inflow of foreign experts. Both Peter's and Catherine's achievements were made possible only by a massive transfer of know-how from Western Europe, a transfer that the communists could not and did not wish to perpetuate.

After the war of liberation against Napoleon, Alexander I focused Russia's energies during the first half of the nineteenth century on territorial expansion rather than economic reform. The perennial key questions for nineteenth-century Russian development were: (1) Are better incomes from agriculture needed to generate internal demand, or should agriculture be taxed more heavily to generate investable surplus? (Export-led growth was not retained as an alternative, given the large size of the country.) (2) Should serfs be freed for the benefit of more rapid development, or not? (This debate was raging at the same time in the United States.) (3) Should the state take the lead in industrial development by investing massively in infrastructure or should the aristocracy be induced to take the lead? Such questions were not fundamentally different from those debated in other countries at a comparable level of development. The real problem was that no consistent answers were forthcoming until the 1890s.

The economy stagnated during the first half of the nineteenth century and industrialisation did not take off until well into its second half, after Tsar Alexander II had set free the serfs in 1861. It then took another thirty years to generate a powerful spurt of industrialisation. The delay is hardly surprising, for even if the freeing of serfs had been expressly designed to set industrialisation in motion, the country simply lacked the administrative, legal and physical infrastructure for an industrial take-off. In particular, communications between the vast stretches of empire were poor and enormous capital resources were needed to build modern means of communication (railways) in what was the largest country on earth.

The underdeveloped domestic market was seen as one of the greatest inhibiting factors for growth. In the 1890s the state attempted to manage development in such a way that the growth of peasant demand for industrial goods would no longer be a prerequisite of successful industrialisation. On the contrary, the prevailing view finally was to curtail that demand in order to increase the share of national output available for investment. This also meant increased exports and better chances of larger and cheaper loans from abroad. It was a policy that was to be confirmed in the twentieth century under communist rule, with one regrettable difference: foreign trade and investment were kept at bay.

The Russian state put the peasantry under considerable fiscal pressure. In the closing years of the 1890s, Russian agriculture produced less bread grain per capita than had been the case three decades earlier. With a growing population and increased exports, domestic availabilities fell sharply. A central principle of governmental policy was to absorb a larger share of the peasants' output rather than to stimulate that output.

Industrialisation in Russia was also conspicuous for the sheer size of both individual plant and individual enterprise – indeed, this was also a prominent feature of later developments in the Soviet Union.[2]

The average annual rate of industrial growth during the 1890s was around 8 per cent, a remarkable success that compares favourably with the growth of other catching-up countries in Western Europe at that time. The very speed of the transformation, however, made for maladjustments of various kinds. The discrepancy between industry on the march and relatively stagnant agriculture was perhaps the most crucial of those tensions.

The years between the 1905 Revolution and the outbreak of the First World War were also a period of fairly rapid growth of industry in Russia (some 6 per cent per annum), even though the rate of change lagged behind that of the 1890s. During those years industrialisation could no longer be the primary concern of government. Wars and revolution had greatly strained budgetary capabilities. Railway building continued, but on a much reduced scale. Nothing underscores more clearly the government's change of mind than Stolypin's reforms in 1906 and 1910. The essence of the 1906 reform was that any peasant could demand a share of the village land, and by 1917 more than half of all peasant households held their land in hereditary tenure. However, a law of 1910 restricted the amount of land any one peasant could acquire by purchase.

Unfortunately, as observed by Voltaire in his *Histoire de l'Empire de Russie sous Pierre le Grand*, then, and again and again, in Russia *tout vient trop tard*. It was left to the regime that finally emerged from the 1917 Revolution, generated in the misery of war and the shame of defeat, to create a different set of conditions and to blend them with some of the old ingredients of Russian economic history into the strange and powerful infusion of Soviet industrialism.

What, then, were the constants of Russian history, preserved under communism? First of all, its relative separateness from the rest of the world, punctuated by occasional openings to accelerate development.[3] Second, a definite imperialist thrust to extend its power in Europe and Asia. This territorial expansion created a permanent conflict between the centre and the periphery and among the various nationalities subjugated by the Russians. The communist regime persuaded the world that the nationalities problem had been definitively solved and that a new species – *Homo Sovieticus* – had been invented. It was only when the empire disintegrated that the nationalities conflict came to the surface again and all its gory consequences with it.[4]

Third, there was never such a thing as democracy in this vast country, either before or after the Socialist Revolution. Central power was propped up before the Revolution by the Church and after it by communist ideology. The administration considerably tightened its grip on the country after the communist takeover but the centralised administration before and after the takeover failed to treat other nationalities on an equal basis and integrate them.

Fourth, specific sectoral misallocations were repeated over and over again. A permanent victim of development was agriculture, whose terms of trade were always unfavourable. The lack of investment in infrastructure also generally disfavoured the countryside more heavily and agricultural producers were always marginals, both before 1861 (the year of their liberation from serfdom) and after.

And last, but not least, there was the importance attached to the military and the vast resources poured into defence.

## 1.2   The Socialist Revolution in Russia

The Bolsheviks staged a classic coup d'état in 1917. Although revolutionary fervour spread from its St Petersburg base across the country, it was unable to prevent the empire from breaking up. Civil war ensued and the rest is history. The USSR was founded by the Treaty of 30 December 1922 signed by Russia, Belorussia, Ukraine and Transcaucasia. The principle of 'self-determination' was highly debated and allowed the Baltic states to gain independence. Lenin was squarely opposed to federalism but determined to save the old empire. That is why he accepted bilateral treaties between Russia and independent republics. The Constitution of 1924 was the consecration of the union of formally sovereign states with equal rights, at least on paper.

With hindsight, much Marxist thinking – the intellectual luggage of European revolutionaries at the turn of the century – appears faulty and half-baked, but in the early part of the twentieth century it was a formidable, sweeping piece of work; one that takes its place even to this day as one of humankind's most influential achievements.

A decisive shortcoming of the Marxist analysis is that it mainly provided a critique of capitalism without proposing a blueprint for a socialist society.[5] It was therefore a more useful instrument for an opposition party than for a party responsible for running a country. The new leaders' task was also complicated by the lack of empirical demonstrations. For want of guidance they turned to the history of developed countries, remembering that 'the industrially more developed country represents to the less developed country a picture of the latter's future' (Marx 1933: Preface).

How useful, then, was the Marxist toolkit to revolutionaries? Despite its shortcomings, it was undoubtedly of outstanding value for several reasons. To begin with, it provided a 'scientific' explanation of 'expropriation' and hence a moral justification for revolutionary activists and 'for expropriating the expropriators'. Second, it offered a theory of crisis that seemed germane to capitalism. Combating a system as imperfect as capitalism, beset by 'fundamental contradictions' and ultimately 'doomed to fail',[6] became a logical necessity, justified both morally and by reason of workers' class interests.

From today's vantage point Marx can be accused of having failed to understand the employment creation and income gains from technical progress and associated rising demand, but it must be borne in mind that many Western intellectuals championed socialist ideas as a humanely attractive alternative to the pallor of early capitalist development and that even today many still perceive technical progress as a threat to employment. Also the devastating European wars were attributed to economic interests not only by Marxists. For more than half a century communist ideology could 'warm the hearts with the fire of words' (Pushkin) in developed and developing countries alike, for the promise of a better and more peaceful world.

The Marxist prediction of the inevitable evolution of capitalism towards socialism did not materialise because the analysis was faulty. In fact what happened was that the less developed countries turned out to be far more (socialist) revolution prone than their rich capitalist counterparts. The main reason is indubitably that the process of accumulation benefited labour in a measure not anticipated by Marx. During the last fifty years and in virtually every country in the world, the share of labour in national income has not declined (see various World Bank *World Development Reports*) and incomes have been multiplying, so that labour has benefited from growth at least proportionately. In addition, employed labour has been able to accumulate wealth so that the distinction between the entrepreneur-capitalist and the worker only 'owning his arms' has become blurred.

During the first half of the twentieth century capitalism was quite dynamic and, particularly in the richest countries, it did not look as though it were about to expire (except during the Great Depression). Happily, Marxists came up with the theory of 'retarding factors'[7] (see Sweezy 1942 and Griffith and Gurley 1985). Some of these factors were seen to destroy even such virtues of capitalism as were associated with competitive capitalism, so that capitalism in its advanced form was destined to become dominated by monopolies and close association with the state and so to degenerate into imperialism. The working class therefore faced two enemies: the capitalists and their agents, the institutions of state.

Although the theory suggested the ultimate breakdown of capitalism without the proletariat having to strike a single revolutionary blow, the outlook was by no means certain in light of these retarding factors. Hence an active revolutionary endeavour was needed to stop prolonging the process. Ideally, on the basis of this analysis, the overthrow of capitalism should have started in England, France or Germany, not in retarded Russia. Why, then, did it happen in Russia?

A first clue is provided by the controversy between Kautsky and Lenin on the question of whether socialism can take the parliamentarian route. By shelving the revolutionary goals Kautsky accepted an initial opposition role for the Socialist Party in Germany. Ever since that day, the Socialist Party has been a major actor on the German political stage, fully accepting the rules of democratic society. Such a role was certainly not foreseen by Marx and it did not have the same potential in countries like Russia with a much less developed middle class and a much less numerous industrial proletariat.

We can therefore turn the Marxist prediction on its head: socialist revolutions are less likely in the most advanced capitalist economies than in the least developed countries, as the latter offer limited scope for democratic evolution. In 1987 35 per cent of the world population lived under communist rule. Most countries were poor in relation to Western Europe and the United States, both before and after communist power took over, so that the share of these countries in world output was less than 15 per cent (see Collins and Rodrik 1991).

Casual empiricism and the data in Kornai (1992) indeed suggest that all socialist revolutions occurred in poor countries, with the exception of Eastern Europe. There, however, socialism was not the result of an internal revolutionary process but was imposed by the Soviet Union. All non-imported socialist revolutions seem to have the following features in common. The countries are poor and have not yet embarked on industrialisation and income distribution is highly biased in favour of a small class of landowners. The political structure is non-democratic and the mass of the impoverished population is deprived of political rights. In some cases external or internal wars unsettle the existing order. As a result, an alternative is sought for a despised and exploitative political system. Socialist ideology provides a 'scientifically' argued critique, associates economic malfunctioning with the political system and offers the perspective of utopia. All the existing value systems can easily be put aside, as 'The ruling ideas of each age have ever been the ideas of its ruling class' (Marx and Engels 1930[1848]). No value system therefore has eternal validity and religion is an instrument of the existing dominant class and the 'opium of the people'.

All these characteristics of a disintegrating society were present in Russia. After the peace of Brest-Litovsk (3 March 1918) the Russian economy was shattered, its aristocracy, law and order discredited, and its empire's outskirts in open rebellion. Even patriotism had evaporated so that the Marxist idea of identification with one's class, as against one's country, came closer to reality. This was not the case in Western Europe, where patriotism was flying high in the victorious countries.[8] The only major country where the empire, the state and the ruling classes were thoroughly discredited was Russia. As in Germany, millions of unemployed, and discharged soldiers without a job, but with arms, crowded into the towns dissatisfied, restless and ready to overthrow what remained of the old regime after the revolution of February 1917. Even if Marx had never written a line, a social revolution would have been in the Russian air.

But as it happened, his analysis was there for the taking. It was not directly applicable as such, since the context was significantly different. The communist utopia of a classless society, without a command structure, without a state and everything in common ownership, simply could not be implemented straight away. Also, lacking widespread popular support, a structure was needed to spread the gospel, to extend and preserve power. This structure was to be provided by the Communist Party. Because the country's administration emerged from the war in tatters, the first important task for the party was to assert its power and to take a firm hold of the administrative reins.[9]

In addition to the traditional tasks of government, the communist regime immediately took control of the economy. Unfortunately, the party's economic management came on top of ever more extensive 'government of the people', which made the overall responsibility that much heavier. For those tasks the new regime had neither the blueprint nor the capital, the skills or general popular support. To gain control, the new regime resorted to unimaginable brutality. Between 1918 and 1922 several hundred thousand workers and peasants were massacred. In 1922 5 million country folk succumbed to a famine that resulted from forced and excessive taxation.

Immediately after the takeover, the communists organised nationalisation and production on an industry-by-industry basis. All firms within a given industrial sector were brought under the umbrella of a department of the Supreme Economic Council. As early as 1920, at the 8th Soviet Congress, enterprises rose in revolt against the excessive concentration of decisionmaking, foreshadowing the new economic policy and repeated reforms in later years under Khrushchev and Gorbachev.

The 1918–20 period was conditioned by the civil war which brought its own special problems. The way production was organised was dubbed 'war communism'. Lenin said in 1921: 'War communism was thrust upon us by war and ruin. It was not, nor could it be, a policy that corresponded to the economic tasks of the proletariat. It was a temporary measure' (quoted in Dobb 1939: 123). The main issue during the years of war communism was how to deal with agricultural production. With hyperinflation rife, peasants refused to deliver and government saw coercion as the only way out of the conundrum. The surplus produce of each peasant farm was subjected to requisitioning. The same was true in industry, but as industry had already been nationalised in the immediate aftermath of the takeover, requisitioning of industrial surplus production was formally less shocking.

From the start the new regime faced two formidable political challenges: to gain control inside the country and to fend off feared interventions from outside as the communist takeover of Russia met with strong internal opposition backed by foreign forces. Civil war broke out in 1918 and lasted until 1920.[10]

Lenin was aware of the difficulty for communism of surviving in a world surrounded by capitalist countries. That is why he attached great importance to social revolution in Germany. When these hopes were dashed in 1921, the theory of peaceful coexistence was developed to cope with the weakness of the Soviet military, to save time and to justify acceptance of support by capitalist countries.

The way in which the Communist Party organised itself and gained control in Russia was often repeated under very similar conditions elsewhere. In order not to get lost in details, it may be preferable to limit the discussion to stylised facts.

Political leadership and economic management is assumed by the Communist Party, which identified with the state. 'Democracy' is exerted through party elections at different levels: local, regional, central. Former political institutions are eliminated right away; the administration is reorganised and staffed with party cadres.

'Expropriation of the expropriators' begins at once. Part of the factories, banks, and other institutions are taken into state or collective ownership. Work starts immediately on centralising production and distribution. The most important of the measures of redistribution is to confiscate the estates of the landowners and divide them among the landless and the poor peasants.

Owing to the disruptive effects of post-war economic turmoil, one of the most immediate tasks is to ensure that food is distributed fairly. Rationing is introduced, so that basic foodstuffs at accessible prices become available to the poor as well. Black marketeers who try to sidestep the rationing system are prosecuted and socially disgraced. In fact, they often serve as scapegoats for economic difficulties. High prices or insufficient supplies are blamed on speculative activities which, to prove the point, are much more harshly punished than in capitalist societies.

No matter how serious the economic problems, a campaign of education covering the entire population is set into motion, free basic health care for all is promised, and holidays for children are organised to gain popular support.

Numerous attributes of the revolutionary period are understandable in the light of prior events and readily explained by them. No less understandable is the fact that this period can only be transitional, since many of the factors that sustain the system are temporary and since only in a few cases do revolutionary fervour and self-sacrifice last a lifetime. It becomes vital for society to encourage people to perform well by dispensing material rewards and, as they are limited, to resort to penalties.

Once all the wealthy have had everything confiscated from them, the scope for that kind of redistribution is exhausted. Production is set back by events preceding and following the revolution and by the confusion of transition. In the Soviet Union, industrial production in 1920 had fallen to little over 20 per cent of the 1917 level.[11] The realisation dawns that production, not confiscation, is the way to continue improving the population's material position.

But delivering the promises of a better life is now hindered by anarchy, lack of law and order and arbitrary local actions. No society, whatever its nature, can function without some degree of discipline. There is a growing demand for order to be restored.

All these altered circumstances prepare the ground for the country to step beyond the socialist revolutionary-transitional system. The spirit of revolutionary heroism gradually fades as the new system becomes institutionalised and bureaucratic, and life returns to 'normal'. The desire for a return to normal was very evident after war communism ended and the new economic policy (NEP) was in the making.

## 1.3   The new economic policy

The call for a new economic policy came most forcefully from three sectors: industrial firms chafing at excessive concentration; trade unions complaining of lack of freedom of action; and agriculture bent under the yoke of requisitioning.

With discontent in the countryside and industrial production paralysed by lack of supplies, Lenin realised the need to turn the peasants into allies again. Groping for a workable solution in the absence of an available blueprint, requisitioning was abandoned and replaced by a proportional tax on all production exceeding subsistence level. On the industrial front, the NEP laid the groundwork for commercially autonomous units called 'trusts', into which smaller enterprises were federated. Private trading and markets were allowed again. When the NEP was brought in, small businesses were denationalised, and a census taken in 1923 indicates that about 12 per cent of workers were employed in private enterprise at that time.

However, from the very beginning all enterprises suffered from underfunding and were forced almost exclusively to rely on self-financing. When the State Bank reopened in November 1921 it was likewise short of resources. Hyperinflation was rampant during 1921 and 1922 and the rouble was devalued twice. A new rouble was created after the second devaluation, equal to 1 million old roubles, and the price level was 200,000 times that of 1913. Barring measurement errors, it therefore seems likely that the new rouble was heavily undervalued. Anyhow, this provided the basis for a hard-rouble policy. In 1923 the State Bank started to issue the chervonetz rouble with a partial gold cover (but not convertible into gold).

During the crisis of 1923[12] Kondratiev explained the sharp increases in the price of industrial goods with supply shortages. The government attached more importance to the monopoly power of state industry and pressured trusts to lower their prices on pain of being refused new credit lines, setting maximum selling prices and opening up markets to imports. Some of these threats were less than convincing, since the government lacked the foreign exchange with which to pay for imports.[13]

Faced with these problems, a plea was made in October 1923 to revert to tighter planning by the 'Declaration of the Forty-Six', drafted by Preobrazhensky and supported by Trotsky. At the other end of the spectrum Bukhanin, Rykov and trade union leader Tomsky argued in favour of opening up to foreign investors and dropping the state's foreign trade monopoly.

The issue was not settled immediately and had to wait for a more deep-seated change in power relations, leading to the end of the NEP.

Lenin had refused to choose a development model favouring either industry or agriculture. In his view, a view that became the basis of the NEP, agricultural and industrial development should go hand in hand. In re-establishing heavy industry the first purpose should therefore be to supply agriculture with the equipment it needed; and support was to be given to small-scale rural industry. Private ownership was to be maintained in small manufacturing and service industries and in agriculture.

If the revolution had effected nothing besides a change in the position of the peasantry, agricultural output might have grown slowly but steadily and the rate of growth in industry would perhaps have slightly exceeded that in agriculture with a massive transfer of un-deremployed farm workers into industrial centres. Stronger peasant demand was bound to effect a change in the composition of Russian industry, with greater stress laid on the 'light' industries.

Through most of the NEP period the high rate of industrial growth camouflaged the fact that little had changed. As long as the problem was to rebuild pre-war industry, largely using pre-war equipment and pre-war-trained technicians, the incremental capital–output ratios were very low and the rapid increases in the supply of consumer goods kept discontent at bay. But the situation was bound to change as Russian factories approached pre-war capacity and further rises in output began to require much more sizeable investment outlays.

This, no doubt, was a crucial and critical moment in the economic history of Soviet Russia. Adjusting to a lower rate of industrial growth would have been difficult in any circumstances. In the specific Soviet conditions of the late 1920s it was aggravated by political factors. To prevent too steep and too sudden a fall in the rate of industrial growth, much higher levels of savings were needed. To increase the rate of taxation carried the threat of resistance; and after the experience of the scissors crisis, when the prices of industrial supplies to the peasantry had had to be lowered in relation to farm prices, an industrial price hike was hardly within the range of practical politics.

With hindsight it is interesting to compare the NEP with reforms in China after the Mao years. Chinese reforms during 1978–81 gradually liberalised prices for agricultural goods with the result that production and productivity increased sharply. Higher rural incomes generated savings that could be used for investment in industry, more specifically in the small and medium-sized town and village enterprises. Why did the NEP not yield compa-rable positive results? A major reason is that Russia was already more industrialised in the 1920s than China in the 1970s and that agriculture was therefore of less importance. Indus-trialisation favoured heavy industry and there was no institutional support for light industry at local level, directly absorbing the agricultural surplus. Dramatically, it took more than fifty years for a demonstration of what could have been done, although the results would have been less spectacular in Russia, for the reasons already mentioned and because total savings were much lower than in China before reforms started.

The economic crisis that followed marked the end of the NEP period. It was, at the same time, a political crisis of the very first magnitude that brought Stalin to the helm. The inability to maintain food supplies to the cities and the growing resistance of millions of peasants seemed set to spell doom to the Communist Party dictatorship. Without further fundamental changes in the country's economic structure, the conditions for a resumption of industrial growth looked inauspicious.

On the eve of the First Five-Year Plan state and collective farms together supplied less than 2 per cent of the total grain crop and covered little more than 1 per cent of the area under cultivation. Although the harvest of 1925–6 was exceptionally good, only 14 per cent of the total harvest was marketed compared with 26 per cent before the war. The prime reason was indubitably the fact that farm prices remained unfavourable, not that the kulaks refused to deliver, as was officially claimed. Indeed, 85 per cent of production fell on middle and small peasants and only 15 per cent on the kulaks (independent farmers). In November 1926 the 15th Party Congress took the historic decision to base the Soviet industrialisation process on large-scale farming on cooperative lines. The decision to strengthen the state's grip over the economy by extending its direct control, by setting up a planning system and by restricting individual ownership further ended the NEP and paved the way for a complete change of direction: Stalinism.

## 1.4   Successes and abuses of the Stalinist era

The NEP became bogged down in serious difficulties that were crying out to be resolved. Either the system had to edge closer to a market economy or else it needed to establish its own clear-cut organised planning solution. Stalin and his supporters opted for extending nationalisation to all productive property and to set in place an integrated planning and command machinery. But in order to do this they first had to impose their views, a task greatly facilitated by the power void left by Lenin's death in 1924.

Agricultural output in 1928–9 was catastrophic, in spite of severe penalties.[14] This made it easy for Stalin to pin the blame on the kulaks and to forge ahead with his plans for reorganisation. The Stalinist reorientation was completed with Stalin's speech of 23 June 1931 in which he condemned the egalitarianism of earlier revolutionary days, and argued against the promotion of workers to positions of higher responsibility as well as pleading for a wider pay range.

Drastic measures were taken in September 1932 to reverse the sharp decline in productivity (28 per cent between 1928 and 1930): generalised introduction of the internal passport and compensation on a piecework basis. Stalin's reward for these moves came at the 14th Party Congress in 1934, when he was proclaimed 'leader of the working classes of the whole world, incomparable genius of our era' and, more simply, 'the greatest man of all times and all people'.

The all-out emphasis placed by Stalin's development strategy on heavy industry at the expense of agriculture and consumers generally sparked rapid urbanisation. The population in some urban centres sky-rocketed, with five-or sixfold increases in the space of just a few years: Dniepropetrovsk in the Ukraine, Sverdlovsk (Yekaterinburg) in the Urals, or Novosibirsk in Siberia.

This massive drift from the land was at the apparent root of numerous difficulties: poor work discipline, alcoholism and delinquency. To foster discipline, the 'work booklet' was copied from Nazi Germany and in 1940 the working week was adjusted from six days of seven hours to seven days of eight hours. Severe penalties were introduced to reduce 'sabotage' (Stalin), including labour camps and the death penalty, which remained in force until 1956. The pay scale widened to a factor of ten between unskilled workers and Stakhanovite worker heroes. For the average worker the real wage declined by 40 per cent during the 1930s, despite much tougher work standards. To stop the flight, farm workers from the villages were not even granted an internal passport and so remained yoked to their *kolkhoz* (collective farms) just as the serfs had been. By the end of the 1930s the number of citizens imprisoned in labour camps was estimated at between 3.5 and 10 million.

In retrospect, the threat to the continuation in power of the Soviet regime during the 'great reorientation' in 1928–31 seems blurred by the indubitable successes achieved subsequently. But the threat was a real one indeed, and it was under pressure of this danger that Stalin embarked upon the gamble of the First Five-Year Plan, planned in 1926 but with its execution delayed until 1928. Viewed as a short-run measure, the declared, but never achieved, purpose of the First Five-Year Plan was to right the industrial imbalance through an increase in consumer-goods output based on an increase in plant capacity.[15] It was a daring scheme if one considers that to bring it off meant accepting a further, albeit temporary, worsening of the situation as an even larger share of national income was deflected into investment and away from consumption. Again, in the best Russian tradition, it was to be a race against time. If the Soviet government could keep peasant resistance down for the relatively short period of a few years, it might be able to offer them sufficient quantities of consumer goods at not-too-unfavourable terms of trade, and so head off the dangers and put village–city relations on a new and sounder footing.

Not unlike the imperial government in the wake of the 1905 Revolution, Soviet leadership was keenly aware of the peasants' hostility to itself. Like its imperial predecessors, it was anxious to find or to whip up a modicum of support in the villages in hopes of facilitating its task in the difficult years ahead. Following suitable adjustments, the collective farms had originally been intended to serve as models to put new heart into the peasant masses. As long as the number of collective farms was kept small, the state would be able to offer sufficient assistance, so that membership of the collective farms would carry real advantages.

These high hopes were dashed, however, when the peasants put up far more resistance than expected. The peasantry, which had emerged victorious from the Revolution and the civil war, had very little in common with the docile masses of the imperial period. The bitter struggles that followed developed a logic of their own. The dogged defence by the peasants of the revolutionary land seizures evoked an all-out offensive by the government.[16] The peasants went down in defeat (and suffered losses of life by the millions through persecution and during the famines of 1932–3) and widespread, though still incomplete, collectivisation followed.[17]

Collectivisation supplied an unexpected solution to the disequilibrium that darkened the last years of the NEP and marked the actual starting point of the great change in Soviet economic policies. But it also profoundly changed the face of the government's industrialisation plans. Once the peasantry had been successfully forced into the collective farming machinery, once it became possible to extract a large share of agricultural output in the form of 'compulsory deliveries' without bothering overmuch about the quid pro quo in the form of industrial consumer goods, the difficulties of the late 1920s were shaken off. The government emerged with its hands freed. There was no longer any reason to regard the First Five-Year Plan as a self-contained, brief period of rapid industrialisation, and the purpose of industrialisation was no longer to relieve the shortage of consumer goods. A programme of perpetual industrialisation through a series of five-year plans was now on the agenda. What had in the earlier stages been conceived of as a brief intermezzo turned into another great spurt of industrialisation, the greatest and longest in the history of the country's industrial development.

This reorientation in favour of industry was also considerably eased by what was initially a favourable response in agriculture. Whereas agricultural production had fallen by about one quarter between 1928 and 1932, and Stalin's brutal reforms uprooted the peasantry, causing the famine of 1932–3, it now rallied and went up by nearly a half between 1932 and 1937, although at the end of the period it was still barely above the 1913 level.

The Second Five-Year Plan (1933–7) was more successful. It was more carefully prepared than the first, building on experience gained, and its implementation went more smoothly. It consolidated rapid growth and gave marginally more importance to light industry. Stalin launched the 'Great Terror' of 1937–8, in which 690,000 perished, including 80 per cent of the country's highest-ranking officers.

The Third Five-Year Plan took off in 1938 but soon had to be revised to accommodate stepped-up defence efforts. In 1940 the allocation for defence was double the 1938 figure and by 1941 it had tripled. Defence and investment together accounted for over 50 per cent of national income in 1940.[18]

The war robbed the USSR of the fruits of its (considerable) growth in the 1930s and the production of consumer goods especially plummeted. In 1946, it was 40 per cent down on the already very low pre-war level. The western part of the USSR emerged from the war a wasteland of wrecked factories, mines, railways, towns and villages. Most of its livestock had been slaughtered and 25 million people were left homeless.

During the war 4 million people joined the Communist Party, which reached a membership of 5.7 million in 1945. Of the country's 9.5 million workers only 2.5 million had been part of the workforce in 1940. With this rejuvenation also came a rise in the level of education. Nevertheless, the difficulties of converting the war economy, the loss of skilled labour during the repression of the 1930s and the vast war losses meant that industrial production sustained a drop of 17 per cent in 1946.

Early in 1946 Stalin projected a trebling of pre-war coal and steel output in the course of the next three Five-Year Plans, a goal that was effectively achieved in 1960. But converting the war economy to peacetime conditions was no easy task. Industrial production topped the pre-war level for the first time in 1948, but at a heavy price: the maintenance of arms production at high levels and continued emphasis on heavy industry rather than re-structuring them to suit a peacetime economy.

Indeed, Stalin had launched a two-tier development plan in 1947: first, to turn the USSR into the world's dominant military power, and, second, to 'transform nature'. Gigantic schemes to create an inland sea in Siberia and to increase Siberia's temperature by redirecting cold currents from the Pacific were developed, but fortunately never materialised.[19]

The speed of post-war recovery was yet again the result of catching up and of victory-inspired identification with the system. Full employment of a smaller labour force was quickly reached, since a large proportion of the male population had been killed in the war. Moreover, only 20 per cent of the 2.3 million homeward-bound prisoners-of-war were reincorporated into Soviet society. The remainder were regarded as a threat to the system since they had been abroad and were able to compare. They were shut up in labour camps that still housed millions of people, comparable to the late 1930s.[20]

Taking advantage of victory, Stalin introduced profound changes with an imperialist overtone, reinforcing his dictatorial powers and cutting the Soviet Union off from the Western world, despite the joint war effort. In a speech on 24 May 1945, Stalin defined the Russian people as the ruling people of the USSR, putting an end to the notion of the Russians as primus inter pares. In so doing he reverted to the pre-revolutionary idea, which saw the Russians as the civilising and protective race.[21]

Economic performance in the Soviet Union and the socialist countries in Eastern Europe was, of course, adversely affected by Stalin's decision to draw down an 'iron curtain',[22] which deprived the socialist bloc of eligibility for Marshall Plan funding[23] and of participation in the European Payments Union, in trade arrangements, in the World Bank and the IMF and, later in the European regional arrangements that eventually gave birth to the European Community. These negative effects were not immediately apparent, but they put a severe strain on the division of labour, on technological transfer and on outside pressure for incessant improvement, impairing the longer-run growth potential.[24]

The apparent success of the Soviet experiment in terms of rapid growth lasted throughout the Stalin years and was frequently hailed as proof of the efficiency of the 'socialist' system: 'It is doubtful whether in any previous age so profound a change affecting so large an area of the world's surface has ever occurred within such a narrow span of time' (Dobb 1966). There was always a good deal of unwillingness to accept the Soviet presentation of rapid growth of its industry because it clashed with the prevailing Western assumption of the fundamental inefficiency of socialism. With hindsight, Western reassessment of Soviet growth proves these sceptics right.

## 1.5    Castles in the sand: Khrushchev's reforms

Like other totalitarian systems, Stalinism assumed an aura of eternity while it lasted. But the sufferings that this regime institutionalised provoked strong reactions that became more open when Stalin left the stage.[25] When Khrushchev assumed the leadership after Stalin's death in 1953, Soviet citizens expected wide-ranging reforms to improve their living conditions and to redress a situation where the nomenklatura had become the new exploiting class of a refurbished (state) capitalism. Stalin had successfully created a non-fascist version of the totalitarian state.

The 20th Congress of the Communist Party of the Soviet Union opened on 14 February 1956 and became a turning point. Khrushchev embarked on a number of revisions of

Stalinist principles with far-reaching consequences. The first was a prudent start with de-Stalinisation, criticising the personality cult of Stalin, the perversions of his 'democratic centralism' and the illegality of his prosecutions. This part of a report, which was leaked to the West, encouraged reform-minded leaders in Central Europe and contributed to the uprising in Hungary that same year. Khrushchev also underlined the importance of *détente*, recognising that confrontation between the communist and capitalist blocs was not a historical necessity and that a pacific coexistence was desirable. Going one step further, Khrushchev recognised that the modalities of socialist construction could vary from country to country. This was a serious break with Stalinist tradition, opening up the possibility of a pluralist socialist camp. Again, reformers in Poland and Hungary felt encouraged.

The reaction of the conservative members of the Politburo was virulent and the Central Committee issued a very watered-down version of Khrushchev's speech. Their position was strengthened by the uprisings in Poznań and Budapest, which Khrushchev was quick to quell.

Khrushchev set out on his economic reforms with commendable zeal. His first target was agriculture – once again. Farming was in a state of chaos, the *kolkhozi* were in dire need of equipment, and production was sagging. Khrushchev pushed through an increase in prices for agricultural goods and smoothed heavy industry's ruffled feathers by stepping up investments in machinery for the agro-sector. Unfortunately, he also launched a major campaign to extend farming to hitherto virgin territories, armed with the necessary agro-chemistry and the enthusiastic help of young pioneers. In the space of three years, the area of land under cultivation increased by 30 per cent.

Initial results were positive and output went up by 25 per cent during the first three years. But with the intensive use of fertilisers and excessive irrigation in delicate soils, by 1963 production in these newly developed areas had fallen back by 65 per cent. A further reason for these agricultural troubles was the attempted reorganisation of the *kolkhozi* into federations, which failed for lack of finance and popular support.

Khrushchev desperately tried to break up the extreme centralisation of the decision-making process. His proposals were repeatedly voted down before being accepted by the Supreme Soviet in May 1957. Eleven industry ministries were closed down and authority was reorganised on regional lines (*sovnarkhozi*).[26]

While he stumbled in his internal reforms, Khrushchev did score some successes on the external policy front, albeit coupled with bad luck and some resounding failures. During 1953–6 Khrushchev nurtured improved relationships with China and Yugoslavia, pursued *détente* with the Western powers and sought greater influence in the Third World.[27]

In this way, Khrushchev successfully pursued de-Stalinisation both at home and abroad.[28] But, as Gorbachev would in later years, he found to his cost that, ugly or no, Stalinism still possessed its own iron logic. Most annoying to Khrushchev was that the waning of Stalinist monolithic power encouraged insurrection among freedom-minded Central Europeans, strengthening the old guard and seriously imperilling his position.

Khrushchev's final undoing was his failure to come to terms with President Kennedy in Vienna in 1961 and his subsequent defeat in the Cuban missile crisis in 1962. It vindicated Mao's early opposition to peaceful coexistence. In reply to a searing critique of Khrushchev's policy by Mao in the *People's Daily* in 1960 entitled 'Vive Leninism', Khrushchev ended Sino-Soviet cooperation on a nuclear bomb and pulled Soviet experts and advisers out of China. This brought about a split in the socialist camp and Romania ended up siding with China. By the time Khrushchev left the scene, not many of his reforms had survived.

## 1.6 Brezhnev's restoration of the socialist idyll

The twenty years following Khrushchev's fall in 1964 have been described variously as 'the era of developed socialism', 'the era of consolidation' and 'the years of stagnation'. Stalin and Khrushchev had fought administrative sclerosis, the former through institutionalised terror and the latter through legal means and reforms. Brezhnev, for his part, made a glorified principle of 'stability and continuity'.

Khrushchev had hardly departed when the administration was recentralised in 1965. The *sovnarkhozis* were abolished, the industrial ministries shut down by Khrushchev put back in business and new centralised state committees created (Gostsen for prices, Gosnab for supplies, Gostekhnika for new technologies, and so forth). The enterprise reform, which had taken economist Liberman years to prepare, was codified in 1965, but abandoned in 1970. After initial improvements it failed to effect any lasting changes in the incentive system. Alongside the production targets, sales targets were introduced as a way of reducing excessive stocks. Part of the surplus was to be left for enterprises to dispose of at their discretion and the bonus for exceeding plan targets was raised. The new team built up a formidable gerontocracy (the average age of cadres went up by ten years during that era) and nepotism flourished as never before in the USSR.

Soaring world oil prices in 1973 and a more than tenfold increase in the market price of gold during the early 1970s provided a substantial windfall for Soviet export earnings, albeit one limited to the relatively small volume of exports outside Comecon (the socialist countries' trade system). In this respect the Soviets treated their vassals with generosity, renouncing sharp terms of trade gains. Between 1972 and 1976 imports of Western capital goods multiplied by a factor of four. New hope was pinned on these imports to effect a transfer of technology and to increase productivity. The results were disappointing, however, as the real problems (resource allocation, management incentives) were never tackled.

When the Brezhnev team took up the reins of power, agriculture was in a very frail condition. From the outset Brezhnev gave top priority to farming – for the first time in Soviet history – and increased its funding (up to 20 per cent of total investment funds). Yet, owing to the earlier failure of extensive farming methods, the need for grain imports kept on rising, and this required foreign currency funding. Whereas agriculture had always been exploited for the benefit of industry, under Brezhnev it turned into a heavy mortgage on the entire economy. Despite high investment, productivity in agriculture declined dramatically during these years.

The problem was that neither peasants nor local party cadres had been willing to trust or cooperate with the state since the brutal collectivisation measures of the 1930s. Although a considerable financial effort was made during the Brezhnev years to accelerate agricultural development, results were disappointing. It was not so much investment funding that was at fault, but rather the planning system and the way in which individual peasants were dissociated from the fruits of their labour. When Brezhnev died, agriculture was still in the same sorry state it had been when Stalin passed away, but its collective cost had sky-rocketed.

Other economic sectors also showed signs of decline: the rate of growth dropped markedly, capital productivity and investments slumped, as did private consumption, and unfinished constructions began to be visible everywhere.

The slowdown in the growth of the working population[29] put a stop to growth based on expansive methods. With the military work discipline of the Stalin years, the parking of peasants without passports in *kolkhozis* and the reserve pool of female workers all gone, the only way to grow was to increase labour productivity. But it was in this area that all reforms failed and where Brezhnev's neo-conservative (some called it neo-Stalinist) approach had nothing to offer. A famous study by the academician T. Zaslavskaia, known as 'The Novosibirsk Report', in 1983 concluded that the origins of crises lay in the system's inability to make efficient use of the human and intellectual potential of Soviet society.[30] While this was nothing new in the USSR, what was different was that it was now happening in a more advanced and more educated society with higher aspirations.

During 1975–85 the system's inability to accommodate dialogue at a time when more sophisticated means of communication were beginning to make information about the malfunctioning of the system more generally available spawned manifestations of dissent, and ultimately led to the need for Glasnost. Among the most important were: ethnic and religious movements (Catholics in Lithuania, the Jewish community, a Muslim resurgence); the cultural dissent of the young, attracted to Western values; non-conformist works of art; an ecological movement opposed to plans for diverting Siberian rivers to Central Asia and to the pollution of Lake Baikal and the Aral Sea; demonstrations against the war in Afghanistan; and criticism of economic management by young technocrats in distant Siberian research outfits.[31]

Brezhnev's restoration idyll came under fire from the reforms instituted by 1968 in Czechoslovakia. The reform package proposed to replace the command planning system by a plan spelling out guidelines and incentives, more autonomy for enterprises, a more important role for the market and more self-management by workers in firms. Brezhnev's solution was to invade Czechoslovakia with a Warsaw Pact army.

A second and even more important challenge to Soviet control reared its head in Poland. In 1970 a jolting increase in consumer prices drove workers onto the streets of Gdańsk in numbers unprecedented in a socialist country. Workers, who could not vote with their voices, voted with their feet (they 'chose to exit', to use Hirschman's term). For the next ten years, Polish policy was lax, avoiding overdue reforms and raising living standards by borrowing abroad. When the rate of foreign borrowing had to be slowed down in 1980 new price hikes became necessary, provoking new and even more massive demonstrations and strikes: the government was forced to tolerate an independent labour union, Solidarność.

The Polish situation in the 1970s was quite different from previous troubles in Poznań, Budapest or Prague. After the reforms instituted by Gierek, the Poles no longer had any faith in reforms from the top down. Solidarność was the first counterweight to the party to emerge in any socialist country. Confronted with this new situation, it became risky for the USSR to intervene and hope to keep loss of human life within acceptable bounds and its already tainted leadership image unscathed.

By contrast, during the 1970s relations between the USSR and Western powers improved dramatically, notwithstanding the threat coming from the new and powerful nuclear missiles aimed at Western Europe, the famous SS-20. A series of treaties normalised relations with West Germany. US President Nixon visited Moscow in 1972 and twenty-three agreements were concluded to facilitate cooperation in a range of areas, including trade. Between 1971 and 1976, US and German exports to the USSR increased by a factor of eight. Nevertheless, the USSR did not obtain the most-favoured-nation clause, which the US Congress made conditional upon the liberalisation of emigration of Soviet citizens of Jewish origin.[32]

The invasion of Afghanistan in December 1979 confirmed the impression of many observers in the West that *détente* was lopsided and that both economic cooperation and military concessions had to be rethought. US President Reagan promised to do so, and by launching 'Star Wars' (a very expensive and sophisticated research project to develop anti-ballistic defence capability) he set to creating major difficulties for the pursuit of Soviet external policy in the 1980s.

## 1.7    The impossibility of reform: Gorbachev's shattered illusions

Brezhnev died on 12 November 1982. His successors Andropov and then Chernenko left no mark on history. The real change was ushered in with Gorbachev in 1985. Contrary to conditions under Khrushchev, reforms were no longer the province of a handful of reformers within the party. The whole nation was aware of the system's shortcomings and avid for a radical overhaul. It was not at all inclined to settle for mini-moves. At stake were the principle of accumulation and of tight regulation of the economy, the need to improve the dismal quality of consumer products and to narrow the distance between the people and the command levels. The catchwords that signposted the change from preceding eras were glasnost, uskorenie and perestroïka.[33]

At the outset these slogans were really no more than a much-needed semantic change. But, starting with semantic concessions and, as usual, with criticism of past mistakes, the dynamic forces developed a dialectic of their own that had not been anticipated. Soon people found it was possible to debate issues outside the party's Holy Grail: the party was overtaken by events. De-Stalinisation was truly completed during this period, when for the first time criticism was no longer stopped dead in its tracks by party interests.[34]

The first reform proposals took their inspiration from the 'Novosibirsk Report' mentioned above. Reformers rallied round the ideas of Aganbegyan, Abalkin, Burlatski and Zaslavskaia and agreed to focus primarily on enterprise reform, with a view to making firms more independent and more responsible. The law on enterprise of 30 June 1987 came into effect on 1 January 1989 and featured many of the reformers' ideas. In practice, however, the administration was in no great hurry to change relationships (after all, they received the enterprises' surpluses and stood to forfeit the power that went with control of these firms).

A law dated 19 November 1986, which was rounded out on 26 May 1988, facilitated private ownership for small crafts and trades and in the service sector. Initially, taxation on such activities was prohibitively high, but in due course taxes were brought down. By 1990 some 10,000 small private enterprises (called cooperatives) had sprung into being and half a million people were registered as 'independents'. Actually these estimates are on the low side, since the number of people employed in the underground economy during that year is estimated at close to 15 million.

In agriculture, leasing contracts were introduced running for periods of up to fifty years. Response was rather timid to begin with and official prices for agricultural output were not adjusted sufficiently to make private investment worthwhile.[35]

Gorbachev was much more successful on the foreign policy front. On 8 December 1987 he signed an agreement to destroy medium-range missiles, with detailed provisions for mutual control. He also put an end to Soviet intervention in Afghanistan. Unilateral retreat was announced in February 1988 and completed early in 1989.[36]

Another landmark in 1989 was the onset of liberalisation in Eastern Europe. Gorbachev had realised that the Soviet Union was now in too weak a position domestically to maintain its iron grip on Eastern Europe and understood that it would be better to concentrate on internal reforms. For the first time in Soviet history imperial aspirations were identified as too costly and ranked below the aim of sustaining party control. In July 1990, the Soviet Union agreed to German reunification, in a move that put a final seal on the Second World War and ended the division of Europe into two camps. It heralded the start of a process to redesign the economic map of Europe, the implications of which are discussed below in the concluding chapter 11.

When the Soviet Union fell apart in late 1991, none of the essential components of reform had been implemented. Among the many reform plans, the famous '500 days programme', drawn up by a group led by Professor Shatalin, came closest to embracing all the elements of comprehensive reform. Although 500 days might be considered a rather protracted 'big bang', this transition period looked pretty ambitious to anyone aware of the enormous number of decisions that would have had to be taken.

Why, then, were none of these programmes implemented? There are at least two fundamental reasons. First and foremost, political structure and economic management were only one side of the coin. The other was the Soviet empire, openly challenged by the republics seizing their historic opportunity. As a result the 'war of laws' developed, under which each republic passed a declaration of sovereignty stating that its laws would take precedence over Union law, whereas the Union government insisted that Union law should take precedence. Second, Gorbachev still attempted to save the basic socialist structure of the economy, ready to reform it substantially, not abandon it.

The macroeconomic destabilisation that developed in the absence of a credible reform programme was a clear sign of fatal crisis, which is further analysed in chapter 7. One explanation for the rapid disintegration is that the Soviet Union operated a system of incentives and controls and of fixing objectives that, although never efficient, worked somehow. When the system itself was put into question by perestroïka, the incentive and command structure began to crumble. The effects of disintegration were all the more negative because the system was excessively centralised. The process of disintegration was further hastened by the uncertainty created when expectations of sweeping changes in the system were repeatedly unmet.

Expectations of liberalisation or of a regime change also made it possible for people to air their disagreements and enabled the open assertion of conflict, something few people had experienced in their own lifetime. The malfunctioning of the Soviet economy had always to some extent been due to lack of motivation and passivity in work commitment. This passivity had increased and become more open and pronounced. Strikes were no longer only (or even mainly) motivated by wage claims; they pursued, first of all, political demands for some sort of reform – decentralisation of power, more individual freedom, and so on. What was often branded as 'sabotage' was in fact simply a way of moving away from a strict enforcement system to one of fewer controls and greater individual responsibility. Such a transition phase is necessarily disorganised, contradictory, and bad for production levels. Particularly worrisome in the Soviet case was the extent of disagreement at all levels and the fact that the structures of the old regime – the party, the KGB and the military–industrial complex – still had enough power to block or even overturn reforms. The process of liberalisation was therefore a drawn-out one, and indeed was never more than a complicated compromise. The more time went by the greater grew the risk of complete destabilisation and of hyperinflation, and the extent to which compromises had to be accepted made even the long-term gains appear doubtful.

The party was clearly unable to make the difficult choices needed to check destabilisation. It never got beyond crisis management. As resources grew scarcer the various groups in society and in different parts of the administration were pitted against each other in a fierce battle for power and resources – the Union v. the republics, the military v. civilians, industry v. agriculture, the various industrial sectors v. one another, and so forth.

Enterprises got into dire financial straits in the process, since the credit mechanism was not designed to cope with rapid changes in domestic and foreign prices. In this way even fundamentally sound firms encountered difficulties due to non-payment or poor credit lines. In many cases the inter-enterprise credit system was stretched to the limit to ensure survival and the state helped by printing money. The absence of export credit facilities, in particular, and of traditional trade patterns represented a serious bias against exports, and the breakdown of foreign exchange allocations made it very difficult to maintain traditional import patterns. Because the Soviet structure of production was highly specialised and lacked sufficient elasticity of substitution, import cuts created bottlenecks, stopped domestic production and fed back into reduced exports. Chapters 7 and 8 provide more in-depth analysis.

## 1.8   The fall of communism: inevitable?

Socialism lasted for over seventy years and reached the height of its extension and glory between the Second World War and the 1980s. Not so long ago, few Western observers would have dared to predict the vertiginous decline of communism that culminated in the liberation of Eastern Europe and the break-up of the Soviet Union during 1989–91. But, writing in 1976, the dissident Andrei Amalrik put the question: 'Will the Soviet Union survive until 1984?', which suggests that, to some insiders at least, the signs of decline were apparent well before the actual fall. Economic factors played an important and probably decisive role, as has been exhaustively argued in this chapter. This view is sustained by the analysis of the slowdown of growth in chapter 2. But it is equally certain that other factors contributed significantly to the ultimate collapse, in particular to its timing, without being essential causes. In eschewing reform of the politico-administrative system, communism signed its own death warrant. And partial reforms as attempted by Gorbachev just did not work. Rather, they sped up the fall.

It was an illusion to believe that the political system could be reformed without touching the economy. And as the Chinese are slowly realising, the reverse is equally foredoomed. Once information flows more freely and citizens are better informed and free to express themselves, they can no longer be kept in check as meek economic robots. They will fight for better living conditions and for the Western consumer nirvana.

As the Chinese experience has demonstrated, partial economic reforms can be very successful. But liberalisation of some but not all markets creates new contradictions, such as underpricing of controlled goods (and restraining their supply) and the generation of huge income differentials ('capitalist speculation and exploitation'). Pressure builds up to extend the scope of reforms until little is left of the command economy. And with resources allocated, goods produced, and income distributed by the market, it is hard to see what would be left of communism.

Why, then, did the system survive for over seventy years? The downfall of communism could easily have occurred sooner, indeed much sooner, or later. In 1918–21, the options were still wide open and virtually anything was possible: a return to a non-socialist society, or choice of a different type of socialism. The period of the NEP was one of trial and error, with cooperative forms of organisation and agriculture left to individual and cooperative producers. The big and decisive turning-point came during the Stalinist takeover (1929–33), with the establishment of the command economy, the extermination of the kulaks, collectivisation of agriculture and acceleration of forced savings to speed up industrialisation. The Second World War placed the country and the survival of its system in jeopardy from external aggression. In their fight for survival, the Soviets and their system achieved one of their outstanding successes. Victorious Stalinism flourished in the first flush of this success. Since the beginning the aspirations of workers for a larger share of income, of consumers for more choice and higher quality and of nationalities for more independence remained oppressed and represented a permanent, latent powder keg, although in terms of a more egalitarian distribution of income the system achieved a success that contributed to its longevity.

It was during the years in which the system had reached maturity (1970–80) that problems not only built up but also came into the open and could no longer be ignored. Revolutionary enthusiasm having faded, there was nothing to take its place to keep citizens in high spirits, and no sufficient progress in welfare to keep them committed to the socialist goal.

As the economy progressively ran out of steam and became less able to pick up the technological and managerial challenge, the problems bedevilling the system started to surface. The Chernobyl disaster in 1986 brutally demonstrated the Soviet lack of technological quality and control and the administration's inability to prevent such accidents or to deal openly with such accidents as did occur.

The Soviet Union had its own Vietnam: with the war in Afghanistan, esteem for the army that had emerged victorious from the Second World War, and which was believed to be the most powerful army in the world, took a serious knock. Possibly even more portentous was US President Reagan's 'Star Wars' gauntlet, flung down in the race for technological supremacy. At that moment, if not before, the Soviet leadership realised that its economy was not powerful enough to enable it to stay in the running. Even military leaders then put their weight reluctantly behind economic reform.

All this was happening at a time when the level of education had increased sufficiently for the people to spot the contradictions of official propaganda, and when telecommunications improved their access to information.

In 1986, when Gorbachev launched perestroïka and insisted on glasnost, the world from a Soviet perspective must have appeared wholly strange. In the USSR, little ever changed for the better and there was no hope in sight. Beyond Soviet borders, Europeans were positioning to create an integrated market spanning a continent, Reaganite and Thatcherite reforms sparked fresh enthusiasm for capitalist exploits in the United States and even in Europe. While Japan continued its rapid growth, its performance was outshone by those of the Asian tigers and China (with the help of a little bit of capitalism).

So, during the 1980s, economic, political and social factors joined forces in speeding up the end. With the benefit of hindsight, it could be said that what disintegrated never made much sense. Politically, the USSR remained an empire of the nineteenth century burdened with problems of over-extension and the difficulties of integrating a large array of nationalities. Militarily, the country overreached itself and bled itself white trying to stay in the arms race. It was brought to bay when economic growth slowed down, the military aura became tarnished and Eastern Europe had to be let off the hook. And ideologically, the system forfeited belief in its Utopian claims.

The fall of communism and the disintegration of the Soviet Union may not have been inevitable, but the forces that built up over time became so formidable that the outcome cannot be attributed to chance. It must be understood as the logic of events.

## Notes

1. See Carrère d'Encausse (1991), Dobb (1939, 1966), Gregory and Stuart (1986), Werth (1990).
2. For one thing, nineteenth-century technology (iron and steel, heavy equipment) typically favoured large plants, and to accept the most advanced technology also meant accepting larger and larger plants. The state, in its promotion of industrial establishments, showed remarkably little interest in small business. A small number of large enterprises were easier to promote than a large number of small ones and bureaucratic corruption tended to reinforce a tendency that was already present for economic reasons. Given the lack of managerial staff, larger plant and businesses made it possible to spread the thin layer of available talent over a larger part of the industrial economy. See Gerschenkron (1962).
3. This seclusion slowed down technological transfer, excluded the country from the gains of the international division of labour and perpetuated inefficiencies.

4. For a detailed discussion see Carrère d'Encausse (1991).
5. Marx did, however, go beyond analysis and elaborated on proletarian revolution in *The Communist Manifesto* and participated in the foundation of the Communist International in 1864.
6. The main contributors to the 'breakdown theory' were Bernstein (1899), Grossmann (1929), Kautsky (1902), Luxemburg (1922) and Tugan-Baranowsky (1901).
7. Retarding factors fall into two categories: those which tend to raise the rate of growth of consumption relative to the growth of the means of production (population growth, unproductive expenditures and state expenditures, imperialistic conquest of markets on the periphery) and those which reduce the disruptive consequences of the growth in the means of production, that is the declining rate of profit (new industries, wasteful investments, monopolisation).
8. Nor was it true in Germany, where the socialists had sided with their country during the war (the *Dolchstoßlegende* attempted to discredit this), a stand that produced the schism of the International Movement. After the war the Germans – including the socialists – closed ranks in convincing themselves that the war was not lost on the battlefield and that patriotism was still an honourable sentiment.
9. That was a formidable task. In 1917 the Communist Party had 40,000 members, no more than a handful of professional revolutionaries, given the size of the country. Of course, there were supporters outside the party. But there were only 8 million industrial workers in a country with a population of 150 million. Clearly, support was most substantial in the cities and from the outset the countryside was left aside.

   With such a small revolutionary group that still boasted only 115,000 party members in 1918 and 250,000 in 1921, control could be assured only by using existing cadres in the administration, army, and industry. This led to the creation of a dual structure that has been maintained ever since. The party planted secretaries in industry and political commissaries in the army and the administration, whose task was to control the class enemies inherited from the old regime but who could not be eliminated because of their skills, which the party members lacked.
10. The new communist government financed the war and met other pressing expenditure largely through inflation. In 1919 the inflation rate tripled and in 1920 quadrupled again. At the end of the civil war the purchasing power of a rouble was just 1 per cent of what it had been three years earlier in October 1917. Wage payments were partially protected through payments in kind. In 1918, 50 per cent of wages were paid in kind, in 1919, 75 per cent and in 1920, 90 per cent.
11. Data mentioned in this chapter are taken from the traditional studies of the Soviet economy: Dobb (1966), Gregory and Stuart (1986), Nove (1969), Ofer (1987). These data cannot be considered as iron-clad and have not resisted current re-examination, although it is still difficult to make a choice among the more recent reassessments. For a comprehensive discussion see, for example, Easterly and Fischer (1994).
12. This crisis is called the 'price scissors crisis', referring to an increase of industrial prices and a decline of agricultural prices. A major contributor to this debate is E. Preobrazhensky. He maintained (correctly) that turning the internal terms of trade against the peasantry increases total savings in the economy. For a modern analysis see Sah and Stiglitz (1992).
13. Austria and Germany, which found themselves in a very similar position, were saved in 1922–4 by foreign loans, while the USSR obtained only very few foreign funds.
14. Both agricultural and industrial production fell markedly in 1928. The system then developed a new, highly meretricious way of explaining away calamities and more worldly bungling. In April 1928 industrial sabotage was discovered (read: staged) in the Shakhty region. The trial created the myth of sabotage instigated by foreign capitalist interests, a very useful addition to the stock of enemy portraits for explaining problems such as the kulak menace and the right-wing peril.
15. For a detailed discussion see Dobb (1966).
16. The Molotov Committee divided kulaks into three categories. The first, of about 60,000 families, were considered as counter-revolutionaries, and the second, of about 150, 000 families, as abusive

exploiters. Both groups were arrested and transferred to Siberia. Their property was confiscated. The third group was composed of kulaks loyal to the regime. They were transferred to the confines of their regions.

17. According to Courtois et al. (1997) 2 million kulaks were deported between 1930 and 1932 and 6 million Ukrainians were killed in the intentionally provoked famine of 1932–3.

18. The emphasis in investment shifted markedly to the chemical, machinery and transport sectors east of the Ural mountains. Just before Nazi Germany assailed the USSR, and in the first months of the war, plants in the western part of the USSR were dismantled and shipped east of the Urals. Over 70 per cent of Leningrad's industrial equipment was evacuated in this way and altogether 12 million people (half of the population of industrial centres such as Kiev and Kharkov) followed suit. Despite the difficulties of reorganisation on this scale, Soviet production of tanks and aeroplanes surpassed that of Germany no later than the summer of 1943. Had the USSR lacked industrial maturity and organisation it would not have been possible to produce up to 2,000 planes and 2,000 tanks a month – more than Germany. Even qualitatively speaking the T-34 tank compared well with the German Tiger tank and the II-1 fighter was claimed to be superior to the Me-109.

19. Stalin's return to the vast – by now megalomaniac – projects of the 1930s ran into considerable opposition. The chief of Gosplan, Voznessensky, attempted a more balanced plan and was duly executed in 1949.

20. Werth (1993), on the basis of data accessed only after the disintegration of the Soviet Union, is able to correct previous estimates. Solzhenitsyn had estimated that at the end of Stalin's era there were 10 million people in the gulags. The correct number is 2.5 million. To this number need to be added 2.7 million 'special workers', that is deported nationalities (Caucasians, Balts, Germans); 800,000 people executed; and those that died in the camps: 250,000 in 1942 alone .

21. Stalin restored the civilian and military titles (in 1946, the People's Commissars became Ministers) that Lenin had regarded as the incarnation of the bourgeois state and had therefore decided to abandon. The Red Army of Workers and Peasants became the Soviet Army and the Bolshevik Party the Communist Party. Yet more important than changing names was the change in the role of the party. Stalin ruled single-handedly and ignored the party. Between March 1939 and October 1952 no Party Congress was held; between February 1947 and October 1952 the Plenum did not meet; and the Politburo never met in full. Stalin operated, illegally, with restricted sub-commissions. Major decisions such as the approval of the 5th Five-Year Plan were taken by the Politburo in a matter of minutes, waiving all discussion for fear of incurring Stalin's displeasure. At the same time, he launched into an exhaustive rewriting of Russian history and science. Most discoveries and mathematical theorems have been credited to Russian scientists in the USSR ever since.

22. Churchill coined this expression in March 1946 in a talk at Fulton, Missouri.

23. Czechoslovakia and Poland had already agreed to participate in the International Conference in Paris held in July 1947 to discuss the particulars of the Marshall Plan. Soviet pressure forced them to withdraw.

24. As Stalin could not hope for transfers from the Western world, he proposed from a very early date to exact large reparation payments from Germany. The United States, and in particular Foreign Secretary Marshall, had not forgotten Keynes's analysis of the implications of the reparation payments after the First World War and refused to go along with this. This meant that East Germany had to shoulder the burden of reparation payments to the USSR on its own, considerably slowing down its own reconstruction effort.

25. It is perhaps difficult now to understand that, during his lifetime, Stalin was widely admired by Western intellectuals. To quote just one, the Brazilian writer Jorge Armado, member of the Brazilian Communist Party and known for his humanity and generosity: 'When I heard of Stalin's death I cried as if my own father had died. The next day when I met my comrades in Santiago de Chile they all had put on black ties' (*Le Nouvel Observateur*, 5–11 August 1993: 72).

26. Some major successes were achieved in advanced technology. The chief Soviet breakthroughs that indeed hoisted the USSR to a level that began seriously to worry the West consisted in mastering H-bomb technology and in securing a temporary lead in space technology with the launching of Sputnik in 1956.

    Khrushchev also attempted to give a little more freedom to artistic expression in the USSR. Here, however, he failed the first test. When Boris Pasternak was awarded the Nobel Prize for Literature in 1958 for a novel he had finished in 1955, he was forced to turn down the prize. *Doctor Zhivago* was resented as anti-Soviet, and even anti-Russian, and had overstepped the bounds of cultural liberalism. In 1962, however, Khrushchev backed up a novel by an unknown writer, Alexander Solzhenitsyn's *One Day in the Life of Ivan Denisovich*.

27. An agreement was signed with China in 1953 in which the USSR granted assistance for the construction of 146 large industrial complexes. The USSR agreed to evacuate Port Arthur and Dairen and to discontinue its activities in Manchuria. The Chinese Communist Party obtained an upgrading of its status in the international movement to virtually equal the role of the Soviet party. In particular, the need for cooperation was recognised and China was given a leading role in the Third World.

    Motivated by the urge to improve external relations, a Yugoslav–Soviet reconciliation took place in 1955. The Joint Declaration of 2 June 1955 recognised that 'the policies of military blocs increase international tension' and that 'development of peaceful co-existence requires the co-operation of all States, without taking into account ideological and social differences'. More remarkably still, 'questions of internal organisation, social systems and different forms of socialist development exclusively regard the people concerned'. Without making the slightest concession on its neutrality, Yugoslavia in addition obtained sizeable Soviet economic assistance.

28. Following the establishment of diplomatic relationships with the Federal Republic of Germany, remaining war prisoners were released. Also under Khrushchev, gulag convicts were released in large numbers.

29. Between 1960 and 1970 the fertility rate dropped by 7 per cent and the mortality rate by 3 per cent. Similarly, the structure of the population changed considerably: the Muslims, who had represented 10.7 per cent of the total population in 1959, accounted for 16 per cent in 1979.

30. The report was secret and discussed only in restricted circles of the Academy of Science and the party. As so often in those days, a copy was leaked to the West.

31. The Brezhnev years were not very happy ones in terms of external relations either. The Soviet leadership was seriously challenged within the socialist camp by Cuba and by China's greater revolutionary fervour. Both severely criticised the USSR for not intervening more openly in the Vietnam War. In 1965 China demanded a public denunciation of the USSR by socialists worldwide. Fortunately for the USSR, China embarked on its cultural revolution in 1966 and the leadership became completely embroiled in its domestic affairs.

32. In 1972, SALT 1 (Strategic Arms Limitation Talks) came to an agreement and in 1974 it was agreed to pursue SALT 2, which was finally signed in 1979. *Détente* reached its zenith in 1972–5, and in 1975 was enshrined in the ratification of the Conference on Security and Co-operation in Europe (CSCE) by all European countries, Canada and the United States.

33. 'Glasnost' can be defined as 'rendering public what was hidden'. Behind that slogan was an appeal for an open discussion of the economic situation, of the crisis in the party, which was indistinguishable from the administration and incapable of imparting new vigour to the evolution of society, and above all of the ideological crises which no official echelon was yet willing to admit openly. In adopting the slogan 'glasnost', Gorbachev promised to reduce controls and to improve access to information. He also repeatedly declared that 'glasnost is healthy criticism of shortcomings, not an assault on Socialism and its values'.

    Along with glasnost there was the call for 'uskorenie': the speeding-up of economic development fuelled by continuous reforms. And to top it all, 'perestroïka' was a call to restructure just about everything.

34. Glasnost obviously also created new problems or rekindled old ones. The old arguments between 'Slavophiles' and 'Westerners', between 'liberals' and 'apparatchiks', between 'Stalinists' and 'non-Stalinists', to name but some, once again reared their troublesome heads. One in particular turned into a major and dramatic issue: the problem of nationalities, which had been stifled for too many years.
35. A detailed account of perestroïka and its failure is given in Goldman (1991).
36. Soviet troops had suffered 13,000 fatalities and 40,000 injuries. According to Podnieks's film. *Is It Easy to Be Young?*, the Afghan war was as unpopular in the Soviet Union as the Vietnam War had been in the United States.

# 2 The obsession with growth

This chapter evaluates the major concern and, ultimately, failure of communism: to catch up with the economic advance of the West. Section 1 discusses the motivation underpinning the major policy objective, common to all socialist economies at all times, namely their excessive emphasis on growth.

Despite the intertemporal injustice that heavily penalised the first generations under socialism through very high forced savings, later generations did not reap the benefits of their forebears' sacrifices. Socialist economies seemed doomed both to fail in their bid for sustained growth and to be quite unable to let their citizens enjoy the fruits of sacrifice.

Section 2 deals with the preliminary issue of measurements, as Soviet accounting standards are not easily reconcilable with Western practices. Section 3 starts from a growth-accounting framework and shows the contributions of the accumulation of factors of production (labour, capital, land) and of productivity growth. If the Soviet economy had been able to put its immense accumulation of productive factors (extensive growth) to efficient use, it would have been at the top of the world's growth league. Unfortunately it was not. Section 4 provides an overview of the successes and failures of Soviet communism and section 5 concludes.

## 2.1    Growth: the overriding plan objective

In all poor countries, catching up with advanced nations is a top policy priority. Socialist revolutionaries came to power on a promise to achieve exactly that (and to redistribute income in favour of the working classes). Faith in the feasibility of catching up is solidly backed up by Marxist theory. Clearly, then, in the view of socialist regimes, catching up would be proof of the superiority of socialism and would also substantiate the socialist leaders' legitimacy. It is worth recalling Stalin's claim in 1947 that he would catch up with Western economies within ten years[1] – a claim repeated by Khrushchev ten years later when he said the Soviet Union would overtake the United States in another ten years – and Mao's desperate bid in 1957 to achieve the 'Great Leap Forward' and to catch up with the United States within fifteen years.[2] These claims were not totally unrealistic. Until the late 1950s, the era of rapid Soviet growth and of the successful Sputnik launch, the main question among Western scholars was: when would the USSR overtake the USA? At that time, specialists such as Bergson (1961) did not exclude the possibility that this might be quite imminent. Now we know that catching up did occur, but only in capitalist economies, notably in East Asia and in China after the 1978 opening-up policy.

Owing to the backwardness of economic conditions, to the shortages of virtually all goods and services and to human nature, which always strives for more, the growth objective is easily passed down the hierarchical echelons and shared by all economic agents. While it is easy to understand that catching up receives undivided popular support, it is much harder to fathom how investment decisions are actually made. None of the mechanisms used in capitalist economies is available. At the aggregate level, in capitalist countries savings and investments are brought into balance by adjustments of the real rate of interest and of expected income. Individual investment projects are judged on the basis of investment costs (inclusive of financing cost), production costs and expected revenues discounted at the appropriate interest rate. Apart from expected sales, not one of these variables is relevant for investment decisions in a socialist economy.

Because government controls investment spending, public sector consumption and wage payments, investment and savings are no longer independent decisions. Once wages are set, the remaining national income is at the disposal of the integrated public sector for consumption or investment purposes. Savings out of wage incomes represent 'voluntary' savings and are additional to the 'involuntary' or forced savings from the integrated budget. As a result, the total amount of savings in socialist countries tends to be far above the levels in capitalist economies and is more easily manipulated by policymakers.[3]

The share of productive investment is much lower than total national savings in socialist countries, as military expenditure (treated as unproductive investment) is much higher (estimated at about 15 per cent of GDP, but possibly as high as 25–30 per cent[4]) than in capitalist countries (5–6 per cent of GDP in the United States during the 1980s and less in Japan and Western Europe). Thus, for the Soviet Union or China, the total savings rates might be above 50 per cent of GDP (of which some 30 per cent is used for investment and some 20–30 per cent for defence). These data suggest that aggregate investment, in general, is maximised in line with the overall growth priority, subject to a level of consumption that the population will accept short of open rebellion. If the ultimate gauge of performance is growth of output, not social utility, the return on investment is of secondary importance.[5] But even output may not have been the prime objective of planners. Ofer (1987) argues that the goal was to maximise growth of GNP less consumption, that is, growth of investment and of military expenditures. Measured that way, Soviet achievements appear much more favourable. The same view is expressed by Berliner (1966): 'But if we are to capture faithfully the aims of the Soviet elite, then we must accord first place to military defence, and derivatively to heavy industry, as the aim of economic development.'

Confronted with virtually unlimited demand for investment funds and no price mechanism to regulate its allocation, administrative rationing is imperative. A first important decision springs from political priorities: the resources needed for defence, production targets of key strategic products and so on. Now bargaining sets in. Each firm belongs to a ministry that becomes its political advocate. The firm may be one that produces inputs needed in another industry and so they form a coalition to improve their bargaining position.

There is definitely a hierarchy of interest groups. The power of each group is correlated with its size in terms of output, its strategic position in the output structure and its strategic importance for the political priorities. For example, the military–industrial complex and the KGB have doubtless been the most powerful interest groups of all, and for a long time their claims went unchallenged and untouched.

As a rule it is difficult to turn down a request for investment out of hand. All firms have some administrative and political support; furthermore, administrations are better at 'satisfying' through acceptable compromises than in making difficult and risky choices. As a result, no investment project meets with a flat refusal and decisions are a very long time in the coming. Funds are spread thin over all projects, with underfunding the inevitable result. This generates hiccups, delays and indeed sometimes projects grind to a complete halt before completion. Owing to very long approval and completion times, and to the dissipation

Table 2.1. *Sectoral distribution of capital stocks, 1987 (by percentage)*

|  | Agriculture | Industry | Dwellings | Other |
|---|---|---|---|---|
| Soviet Union | 14.2 | 32.2 | 18.6 | 35.0 |
| Industrial market economies | 5.0 | 23.4 | 35.9 | 35.6 |
| United States | 2.8 | 22.4 | 45.6 | 29.2 |
| F. R. Germany | 3.6 | 20.1 | 44.2 | 32.1 |

*Source*: USSR-Soviet data; industrial economies-OECD data. Easterly (1993).

of funds, projects more often than not are technologically obsolete by the time they are completed and their cost is many times what it would have been had they been carried out without hindrance or delay.[6]

While bargaining and power relationships certainly influence the choice of investments and the investment process itself, the planning process has developed a system of priorities. These priorities concern the sectoral structure of the economy and, within sectors, certain types of products.

Among the productive activities top priority goes to industry, which has always been regarded as the engine of economic development. It leaves agriculture behind, but farming in turn does better than services.[7] By and large, a lack of balance in development strategy is not to be condemned as such. Hirschman (1958) and Streeten (1959) have argued that a poor country simply cannot tackle everything at once and that it would be wise to concentrate on a few key sectors that are able to pull along connected activities. Owing to their upstream and downstream linkages, progress in these sectors will spread to others, aided by the incentive effects of imbalances in technology and incomes. What is questionable, however, is a strategy that by design maintains an unbalanced approach for generations, and hinders the spread of investment flows into other areas of economic activity.

In the realm of industrial activity there are priorities both by sector and by type of product. Investment goods prevail over consumer goods, as investment is seen as the prime condition for growth. The development of heavy industry has been singled out as the basis for successful growth since long before the Revolution. Because large quantities of steel are used in the production of machinery (and mechanisation is the road to greater productivity and technological progress) and, incidentally, in arms production, the iron and steel sector and heavy equipment has always played a special role. This role was most ruthlessly developed by Stalin,[8] but has been maintained ever since. According to one statistical source, the share of heavy industry in total investment in industry between 1917 and 1976 amounted to 84 per cent.[9]

Table 2.1 confirms the allocation bias in favour of industry and capital-intensive agriculture to the detriment of housing and the service sector. Spending so much less (in proportion) on housing than Western consumers can hardly be due to Soviet citizens' preference. This biased structure with its excessive emphasis on heavy industry has been blamed for stagnation in the 1980s and, in particular, for the technological slowdown. See Gomulka (1986) and Ofer (1987).

One might expect that, with growth given such overriding precedence over consumption and the quality of life, socialist countries would have outperformed Western countries on that score at least, as they did in the Olympic Games. Unlike the world of sports, however, there is a major obstacle in comparing growth performance: the problem of measurement to make the data internationally comparable.

## 2.2 Measuring growth

The Commission of the European Communities (1990b) provides measures of historic growth performance in the Soviet Union, both on an official and on an adjusted Western basis. Several interesting facts emerge from these data. Average growth during the twentieth century was virtually identical for the former Soviet Union and the United States. If one takes the period 1929–87, in order to exclude the pre-socialist, war and NEP years, then the Soviet Union did better by one percentage point, despite the Second World War, which benefited US but harmed Soviet growth. Western estimates consider that the official figures considerably exaggerate growth. The question is: Is this a coincidence or is it a systematic feature of Soviet statistical endeavour?

On an adjusted basis the Soviet growth record is not exceptional by Western standards but, until 1970 at least, was quite respectable. Two periods of rapid growth occurred, from 1922 to 1940 and from 1950 to 1960 (in fact, from 1946 to 1960). Growth rates close to 10 per cent are typical for capitalist economies emerging from depression or war, as witnessed by the growth rates of European and some Asian countries in the 1950s. Each of the two periods of rapid growth in the Soviet Union was preceded by a war period during which production plummeted. When peace and order were restored, work-eager labour was in abundant supply, as was capital stock, which, at least in part, needed only to be repaired and brought back on stream.

We are forced to conclude that, notwithstanding its tremendous growth effort, the Soviet Union never succeeded in matching the best Western performances. Before explaining why, we need to make sure that the official data are indeed overestimated and that the adjusted data offer a more reliable basis for comparison.

Official statistics suffer from measurement errors (which include neglect of the underground economy), over-reporting by plant managers and political manipulation, but this is hard to verify. Major biases are, however, created by the conceptual treatment of value creation. First, the Marxist distinction between productive and non-productive activity creates a sizeable difference between Western national income accounting and material product accounting. Net material product (NMP) does not include most services. This at any rate underestimates GDP and is likely to overestimate growth. Because services receive a lower priority in the socialist growth process, their growth rate over long time spans is definitely lower than growth in the 'productive' sphere. Hence, if services were included, this would increase GDP but might lower the overall growth rate.

Another major distortion is created by the pricing system. The prices of many industrial products are overvalued in relation to agriculture and services. Because they also enjoy a higher growth rate, the upward bias in their weight (which depends on the *value* of output) tends to bias upwards the aggregate growth rate. A similar bias results from hidden inflation. GDP deflators used are the official price indexes, which are underestimates of true price trends, even though there were periods of pronounced price adjustments (see Nuti 1986, and United Nations 1990). What is presented as the real rate of growth may, in fact, be closer to a nominal rate of growth.

Finally, the statistics fail to reflect changes in the quality of products. Western statisticians also find it difficult to take into account quality changes, but approximations are used much more systematically than in socialist economies. Moreover, the problem with Western statistics is that they tend to take only partial account of quality improvements, so that GDP figures underestimate the true figures. By contrast, socialist statistics fail to take account of declining quality so that NMP figures overstate the true index. For a detailed discussion of statistical and conceptual problems with socialist national accounts, see Bergson (1991), Desai (1986) and Ofer (1987).

## 2.3   Factors contributing to growth

'Extensive growth' refers to the accumulation of the factors of production (labour, capital, land) and 'intensive growth' to increases in the productivity of production factors.[10]

### *Labour accumulation*

Socialist planners had banked on maximising labour mobilisation. Data in Ofer (1987) suggest that from 1928 to 1985 population increased at an average annual rate of 1.3 per cent, the number of employed by 1.9 per cent and hours worked by 1.8 per cent. In this way the growth in labour contributed not only to GNP but also to the growth of GNP per capita. When the Soviets came to power, unemployment in urban centres was high and so was underemployment in agriculture. Up to the Second World War, there was no shortage of unskilled labour and the investment strategy served to equip the available excess labour supply. This is a major reason for the growth sustained during the 1920s and 1930s. Misallocation of investment was less important as all capital was in short supply and could be put to good use. What was lacking was skilled labour, in particular in management. It took the regime at least until the 1950s to replace the trained elite inherited from the tsarist regime and offset the losses suffered during the Second World War.

The loss of human capital throughout the history of the Soviet Union was one of the highest in world history and inflicted incalculable economic costs. When the socialists took over in 1917 the country suffered from the loss of human lives during First World War. Socialist reorganisation of the society withdrew traditional cadres from their responsibilities, in effect reducing their social utility dramatically. Some of the greatest talents emigrated before and after the internal war between the progressive (red) and reactionary (white) forces. It is estimated that between 1 and 2 million Russians emigrated between 1917 and 1925, the intellectual elite of the country. During the famine of 1933, between 3 and 5 million people died and the kulaks were executed, put into labour camps, or transferred to distant regions to carry out low-productivity tasks.

Millions ended up in gulags or were executed during the Stalin years. At the death of Stalin, 2.5 million were in gulags (Werth 1993). The Second World War cost an estimated 20 million Soviet lives, and, of returning war prisoners, 1.5 million were executed or deported. After Stalin's death over a million Jews and dissidents emigrated. This extensive and continuous destruction of people, including the intellectual elite of the country, is above all a human tragedy, but also an immense economic cost, which can be appreciated by the huge gain realised by immigrant-receiving countries such as the United States.

In order further to augment the available labour force, particularly during the war and thereafter, the socialist economies achieved exceptionally high participation rates in the labour force. In 1980 the Soviet participation rate, measured as a ratio of all those working to the population aged 15–64, was 86.9 per cent, compared to 66.5 per cent in the OECD and 70.9 per cent in the United States (Ofer 1987). Much of this came from a higher female participation than in capitalist countries. If one disregards the marginal disutility of work then, even in a labour-abundant country, it makes sense to stretch working time to the maximum acceptable level. As so often happened, Marx's analysis of the capitalist system was applied with a vengeance by socialists. He had argued that the only limit to capitalist exploitation of workers was the physiological need to rest in order to keep the variable capital (labour) intact. Working conditions in capitalist countries throughout the nineteenth century were indeed dismal, but they were no better in the Soviet Union in the twentieth, at least until the 1960s.

As long as there is unemployment and the participation rate can be increased, the contribution of labour to growth is a dominant factor. But at some time or other this potential is exhausted. It then needs to be replaced by qualitative improvements in labour skills. The absence of competitive conditions, the lack of a market for services and the limitations to wage differentials seriously hampered the development of skills, so that socialist economies suffered more from the labour constraint of a fully employed economy than capitalist economies.

## Capital accumulation

Table 2.2 provides a comparison of official and Western estimates of growth rates of output per worker and of capital per worker. Overall, both data sources confirm that the capital–output ratio was increasing during the entire period 1928 to 1987. The Soviet capital stock grew after 1928 at an annual rate of 7 per cent (and at 7.5 per cent if the Second World War years are excluded) until 1985. Extensive growth (i.e. rising capital–output ratio) is doomed to be slowed down by diminishing returns and implies that the investment ratio has to increase over time. Indeed, the Soviet investment ratio doubled between 1950 and 1975 (Ofer 1987). The level reached by the capital–output ratio in the USSR in the 1980s was among the highest in the world (Easterly and Fischer 1994). Thus, although many countries exhibit increasing capital–output ratios over time (Japan is a prime example, also the EU), the USSR was an extreme case.

So extensive growth contributed to the slowdown of Soviet growth after the 1950s. Furthermore, as argued below, the translation of extensive growth into diminishing returns

Table 2.2. *Soviet growth data, 1928–87 (by percentage)*

| Period | Industry, official | Industry, Western | Total economy, Western |
|---|---|---|---|
| Growth rates of output per worker, alternative estimates | | | |
| 1928–87 | 6.3 | 3.4 | 3.0 |
| 1928–39 | 12.5 | 5.0 | 2.9 |
| 1940–49 | 0.1 | 21.5 | 1.9 |
| 1950–59 | 8.9 | 6.2 | 5.8 |
| 1960–69 | 5.7 | 2.8 | 3.0 |
| 1970–79 | 5.2 | 3.4 | 2.1 |
| 1980–87 | 3.4 | 1.5 | 1.4 |
| Growth rates of capital per worker, alternative estimates | | | |
| 1928–87 | 6.2 | 3.2 | 4.9 |
| 1928–39 | 11.9 | 6.5 | 5.7 |
| 1940–49 | 1.5 | 20.1 | 1.5 |
| 1950–59 | 8.0 | 3.9 | 7.4 |
| 1960–69 | 6.1 | 3.4 | 5.4 |
| 1970–79 | 6.3 | 4.1 | 5.0 |
| 1980–87 | 5.6 | 4.0 | 4.0 |

*Note*: Growth rates are logarithmic least-squares estimates.
*Source*: Western data is based on Powell (1968), CIA (various years), Kellogg (1989). Easterly and Fischer (1994).

was, by Western standards, extremely pronounced. The reason was a very low elasticity of substitution between labour and capital.

## Land

The third factor of production is land, which serves as shorthand for agricultural land, forests, minerals and so on. Land under cultivation increased by 0.8 per cent on average during 1928–83 (Ofer 1987), reflecting territorial acquisitions in 1939, and Khrushchev's Virgin Land Programme during the 1950s. The Soviet Union is particularly well endowed with natural resources, although geographical dispersion, vast distances and climatic disadvantages lower the economic value of available natural resources. Because prices bore no relation to production costs, relative scarcity and interest rates, the Soviet economy exploited nature (forests, water, soil, mineral wealth) excessively.[11] This policy bias produced the situation that Feshbach and Friendly (1992) describe as follows:

> In the last decade of the 20th century, there are no leading industrial cities in the Soviet Union where air pollution is not shortening the life expectancy of adults and undermining the health of their children. The growth that made the USSR a superpower has been so ill-managed, so greedy in its exploitation of natural resources and so indifferent to the health of its people, that ecocide is inevitable.

In fact, the socialist system generated and fell victim to a major inconsistency in managing its natural resources.[12] If the rate of interest (the expression of the intertemporal time preference) is high, then a society prefers to transfer more to future generations than when the rate of interest is low. The high level of forced savings reflects considerable concern on the part of socialist planners for the welfare of future generations and is inconsistent with low real interest rates, that is it is inconsistent with time preferences that give priority to the present. Several generations of Soviet citizens have been sacrificed since the 1920s in order to build up an industrial power basis to enrich future generations. By the same token, low rates of interest and high concern for future generations should have been reflected in great care for natural wealth and a low pace of exploitation of mineral resources. In fact, however, the Soviets exploited their mineral resources and nature recklessly.

Such an inconsistency can occur only in a context where interest rates do not matter and where prices do not reflect costs and demand. The best productive sites for oil and many other minerals are already exhausted and the marginal cost of production now makes many resource sites uncompetitive even at world market prices. The same is true for agriculture in certain parts of the former Soviet Union. Considerable investment will be needed to bring ecological conditions in overused areas back into balance.

## *Factor productivity*

The data in table 2.2 summarise the growth of output and capital per worker. These are the basic data for the estimation of total factor productivity (TFP).

Easterly and Fischer (1994) estimate a CES (constant elasticity of substitution) production function and calculate TFP growth rates for 1950–87 (assuming Hicks-neutral technical progress). They find elasticities of substitution as low as 0.13 for the industrial sector and 0.4 for GNP on Western data for the period 1950–87. For the entire data range 1928–87, elasticities of substitution are higher but not statistically significant. These rates of substitution are much lower than those estimated for Western countries, and even lower than those obtained for developing countries. This implies that extensive growth resulted in returns to capital that were diminishing at an abnormally high rate.

This, of course, makes one ask why extensive growth was not corrected and why the elasticity of substitution was so abnormally low.

The answer to the first question is much more straightforward than the answer to the second. The traditional mechanism of a market economy, where investments need to generate a return superior to the cost of capital, did not operate in the Soviet Union. The problem was the absence of a proper pricing mechanism.

The answer to the second question is more of a conjecture. Under the planning system, additional equipment did not displace workers. Employment in productive units has been relatively stable so that more capital generated more underemployment but not less unemployment. Furthermore, the optimal mix of factors of production in terms of skill requirements and support services was rarely achieved. Planning consisted above all in adding more equipment, not in restructuring to achieve the optimal mix.

## 2.4   Failures and achievements

We shall start this section on the positive side, as the regime also produced some positive achievements. The Soviets' overriding priority, as in other developing countries, was growth, but propelled by the need to demonstrate the superiority of the communist regime. Western revisions of the official Soviet growth records demonstrate that the official data vastly exaggerated the growth rate. Nevertheless, growth during the 1950s was remarkable, and respectable during the 1930s and 1960s. The 1920s record can be pardoned by the turmoils of the civil war and the groping for a model to organise the economy. Similarly, the 1940s suffered from world war. The ultimate failure of the system was, however, the dramatic slowdown of growth during the 1970s and 1980s.

The system was able to generate full employment rapidly and maintain it over time. This is still perceived today by the citizens of the former Soviet Union as a success. The price for this 'success' was, of course, quite high: underemployment and a very low growth of consumption. The share of consumption (in current prices) declined from 73 per cent in 1928 to 64 per cent in 1950 and 55 per cent in 1980 (Ofer 1987). Consumption here includes household consumption and communal services, such as education and health. The share of consumption in the Soviet Union was, therefore, below levels in the West by at least ten percentage points.

Another (partial) success was income distribution, not as egalitarian as claimed by communist ideology but still less skewed than in market economies. Box 2.1 provides details.

We now turn to the slowdown of growth during the 1970s and 1980s. Some insights can be gained from an international comparison, as certain factors (world demand, extensive growth) affected other countries as well. Easterly and Fischer (1994) compare the Soviet Union with 102 countries. Over 1960–89 Soviet per capita growth was, in fact, slightly above the global average, but well below the upper range performers.

Given the strong accumulation of productive factors (capital, labour) in the Soviet Union, it is desirable to control for these factors to derive information about the efficiency of the growth process. Running a regression of per capita growth on the standard growth determinants (initial income, population growth, schooling and the investment to GDP ratio), Easterly and Fischer show that the growth performance, once one takes these factors into account, was dismal. Secondary education (a big Soviet success) and the investment ratio are near the top of the sample distribution. Had the Soviet economy operated like the average of the sample, it would have had one of the highest growth rates. Or, in other words, Soviet per capita income in 1989 was only half of what it would have been if it had performed according to the sample average during 1960–89. As it turned out, 'the Soviet economic performance conditional on investment and human capital accumulation was the worst in the world over 1960–89' (Easterly and Fischer 1994:1).

What, then, are the reasons for the slowdown of growth during the 1970s and 1980s? There is no single explanation, although it all boils down to the regime's objectives (autarky, military superiority, restrictions on individual freedom) and institutions (planning, social ownership).

---

### Box 2.1   *Income distribution in the Soviet Union*

Incomes in the USSR were radically equalised in the earliest post-revolutionary years, but have become progressively more unequal ever since. There have been three cycles of contraction and expansion of inequality. The initial one occupied essentially the first decade after the Revolution, thus embracing first the years of war communism and then those of the NEP. The second cycle occurred during the first two decades of Five-Year Plans and war under Stalin. Having become extraordinarily marked by the early post-Second World War years, inequality in pay had again tended to decline afterwards.

Calculations in Bergson (1984) indicate that inequality of wages in 1928 tended to be less than that in the United States in 1904, though not as markedly so as between the USSR in 1928 and Russia in 1914. Under Stalin, income inequality increased to reach its pinnacle in 1946. A decade later, however, it had markedly decreased. The decline continued until around 1968. At that time inequality measures were comparable to those of the most egalitarian income distributions in capitalist countries such as Sweden. More recently there has been something of a reversal, though the inequality still does not compare with that of 1956, let alone that of 1946.

In contrast to the Western experience, high incomes did not appear to be perpetuated on any scale through inheritance in the USSR, though the intergenerational transmission of such wealth as was privately owned was permitted. Children of elite personnel and of better-placed individuals generally, however, were inordinately represented in admission to higher educational institutions. They also appear to have been over-represented in posts such as their parents occupied.

There is considerable difference in average earnings between the Soviet republics and there is no clear evidence that this has become less over time. In the late 1980s there was, in fact, a sharp widening of the gap with Russia.

In the official Soviet view, Soviet society was destined to become fully egalitarian. That followed at once from Marx's famous scheme of post-revolutionary social evolution. Thus the USSR was admittedly still in Marx's egalitarian 'lower' stage, but was seen as bound to advance in time to his egalitarian 'higher' one. Confronted by the Soviet experience, one imagines, Marx himself might have been surprised at how protracted the lower stage was proving to be, and disconcerted by currents manifestly at odds with attainment of the higher one.

The results for the USSR cannot be taken as applying equally to all socialist economies. There is considerable variety across countries and across time. In 1986 Czechoslovakia had the lowest degree of earnings dispersion (a Gini coefficient of 19.7), followed by Hungary (22.1) and Poland (24.2). Russia had a Gini coefficient of 27.6, slightly higher than the UK (26.7). (The Gini coefficient is half the expected absolute difference in incomes, relative to the mean, between any two persons drawn at random from the population. A Gini coefficient of 30 per cent, for example, implies that the difference, on average, between the incomes of two persons is equal to 60 per cent of the population's mean income.)

Worldwide growth declined during 1970–90, but by less than in the Soviet Union. As the Soviet Union remained virtually closed and benefited rather than suffered from the oil price increases, there is no negative feedback of slower world growth to the socialist camp.

Of course, the absence of wide-ranging foreign trade had other effects which were much more dramatic. The transmission of technological and managerial know-how, which is a major source of gains from international trade, in addition to the signalling of competitive advantages and the real value of resources, was cut off. This may not have been crucial before the 1970s as the Soviet Union built up a traditional economic structure centred on heavy industry. But it became a crucial shortcoming for the next step forward to an advanced economy. Human skills, market knowledge, distributional systems, consumer satisfaction, rapid change, development of services are all features of a modern, advanced economy for which the Soviet Union was not geared up, and lack of openness prevented it from importing 'ideas'. Because of the system's failure to respond positively to these challenges the labour force became increasingly demotivated so that the country suffered both from a slowdown in the growth of the labour force for demographic reasons and a lower average performance. Emigration of the most highly trained ethnic group, the Jewish population, and of dissidents only made matters worse.

Military expenditure increased in a vain attempt to stay at par with the United States and to cope with the Afghanistan adventure. Some economists have used the share of military expenditure in GDP as an explanatory variable in growth regressions and find no significant contribution to slower growth (see Easterly and Fischer 1994). However, the estimates of Soviet defence expenditure do not usually include the real cost of the military–industrial complex, whose cost is closer to 25–30 per cent of GDP than to the 15 per cent usually advanced. The argument that sustained military efforts have contributed significantly to the growth slowdown can therefore not be put aside, although quantification still needs to be made.

The major explanation for the slowdown was that growth was extensive, as shown in the previous section, with a dramatic decline in returns to capital and, more controversially, a slowdown in total factor productivity. These in turn, are the consequences of the planning system, the absence of a price regulator and the closed nature of the economy.

## 2.5  Conclusions

The superiority of socialism under the guidance of the USSR had been proclaimed by the Soviet leadership ever since the victory at Stalingrad. We have highlighted the contradictions and failures of the system. What, then, are the real or perceived successes of the Soviet Union?

An empire that matched Europe's mightiest fell to pieces in 1917. What was subsequently reconstructed by the Soviets became one of the two largest military powers the modern world has known, equipped with an ideology that gave hope to the Third World. Its technological exploits were remarkable, though limited to specific goals mainly in areas related to the military. Economically, its track record is less impressive, yet not without its successes. Unemployment (unlike underemployment) became a thing of the past, and citizens' basic educational and economic needs were satisfied. Income distribution was less uneven than in capitalist countries, although the reality fell significantly short of Marxist goals. But it is nevertheless hardly surprising that there are many citizens of the former Soviet Union who today look back with nostalgia to the mediocre but stable conditions of Soviet times.

After the Second World War socialism benefited from its participation in the victory over Nazi Germany and its elevation to world-power status. While this undoubtedly gave Soviet citizens self-confidence and demonstrated the Soviet Union's potential capacity to become a world leader, it was the beginning of the end. The country's one besetting constraint had always been a lack of skilled labour. After 1945, a power base expanded within the Soviet state that absorbed the best and the brightest: the military–industrial complex.[13] This complex achieved world-class performance, catching up with US nuclear domination and at times even taking the lead in space technology. But while the USA could afford such costly aspirations, the USSR could not. The best scientists, engineers, managers and the best machines and raw materials were poured into the military–industrial complex. Between 25 and 30 per cent of GDP was funnelled into that sector, and the rest of the economy had to be content with the leavings.

Lack of competition inside the economy, protection from foreign trade and limited access to Western high technology increasingly hindered growth as technological development accelerated and the international division of labour in the West deepened. The effectiveness of investment gradually declined, and white elephants became the most prolific Soviet species. Making the right investment choices becomes more essential in a mature economy than in a closed, underdeveloped economy. Therefore, the same procedures that had worked reasonably well during the initial stages of development grew increasingly inadequate. In particular the cut-off from the trade in 'ideas', which did not hold back the post-war reconstruction effort, stifled the economy increasingly and aborted its attempt at achieving promotion to the class of 'modern' economics. Extensive growth resulted in dramatically diminished returns to capital during the 1970s and the 1980s, a process that could not be stopped as planning ignored such signals and there was no pricing system for the allocation of capital.

The overall growth rates of output were respectable since they were usually above those of the developed market economies. However, they were achieved at a very high price in terms of consumption that had to be sacrificed. Furthermore, the output statistics (which suggested that the former Soviet Union had slightly narrowed the distance to the USA) turned out to be misleading once the borders were opened. The verdict of consumers and the markets showed that Soviet output was worth much less than was assumed in the statistics. In the 1980s it was estimated that Soviet income per capita was about 50 per cent of that of the USA. When the markets were allowed to value the output of Russia (one of the better parts of the Soviet Union) the result was that income per capita turned out to be about 10 per cent of the US level, about the same level as Turkey. In this perspective it becomes understandable why, by the end of the 1980s when the growth potential of socialist economies was exhausted, citizens despaired because they could only look back in anger, received no comfort in the present and saw no promise in the system's future.

## Notes

1. Berliner (1966) quotes an earlier call by Stalin from 1931: 'We are fifty or a hundred years behind the advanced countries. We must make good the distance in ten years. Either we do it or they crush us.'

2. This hope and naivety persisted until the Brezhnev years, despite mounting evidence that things just were not working out that way. Here is an example of the kind of utopian visions still marketable in the socialist countries in the 1950s and 1960s: 'Our table will be covered with the best nature can offer: prime meat and milk products, the best of the orchard, strawberries and tomatoes at a time when they are not yet ripening on our fields, grapes in winter and not only when in abundance in autumn. As socialists we know perfectly well that in the socialist camp an excess of food products will be available by 1965 . . . To imagine that future abundance in the retail outlets, mighty and ever-growing waves of food and specialities from the four corners of the earth, of clothes and shoes of marvellous new materials, of kitchen appliances and working machines, cars big and small, handicrafts and jewellery, cameras and sports equipment . . .' Walter Ulbricht, *Unsere Welt von Morgen*, Berlin: Verlag Neues Leben, 1961 (our translation). How anyone could forecast in 1961 that by 1965 would exist such a paradise – which, in fact, more closely describes conditions in the developed capitalist world in the 1990s – after forty years of unsuccessful attempts in the Soviet Union is quite incomprehensible.

3. Another interpretation of the term 'forced savings' refers to a lack of goods available for purchase, so that agents are 'forced' to save.

4. Estimates by Brada and Graves (1988) and Steinberg (1987) range from 12 to 16 per cent of GNP. But as we now know, GNP was vastly overestimated at more than 50 per cent of US GNP, and therefore the share of defence was underestimated. These studies neglect, moreover, the resource cost of the military–industrial complex, absorbing the best brains and material resources for which no correct opportunity cost is imputed. Connected areas of nuclear and space technology are also not fully accounted for in these studies. If the strength of the Soviet army was comparable to that of the United States, then the 5 per cent defence budget of the USA, which enjoys a GDP at least five times that of the USSR, must translate into a share of Soviet defence in GDP of at least 30 per cent.

5. 'The system stressed production for production's sake. Whether the goods were actually used by a purchaser was immaterial. Presumably someone would find a use for them sooner or later. Since everything always seemed to be in short supply, it was usually sooner. Therefore, the system put a premium on good production engineers who knew how to prevent production breakdown, issue a steady flow of supplies and maximise the production process. Those who excelled at quality control or sales served no purpose and thus, more often than not, were flushed out of the system. Inevitably, economic growth became the chief gospel of the Soviet Union, and Gosplan became its chief prophet' (Goldman 1983: 32).

6. According to Judy and Clough (1989) about 25 per cent of the projects completed during the first part of the 1980s had been on the drawing-board ten to twenty years earlier. Projects took up to five times as long to complete as in Western economies. These delays became longer over time.

7. Marxist theory insisted on the distinction between 'productive' and 'non-productive' activities, with the latter comprising most services. As a result, services rank very low on the scale of investment priorities. It is of course true that many services can manage without major investment outlay, but as independent businesses (hairdressers, restaurants, bars, street peddlers, repair shops, etc.) are not built up in socialist economies, such services remain underdeveloped. Other services, such as financial intermediation, are altogether unavailable, partly for ideological reasons. Finally, some of the more investment-intensive services, such as housing, tourism, health and education, remain seriously underdeveloped because they are firmly stuck at the lower end of the scale of priorities. See Aganbegian (1989).

8. In the 1920s, during the NEP, there was extensive discussion among party members about the optimal growth strategy. Stalin was certainly much influenced by Preobrazhensky, who adopted Marx's theory of primitive capitalist accumulation to the socialist context (this is another illustration of our general point that Marxist political theory of capitalism found application in socialist economies). To realise a 'big push', consumption must be cut back to free resources for investment (forced savings). The prices for agricultural products must be lowered and those of industrial products raised. Agriculture needs to be collectivised to free labour for industrial expansion. Investment is thus concentrated on industry and, as consumption is set back, on heavy industry. Ironically, Preobrazhensky and many of his disciples fell prey to Stalin's furore, who then applied their ideas with a brutality not foreseen by his intellectual forebears.

9. *Statistika*, Moscow (1977) p. 436 as quoted by Kornai (1992: 173).

10. Extensive growth is defined by Ofer (1987) more restrictively as a rising capital–output ratio and is used in this sense in the rest of this chapter.

11. In Western terminology, the real problem was incorrect pricing, in particular of the rate of interest. A standard result of non-renewable natural resources theory is that, in equilibrium, the price must increase by the rate of interest. That is, it pays to sell a resource now if the future price increases at a rate below the rate of interest. By contrast, if the price of the resource increases at a rate above the rate of interest, then the resource should be left in the ground. In equilibrium, any increase in the price of the resource needs to equal the rate of interest.

12. In Soviet national accounting there were no capital charges other than depreciation. Rents on land and natural resources were introduced only after 1966, and then only half-heartedly.

13. Before the Second World War, defence made large claims on heavy equipment but not on the country's best scientists, engineers and managers. Increasing technological sophistication shifted requirements over time to absorb an increasing share of human capital.

# Part II

## Transition: 1990–2000

'The doors of Heaven and Hell are adjacent and identical.'

(Nikos Kazantzakis, *The Last Temptation of Christ*)

# 3    Transition: the job

Transition

The year 1989 was christened 'annus mirabilis'. Policymakers and their advisers were not trained anywhere to deal with miracles. In order to gain insights into the problems of transition, economists turned to related, but not strictly identical, experiences. Western Europe's post-war reconstruction; the problems of development and the success of certain emerging countries; China's drifting away from a centralised command economy; and Latin America's problems with institution building and inflation control. Now, over ten years later, we have much more experience and this is the topic of the next chapter. But it is still important to understand the mindset of the early 1990s to interpret what has happened.

From the start, transition countries fell into three categories. The first included only East Germany. With generous West German financial support and extension of West Germany's institutional framework to the east, the policy dialogue was closed. In the second class were all the other socialist economies outside the FSU. These were mostly small economies that could expect a lot of support from the European Union and to gain substantially from reorienting their trade from former Comecon countries to Western Europe. And the third class was composed of the successor states of the FSU. They first had to cope with the political job of creating a state and an administration and then look around for a place in this new world. Clearly, their job was the hardest.

Despite very different starting points, the main elements of a reform programme are common to all countries. However, the problems that arise in the implementation of reform programmes vary from country to country. They depend on the strength of the administrative machinery inherited by the reformers, the overall political situation and the popular support for reforms. Differences in these factors are in our view more important in explaining the huge differences in the fate of the reforms in Central and Eastern Europe than differences in the intellectual concepts behind the reforms. Hungary and Russia might serve as the two extremes.

In Hungary the reforms were successful mainly because there existed an efficient and loyal administration that did implement the new laws as intended, state managers were effectively controlled by the government prior to privatisation and the newly created fiscal administration was able to produce enough revenues to balance the budget. Moreover, strong support from most political parties and the population at large made the reforms credible in the sense that the perceived risk of reversal or macroeconomic destabilisation was close to zero. The political spectrum was, and still is, quite centralised and strong centrifugal tendencies are absent.

Contrast this to Russia: Since in the Soviet Union all power came from the party, which was organised mainly at the union level, the Gaidar government of the Russian republics, which was committed to a big bang, could not rely on an effective administrative machinery nor on support from the various stakeholders. The first Russian parliament, the 'Supreme Soviet', was dominated by representatives of the old order (the army and the military–industrial complex) that were bound to lose from reforms. As a result the decisionmaking power of the government was neutralised and reforms were not implemented. With the old order in shambles the result was chaos. This explains why, during the first year of the reforms, the Russian government could achieve only price liberalisation. Without parliamentary support and a weak bureaucratic apparatus the government could not recover control over state-owned enterprises (the government had already lost control during Soviet times) and the new tax system brought in only a fraction of the revenues that were needed. One result was total macroeconomic destabilisation. Another result (and a further cause of macroeconomic destabilisation) was that state enterprises did not adjust; they just kept producing the old goods with the same techniques while they were financed by cheap credit from the Central Bank. Moreover, there was no widespread popular support for quick structural reforms, partly because of the lack of success of the reforms. There were thus continuing debates about the desirable speed of reform and a reversal of the reform strategy always seemed possible. In other words, the programme was not credible.

To be successful a reform plan must take into account political and economic reality. A plan that can be executed successfully in Hungary is not necessarily a good recipe for Russia.

The real-world difficulties in implementation are also the reason that some sequencing of reforms is unavoidable. Some steps need more preparation and take more time to implement than others. Prices and external trade can be liberalised quickly. But privatisation and the creation of a fiscal administration take more time.

Another way to express the same idea is to say that any reform programme comprises both 'negative' and 'positive' steps, measures to dismantle old and create new structures. Destroying first and creating afterwards produces chaos in the interim. Yet, as creation always takes longer than destruction, some disorder is unavoidable in the transition. The amount of chaos created by destroying first, and the amount of chaos that can be tolerated, varies from country to country.

This chapter starts with price liberalisation (section 1) and external liberalisation (section 2), which are typically the beginning of reforms. Then follow the more complex reforms: establishing property rights and a market for trading them (section 3) and the role of governments in establishing stability and a fiscal system (section 4).

## 3.1   Price liberalisation

Reform of the price structure is the cornerstone of internal reforms. Prices must be determined by 'scarcity', i.e. by the market. If prices, or a large set of prices, for goods of social or national importance remain bureaucratically fixed, then the other elements of economic reform do not make much sense. The bad experiences of socialist Hungary, Poland and Yugoslavia, which had a 'neither-plan-nor-market' system at different points in time, support this thesis.

Technically, price liberalisation is easy to implement: the government just announces that henceforth all households, enterprises etc. can set their own price. The real difficulty is political, as price liberalisation inevitably entails income redistribution.

Price liberalisation must also be accompanied by the freedom to trade, i.e. people have to be able to buy low and sell high. Freedom for commerce is essential to ensure that the goods that are produced reach those consumers that have the best use for them. In the very first phase of the transition this, and the elimination of queues, are the only efficiency gains that are available, because even under the most favourable circumstances enterprises need time (months, if not years) to produce different products and to become more efficient.

In order to avoid a damaging burst of inflation, the liberation of controlled prices and removal of producer subsidies have to be complemented by monetary and fiscal discipline, and the establishment of a new market-conformable tax system.

It should perhaps be pointed out here that price reform per se cannot be a cause of inflation. If subsidies and production taxes are eliminated simultaneously, this should not affect the overall price level. Some prices would go up (foodstuffs, rents), while others would go down (many tradable industrial goods). What happened in the ex-GDR (this is discussed in chapter 6) is a case in point: only months after the Deutschmark was introduced in July 1990 (a move accompanied by comprehensive price reform), the overall price level had already dropped from the previous year's level. But, price reform can transform repressed inflation into open inflation if there is a monetary overhang.

Price liberalisation (coupled with freedom for commerce) is initially often difficult to sustain politically. As the old distribution system breaks down a few well-connected individuals will become rich very quickly because they know where the scarce goods can still be obtained at low prices. Over time a new market-based distribution system will evolve and profits in that sector will stabilise at the normal rate. But in the beginning very high profits from this apparently unproductive activity might cause popular resentment.

Why undertake price reform? The obvious answer is that price reform yields economic gains. We discuss the nature and the size of these gains in a short-to medium-run context in order to find out the impact price reform can have at the beginning of the reform process. We thus concentrate on the adjustment in consumption that can occur immediately when prices change, as it takes much more time to change production. The other parts of the reform package aim at providing the right environment for firms so that they are restructured and new investment can take place. They will thus take much more time to have an impact 'on the ground'. The efficiency gains in consumption are thus the only ones available immediately, and are thus important in maintaining popular support for the reforms.

How large can the efficiency gains from price liberalisation be if only consumption can adjust? Imagine a closed economy in which there are queues for most goods. Before price liberalisation each household consumed up to the point where the total cost (price plus waiting time) was equal to the marginal utility it could get from consuming this good. The marginal utility was presumably different from the marginal cost of production (at the level of production decided by the planners). After price liberalisation markets clear so that queues are eliminated (and the price is equal to the marginal utility for consumers). While each individual household can adjust the consumption of each particular good, all households together can consume in the aggregate only the same amount as before if production does not adjust instantaneously. Before production has adjusted, the elimination of queues is thus the main welfare gain from price liberalisation.[1] If trade liberalisation is also among the first measures, this argument is, of course, valid only for so-called non-tradable goods because for all tradable goods an excess domestic supply can be exported and an excess of domestic demand can be satisfied through imports. For goods that are tradable, consumption can then adjust in the aggregate even if production is initially slow to react. For these goods the domestic price is determined by the world market, and the world market price represents the marginal cost for the economy. After price liberalisation marginal cost will thus equal marginal utility. With price liberalisation consumers will reorient their consumption pattern, increasing demand for goods whose prices fall and decreasing demand for goods whose prices increase (e.g. oil). The lower consumption of the latter pays for an increase in imports of the former and other goods.

However, even for non-tradables there should be gains that go beyond the elimination of queues. After price liberalisation consumers should be able to find, within their budget, the product they prefer. People who prefer potatoes should no longer end up with onions and vice-versa.

Since consumers will reduce their consumption of goods with a low marginal utility and increase consumption of goods with a high marginal utility, this reorientation of consumption (and implicitly trade) must make them immediately better off.

Over time, production can begin to adjust. And if production can change, aggregate consumption of non-tradables can also change. This yields additional welfare gains. The basic economic mechanism is that, before price liberalisation, marginal utility in consumption does not equal marginal cost of production. A net gain is available to producers and consumers for any increase in the production (and consumption) of a good for which marginal utility exceeds marginal cost.

Reducing the consumption (and production) of previously overpriced goods and vice-versa thus yields net welfare benefits to society. How large are these gains? No comprehensive estimate has been attempted so far. It would anyway be not only very difficult, but also conceptually wrong just to add the individual gains ('Harberger triangles') from all different markets. The fact that distortions are omnipresent makes it conceptually difficult to measure the gains from price liberalisation. The demand curve for any one product is affected by the prices of other products. A simultaneous change of all prices could thus shift the entire aggregate demand curve and lead to other effects, which could potentially outweigh the direct effect from the change in the price of the particular product concerned.

While it seems impossible to give a precise estimate of the welfare gains from overall price liberalisation, it is still possible to estimate the order of magnitude of the gains in some sectors. We do this using one of the most important distorted sectors of the economy under socialist planning, i.e. energy. Box 3.1 shows that liberalising prices in this sector alone should, in the long run, lead to welfare gains in the countries of the FSU equivalent to between $60 and $135 billion at least, or more than 10 per cent of income of these countries, even if their GDP is estimated generously. Since the intensity of energy use was about the same in the other Central and Eastern European countries, one can assume that for most former socialist countries in Europe the welfare gains from liberalising this sector are similar as a proportion of income.

The welfare gains calculated in box 3.1 represent a lower bound since they take into account only the consumers' surplus. In order to obtain the overall welfare gain one would have to add the producers' surplus. However, this would require more information about the energy production conditions in the FSU. The important point about these calculations is not so much the precise number, but the order of magnitude. For example, the potential welfare

---

*Box 3.1    The welfare cost of underpricing energy*

The starting point is provided by estimates of the underpricing of energy that indicate that the world market price was about 150 per cent above the domestic price in the FSU. This indicates the height of the welfare triangle. In order to estimate the base of the triangle, i.e. the reduction in consumption, it is necessary to estimate the shape of the demand curve. Econometric studies for the West suggest that, in a market economy, the long-run price elasticity of demand for energy is about 0.5. This implies that an increase in the price by 150 per cent should lead to a reduction in demand of 75 per cent. The overall amount of energy production can also be measured. Applying world market prices to the individual components oil, gas and electricity yields a total value of the FSU energy production of about $240 billion p.a. in the years up to 1990.

The welfare gain, due to the change in consumption, is equal to the triangle under the demand curve. This area is given by: one half of (the absolute value of) the product of the change in demand and the change in price (i.e. 0.5 × change in quantity × change in price).

Since only the elasticity of demand is known (elasticities link proportional changes in price to proportional changes in demand), it is necessary to render the absolute changes in proportional or percentage terms. The welfare gain is then equal to half the proportional change in price times the proportional change in quantity times the value of initial production.

With the numbers mentioned this yields: 0.5 × 1.5 (increase in price) × 0.75 (fall in demand) × $240 billion = $135 billion. If the distortion in the FSU is assumed to have been 'only' 100 per cent, the estimated welfare gain would still be 0.5 × 1 × 0.5 × $240 billion = $60 billion.

In order to relate these dollar figures to FSU income one has to estimate the value of the FSU economy. Generous estimates put the GDP per capita in the FSU at about $2,500 to $3,000. The first estimate of the welfare loss is thus considerably above 10 per cent of GDP. Given that the actual combined GDP of Russia and the other FSU republics is much lower than the estimate used here, the welfare gain might turn out to be more than 10 per cent of national income even for the second estimate. However, since the demand elasticity refers to long-run effects, it might still be appropriate to use the higher GDP estimate.

*Source*: Gros and Jones (1991).

---

gains calculated here for only one sector, of 10 per cent of income, are a multiple of the gains the European Community expects from its internal market programme.

The demand elasticity used here refers to the long run. In the short run it is much more difficult to economise on energy. This implies that in the very short run the welfare gains will be much smaller. Studies of demand for energy in the West indicate that it takes ten years for the adjustment to be complete. If one accepts this and assumes that the adjustment is evenly spread over time, the welfare gains from price liberalisation in the energy sector would be 'only' 1 per cent of GDP in the first year, 2 per cent of GDP in the second, and so forth. Even though the initial gains are more modest, but still substantial, there is no reason to delay price liberalisation because the adjustment will start only if prices change (and are expected to remain free).

The welfare effects of sectoral exemptions to price liberalisation are thus likely to be substantial. Experience has shown, however, that there are three sectors that are often, at least temporarily, exempted from price liberalisation, namely foodstuffs, housing and energy.[?] The underlying argument is always one of income redistribution: higher prices of these goods will make parts of the population worse off and that is often deemed socially unacceptable. Since the above-mentioned sectors cover a large part of overall consumption and since their demand is rather inelastic in the short run, the income effects can indeed be large for those parts of the population that do not receive higher prices for their production, i.e. mainly pensioners and state employees.[3] However there are always better ways of achieving the desired redistributive effect than to fix the price of these goods at a distorted level. We show this briefly with respect to these three sectors where, indeed, liberalisation has been slow in most transition countries.

### Food

In the case of foodstuffs, one way to avoid the redistribution of income that goes with price liberalisation would be to offer direct income support to people in need. Alternatively vouchers which give the right to buy certain foodstuffs at low prices (presumably in a limited number of state stores) could be issued which, if transferable, would maintain the scarcity signal of prices.

The main problems for post-socialist agriculture are land reform and the food processing industry. A number of studies have shown that, under socialism, food processing was particularly inefficient. In some cases food processing even subtracted value (see, for example, Hughes and Hare 1992a). Inadequate domestic food processing is the main reason that most post-socialist countries spend a large part of their total hard currency earnings (about 30 per cent) on high-value Western food (sweets, yoghurt, etc.).

### Housing

Continued rent protection would freeze the housing market in its sorry state. Since construction is potentially an important source of unskilled jobs, such a policy would make no social sense either. If it is felt that the redistributive effect of an unavoidable (and economically appropriate) increase in rents must be tempered, the answer might be to give current occupants the opportunity of buying their homes at an income-related price. Once private ownership is secure, rents and house prices set by the market will ensure that construction can take off, and owners will have an interest in renovating their homes. Unemployed workers would then have something useful to do. In post-war Western Europe, the unemployed contributed significantly to rebuilding the housing stock destroyed during the war.

*Energy*

We have already discussed the exceptional importance of the energy sector. Exceptional because the level of production was high, reflecting endowments and the emphasis of central planners on heavy industry and the fact that planners also assigned a low shadow price to energy. At the level of the consumer, the price of energy (petrol, electricity), in terms of other tradable goods, was much lower than in the West. The upshot of all this was that the use of energy per unit of output was several times higher in the post-socialist countries than in the West.[4] This implies that proper pricing of energy is both economically more important, and politically more difficult, than in the West.

To increase prices for household heating is, of course, very difficult in countries where badly insulated apartments have no individual meters (as in the FSU area). However, energy (in the form of gas, oil or electricity) is a homogeneous product, which has a well-defined world market price. The shadow price of energy can thus be measured easily in terms of hard currencies. This holds for energy-importing as well as for energy-exporting countries.

The real exchange rate of most post-socialist countries was usually at a very low level in the period immediately following the reforms. This implies that world market prices for energy lead to massive price increases in terms of non-tradables. For example, in Russia the cost of heating would be several times the rental cost and higher than the income of many pensioners if electricity and other forms of energy were priced in hard currency. This is why energy price liberalisation is so much delayed. The solution to this political problem would have been to allow households to consume a certain fixed amount (e.g. 50 per cent of previous consumption) at low prices and to charge world market prices for the remainder, so that at the margin consumers would pay the appropriate price.[5] This would allow the country still to reap the welfare benefits calculated above. Another efficiency-compatible solution, applied to the situation in Serbia in 2000–1, is given in box 3.2.

A further argument against the continuation of price controls is that once prices are set at the political level it becomes very difficult to change them and keep them at least constant in real terms. Governments are often tempted to use the controlled prices to slow down inflation. A good example is Russia, where energy prices (petrol, household electricity) were kept constant in nominal terms for months while inflation was running at 20–30 per cent per month (annual rates of over 500 per cent). One result was that the price of electricity was at times 100 times lower than in the West (at market exchange rates). This mechanism magnifies the distortions caused by continuing price controls.

## 3.2    External liberalisation

Price and trade liberalisation are Siamese twins. One without the other does not make sense. Moreover, trade liberalisation is easy to achieve: all that is needed is a stroke of the pen that eliminates all restrictions to export and import. However, in reality the issue is a more complex one because for trade liberalisation one can make a good case for gradualism. While economists generally agree that all quantitative restrictions should be eliminated

---

**Box 3.2    *Efficient energy pricing***

One of the most urgent problems facing the new democratic republic of Serbia was a severe electric energy crisis during the winter of 2000–1. This was due to many reasons: a decade of mismanagement, the NATO bombings, a drought and ill-considered exports of electricity during the last days of the Milošević regime. But behind the headline crisis lurked the larger problem that energy consumption was simply out of line with the income of the country. Systematic underpricing of energy led firms and households to demand more energy than the country could afford, as happened in most transition countries.

The medium-term challenge in 2001, as in many transition countries ten years earlier, was to ensure that consumers face the true market price for electricity, which would be 5–8 eurocents per kwh, instead of the 1 cent paid in Serbia. Five eurocents is the marginal cost in the EU for residential consumers. How could this be achieved in a country where pensions were so low, often below 50 euros per month? The electricity bill could not be paid if prices were suddenly increased to the true cost level, but it was still imperative that consumers faced the true price.

An interim solution was simply to apply the higher price only to *changes* in consumption. All households would pay, as the basic bill, only the old price for the amount consumed during the same period last year. But if they were to consume more they would have to pay the new price, say 5 eurocents for each additional kwh. If they managed to consume less, their bill would be reduced by the corresponding amount: they would receive a credit equal to the number of kwh saved (compared to last year) times the new price. All households would therefore have an incentive to save energy immediately.

The obvious drawback of this approach is that the receipts of the electricity company will fall if people were to start really saving energy. But this could be accepted during a special transition period and is more than offset by the advantage that the system can be implemented quickly, ensuring that pensioners and other poor people do not suffer from higher energy prices. If a household saved so much that the energy bill became negative, this would be allowed up to a (small) maximum amount per household, as it would give low-income families an additional source of income during this difficult transition period.

After one year the basic bill would then be increased by reducing by one-third the kwh counted at the old price. Continuing in this fashion for another two years, the electricity company's full revenues would increase to reflect full market pricing after three years. But consumers would have the incentive to start saving immediately, without having to face crippling bills.

---

immediately, there are respectable arguments for retaining some tariffs. Completely free trade has never existed, and over time progress has been achieved only gradually throughout the world, through a succession of difficult and drawn-out GATT rounds.

Table 3.1. *Trade dependence of some Eastern and Central European countries during 1992*

|  | Imports (as % of GDP) | Exports (as % of GDP) |
|---|---|---|
| Czech Republic | 38.4 | 32.7 |
| Hungary | 31.6 | 29.6 |
| Poland | 17.8 | 14.6 |
| Russian Federation | 41.7 | 47.7 |

If one takes into account how trade was repressed and regulated in socialist economies it becomes clear that, to liberalise foreign trade, a number of practical steps must be taken. The most pressing of these is to abolish the state monopoly on foreign trade, unifying the exchange rate so that all exporters and importers transact at the same rate, eliminating all quantitative restrictions (or converting them at least into tariff equivalents); and moving to unrestricted foreign exchange convertibility for current account transactions.

There is no need to provide special arguments for the abolition of the state monopoly concerning foreign trade. The rationale for exchange rate unification is also clear. It eliminates the many different implicit export taxes (usually on energy and other material inputs) and import subsidies (usually on so-called 'essential' imports). One immediate result is that the domestic currency prices of these goods rise to the world levels.[6] In the short run, producers in manufacturing have an incentive to begin economising on energy and other material inputs.

The unified exchange rate can transmit world market prices to the economy only if exporters and importers actually have access to foreign exchange. This is why 'current account convertibility' for residents is an additional required step.

The net effect of the initial steps is 'only' to convert implicit protection by direct controls into explicit protection by tariffs – possibly still rather high tariffs. The final step is to decide on the appropriate level of the explicit protection. In the long run, free trade is the appropriate complement to price liberalisation. However, during the transition period some tariff protection should be maintained through a *uniform ad valorem import tariff* in the 20 to 40 per cent range. Needless to say, no transition country followed this advice: tariff protection is a concession to interest groups. As the strength of interest groups varies greatly across sectors, tariff rates vary accordingly.

Why temporary tariff protection? One argument is that tariffs can yield substantial revenues for the government. This is an important source of revenue for a government that has to create a new fiscal system from scratch and will thus have only a very uncertain revenue base at the beginning of the reform process.[7]

An order of magnitude of the potential revenue can be calculated easily. For a country with a ratio of imports to GDP of about 30 per cent (e.g. Hungary in 1992, see table 3.1), a tariff of 25 per cent would yield a revenue of about 7.5 per cent of GDP. Since total government revenues have usually been around 40 to 50 per cent in the transition economies, this implies that tariffs could easily provide between 15 and 20 per cent of total government revenues. This would actually not be outside the range spanned by the experience of a number of

Table 3.2. *Share of central government revenue from taxes on international trade*

| | |
|---|---|
| Bulgaria | 6.0% |
| Czech Republic | 2.3% |
| Hungary | 3.6% |
| Poland | 3.1% |
| Romania | 5.6% |
| Slovakia | 5.2% |
| Russia | 8.7% |

*Note*: 1998 data.
*Source*: International Monetary Fund, *Government Finance Statistics Yearbook, 1999.*

Table 3.3. *Shares of output in industries with negative value-added (at quality adjusted world prices)*

| | |
|---|---|
| Bulgaria | 50.8% |
| Czech Republic | 34.8% |
| Hungary | 34.6% |
| Poland | 8.4% |
| USSR | 22.3% |

*Source*: Hughes and Hare (1992b).

other 'emerging' countries. As shown in table 3.2, actual tariff revenues are much smaller, mainly because import tariffs are lower and because tariffs are not always paid.

The fiscal argument would suggest that the degree of tariff protection, and its reduction over time, should be a function of the fiscal 'needs' of the government.

Another argument for retaining some tariffs comes from 'second-best' considerations. It could be argued that some of the 'senile' state-owned industries need temporary protection to prevent them from failing all at the same time. According to McKinnon (1991) and Hughes and Hare (1992b), many industries in Eastern Europe generated negative cash flows (and sometimes even negative value-added) at world market prices in the short run, i.e. before input combinations and product quality can be adjusted (see table 3.3). Hence a devaluation coinciding with the move to free trade would simply raise material input prices in tandem with the prices of finished goods, and negative cash flows would persist. Moreover, with incomplete financial markets, firms with negative cash flow (but positive value-added) today might go bankrupt even if they are perfectly viable and competitive in the long run when the scale of production and the input mix are adjusted. Because manufacturing absorbs a very high proportion of the East European labour force and firms with a negative value-added constituted a large fraction of all firms, a wholesale collapse of the industrial fabric would lead to huge unemployment.

How much protection is needed according to this argument obviously depends on the level of the real exchange rate. A much-depreciated exchange rate reduces the need for tariff protection if undervaluation can be sustained. Trade policy during the transformation should thus be discussed together with the exchange rate regime (we do so below).

Opening up economies to international trade also partially solves another problem, namely that even when reforms are complete, many firms will still be the only domestic suppliers of certain products. Strong international competition should prevent domestic monopolists from charging more than the world market price (see Lipton and Sachs 1990).

Tariff protection is very much a 'second-best' approach, but this is the world we are living in. An import tariff raises the real exchange rate and therefore hurts export industries. By abstracting from intertemporal considerations, we can go even one step further: simple arguments can show that an import tax is equivalent to an export tax. The equivalence can be established if it is taken into account that, for a small country that cannot affect world market prices, the import tariff increases the price of imported goods relative to exported goods. An export tariff, at given world market prices, lowers the price of the exported good at home, relative to the imported good. Lowering the price of one good relative to another, or increasing the other price, leads, of course, to the same relative price.[8]

This equivalence between export and import tariffs is revealing. It shows that perhaps the most important side-effect of trade protection is the reduction in the growth of trade, both of imports and of exports. This is crucial because export-led growth is the only way Central and Eastern European countries can hope to catch up with Western standards of living. This is another reason why the protection we advocate for the transition has to be temporary and modest.

The Central European countries were in the fortunate position that, for general political reasons, their hands had already been bound, by their signing the new style Association Agreements with the European Union in the mid-90s. These agreements provided for the establishment of a (bilateral) free trade area between the EU and the country in question. Although this 'hub and spoke' approach is not ideal from a theoretical point of view, these agreements had the immense advantage of being preparatory for membership of the EU, and thus providing institutional certainty.

Liberalising foreign trade should bring efficiency gains such that everybody could be better off. However, if the initial price structure is quite different from world market prices, trade reform also implies large shifts in income distribution. The main redistributive effect has come from the repricing of (initially Soviet, then) Russian energy exports. The Soviet Union sold relatively cheap energy and other material inputs to East European economies in return for manufactured goods of lesser quality than those traded in Western markets.

The Central European countries and most former Soviet republics lost the subsidies for their material inputs. However, Central European countries suffered much less from the negative-value-added (at world market prices) syndrome, despite the fact that their extensive manufacturing and agricultural industries had become dependent on cheap material inputs – particularly energy. In fact, some of them were able to sell their manufactures to the West. The examples of Poland, Hungary and the Czech Republic are encouraging. Within just a

Table 3.4. *East European countries' share of the OECD market (percentage change of market share over the period)*

|  | Bulgaria | Czechoslovakia | Hungary | Poland | Romania |
|---|---|---|---|---|---|
| 1979–89 | −18.5 | −44.0 | −7.8 | −32.3 | −46.3 |
| 1986–89 | −19.9 | 0.9 | 1.5 | −23.5 | −27.8 |
| 1989–92 | 59.1 | 82.4 | 36.4 | 49.2 | −55.1 |
| 1992–97 | 0 | 50.0 | 50.0 | 37.0 | 38.0 |

*Source*: IMF (various years).

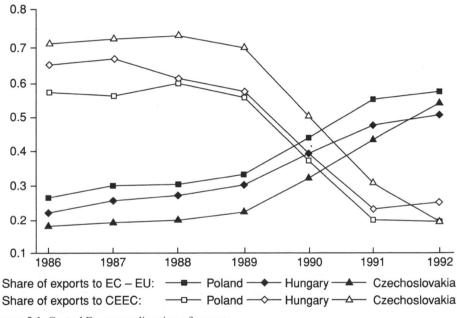

Share of exports to EC – EU:  ——■—— Poland  ——◆—— Hungary  ——▲—— Czechoslovakia
Share of exports to CEEC:  ——□—— Poland  ——◇—— Hungary  ——△—— Czechoslovakia

**Figure 3.1** Central Europe: redirection of exports

few years they have managed to redirect their exports from the CMEA area to competitive Western markets (see table 3.4).

Before 1989, Central and East European trade was predominantly conducted within the socialist block (see figure 3.1).[9] This inward concentration became even more marked in the 1980s, accounting for about 60 to 70 per cent of Central Europe's foreign trade by 1988. Until the demise of CMEA all these trade flows were managed bilaterally and subject to one- or five-year horse-trading between governments. The data for 1992 show convincingly that not much time is required to redirect trade. Industrial countries already accounted for two-thirds of the exports (and imports) of Central European countries by then.

Gros and Gonciarz (1994) show that the distribution of trade of the Central European countries in 1992 was already quite close to that of European Union countries of similar size. In this partial sense these countries managed very rapidly to integrate into the Western European economy.

### Liberalisation of the capital account

Trade liberalisation requires 'current account convertibility',[10] i.e. exporters and importers have to be able to buy and sell foreign exchange for their transactions. 'Current account convertibility' thus makes the domestic currency convertible only for trade, or other 'current' transactions. A much-debated question is whether foreign currency should also be made freely accessible for capital account transactions.

Why should trade transactions be free (subject at most to a uniform tariff), whereas capital transactions remain restricted? The main issue here is macroeconomic stability and the state of the domestic financial market. In an ideal world there would be no need to impose restrictions on capital movements. However, the creation of an efficient domestic financial market is the part of the overall reform that might take the most time. Transition countries are thus likely to be for some time in a second-best world, in the sense that the domestic financial market is not working well.

In many reforming economies macroeconomic stabilisation was delayed. In these cases interest rates were often kept very low; lower than the rate of inflation or the rate of depreciation of the currency that could be reasonably expected. Russia provides the best example of this situation: in 1992–3 interest rates on the interbank market and those charged by the Central Bank of Russia, were about 100 to 200 per cent p.a. while inflation was running at 2,000 per cent and the exchange rate was depreciating at a similar rate. In such circumstances anybody with access to credit could make a huge profit by just investing the proceeds in foreign exchange. This was clearly not in the interest of the country as a whole, since the government was at the same time desperately seeking funds on the international capital market. For the individual concerned it was, of course, completely rational to invest in the world capital market (and thus give a credit to foreigners). But the country as a whole lost from these operations because the social return for Russia would have been much higher if this capital had been invested at home. Prohibition of foreign exchange transactions not related to foreign trade can reduce this loss. Of course, it would be better still for the country to raise nominal interest above the inflation rate. In that case there might not be a massive capital outflow and hence no need for prohibition.

Another, related, circumstance in which limitations on capital movements can be justified arises when budget constraints on some sectors of the economy are not yet hardened. For example, large enterprises that are nominally owned by the state, but de facto no longer under its control, or enterprises taken over by influential oligarchs might have access to the banking system under the assumption that they are 'too large to fail'. These enterprises might also borrow large sums that they invest abroad. If the country as a whole is at the same time refused additional credit from abroad, this type of operation reduces social welfare. This has been a problem in Russia.

There can thus be situations in which it is not in the interest of the country to permit full capital account convertibility. The best solution would, of course, be to eliminate the distortions in the domestic financial market. However, this might not always be feasible immediately. If these financial market distortions cannot be eliminated, a second-best measure remains to limit capital account convertibility. These limitations will, in practice, to some extent be circumvented through overbilling of imports, underbilling of exports and in many other ways. Effectiveness is always curtailed.

Even as a second best response, restrictions on capital movements have a drawback: they need to be enforced. By contrast, full convertibility has one big advantage: it does not require any controls. Countries with a sound macroeconomic balance should thus move to capital account convertibility. Estonia is a good example. It would have been difficult for the Estonian authorities to control capital movements when the country re-emerged from the FSU, because the government had to be organised from scratch. Moreover, the government was able to balance its books quite quickly, and hard budget constraints were effectively imposed on state-owned enterprises. This is why, in this case, it was sensible simply to lift all controls on foreign exchange transactions, which is tantamount to capital account convertibility.

### Currency convertibility and the exchange rate regime

When liberalisation started in 1989–90 it was often argued that an immediate move to (current account) convertibility was not possible because the countries concerned (Poland, in the first instance) did not have enough foreign exchange reserves. However, subsequent events proved that this argument was wrong. Provided the exchange rate is low enough, convertibility does not require large reserves. Indeed, a purely floating exchange rate does not need any support in terms of foreign exchange reserves. However, for reasons discussed below, most reforming countries initially opted for a fixed exchange rate.

The classic options regarding the exchange rate regime are: a free float, a fixed but adjustable peg and a dual exchange rate system combining the first two options. More extreme solutions have also been adopted: Estonia chose the currency board solution, copied by several other countries.

The free-floating option has gained little support among reformers. The governments of reforming countries must guarantee, among other conditions, stability and, in particular, reduce uncertainties about their exchange rates if they want to increase external trade and attract foreign investment. With the limited financial instruments that are available, flexible exchange rates are likely to create an uncertainty for traders that cannot be hedged as easily as among currencies with more developed financial markets. No country in Eastern Europe has refrained from interventions in the foreign exchange market. Even in Latvia, which formally had a free float until February 1994 (since when the Lat has been pegged to the IMF's Special Drawing Right), the central bank intervened heavily to slow down the appreciation of the Lat.

With weak financial markets, fixed exchange rates have to be adjustable and have to be supported by capital controls; otherwise, the exchange rate commitment could be undermined at any time by speculative flows, owing to political and economic uncertainties that cannot be eliminated during the transition.

One solution for the transition is, therefore, an intermediate regime between fixed and flexible exchange rates, i.e. a dual exchange system. This solution is economically equivalent to fixed exchange rates with varying capital levies on capital transactions.[11] In such a system, current account transactions are treated at the controlled, and usually fixed, exchange rate, while financial funds flow in and out of the country at a freely flexible exchange rate. Such a system was introduced temporarily in Poland and Romania.

The underlying aim of such a system is to shelter the domestic real economy from external and domestic financial shocks. At the micro level, capital can flow in and out of the country in pursuit of the most favourable return–risk trade-off. However, at the macro level there can be no net capital flows unless the central bank chooses to intervene in the market for capital account, i.e. financial transactions. The free, financial rate has to adjust in such a way that the capital account is always in equilibrium. In such a system the domestic monetary authorities do not have to react to financial shocks from the outside. The system automatically redirects the burden of adjustment to the financial exchange rate instead of to the domestic interest rate. The current account exchange rate can be kept constant, thereby maintaining stability for the relative prices of goods and services, provided domestic prices are stable.

In fact, by imposing a varying tax on capital transactions (equal to the flexible gap between the controlled and uncontrolled exchange rates), such a system reduces the substitutability between domestic and external assets, without erecting any barrier to capital flows at the level of individual transactions. This imperfect substitutability confers some latitude on domestic monetary authorities. In practice, however, the latitude of the domestic monetary authorities is limited because the spread between the controlled and the uncontrolled rates is constrained by the impossibility of a leak-proof separation of both exchange market compartments.[12] On reflection, this is an advantage rather than a disadvantage: when the free rate moves far away from the fixed rate then it is unlikely that the fixed rate is still an appropriate rate. This tension would suggest the need for a fixed rate adjustment and policymakers cannot sustain the fixed rate at the wrong level for too long.

An essential feature of the dual exchange system is that there cannot be any net capital inflow or outflow unless the central bank decides to intervene in the financial exchange market. The central bank is therefore released from financing net capital imbalances but has to support current account disequilibriums.

Such a regime should, however, be strictly temporary. Given the flexibility inherent in such a system, it would be straightforward to wind it down gradually by eliminating the implicit capital controls through a commitment to keep the spread between the two rates within certain limits that are reduced over time. Belgium operated a dual exchange rate system for over forty years with considerable success. Its discontinuation in 1991 was not even noticed by market participants.

Two decisions are of overriding importance in fixing the (commercial) exchange rate. First, the choice of currency to which the national currency is pegged and, second, the rate for the peg. This second choice is mainly an empirical question and we only wish to stress that the frequent error of maintaining an overvalued exchange rate needs to be avoided. In this respect, West European experience after the Second World War is a good lesson: growth resumed only when overvaluation ended and was highest in those countries with currencies close to or below purchasing power parity rates. Unfortunately, only a few transition countries could maintain the initially favourable real exchange rates (Hungary, Slovenia, Slovakia). Most had significant real exchange appreciations during 1993–8.

Under fixed exchange rates, a small country can, at best, only achieve the monetary stability of the currency to which it is pegged. It can, of course, do worse. This constraint suggests that if a country aims at monetary stability then it should peg to a stable currency that becomes the anchor for its national monetary system. The DM or the euro were therefore more promising than the US dollar, for considerations of both stability and trade structure.

## 3.3   Property rights and financial markets

Price liberalisation can only stimulate the production (as opposed to the distribution) of scarce goods by the private sector if individuals and enterprises can engage in this activity and can own factors of production. This freedom is thus another indispensable ingredient of any transformation programme, which can also be achieved at the stroke of a pen. To be effective, however, it must be accompanied by private ownership of factors of production. The supply responses to price reforms will thus remain weak unless the restrictions on private property rights of the means of production are eliminated.

But private ownership is no more than a starting point. What counts are the rights and obligations attached to ownership and how stable they are expected to be. Property rights are the fundamental defining elements of any organised society.

In agriculture, the main factor is land. Land ownership by individuals is taken for granted in the West and in Central Europe, and re-establishing the unlimited freedom to own, sell and buy it posed no problem there. However, in Russia and other CIS states with a different tradition this issue has not been settled, with the result that production and investment have declined sharply.

In industry the main factor is physical capital (human capital has always been privately owned, although the attached property rights were severely limited under communism: the freedom to choose a profession or employment). Private ownership of factors of production and the availability of labour are thus essential ingredients of a market economy.

But not only the laws have to be changed to make private ownership economically viable. The practical guarantee of equal treatment of private and state-owned companies is no less important. This is again a question of implementation.

This much is obvious. However, the real problem arises with the ownership of the existing stock of capital. Since at the beginning of the transition all land, buildings and machinery are owned by the state, the private sector can develop only very slowly (through the accumulation of capital) unless a large part of the state-owned capital is transferred quickly into private hands.

Privatisation (of land and capital) is thus a crucial part of the transition programme. However, experience has shown that privatisation is different from price liberalisation and freedom to enter a business. Experience in a number of post-socialist countries has shown that it is comparatively easy to privatise quickly small enterprises (essentially shops and restaurants) and small agricultural plots, because the new owner can immediately assume effective control over the enterprise. That this small enterprise privatisation frequently only changes the nature of the property rights contract (typically from leaseholder or employed worker to owner-worker) without calling for complicated reassignments of rights and re-distribution creates a favourable and largely non-conflictual political backing.

Privatisation of large enterprises (the majority of all manufacturing units had more than 100 employees under the socialist regime) is much more difficult: the state and existing management lose control and therefore rents; employees fear loss of employment or loss of shirking; and society at large is worried about the 'nouveaux riches'. Also from an economic viewpoint efficiency is not ensured by mere privatisation, as formal ownership does not necessarily also imply effective control. This problem exists also in market economies and it has never been fully resolved. Different countries have developed different institutions to deal with the effects of corporate governance: that is, the fact that it is difficult for a large number of shareholders to control effectively the management of large enterprises.

Intimately linked with the privatisation of the existing state-owned stock of capital is the question of the organisation of financial markets. To privatise means to sell capital, so that privatisation helps to create a capital market. If it is well done, an efficient capital market will develop. Such markets have never existed in centrally planned economies and there is a lack of experienced native specialists. But privatisation cannot really proceed in a void. If there are no banks and no other institutions that can provide capital for investments, the government will de facto continue to dominate the economy. Privatisation must thus go hand-in-hand with financial market reform.

## *Why privatisation?*

In Eastern Europe, the success of Western economies is perceived so overwhelmingly that market-based capitalism appears as the only widely shared objective for social organisation. History has shown that a market economy based on private property performs much better than socialism. Yet the theoretical support for the transformation of non-market economies into capitalist ones is less solid than is often assumed. See Stiglitz (1987) and Arrow (1987).

Any privatisation programme should set out to achieve a range of objectives. First and foremost, privatisation should be viewed as an instrument for promoting efficiency by creating an incentive-based economy. Second, privatisation should lead to a distribution of ownership that is accepted as fair. This is important because otherwise political support for the reforms could diminish and turn into a general climate of resistance to change. Third, the privatisation process should serve the creation of a market structure compatible with the expectations of a decentralised and ultimately democratic society. Private ownership is necessary to achieve separation of political and economic decisions and in this separation lies the scope for efficiency and stability gains.

The first aim, increased efficiency, cannot be achieved at the stroke of a pen through a change of ownership. West European experience clearly shows that ownership per se is not really the issue. Indeed, if enterprises are to be compelled to behave more efficiently, they must face competitive pressures in markets with rational prices and hard budget constraints (Newbery 1991). Therefore, as shown by Vickers and Yarrow (1988), the major determinant of success in transforming the performance of state owned enterprises (SOE) is not just ownership, but the entire economic environment in which they operate.

The success of privatisation hinges on owners' ability to monitor managers' performance properly. A firm is the result of incomplete contractual arrangements under asymmetric and incomplete information (Coase 1937). Except in the case of the owner-manager, all enterprise structures are subject to some form of principal–agent problem. Whilst there is no ideal institutional solution, it is possible to do better than in Russia.

The principal agent conundrum is not only a microeconomic problem. It has often been noted, for example in Lipton and Sachs (1990), that wage earners in reforming economies are not confronted with principals who effectively oppose wage increases or reduction in work efforts. Failure to address this problem can lead to macroeconomic destabilisation, as became clear in Russia.

In the early period following privatisation, the stock market is also unlikely to provide sufficient discipline to ensure the strict control of large firms.[13] The most promising corporate governance mechanism is likely to be a combination of widespread shareholdings, with the shareholders assisted in their role of principals by institutions acting on their behalf. There is some choice as to the type of institution: banks acting as equity investors ('universal banks') is one example, the unit trust (investment funds) is another. To guarantee further the efficiency of the principal's role, foreigners should be allowed to participate in the management of institutional funds.

## Valuation of firms

The valuation of firms in reforming economies is considerably more complex than in mature market economies, as their future viability and performance is hard to assess in a highly unsettled environment. We discuss two aspects: market structure and macroeconomic uncertainty.

### Market structure: is there a need for competition policy?

In reforming economies many large SOE face no domestic competition at all, simply because there are few or no other firms which produce the same kind of product. In the FSU it is estimated that, for two out of every three products, a single plant was the main supplier (Bennett and Dixon 1992). This situation was due to the fact that SOE were generally highly integrated both vertically and horizontally. The peculiar production structure that led to this monopolistic market structure will, of course, change over time, but in the meantime the market structure will remain different from that in the West. It needs a drastic overhaul if privatisation is to generate the full advantages of competition.

This has important implications for privatisation since, whether public or private, monopolies behave in much the same manner (Vickers and Yarrow 1988). It should be borne in mind that for most products monopolies can exist only by the grace of government. If governments do not want them to exist, the most effective means of ensuring competitive behaviour is to introduce a measure of 'contestability' through foreign trade.

There are two main ways of avoiding uncompetitive market practices: regulation and openness. In the particular case of Eastern Europe, regulation is the more debatable method, chiefly because the authorities' decisionmaking prerogatives are in danger of being captured by interest groups. The recommendation of the classical maxim 'Competition where possible, regulation where necessary' is the safer alternative. For the tradable goods sector, competition can be ensured by liberalising foreign trade. Only sectors that because of technical constraints cannot be exposed to foreign competition (e.g. the electricity grid) are in need of regulation. Nevertheless, since a fair and sound regulatory system is never easy to design, contestability should be promoted in preference to regulation wherever possible.

Product markets are not the only ones that should be made competitive. A well-functioning labour market is also crucial to successful restructuring. Since substantial unemployment must be contended with, at least in the short term, the whole reform process could be in jeopardy if firms' employment choices were straitjacked. Unless employment levels are adjusted, productivity gains will be minimal, and the reallocation of labour across the economy and the acquisition of new skills made more difficult. Liberalisation of the labour market will meet with dogged resistance on the part of workers unless the overall reform package is perceived as fair and credible and offers a secure safety net. Experience shows that during the first year or two of reforms unemployment rises only slowly, suggesting that initial restructuring is de facto quite limited and workers are kept on the payroll even when output declines strongly. This explains the low levels of unemployment even in reform-minded areas like the Czech Republic and the CIS countries.

### Macroeconomic uncertainty

Given the highly uncertain environment in which firms – domestic and foreign – will have to operate, macroeconomic instability presents awesome risks. The longer it takes the authorities to establish credibility, to temper the surrounding uncertainty and to stabilise the economy, the slower adjustment will be. As demonstrated by Dixit (1989), uncertainty can be a powerful disincentive to grasp investment opportunities. Indeed, in a turbulent environment, there is great pressure on potential entrepreneurs to delay even attractive projects, if part of the investment is irreversible.[14]

A 'wait and see' attitude by investors is an optimal response to uncertainty. In the laggard transition countries the only way to induce more domestic and foreign investment is to reduce uncertainty. Indeed, a potential investor when deciding whether or not to go ahead with a project, is faced with three options: to invest now; not to invest at all; or to keep the investment opportunity open for future reference. It is this third possibility that makes the investment opportunity resemble a call option. If the excess rate of return of the investment over the opportunity cost of capital is not high enough to compensate for risk, it is optimal not to exercise the option and to wait and see how economic conditions evolve. Investment will therefore not be forthcoming unless the option is sufficiently deep in the money. Furthermore, Dixit's calculations show that the excess current return necessary to induce investment is a positive function of both the level of uncertainty and the degree of investment irreversibility. Even for small amounts of uncertainty and irreversibility, the premium required to undertake the investment project can be considerable. Macroeconomic uncertainty thus not only increases uncertainty about the value of the firm, it also reduces the amount of investment potential all private owners (domestic or foreign) will undertake.

This discussion clearly shows that the valuation of East European firms is fraught with enormous difficulties. Any attempt to sell a significant number of large companies all at once is likely to lead to rock-bottom prices. Another reason why it is difficult to sell large enterprises rapidly is that domestic savers will not be able to bid large amounts if they have to pay in cash. The flow from domestic savings is limited for each time period and quite small relative to the value of the stock of capital of the entire economy. Sinn and Sinn (1991) stress this effect in their analysis of the sell-off of state-owned enterprises (SOE) in the former German Democratic Republic. It is clear that any attempt to sell 100 per cent of the capital stock of an economy within a short period, say a year, must depress prices below the value of firms. The only way out of this conundrum would be to allow investors to pay later, i.e. for the government to accept IOUs in exchange for control over the assets of the SOE. But this would entail major risks, since it would always remain uncertain to what extent investors would actually pay up later (they have every incentive to take the assets and run; see Russia).

Insufficient domestic savings can be overcome by selling SOE to foreigners. The potential of a 'sell-out' to foreigners has, however, been strongly resisted everywhere. Politically it has proved unacceptable to sell a large portion of industrial assets, notably the 'jewels', to foreigners owing to the fear of losing national control. Foreign investors are anyway likely to buy in most countries only at rock-bottom prices, since the risk of a reversal of reforms or a future (re)nationalisation can never be eliminated. In the Central European countries that are to become members of the EU, these problems have been marginalised. But in the countries of the FSU, which had just become independent, the desire to safeguard 'sovereignty' proved too strong.

## *The case for giveaway privatisation*

As we have seen, to all intents and purposes it is not possible to sell quickly all SOE on a one-by-one basis. Is it preferable, then, to drop the one-by-one approach or, at least, accept a slower pace of privatisation?

What matters most on both economic and political grounds is that the privatisation process should be swift and comprehensive.[15] The attitude taken by the SOE themselves is paramount in determining the success of adjustment in Eastern Europe, because SOE dominate industry inevitably in the short-run. At the outset of the reforms the ownership structure will certainly not be ideal, but if managers and workers know that privatisation and a competitive environment are around the corner they will start immediately to adjust (provided they are prevented from running off with the firm's assets). A clear, realistic timetable for reform is thus crucial in ensuring that the SOE respond from the beginning to market signals.

Experience has shown that the transitional phase, in which the economic incentive system associated with central planning has been jettisoned but no market economy is yet in place, is the most dangerous phase. In the resulting fog of uncertain property rights and effective lack of management supervision, it is child's play for managers to dispose of enterprise assets for their personal benefit, bringing decapitalisation and collapse of the production process in its wake.

Of course, a rapid change of ownership structure also has a price. One of the consequences will be a sharp increase in unemployment as the newly privatised firms shed excess labour and become more efficient. Another possible consequence is a highly skewed redistribution of income, which, in turn, might produce a political backlash. These consequences may well arise, but there are steps to mitigate the cost of transition by retaining some of the alternatives mentioned below.

Moreover, one also has to consider the cost of a more soft-pedalling alternative. What would be wrong with, say, privatising a handful of firms every now and again, so that it would take several years for a substantial proportion of firms to move to the private sector? The state would then continue to control most of industry and one could argue that this would be as in some West European countries, where the privatisation drive of the 1980s left public sector enterprises in partial charge of certain industrial sectors. The hitch in this argument is that public sector companies in the West are a small part of the overall economy and have to reckon with market signals if they are to hold their own against private enterprises. They operate in an established market economy with all the trappings of financial markets, ownership structures and control machinery firmly in place.

The gradualist and piecemeal approach would also mean that the least efficient enterprises would be the last to leave the public sector arena, if indeed they were sold off at all. This is amply illustrated by the Treuhand experience in Germany. The point is that such enterprises are both large and numerous. They would constitute a significant drain on public sector finances for some time to come, as it would be politically costly to close them down.

After the chaotic privatisations in many transition countries, a few lessons emerged. First, hard budget constraints need to be established prior to privatisation. Second, the legal and regulatory framework needs to be prepared beforehand. Third, the distributive effects should not be ignored to maintain popular support for the creation of a 'capitalist society'.

Given the pitfalls of standard privatisation procedures in Eastern Europe, a number of alternative proposals have been put forward. These typically rely on some sort of distributive scheme involving the free distribution or sale at a nominal fee of a share of the ownership in SOE to private citizens. This obviates the need for valuing enterprises, a task of Herculean proportions, as was argued above.

We now elaborate in some detail a proposal already submitted in Gros and Steinherr (1990). Although most SOE are by now already privatised in most transition countries, privatisation is nowhere complete. We propose that whenever a large public-sector company is privatised, a percentage of its capital (perhaps 30–50 per cent) would be given away. There are two ways of doing this, which are not mutually exclusive and could therefore be combined:

(a) The number of shares to be given for free is set equal to the number of eligible citizens, with everybody receiving one share, either directly or indirectly, as part of a national investment fund.
(b) The number of shares is set equal to the number of workers in the firm, each of whom receives one share.

Under alternative (a), each citizen would receive one share in the form of a book entry. Over time, as privatisation progressed, each citizen would hold an increasingly diversified portfolio. Obviously, not all citizens would be interested in holding all the shares they received and an informal market would therefore quickly be established. This would provide the basis for an over-the-counter market that could eventually blossom into an organised stock exchange. An investor wishing to obtain control over a company would have to acquire shares at market rates or with a takeover proposal. Whether the investor was a resident or a non-resident would then be a question of secondary importance. Citizens, as shareholders, would decide whether to cash in now rather than later – or not at all – as in a referendum, about each sale to foreigners, with the clear advantage that each citizen would have the same endowment of 'voting' rights (one share). A possible sell-out to foreigners could not be criticised because it would not be a decision taken by the old or a new nomenklatura.

Such a privatisation programme would be flexible enough to accommodate worker participation, if desired, by combining it with alternative (b). Instead of strengthening union power along the lines of the German *Mitbestimmung*, workers could be allocated shares in their firm, which would give them voting rights and a stake in the firm's results. Needless to say, there should be no ban on disposing of such shares, so as to allow for better risk diversification.

One implication of such a scheme would be that all workers would receive shares in all firms slated for privatisation, plus a special allocation of shares in their own firm. Public sector employees would be excluded from that special allocation. Economically speaking, the firm-specific allocations might be likened to a risk premium, since the risk of bankruptcy or layoffs is higher in the private sector. Moreover, as the public administrations inherited from the old system present a bad case of hypertrophy anyway, some sort of incentive to leave public sector employment might be useful.

Finally, it might be a good idea if, for a limited time, governments maintained a minority share of 10–30 per cent. The government could in this way make sure there is no abuse during the restructuring phase. The countervailing power of worker-shareholders and of outside shareholders should suffice to prevent the government from pursuing objectives too antagonistic to long-term value maximisation. Moreover, the government would automatically receive a part of future profits. All shareholders, including the government, would participate even in profits that are hidden from (initially imperfectly administered) corporate taxes, as share values over time would reflect these hidden profits.

Privatisation along these lines offers several attractive advantages, three in particular:

• First, it would be consistent with social justice. In fact, the concept of 'social ownership of the means of production' would for the first time have real, as opposed to rhetorical, meaning.

- Second, to launch into a market economy with some social capital distributed to all has definite political appeal. Capitalism would then also be perceived as a system with the potential not only for greater dynamism but even for greater social justice than the defunct 'social ownership'. This is a notion much prized in Western Europe, where privatisation often aims at spreading share ownership as widely as possible. It might be argued that citizens owning a portfolio of shares in national industry turn into convinced 'capitalists' and recognise its 'human face'.
- Third, private ownership, if widely distributed at the starting-point, is liable to command stronger support than alternative property rights proposals. Recent difficulties with privatisation everywhere in Eastern Europe confirm this view. The right of governments to privatise, the prices negotiated, the neglect of workers' interests (and more generally those of the general public) have all run into fierce criticism.

A major objection to all variants of the giveaway solution is that it deprives governments of the revenue that would be generated by selling off SOE. In theory, selling SOE and redistributing the revenue to citizens in the form of lower taxes or better services amounts to the same thing. In practice, however, governments could retain privatisation revenues to limit the deficits they usually run during the transition. At any rate, government receipts from selling SOE have been negligible in most countries.

The whole point of privatisation is to achieve better control over the productive sector. Diffuse share ownership carries the risk of leaving effective control in the hands of the existing nomenklatura. That is why it is important that voting rights be exercised effectively until stock market control is established – a process that will require time. To this end one could set up financial investment companies entitled to acquire shares, up to certain limits, in a restricted number of firms (e.g. one firm per industry). Citizens and the state would jointly own these financial companies or, alternatively, they could be privately owned and manage shares directly owned by citizens.

The 'giveaway' approach has been criticised for not providing efficient corporate governance. However, actual privatisation outcomes certainly fail the corporate governance test in most countries. If 10 per cent of the shares of a company were retained by government, 10 per cent given to the workers and 29 per cent to citizens, then any investor could acquire 51 per cent of capital and so control the firm. Over time shares may be acquired from the other shareholders to gain even more control. It would, however, be much easier to obtain a higher acquisition price with this approach than by selling out immediately.

## 3.4   The remaining role of the government: macroeconomic stability and an efficient fiscal system

Even if the basic elements of a market economy are established, a private sector will not emerge if the monetary and fiscal systems are not reformed. Confiscatory tax rates are equivalent to a formal prohibition of private ownership and must thus be abolished. However, with the establishment of a market economy the state does not disappear. It still has to produce some public goods (defence, police, justice, etc.) and it therefore has to levy some taxes. It is thus not possible to maintain or simply eliminate old taxes, instead a new 'market conforming' fiscal system needs to be created.

Another task for the government is to maintain a stable macroeconomic environment. The experience of transition countries shows that high and variable inflation rates have very damaging effects on investment and growth. While a private sector can work in almost any macroeconomic circumstances, growth will really start only if investors can rely on a minimum of macroeconomic stability. This minimum requires a stable inflation rate. History demonstrates, however, that it is near to impossible to stabilise the inflation rate at levels much higher than a few percentage points. It is therefore more practical to aim at price stability. Price stability can be realised only if the fiscal accounts are more or less balanced. This is difficult to achieve at the beginning of the transformation process because expenditures continue to be high and the new fiscal system might not yield immediately all the potential revenues.

Experience has shown that the most dangerous phase comes during the beginning of the transition, when the old controls no longer operate (prices and wages have been liberalised) but the new macroeconomic tools are not yet in place. In this vacuum, compounded by uncertainty about the future, temporary disruptions in the production process, loss of traditional export markets and a long list of related problems, chances are high that inflation will go out of control. When this happens, all the other parts of the reform programme are threatened as well. One therefore has to draw a limit and consider both sides of it: the cost of hyperinflation and chaos on the one hand, and the cost and temporary hardship of stabilisation on the other. Hyperinflation is generally defined as inflation of 50 per cent per month or more. By this definition hyperinflation is a rare phenomenon; but among reforming countries all CIS countries have already experienced hyperinflation at some point.

The so-called 'monetary overhang', which was considered an obstacle to price liberalisation at the very beginning of the reforms in Central and East European countries (CEEC), presented two dangers for macroeconomic stabilisation that are specific to economies in transition. First, how to assert some control over nominally still 'state-owned' enterprises, which in fact no longer follow the orders of the state. And, second, fiscal reform, i.e. how to obtain enough revenues for the state that the recourse to the inflation tax can be limited.

## *The monetary overhang*

In a number of socialist countries the so-called 'monetary overhang' (see box 3.3) was seen as a serious obstacle to price liberalisation. It was argued that after price liberalisation consumers would spend all their accumulated excess cash balances and this would lead to inflation. It would have been more appropriate to speak of a jump in the price level, but the discussion was usually in terms of inflation. Price liberalisation led, indeed, in all cases to a jump in the price level. However, the size of the initial jump differed greatly, from about 50 per cent in Czechoslovakia to over 300 per cent in Russia (see table 3.5). There were also great differences in terms of the subsequent performance: prices stabilised in some countries (Czechoslovakia, Latvia), but in Russia and to some extent Poland prices continued to increase rapidly even after the initial jump.

Table 3.5. *Countries in transition: consumer prices (annual % change)*

|  | 1989 | 1990 | 1991 | 1992 | 1993 |
|---|---|---|---|---|---|
| Czechoslovakia | 1.4 | 10.8 | 57.7 | 10.8 | 20.8* |
| Hungary | 17.0 | 28.9 | 36.4 | 23.0 | 22.5 |
| Poland | 251.1 | 585.8 | 70.3 | 43.0 | 35.3 |
| Russia | 2.3** | 5.6 | 92.7 | 1353.0 | 895.9 |

*Notes*: * Czech Republic; ** USSR.
*Source*: IMF, *World Economic Outlook*.

---

### Box 3.3   *Monetary overhang*

A monetary or liquidity overhang is defined as an excess stock of cash or savings deposits (and the sight deposits of firms) because the population has been 'forced to save'. In order to speak of an 'overhang', it is first necessary to establish that the actual holdings are somehow excessive. A monetary overhang is usually diagnosed if the actual ratio of cash (or savings deposits) to income exceeds that observed in market economies.

There are two reasons why the ratio of cash or financial assets to income may be much larger in socialist than in market economies. They are basically dissimilar, and only if we understand the difference between the two can we predict with some confidence what might happen during stabilisation.

The first reason is excess demand and rationing, in particular in goods markets. This may prompt consumers to hold both a large volume of goods ('buy when you can, not when you need') and of cash (so as to be able to seize the opportunity of buying things). Such behaviour is well documented, not only for consumers, but also in the case of East European firms, which tended to carry unusually high levels of raw materials and goods in process to avoid breaks in production.

The second, more widely emphasised, reason is forced savings, i.e. the fact that consumers are not able to spend their money on what they want. A closer analysis suggests, however, that 'forced savings' are likely to be temporary and will arise only under extreme conditions from a microeconomic point of view (the incentives faced by an individual household), but from a macroeconomic point of view very different conclusions emerge.

At the *microeconomic* level it makes sense to speak of forced savings if *all* prices are fixed and *all* goods are rationed, because only in these circumstances would people be forced to save what they could not spend anywhere. But even in the worst days of the Soviet Union, some goods were available, and there was a thriving black market, operating at market-clearing prices, for a range of products. Households could, then, always find some goods on which to spend 'excess' savings. Forced savings should thus be only temporary since, if people do not expect shortages to ease, there is no reason for them to keep saving, for tomorrow will be no different from today.

In other words, sustained forced saving means either that many people are incurable optimists, or that they have no access to the black market (including the black market for foreign exchange), or that they have no use at all for the goods available at market-clearing prices. Only when liberalisation is actually in the air does it make sense to build up an excess balance. But why should the public accumulate domestic currency (in cash or ill-remunerated deposits) when it has to expect that the prices of most goods will go up? On the contrary their attempt to spend just before price reform ensures that the queues will get even longer (and the shelves even emptier), as could be observed in the Soviet Union towards the end of 1991.

The reasoning so far looked only at the incentives of individual households to accumulate savings. However, the term 'forced savings' does make sense from an economy wide, or *macroeconomic* point of view. The underlying cause for the monetary overhang is a mismatch between wages and the amount of goods available at the state-controlled price level. In many socialist economies the sum of all wages in the economy exceeded the available supply of goods at the price level fixed by the government. Imagine a socialist economy with 1,000 workers that produces 1,000 widgets (one per worker, per unit of time). The government fixes the price of each widget at 1 (rouble). However, workers receive a salary of 2 (roubles); the total salary mass is thus 2,000 (roubles). Workers will try to spend all their salary, but on average they will not be able to do so since only one widget per capita is on sale in the shops. (On average, of course. Some workers with better connections might be able to get two widgets; others might have to do without.) At the aggregate level the population is therefore 'forced' to save the difference between the total wage bill and the value of the total supply of goods sold through state stores. Trade, even at market clearing prices, between households does not affect the aggregate equilibrium since the only way cash can go back to the government is via the state-owned stores or savings accounts.

At the aggregate level households are thus 'forced' to save. However, they will do this only if prices and expectations are such that each individual household does so voluntarily. Expectations about the future become crucial in this respect: if households perceive that the supply of goods (especially consumer durables) will increase in future they will want to put part of their income into savings accounts until the goods arrive. If they expect the shortages to increase, they will bid up prices on the black market to the point where they are indifferent, at the margin, between consuming black market goods or saving the money after all.

The inflationary pressures that did in fact persist in most, but not all, post-socialist countries after the initial price shock were thus due not just to the combination of price liberalisation and monetary overhang. Theoretical considerations and empirical evidence suggests that the main cause of continuing inflation were lax financial policies, in turn due to a lack of control over SOE and an inefficient fiscal system.

How large was the monetary overhang in the various CEEC? In most socialist economies planners were able to keep the difference between the wage bill and the value of the available consumer goods relatively small. This should not have been difficult since there was little pressure for higher wages and the monetary value of the supply of consumer goods could

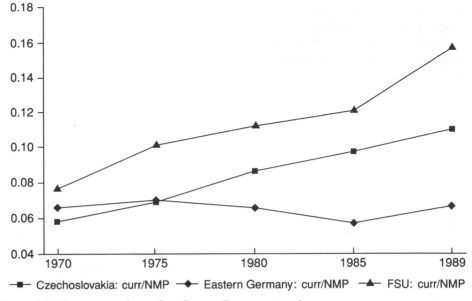

**Figure 3.2**  Monetary overhang: three Eastern European experiences

be calculated easily. However, in most socialist countries the growth rate of money (cash and savings deposits) exceeded that of nominal income by a little, and even small flows can grow to considerable stocks over time. Households might have been quite content to accumulate considerable savings during the 1960s when growth was still satisfactory. However, as growth slowed and turned into stagnation during the 1980s expectations changed and households were willing, or rather forced, to keep their savings balances only because queues got longer and longer. Moreover, as perestroïka proceeded in the USSR and political control became weaker in some Central European countries, workers demanded and obtained higher wages. The final straw came when price liberalisation was imminent. At that point one had to expect that prices were going to increase and people were willing to stand in line (or bribe shop employees) up to the point where the value of the time lost in the queue (or the bribe) was equal to the difference between the current price and the expected future price. At that point the stock disequilibrium became very large. This is why the so-called monetary overhang did indeed represent a serious problem in a number of countries. Figure 3.2 shows the ratio currency to NMP for the few countries for which long-term series are available. This graph shows that in the FSU disequilibrium was clearly building up, but that the problem was much less severe in the CSFR and in East Germany.

Widespread rationing, queues and a large price differential between official prices and black markets are sure indicators of a monetary overhang, but it proved extremely difficult to estimate the size of the jump in the price level that was required to eliminate the overhang. In all countries the increase in the price level that followed price liberalisation was larger than expected. The biggest error was made in Russia, where the IMF estimated an overhang

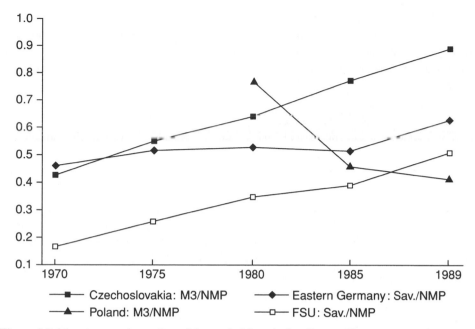

**Figure 3.3** Monetary overhang: financial asset holdings in four Eastern European countries

of about 50 per cent (in 1991), whereas prices jumped by almost 300 per cent in January 1992.[16]

How was it possible that most estimates were so wrong? Many advisers relied on sophisticated models of the demand for financial assets that work quite well over the long run in developed market economies. However, these models proved useless in predicting the behaviour of households in transition economies who had basically only three assets: cash, savings deposits and foreign currency. Velocity of savings deposits, which are an imperfect substitute for foreign exchange, turned out to be rather variable and there were important cross-country differences, as shown in figure 3.3. Chapter 8 discusses in more detail the case of Russia, which had the largest one-month jump in prices, and compares it to the Polish experience. It is shown there that for the short-run dynamics one could have made more accurate predictions if one had relied on the velocity of cash instead of that of savings deposits (M2). This is also confirmed by a comparison between figures 3.2 and 3.3. The first is correlated with the price jump after price liberalisation (none in the ex-GDR, 50 per cent in the CSFR and 250 per cent in Russia), whereas the second is not.

However, while the exact size of the overhang was not known ex ante, the reformist governments knew that they had to face this problem. They had a range of options: from confiscation – explicit or implicit (through inflation) – to consolidation. De facto confiscation was the approach that was actually followed in most countries, but we briefly discuss others as well.

Explicit confiscation by declaring *part* of the outstanding stock of money to be no longer legal tender was likely to be politically risky, as shown by the experience of the ill-fated attempt by the Ryzhkov government of the FSU to withdraw certain high-denomination rouble notes from circulation in early 1991. This approach was never again seriously considered. Currency reform, i.e. confiscating the *entire* stock of money, is the fast way of getting rid of the overhang. The German monetary reform of 1948 is one example of how this method has been used successfully in the past. But there is a catch. Since the 'incidence of the tax' associated with monetary reform is not distributed evenly across the population, the political support needed for a successful implementation of the tough follow-up policies may fall off. Governments may then be forced into income policies to provide social safety nets. As emphasised by Calvo and Frenkel (1991), the income policies that have to go with confiscation will reduce economic efficiency; the net advantage of confiscation might thus be reduced.

At the other end of the spectrum is consolidation, which can be achieved by making money, i.e. domestic liquid assets, attractive enough to households so that they want to hold the entire stock. The obvious way is to increase the rate of interest paid on domestic currency deposits. This should induce households to hold these assets (i.e. M2 or M3) instead of trying to use them right away to buy goods.

In choosing this approach, i.e. by raising the interest rate on bank deposits, governments are taking their chances in budgetary terms, at least while banks are still government-owned or government-backed. Bank deposits are to all intents and purposes public debt, and the interest on deposits may be regarded as public-debt service. Viewed from this angle, credit and budget policies are closely linked, and a rise in the deposit rate will need to be financed through new taxes. Whether or not consolidation is possible depends on the ability of the tax system to generate the necessary tax revenue, and on the distributive and efficiency implications of the associated 'incidence of the tax'. In this respect the situation in transforming economies is very different from that of post-war stabilisations. In Germany in 1948 the pre-stabilisation money-to-GDP ratio was considerably higher than the ratios in Central Europe or Russia (including or excluding savings accounts). Consolidation was clearly not an option in Germany at that time because paying a real interest rate of 2–3 per cent would have cost 10–15 per cent of GDP. It might have been an option in Central Europe and the countries of the FSU where this ratio was close to 1.

Instead of enticing people to hold large liquid balances, the government might also achieve a reduction in liquidity by enticing people to exchange their money balances for other assets, e.g. assets sold by the government on the open market. In Eastern Europe, the elimination of monetary overhang through open market sales was made difficult by the lack of conventional financial instruments and poorly developed capital markets. At the start of the reforms, it was often thought that the most promising way of absorbing excess liquidity would have been to sell off the housing stock and SOE. This was discussed in depth (especially in the FSU), but not carried out on a large scale anywhere. The receipts from the sale of housing and of those enterprises that could be sold quickly turned out to be too small to have a real effect on the monetary overhang.

Implicit confiscation through an upward jump of the price level was the course of (in)action actually chosen by most governments in Central and Eastern Europe. The main concern was the required jump in prices. It turned out to be difficult to predict how households would reorganise their assets and change their consumption behaviour. A priori, however, it was clear that a variety of considerations would have to come into play as outlined in Blanchard et al. (1990). The main considerations are that, in response to the removal of micro-rationing, people want to run down their stock of hoarded goods and reduce their cash holdings. They do this by shifting from cash to interest-yielding assets, and by consuming the goods they were hoarding, thus for a while reducing their consumer demand. In response to the removal of macro-rationing, they want to decrease their stock of financial assets and so bump up consumer demand. But, with the outlook for the future highly unsettled, they may also want to save, to prepare against future contingencies. How people behave at this juncture is thus difficult to predict. In general, the macroeconomic environment and the nature of the financial instruments available should be the main factors.

What happened in reality was that the future course of inflation was the chief source of uncertainty and lack of inflation-proof assets did prompt people to plump for consumption rather than saving. The demand for financial assets thus fell dramatically in countries where inflation was not brought under control, but even in these cases the holding of cash turned out to be quite predictable.

## *Sources of destabilisation*

All reforming countries had to deal with the monetary overhang. They chose to liberalise prices and the result was a jump in prices. In some cases this was the end of the story. For example in Czechoslovakia prices rose by about 25.8 per cent when prices were liberalised in January 1991, but during the remainder of the year inflation fell to about 1 per cent per month and stayed at that level during 1992 and 1993. In this case price liberalisation led mainly to a jump in the level. However, this turned out to be the exception, rather than the rule. In most other reforming countries the first years were characterised by macroeconomic problems in the form of rising fiscal deficits and substantial inflation rates. In Russia the initial jump in the price level was followed by monthly inflation of about 20 per cent per month and fiscal deficits in excess of 10 per cent of national income. Russia is an extreme example, but most reforming countries had similar problems.

The root of macroeconomic destabilisation was the uncontrolled price-push taking place in Eastern Europe during the last days of the *old* regime. Inflation arose because the declining political regime could not constrain unrealistic income aspirations. This situation fuelled inflation in two ways. First, it had a direct impact on the financial position, leading to budget deficits and monetisation. Second, the government, not keen for political reasons to countenance the economic contraction needed to reconcile income claims, instead accommodated wage and price increases through monetary expansion and so set the stage for a wage–price spiral.

Under the post-socialist regimes similar difficulties arose. But the visible, proximate cause for inflation was different from case to case. For the transforming economies there were three main dangers for macroeconomic destabilisation: (i) enterprises that did not accept a tight budget constraint, (ii) workers that did not accept the apparent decline in real wages that comes with price liberalisation and demanded wages that exceed productivity, and (iii) a fiscal deficit that exploded because profit transfers from SOE declined.

The first danger for stabilisation arose in most transforming economies immediately after price liberalisation when enterprises stopped paying each other. This led to a chain accumulation of so-called inter-enterprise arrears, as firms that were not paid by their clients were in turn unable to pay their suppliers. If this process had become widespread the price level could no longer have been controlled by monetary policy since enterprises could have financed any level of transactions by using inter-enterprise arrears as a substitute for money. In a certain sense the managers of the SOE had an interest in such a process freeing them of the budget constraints that had, in principle, also to be introduced with the reforms.

Calvo and Corricelli (1993) point out that there is an external effect in the arrears phenomenon in the sense that for each individual enterprise the cost of incurring arrears, i.e. the cost of not paying a bill, is a function of what other firms do. Consider a situation in which most enterprises pay on time. In this case it will not be too difficult for the creditor firm to put pressure on the few recalcitrant debtors, cutting off supplies or even initiating bankruptcy proceedings. Moreover, a non-paying firm cannot expect to be bailed out by the government because the presumption that it is not profitable is strong if all other firms pay. All this will be different when most firms do not pay their bills. In these circumstances it will be difficult for the creditor to put pressure on the debtor. Cutting off supplies does not help because nobody is paying anyway. Initiating bankruptcy proceedings would be difficult because the courts would not be able to handle thousands of cases and because the non-payment of bills might not be accepted as a cause for bankruptcy proceedings if it was common and if the debtor enterprise could claim that it could not pay because it was owed money by other enterprises. Finally, if arrears were widespread, firms could expect that the government would bail them out because the political costs of wholesale failures would be prohibitive.

The cost of not paying should thus be high when arrears are rare and it should be low when arrears are widespread. This suggests that two equilibria might exist: a low-arrears equilibrium in which firms pay their bills because the cost of not paying is high; and a high-arrears equilibrium in which few firms pay because the cost of not paying is negligible.

In the high-arrears equilibrium enterprises effectively no longer have a budget constraint (consumers still have one because they have to pay in cash). An ever-increasing chain of inter-enterprise arrears would thus not only threaten macroeconomic stabilisation, but the cornerstone of all reforms, i.e. the introduction of hard budget constraints. This is why the emergence of arrears caused considerable anxiety among policymakers.

It was also recognised early (see, e.g., Begg and Portes 1992) that inter-enterprise arrears also exist in developed Western market economies, where they are called suppliers' credit. The latter can be an efficient market mechanism that substitutes for bank credit because in some cases the supplier might know the financial conditions of his clients better than a bank. The real question was thus whether the arrears in the transforming economies went beyond this voluntary extension of suppliers' credit. Since there were vast differences in the experience of different countries it is not possible to assert that the extreme arrears equilibrium outline above was avoided globally. Many CIS countries are still in an extreme arrears equilibrium. With hindsight, however, it is clear that the problem was in most other cases less severe than initially thought.

The experience of Poland is instructive because the problem was most acute *before* the reforms were implemented (the level of arrears peaked at 18 per cent of GDP at the end of 1989). Once the reforms were implemented arrears declined to about one half of this value. In this case the reforms apparently created a credible budget constraint. In other countries, however, the arrears started to grow with the implementation of reforms. Apart from Romania, the most spectacular case was Russia. In mid-1992 the stock of arrears was equivalent to the GDP of Russia during that period. If one assumes that for each rouble of GDP (which is a value-added concept) there are two roubles of transactions between enterprises, then during the first half of 1992 every second transaction was not paid. This comes close to the bad equilibrium of a generalised 'no payment' environment without a budget constraint.

A second danger for stabilisation that arose in many instances was that workers did not accept the (largely) apparent cut in real wages that came with price reform. This raises the issue of income policies in the form of price and wage guidelines. Gros and Steinherr (1995) discuss this issue in detail.

## State-owned enterprises: a roadblock to fiscal stabilisation?

Once liberalisation gets underway, a serious fiscal problem typically arises because the formal central planning machinery is progressively weakened as decisionmaking and effective property rights pass to the SOE themselves, and perhaps to a newly enfranchised private or cooperative sector. Price controls may or may not be removed in this transitional period. The government is in effect surrendering its tax base by relinquishing control over state property. As the old taxation system was implicit rather than explicit, there is no formal tax collection service at the beginning of the transition that can claw back revenue from entities no longer under government control.

Profits from SOE were one of the major sources of revenue for the government. This source was subject to very large fluctuations in the initial transition period. Immediately after price liberalisation most SOE increased their profits because many of them were monopolies. Governments were often able to obtain part of these profits because they still conserved some effective control over SOE at the outset of the reform. This effect was important in Poland and Russia. Increased profits from SOE allowed the budgets in these two countries to be roughly balanced during the first few months after price liberalisation. However, as competition (especially from imports) increased, and as workers also demanded higher wages, the profits of SOE fell. Moreover, the control of the government over managers fell and some of the most profitable SOE were privatised. For all these reasons transfers of profits to the budget fell sharply after the first few months were over.

Of course, the transfer of some property away from direct government control is only the tip of the iceberg. There are other factors that hasten the decline in revenue. Central and local governments do not just sit back and let liberalisation run away with all their traditional industrial firms. They will, on the contrary, try to hang on to as many as possible. Yet as soon as goods and service markets are given a freer rein, the government's revenue position suffers. Industrial enterprises face new competitive challenges from newly enfranchised

Table 3.6. *Profit taxes in Russia (billions of roubles)*

| Year | Profit taxes | Total revenue | GDP | as % of GDP | |
| --- | --- | --- | --- | --- | --- |
| | | | | Profit taxes | Total revenues |
| 1992 | 1566.8 | 5327.6 | 18064.3 | 8.7 | 29.5 |
| 1993 | 16773.5 | 41449.1 | 162300.0 | 10.3 | 25.5 |
| 1994 | 18007.5 | 60012.0 | 245000.0 | 7.4 | 24.5 |

*Source*: 1992 and 1993: Ministry of Finance of Russian Federation; 1994: average of first two quarters in 1994 for profit tax/GDP; 1994: data first half year for total revenues/GDP

private or cooperative firms and, possibly, from freer imports. The industrial profit base contracts as the monopoly positions of the old SOE are undermined.

As revenue declines, the pressure increases on governments to slash expenditure. Since government-financed investment expenditure is usually the first casualty, local governments in particular press the banks to lend to the firms they own or control to finance their infrastructure investments. Not only does this foster unhealthy fiscal competition among parts of the government to whom control over enterprises means fiscal revenue, but, in addition, the forced extension of bank credit undermines monetary control. We return to this issue below.

With the transition to a market economy the government thus loses one of its most important sources of revenues. But, as mentioned above, in the very short run the reforming government typically experiences a windfall gain as revenue from profit taxes soars because prices initially increase by more than salaries. The experience of the first years in Russia confirms this, as shown in table 3.6, which refers to the consolidated government, i.e. the federal and regional governments together.

If profits decline because wages go up the government should receive higher wage (income) taxes that should offset the loss of profit taxes. However, it appears that this was not the case in Russia since profit taxes made up almost 80 per cent of all direct taxes throughout the period. Household income tax never accounted for more than 20 per cent of the profit tax.

In Poland the fall in profit taxes was even more striking: between 1990, the first year of the reforms, and 1991 the revenue from income tax fell by over 8 percentage points of GDP, from 14 per cent of GDP to 5.8 per cent.

The data presented in table 3.6 do not capture two other important elements of the short-run developments on the fiscal side that were mentioned so far:

(i) We argued that the federal government, responsible for setting macroeconomic policies, has to take the interests and possible reactions of local governments into account. This emerges most clearly in the case of Russia where about 44 per cent of all government revenues were raised at the regional level; for profit taxes the proportion was even above 60 per cent. In Poland local government levels were much less important, they accounted for only about 12 per cent of all government expenditure and receipts.

(ii) Another development concerns the expenditures that support SOE. During 1992 the Russian government received a total of 1,567 billion roubles in profit taxes, 8.7 per cent of GDP, but during that same period it spent 2,059 billion roubles, about 11 per cent of GDP, under the heading 'national economy', half of which constituted subsidies.[17] Since the economy was still dominated by SOE in 1992, most of these subsidies must have gone to the state sector. Moreover, since almost all the profit taxes must also have come from SOE, the '*net*' revenue from profit taxes (i.e. net of expenditure on subsidies of SOE of 1,000 billion roubles) was only about 500 billion roubles, about 3 per cent of GDP and less than 10 per cent of all government revenues.[18] In Poland the subsidies that survived during the first year of the reforms were also substantial since they were equivalent to about 50 per cent of the revenue from income taxes.

Thus the initial fiscal honeymoon did not last. Wages quickly recovered most of the ground lost relative to prices and profits therefore declined rapidly. Moreover, another dangerous development arose once the initial boom in profits was over: in some cases the 'soft budget constraint' threatened to reappear.

Just before the onset of reforms, i.e. once central planning was dismantled but the uncodified tax system based on the seizure of accumulated enterprise surpluses was not, managerial incentives came to grief. The syndrome of the 'soft budget constraint' was worse than ever: firms making incipient losses received subsidies for their pains (including cheap credit), while 'successful' firms were stripped of their surpluses. In addition, the government was in such dire need of revenue that it could not keep itself from intervening at random in order to extract more surpluses, a task considerably facilitated when enterprises' highly visible deposits with the state bank would be (re)frozen or seized.

The transition from this situation to one where banks lend only for viable projects and the government takes only a clearly identified part of profits requires some time.

Loss-making enterprises continue to borrow from the state bank, refuse to pay taxes or do not pay their suppliers to avoid layoffs, contributing to the loss of control over the money supply. A further complication is that once planning controls are removed, profitable enterprises will be anxious to spend the cash balances they could not previously touch lest they be seized or refrozen, adding to inflationary pressure. Luckily, however, this is only a once-and-for-all effect.

Another problem is that the productivity of physical capital – both fixed assets and inventories of inputs and goods – typically falls immediately after the reforms. As attractive monetary assets, whether liquid cash or time deposits bearing a positive real rate of interest, are not usually on offer, newly liberalised firms will overbid for storable material inputs, foreign exchange, capital goods and so forth. In effect, decentralised enterprises will carry 'excess' inventories of all kinds as substitute monetary stores of value (McKinnon 1991). The problem arises from the starting point for reforms that was in many cases catastrophic.

It was often alleged that managers of SOE would constitute a roadblock for reforms because they would not understand how to operate under market conditions and because their own interests were threatened by privatisation. The first argument is difficult to assess a priori. SOE worked in an environment that was, in a certain sense, even more difficult than a

Western market because supplies were erratic and workers could not always be disciplined. The limited evidence available from Poland, which managed to increase exports to the West by over 50 per cent during the first years after the reforms, suggests that, indeed, SOE managers were able to operate in a market economy since over 70 per cent of exports came from SOE. The second argument is rather weak, since any competent manager (who was not politically compromised) must have reckoned that his or her income could only increase in a market economy. Pinto, Belka and Krajewski (1993) suggest, furthermore, that the performance of SOE in Poland was much better than often expected. Interviewed, managers repeatedly did not express fundamental opposition to the reforms and did not object to the principle of hard budget constraints.

This confirms that the crucial element in determining the performance of enterprises is the hard budget constraint. In Poland the availability of cheap credit diminished sharply at the outset of the reforms. Since it took the banking system some time to become competitive, and competent enough to be able to distinguish between good and bad borrowers, large SOE continued for some time to have privileged access to credit. But even this did not last for more than one year. In contrast, in Russia, during the twelve to eighteen months following the Gaidar stabilisation of early 1992, SOE had ample access to cheap credit that came ultimately from the central bank. Under these conditions it is not surprising that little adjustment took place. SOE cannot threaten stabilisation if the central bank reins in overall credit expansion and if there is some discipline on the banking sector.

### Fiscal and monetary destabilisation

An interesting question is whether the fiscal problems just discussed led to inflation. A priori, one would expect this to be the case since fiscal and monetary policy are closely intertwined. The latter often serves to finance fiscal deficits and the former exerts an influence on aggregate demand in a way that may contradict the monetary objectives. A truly independent central bank, in control of monetary policy and responsible for regulating banks and financial markets, could, in principle, achieve sustained price stability. But granting independence to a central bank is one thing and maintaining it another. It is not enough merely to wave the constitutional wand: unwavering political and popular support are indispensable to continued independence. In the long run, independent central banks should not find it more difficult to achieve price stability than their Western counterparts. In the short run, the task is much more complex.

The problem for the central bank is that, in the very short run, the public sector has no alternative to monetary financing and reforms might seriously destabilise fiscal revenues, at least until revised tax laws succeed in broadening the tax base. In time, as growth picks up and the new tax system comes into full swing, these transitory deficits will evaporate. They can therefore be regarded as specific to a once-and-for-all change of regime, and a one-off financing method is justified. One such opportunity is to sell off housing and land to citizens with payments spread out over the years, as with mortgage financing. To encourage sizeable downpayments, a variable but positive real interest rate could be imposed without great difficulty on a scale sufficient to stabilise the initial budget.

Table 3.7. *Fiscal policy and inflation*

|  | Fiscal balance (% GDP) | Inflation (CPI annual % change) | Seigniorage (% GDP) |
|---|---|---|---|
| **Poland** | | | |
| 1989 | | 251.1 | 23.4 |
| 1990 | + 0.4 | 585.8 | 9.2 |
| 1991 | − 3.8 | 70.3 | 2.5 |
| 1992 | − 6.0 | 43.0 | 4.0 |
| **Hungary** | | | |
| 1989 | − 0.1 | 17.0 | 3.4 |
| 1990 | − 4.9 | 28.9 | 7.9 |
| 1991 | − 7.4 | 36.4 | 10.3 |
| 1992 | − 5.6 | 23.0 | 0.9 |
| **Russia** | | | |
| 1991* | − 15.0 | 92.7 | |
| 1992 | − 3.5 | 1353.0 | 21.03 |
| 1993 | − 9.7 | 859.9 | 10.65 |

*Note*: * Data for former Soviet Union.
*Source*: Fiscal balance: UN, ECE, *Economic Survey for Europe 1992–1993*; *Russian Economic Trends*, various issues; Inflation: IMF, *World Economic Outlook*, various issues; Seigniorage: Gros and Vandille (1994) and own calculations.

However, this solution was not adopted anywhere on a large scale. The main danger then arises from fiscal deficits not financed by the sale of bonds to the public. When this happens, the central bank will be unable to resist pressure to cover part of the deficit through the printing press. Experience has shown, however, that the amounts that can be raised through such an 'inflation tax' come to little more than 3–4 per cent of GDP in the long run (see Fischer 1982). Since money demand is sensitive to high inflation rates, there is a strong 'Laffer curve' effect beyond certain thresholds (i.e. beyond inflation rates of 20–30 per cent, the revenue from inflation tax declines rapidly). Attempts to finance even larger deficits lead to hyperinflation (because they destroy the base for the inflation tax).

The experience of the reforming countries has, however, been extremely varied on this account. Russia financed more than 15 per cent of GDP from this source, but in Central European countries the scope of the inflation tax has been more modest. Moreover, the link between deficits and inflation was not as strong as one would have expected.

Table 3.7 reports the data for Poland, Hungary and Russia and shows that there was no direct link between the fiscal deficit and inflation once the reforms were under way. Poland is an interesting case because during the first three years following the 'big bang' of 1990 the officially recorded fiscal position of the government continued to deteriorate as it went from a small surplus in 1990 to a deficit of about 4 per cent of GDP in 1991 whereas inflation declined from 95 per cent in 1990 to 70 per cent in 1991 and 43 per cent in 1992. The Polish case is intriguing because of the clear inverse relationship between fiscal deficit and inflation. Hungary is somewhat different in that there is no clear direct relationship at all between fiscal position and inflation.

How can these facts be reconciled with the general presumption that the root cause of inflation is monetary financing of a fiscal deficit? The last column of table 3.7 shows that monetary financing indeed took place on a very large scale.

Monetary financing can essentially take two forms: (i) printing of additional cash, or (ii) requiring commercial banks to hold more reserves with the central bank. The column entitled 'seigniorage' shows the sum of these two forms of monetary financing as a ratio of GDP. The values that appear in table 3.7 are extraordinarily large in relation to those even in highly inflationary market economies. The main reason why seigniorage was so high in Hungary is that during the first years following the reforms the reserves of Hungarian commercial banks with the central bank increased considerably. In Poland (and Russia) the cash component contributed about half of the total, but another reason why seigniorage was so high in Russia was that the slow payments system forced banks to keep large zero-interest-bearing reserves at the central bank.

### The external anchor

In a market economy price stability demands a nominal anchor. In principle there are two ways of anchoring prices: through the money supply or through the exchange rate.

As our previous discussion has shown, during transition it is extremely difficult for the central bank to resist pressure from government to monetise the deficit. The only possible improvement would consist in rendering the central bank independent and to anchor this independence in the constitution. This is no guarantee for success, as public opinion may turn against the central bank and make it responsible for economic hardships, but it could be helpful. The other innovation needed to decouple monetary policy from fiscal policy is to create a market for government paper.

If stabilisation is successful and inflation is wiped out, people will be willing to hold money again and demand for money will go up. At a given price level, increased demand for money would require a one-off increase in nominal money supply to accommodate rising demand. To engineer such an increase without making it look like a resumption of money growth is difficult. Yet if the money supply is not increased, very high interest rates will have to be contended with for some time. Moreover, we showed previously that during transition velocity is highly unstable, so that it is difficult to estimate the money supply growth that is compatible with price stability.

The main alternative anchor – fixed exchange rates – is also fraught with difficulties. The possibility that policy laxity can ex-post be corrected through a devaluation can never be excluded. Even if this does not happen, capital controls are used to soften the disciplinary effect of fixed exchange rates and give domestic policymakers considerable freedom. The constraint of a fixed rate on monetary policy will then be felt only when the gap in competitiveness becomes sizeable. And as the disciplinary device is imperfect, fixed exchange rates with capital controls present major risks. The first is that, as long as the outcome of stabilisation is in the balance, very high nominal (and, if prices are stable, ex-post real) interest rates may be required in defence of the exchange rate. And if prices continue to rise for a while, the real exchange rate will steadily appreciate. Corrective devaluation halfway into the stabilisation programme also raises questions as to credibility and risks fuelling inflation. In fact, a precondition for successful nominal anchoring is a monetary and fiscal reform without which the nominal exchange rate will quickly have to be abandoned.

In view of these dangers, it is wise to fix initially the exchange rate at an undervalued level. This creates room for some slippage in competitiveness, and avoids immediate credibility problems. In addition, undervaluation gives a boost to exports and makes imports more expensive. The reorientation of production to the external sector is thereby facilitated. In fact, initially, all Central European countries strove for an undervalued exchange rate, as did Russia after 1998.

Of course, undervaluation should not be pushed too far. One obvious cost is the adverse terms of trade that may result from undervaluation. Another possible problem is the destabilisation of domestic inflation brought about by the feedback of devaluation on domestic prices. This was a problem Poland had to face in 1990–1.

One way of tying the policymakers' hands more tightly is to forgo the use of monetary policy – thereby convincingly constraining fiscal deficits to non-monetary financing – and exchange rate policy. This can be done by adopting the 'currency board' solution, i.e. by making domestic currency equivalent to a chosen foreign currency, and anchoring this decision in the constitution. Estonia was the first transition country to adopt this option and has locked its currency to the DM. Price stability was achieved by Estonia within less than one year. But Argentina provides a warning: without acceptance of the rules of the game for fiscal policy a currency board may end in tears. For technical details see box 3.4.

### The sustainability of stabilisation and the need for social safety nets

Stabilisation programmes notoriously fall short of expectations because there are simply too many things that can go wrong. And, when stabilisation does succeed, the need to restrain inflation often engenders deep economic contraction.

Can post-stabilisation economic depression be avoided? In principle, the answer is yes, as argued by Blanchard et al. (1990), but in practice it requires a combination of several happy circumstances. Once the initial transformation shock is over, in theory, all that is required is a change in taxation and spending structures, typically, the elimination of the inflation tax offset by a cutback in subsidies. As a rule, we do not think of tax changes as a major contractionary factor. The cut in subsidies to consumers will scale down disposable income, and the cut in subsidies to firms (which firms have to compensate for by increasing prices) will reduce real wages. But if the subsidy cut and the inflation tax are of equal magnitude to start with, real income, i.e. income including losses on money balances, will be unchanged. There may be distributive effects, with income distribution moving away from, presumably, the poorest people, those who held the least money and bought the most subsidised goods. These effects are unlikely to be substantial or imply a major downturn in demand. By the same token, the removal of distortions and the improved climate overall might be expected to induce firms to invest more and reassure consumers as to the future and so to spend

## Box 3.4    The currency board solution

How does such a system work? A law, or, better, a constitutional amendment, obliges the monetary authority to exchange unlimited amounts of foreign currency into domestic currency at a certain rate (8 kroons for 1 DM in the case of Estonia). This will be credible if the foreign currency reserves are equal in value to the sum of all the liabilities of the monetary authorities (i.e. cash and deposits of banks). The law also declares that the monetary authority will create additional currency only against foreign currency receipts. Variations in the domestic money supply are then exclusively caused by net inflows or outflows of foreign exchange. Which currency should be the anchor? The best anchor is in the currency most widely used in the country's foreign trade and offering the price stability to be copied.

The monetary authority ('the currency board') holds its assets exclusively in liquid interest-earning foreign assets in the anchor currency. Its liabilities are restricted to the 'monetary base', i.e. cash in circulation and deposits by banks (including required reserves). As the monetary base is only a small share of all deposits and savings accounts, typically 20–40 per cent, the required foreign exchange backing is not very large relative to the overall money supply and GDP. It usually corresponds to about 10 per cent of a year's income.

One important difference between the clear currency board approach and a fixed exchange rate is thus that the balance sheet of the 'currency board' does not contain advances to government and holdings of government debt instruments. This would be somewhat different if, at the starting point, foreign exchange reserves were insufficient. The rules could then be modified as follows. Some of the initial money supply would be backed up by credits to the government. Any *increase* in the money supply would, however, have to be fully backed up by foreign exchange and, over time, government credit would have to be replaced by foreign exchange holdings according to a binding rule drawn up in advance.

The requirement that only the monetary base is to be covered with foreign exchange holdings, and not the entire money supply, takes into account the fact that the monetary base corresponds to currency in its strictest sense. Interest-earning deposits are close substitutes for both monetary and financial instruments. As long as banks incur a resource cost of collecting and remunerating deposits they are forced in a competitive banking market to allocate these funds rationally. Clearly, independence of commercial banks and competition, enhanced by the presence of foreign banks, are essential ingredients.

Could the foreign exchange constraint cause insufficient liquidity? Suppose that, owing to initial foreign exchange scarcity, there is a lack of domestic liquidity. Banks would have to borrow abroad to satisfy their clients. With the credibility achieved by the reform, and as long as the quality of banks' balance sheets remains intact, they will be able to borrow foreign exchange, convert at the board and obtain liquidity in domestic currency.

The currency board, as would any central bank, would have the benefit of domestic seigniorage: its assets are remunerated whereas its liabilities are not (or only partly on bank deposits). The social cost of foreign exchange backing is also very low: private banks borrow foreign exchange abroad, which is reinvested by the currency board in international markets. The cost is equal to the spread between interest rates paid and received, which should be equal to a small premium for differences in liquidity and risk. The social benefit can, however, be enormous in terms of monetary stability, and hence is a better base for sustainable growth.

The only macroeconomic policy available is fiscal policy. Some independence is lost even for fiscal policy because it must ensure that domestic inflation is in line with the currency of attachment. If this restriction were not politically accepted then it would be unwise to set up a currency board. Of key importance is also a competitive starting value for the exchange rate.

more. This optimistic view does not, however, reckon with four crucial factors in Eastern Europe.

First, uncertainty about the future does not disappear with the inception of a stabilisation programme. Once the initial relief resulting from temporary stabilisation wears off, scepticism returns with a vengeance. Even the best stabilisation programmes sometimes fail, and firms will probably prefer to wait and see which way the wind blows rather than embark on an investment spree.

Second, inflation may not come to a dead halt either, owing to the coordination problems outlined above or because the stabilisation programme is not perceived as wholly credible. In that case, developments will depend on the choice of nominal anchor. In the event of a fixed exchange rate, for example, suspicion of the programme, and the odds of devaluation later, may have to be paid for in very high interest rates to defend the exchange rate, and these may in turn affect demand and lead to contraction.

Low credibility leads to expectation of devaluation, contraction and abandonment of the programme, which, in turn, make the programme less likely to succeed. High credibility may be self-sustaining as promises are being delivered.

Third, the initial shock that triggered the process to start with may not yet have worn off. In that case, unless workers and firms have learned about inflation the hard way and can be persuaded to agree on the distribution of income between profits and wages, unemployment is the only way of keeping wages and prices consistent with price stability. Otherwise, all that stabilisation can achieve is to set the clock ticking again.

Finally, stabilisation also has repercussions for the supply side itself. Certain unprofitable firms may not be able to weather the changes brought about by the removal of subsidies and the revamping of price structures; if they close it will lessen the economy's ability to respond to demand in the short run.

All these risks are a potential threat to sustained stabilisation. Success depends on the overall consistency and credibility of the stabilisation programme and the political support it receives. For widespread political support a safety net is required.

In choosing among alternative safety nets, it should be borne in mind that there is no way of protecting all segments of society. A comprehensive reform programme may involve sacrifices by a substantial share of the population, and therefore needs to be seen as fair and efficient. Furthermore, in designing the mechanism through which the safety net operates, the introduction of new distortions should be avoided to the utmost. In this regard, the safety nets should not interfere with the incentives to work, save and invest, nor should they tamper with monetary and exchange rate policies. Rather, allowance should be made for them in the budget and they should be effected through income transfers.

The safety net we strongly prefer is a giveaway privatisation programme that provides citizens with real assets to compensate for the reduction in income streams. Such assets may be used as collateral for borrowing in bad times, making saving less mandatory, and to fund maintenance and improvement (e.g. of the housing stock), which would allow underemployed workers to minimise the opportunity cost of underemployment.

## 3.5  Conclusions

We have shown that a functioning market economy needs a number of institutions that are all linked and do not function well in isolation. This, in our view, is the main argument for a comprehensive, or 'big-bang', approach: at the very beginning a comprehensive set of new ground rules should be laid out signalling an irreversible and clear-cut regime change with a new constitution and legal system, redefined property rights and redesigned economic institutions. In essence, what is needed is a new social contract based on the rule of law.

The fundamental problem is thus not simply to change some rules of the game but rather to change the nature of the game that is played. The entire legal structure in a centrally planned economy is in fact inappropriate in a market economy: the constitutional, civil, business, commercial and social laws must all be tailored to a different economic and social order. A market economy can only work if the doctrine that *salus publica suprema civitatis lex est* becomes as clear to leaders in Eastern Europe as it was to Kant.

Integrating new laws into old legal structures is not good enough. Such a course would create confusion and convince neither citizens nor outsiders (foreign lenders, investors and traders). The entire legal structure has to change and the state itself must subject itself to the rule of law, or confidence in the reform programmes will be short lived. To ensure domestic peace, a social contract is needed: a new constitution has to be accepted implicitly or explicitly by the majority of people. Property rights must be clearly defined to boost incentives, long-term commitments and 'book-entry trading' and the whole judicial set-up constructed so as to guarantee that these rights would be respected in the long term.

Recognising that reforms need to be comprehensive does not imply, however, that all reforms must be implemented at the same instant.

We have emphasised the linkages between price reforms, privatisation, financial market reforms, fiscal reforms and the legal framework (contract law, property rights, banking regulations, tax legislation and the like). Some of these reforms take relatively little time (say, revising a law), others may take years (the creation of an efficient banking system). This serves to reinforce our preference for an all-embracing, comprehensive reform, but it hardly implies that every single thing has to be changed on the spot. The government needs to set priorities for its agenda and thus there will be some sequencing of reforms.

# Notes

1. The elimination of queues is a tangible saving in time for everybody. However, with market clearing prices, people with a higher monetary income (but less time to spare to wait in line) will be better off relative to people with a lower monetary income (and more time to spare), e.g. pensioners. The overall economic efficiency gains from price liberalisation will thus be unevenly distributed across the population.

2. Even a reformer with a historic reputation for his pro market convictions skidded on this point: 'I am convinced that the best solution is to proceed from a currency reform to a market economy with prices set by the market. Of course, in practice, we would not do that (especially not for food, rents and coal), but the trend is the correct one.' Ludwig Erhard, the father of the German miracle, on 14 January 1948.

3. In socialist economies the accumulation of real or financial assets was very limited. Therefore, people were unable to fall back on accumulated savings to bridge difficult times. Safeguards for their incomes are therefore even more necessary than in Western economies.

4. See Gros and Jones (1991) for further details.

5. A reminder: to ensure efficiency in allocating resources, prices need to be market prices only at the margin. That determines the amount of production or consumption, independently of the subsidised price of intramarginal quantities. They have only redistributive – and not allocative – effects.

6. The revenue position of the government would be greatly enhanced if it retained a full claim on the profits or surpluses being generated by natural resource-based industries at the higher domestic prices. For that, it need not retain ownership. Appropriate taxes can transfer the natural rents to the government.

7. Typically, the uniform tariff rate that maximises tariff revenues is higher than the rate that maximises welfare of consumers and producers through international trade. For a small economy, and abstracting from distortions, this optimal rate is zero.

8. Formally, this can be shown by observing that, with an ad valorem import tariff of $t$, the domestic price ratio is: $P_{imp}(1 + t)/P_{exp}$. With an ad valorem export tariff of $t$ the domestic price ratio is $P_{imp}/(P_{exp}/(1 + t))$, which is equivalent to the result under an import tariff. See Lerner (1936).

9. As trade within the CMEA was conducted in transferable roubles, which are not convertible, aggregation of global trade flows depended heavily on the implicit exchange rate used in the analysis. The data in figure 3.1 should therefore be interpreted with care and are best seen as a rough guide for analysing the change in East European trade patterns.

10. Internal convertibility refers to the right of residents freely to acquire foreign exchange; external convertibility gives to non-residents the right to convert domestic currencies; both may be subjected to specific conditions or limitations so that convertibility is called restricted or limited.

11. For an assessment of dual exchange rates, see Decaluwe and Steinherr (1976).

12. For an analysis of the effects of arbitrage between the two exchange-rate markets, see Gros (1988).

13. Even in developed market economies the effectiveness of owner control of firms is debatable. For a very positive assessment of the US experience, see Jensen (1988); for a more reserved evaluation of the German variety, see Steinherr and Huveneers (1992).

14. This may explain why the bulk of investment by nationals and foreigners alike currently concentrates on trading companies and plant needing little new fixed investment.

15. It has indeed been suggested that the difficulties faced by the 1990 Balcerowicz Plan in Poland were at least partly due to the absence of privatisation. See Lipton and Sachs (1990) and Frydman and Rapaczynski (1991).

16. Prior to the reforms many economists specialising in Soviet economies had, of course, produced estimates of the monetary overhang. Some of the estimates relied on the difference between controlled and free prices for food (in those countries where there existed small markets for

privately produced food). This approach assumed in general that eventually the price level would be somewhere between the controlled and the free prices. However, it turned out that the overall price level went straight to the free price level.

17. See *Russian Economic Trends*, 1993.

18. However, in Russia the subsidies that went through the budget were actually secondary to those coming from another source, namely the Central Bank of Russia; this is discussed in more detail in chapter 8.

# 4     Transition: ten years later

"Slowly, slowly, repeat: God, the market economy and EV membership are good for me..."

As chapter 3 made clear, economists could not agree on a detailed optimal blueprint for reforms. Different countries opted for different approaches. Now, more than ten years later, one can attempt an evaluation of how successful different approaches to reform have been.

We start this chapter with the question in section 1 whether rapid or slow reforms were more successful. Here the evidence is unambiguous: it paid to reform quickly and comprehensively.

One experience common to all transition economies and not anticipated by Western economists was the initial collapse of output. Was the depth or duration of the output collapse avoidable?

Most countries liberalised the price system as one of the first (and administratively easiest) reform measures. The combination of relative price adjustments, lower production and a monetary overhang propelled inflation, in some countries degenerating into hyperinflation. Macrostabilisation became important and urgent, as argued in section 2.

All transition economies liberalised their foreign trade early on and, to varying degrees, capital movements. The rapid reorientation of trade to Western markets is a salient result; foreign direct investments were initially much more modest. The Russian crisis of 1998 was a dramatic reminder that liberalising capital flows is altogether a different matter from liberalising trade. With the opening up, the choice of exchange rate regime became important. From currency boards to 'dirty' floating, all regimes were tested somewhere. Section 3 asks whether there are conclusions to be drawn.

All these options for macroeconomic policy are delicate choices and mistakes can entail disproportionate penalties. But, in a way, these were the 'easy' issues. Easy in the sense that not much effort or political will is required to choose an exchange rate regime, a particular monetary target or a tariff schedule.

The more difficult issues concern institution building. Privatisation has made progress in all transition countries, but the results were often disappointing. Success is measured not by the share of enterprises privatised, but by the efficiency of resource allocation. To score well by that benchmark requires more than changing ownership. It requires clearly defined relationships between the state and enterprises, a level playing field, transparency, and solutions to the corporate governance issue.

The most important economic player, even in a market economy, remains the state. Redefining the role of the state is perhaps the single most difficult issue and a source of problems, particularly in the laggardly transition countries. Part of the problem is that the state has not withdrawn from functions where the private sector should be responsible; the other part of the problem is that the state does not discharge efficiently its responsibilities in areas such as taxation, social security, creation of fair and easy-to-understand legal rules and their enforcement. Section 4 notes some of these problems.

In section 5 we ask the question, ten years after the fall of communism, is transition over? The answer is not obvious and requires some work.

## 4.1  'Big-bang' versus a gradualist approach

The economics profession was unanimous about many things that had to be done: to privatise, stabilise inflation, control the budget, open-up to trade. Diverging viewpoints concerned the 'how' and, above all, the 'when'.

The actual stepping-stones of reform will vary according to the state of the economy, to the level of popular tolerance for the disruptions that are sure to accompany reform, and to the political situation. In order to be more concrete, we show briefly the prototype reform for a representative European socialist economy with initial conditions close to those of Poland and Czechoslovakia.

The order of priorities reflects the time and effort needed to achieve reform goals. We put macroeconomic stabilisation first because, in countries with high inflation and non-sustainable balance-of-payments deficits, the government will have to devote a lot of effort to macroeconomic stabilisation provided, of course, prices and foreign trade have been liberalised. How tough the programme and the range of accompanying structural reforms will be depends on the magnitude of the initial imbalances and on how much voters can be expected to swallow. A new government, or a government with broad-based support for radical change, has considerable room for manoeuvre, but experience has shown that it does not last. It should therefore use the brief period of time available to push through tough measures that may be unacceptable later on. Countries that do not enter the reforms with macroeconomic imbalances have the advantage that they can concentrate immediately on the more long-run issues like privatisation.

Figure 4.1 highlights how much needs to be done right at the start. Virtually all the reforms, or preparations for them, must be launched quickly, even if they take a decade to implement. Of course, figure 4.1 exaggerates the precision of the process, and makes no allowance for the inevitable setbacks that occur in any economic reform programme.

There is another vital element that does not show up in figure 4.1. A government that sets out on the road to reform with a clear idea of what it wants to achieve and with a popular mandate to forge ahead is bound to be more successful than a government and a society that are not sure of what they want.

Figure 4.1 is consistent with a pragmatic interpretation of a 'big bang' and with swift gradualism. (For theoretical arguments in favour of gradualism, see Roland 2000.) In the end, the proof of the pudding is in the eating, and the proof of a good reform package is better economic performance. Enough time has passed by now to judge which approach to reform did, in fact, yield the best results. The experience of Poland was often used to argue that 'big-bang' reforms plus stabilisation lead to large output declines. However, the experiences of Russia and Ukraine have shown that slow reforms do not give better results. On the contrary!

A systematic econometric analysis of the experience of the twenty-five countries in Central Europe and the former Soviet Union by Gros and Vandille (1997) shows that there is no link between the speed of reform and the size of the initial output decline. The size of the decline of output seems to be determined mostly by the amount of time the country spent under communism (the output decline was much higher, on average, for FSU countries).

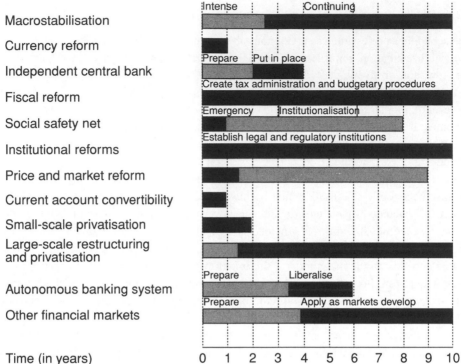

**Figure 4.1** Sequencing of reform
Source: Adapted from Fischer and Gelb (1991).

The argument that quick macroeconomic stabilisation had a negative effect on output can also be easily refuted. Experience has shown the contrary. The first row of regression results in table 4.1 shows that countries with higher inflation have experienced a steeper decline in output. These results suggest that the price of each additional percentage point of inflation (average monthly rate) was a reduced output of 3 per cent.

A package of quick stabilisation and comprehensive reforms did thus not increase the pain; on the contrary it mitigated the output decline. Did it also accelerate the recovery? Here the evidence is again strong. The second row in table 4.1 shows that the recovery that started in 1993 was also negatively affected by inflation. But is there a link between reforms and growth? The empirical investigation is handicapped by the fact that it is difficult to measure the speed of reforms. We used the only objective indicator available, namely the reform indicator from the Transition Report of the EBRD which grades for all transition economies the degree to which different elements of the economy (foreign trade, prices, privatisation, etc.) are liberalised. All transition indicators are strongly correlated with the recovery in output. Table 4.1 reports just the two most striking results: the third row shows that an increase in the share of the private sector by one point was associated with output growth of 0.6 per cent in 1994. The *t*-statistics indicate that this association is statistically

Table 4.1. *Causes of output decline and recovery*

| Dependent variable | Explanatory variables: point estimate (*t*-statistics in parenthesis) | | Summary statistics |
|---|---|---|---|
| Output decline | Inflation: | 2.99 | $R^2 = 0.50$ |
| | | (4.59) | |
| GDP growth in 1994 | Inflation: | −0.697 | $R^2 = 0.45$ |
| | | (−4.33) | |
| GDP growth in 1994 | Share of private sector: | 0.61 | $R^2 = 0.55$ |
| | | (5.36) | |
| GDP growth since trough | Share of private sector: | 0.44 | $R^2 = 0.63$ |
| | | (6.25) | |

*Note*: In the first regression for each country only the years of output decline (up to 1994) are retained. In the fourth regression are all the years since the worst year up to 1994.
*Source*: Own calculations based on data from EBRD, Transition Reports 1994 and 1995.

very significant. That the recovery was stronger in countries that had liberalised most thoroughly is shown also convincingly in the last row of table 4.1: the share of the private sector in the economy explains over 60 per cent of the variation in the size of the recovery. The *t*-statistic on this reform indicator is even stronger. It bears repeating that other reform indicators, e.g. those that describe the degree of external liberalisation or of enterprise reforms, gave similar results.

One of the most baffling outcomes in transition countries is the depth and duration of the initial output collapse. Western economists had certainly underestimated the coordination problems for economies that discarded an inefficient but working system and groped towards the establishment of a market-based system. As shown by the regression results in table 4.1, output recovered earlier in countries that opted for rapid reforms. But what accounted for the severity of the collapse? There are two contenders: initial conditions and reform implementation.

As shown in table 4.2, the collapse of production was more pronounced in CIS countries (the only exception is Uzbekistan) than in Central and Eastern Europe. By 1998 real GDP in Central and Eastern Europe reached, on average, 95 per cent of its level of 1989 and surpassed this level around 2000. By contrast the CIS countries were in 1998 still only at about half the 1989 level (on average 53 per cent) and, while growth in the CIS has subsequently picked up, these countries are still way below their starting point.

We hasten to add that all comparisons with output in 1989 must be taken with a large *grano salis* because the value of output produced under a non-market system is impossible to determine with any precision. However, as one can assume that the mis-measurement of 1989 output is the same across countries, one can still take the differences in the ratio GDP 2000/GDP 1989 as a reliable indicator of the relative success of different countries.

What caused these differences in performance? Starting conditions seem to matter, but it has been surprisingly difficult to relate initial *economic* indicators to the ensuing fall in

Table 4.2. *Inflation and output performance in transition economies*

| | Year in which inflation peaked | Maximum end-year inflation rates[1] | Stabilisation programme date | Exchange regime adopted at date of stabilisation | Year in which output was lowest | Ratio of lowest registered GDP to 1989 (%) | Estimated level of real GDP in 1998 (1989 = 100) |
|---|---|---|---|---|---|---|---|
| *Central and Eastern Europe and the Baltic states* | | | | | | | |
| Albania | 1992/1997 | 236.6/42.1 | Aug. 92 | Flexible | 1992 | 60.4 | 86 |
| Bulgaria | 1991/1997 | 338.9/578.6 | Feb. 91 | Flexible | 1997 | 63.2 | 66 |
| Croatia | 1993 | 1149.0 | Oct. 93 | Fixed | 1993 | 59.5 | 78 |
| Czech Republic | 1991 | 52.0 | Jan. 91 | Fixed | 1992 | 84.6 | 95 |
| Estonia | 1992 | 953.5 | Jun. 92 | Fixed | 1994 | 60.8 | 76 |
| FYR Macedonia | 1992 | 1935.0 | Jan. 94 | Fixed | 1995 | 55.1 | 72 |
| Hungary | 1990 | 33.4 | Mar. 90 | Fixed | 1993 | 81.9 | 95 |
| Latvia | 1992 | 959.0 | Jun. 92 | Flexible/Fixed[2] | 1995 | 51.0 | 59 |
| Lithuania | 1992 | 1161.1 | Jun. 92 | Flexible/Fixed[2] | 1994 | 53.3 | 65 |
| Poland | 1990 | 249.0 | Jan. 90 | Fixed | 1991 | 82.2 | 117 |
| Romania | 1993/1997 | 295.5/151.4 | Oct. 93 | Flexible | 1992 | 75.0 | 76 |
| Slovak Republic | 1991 | 58.3 | Jan. 91 | Fixed | 1993 | 75.0 | 100 |
| Slovenia | 1991 | 247.1 | Feb. 92 | Flexible | 1992 | 82.0 | 104 |
| *Commonwealth of Independent States* | | | | | | | |
| Armenia | 1993 | 10896.0 | Dec. 94 | Flexible/Fixed[3] | 1993 | 31.0 | 41 |
| Azerbaijan | 1994 | 1788.0 | Jan. 95 | Flexible/Fixed[3] | 1995 | 37.0 | 44 |
| Belarus | 1993/1998 | 1996.0/181.7 | Nov. 94 | Flexible/Fixed[3] | 1995 | 62.7 | 78 |
| Georgia | 1993 | 7487.9 | Sept. 94 | Flexible/Fixed[3] | 1994 | 25.4 | 33 |
| Kazakhstan | 1992 | 2984.1 | Jan. 94 | Flexible/Fixed[3] | 1998 | 61.2 | 61 |
| Kyrgyzstan | 1993 | 1363.0 | May 93 | Flexible/Fixed[3] | 1995 | 50.4 | 60 |
| Moldova | 1992 | 2198.0 | Sep. 93 | Flexible | 1998 | 32.1 | 32 |
| Russia | 1992/1998 | 2506.1/84.5 | Apr. 95 | Flexible/Fixed[2] | 1998 | 55.3 | 55 |
| Tajikistan | 1993 | 7343.7 | Feb. 95 | Flexible | 1996 | 39.2 | 42 |
| Turkmenistan | 1993 | 9750.0 | Jan. 97 | Flexible | 1997 | 42.0 | 44 |
| Ukraine | 1993 | 10155.0 | Nov. 94 | Flexible | 1998 | 36.6 | 37 |
| Uzbekistan | 1994 | 1281.0 | Nov. 94 | Flexible | 1995 | 83.4 | 90 |

*Notes:* [1] For countries with inflation reversals (an increase in inflation from below 30 per cent to above 30 per cent) both the initial peak inflation and the subsequent peak during the reversal is shown.

[2] The Latvian currency was pegged to the SDR in February 1994. Lithuania adopted a currency board in April 1994. Russia announced an exchange rate corridor in July 1995. All three countries had flexible exchange rate regimes prior to these dates.

[3] As of 1995 these countries adopted a de facto peg to the US dollar.

*Source:* EBRD (1999).

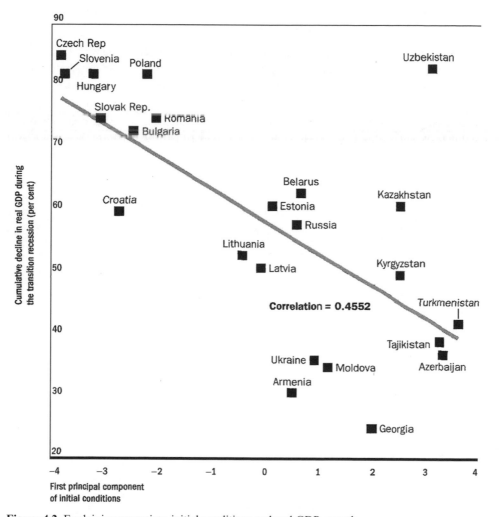

**Figure 4.2** Explaining recession: initial conditions and real GDP growth
Note: The transition recession is defined as the period in which annual growth was negative. The cumulative decline in GDP is thus measured over all years since 1989 (= 100 per cent) until the first year of positive growth. Albania and FYR Macedonia are excluded because of missing values on initial conditions. Initial conditions are represented by the first principal component of a factor analysis.
Source: EBRD *Transition Report* (1999).

output. The EBRD (*Transition Report*, 1999: 62) claims to have found a very significant contribution of initial conditions to the depth and length of output decline. The four factors found to be most important in explaining the initial output decline were dependence on intra-communist-bloc trade, level of development, macroeconomic distortions and distance from Western Europe. By using a principal component analysis the EBRD arrives at the result displayed in figure 4.2.

*Box 4.1  'Big bang' versus gradualism*

The academic discussion of this issue now seems definitely, well, academic. Experience has shown that slow reformers were just that, slow reformers. The tortoises did not overtake the hares. Countries that implemented reforms early usually stayed ahead of the others. Figure 4.3 shows this by plotting simply the overall EBRD reform indicator (the average of all the indicators available) for 1994 (the first year this indicator was published) against the value of the same indicator in 1999. It is apparent that countries with high indicators in 1994 also had higher values five years later.

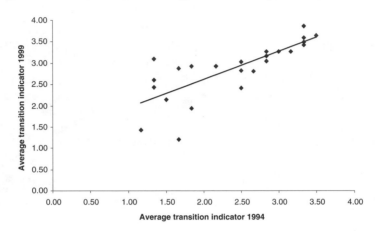

**Figure 4.3**  Progress in transition

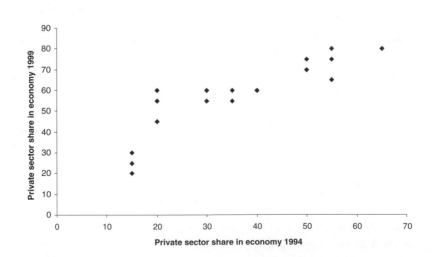

**Figure 4.4**  Progress in privatisation

Figure 4.4 makes the same point with respect to privatisation. In this figure we put the private sector share of the economy in 1994 on the horizontal axis and on the vertical axis the share in 1999. This figure suggests that countries that were late to begin privatisation also did not make up the lost ground later. Slow privatisation meant in reality no privatisation. By contrast, countries that privatised early continued to privatise the remaining parts of their economy at a faster pace.

Using more recent data would confirm this pattern, but with one exception: a number of the early reforms have stopped progressing because they reached their destination: a fully fledged market economy integrated in the EU.

While there is a strong overall relationship between initial conditions (measured by their first principal component) and the output decline it is also clear that there are two distinct groups: on the lower right-hand side one finds all the former Soviet republics (including the Baltics) and on the upper left-hand side one finds all the candidate countries for EU membership (minus the three Baltic countries, plus Croatia). Among this latter group there is a link between initial conditions and output decline, but among the FSU states there is no correlation at all, even if one ignores the special cases of Uzbekistan (no reforms) and Georgia and Armenia (civil wars).

It is also interesting to note that it has not been possible to establish a link between the size of the initial output decline and the symptoms of central planning, e.g. an excessive build-up of heavy industry, energy intensity and the preponderance of large firms.

All in all it is thus difficult for economists to explain the wide variations in the initial output decline. The decline was, on average, much larger throughout the FSU, but the wide variations within this group do not seem to be related to clearly identifiable economic factors. The one factor that seems to have been important is distance from Western Europe: the closer a country is to Europe the smaller has been the output decline. We discuss in chapter 9 the importance of geography and show that the pull of the EU market can determine the fate of countries in Central and Eastern Europe. But while distance to an important market can explain why a country trades little, it should not be a factor in the size of the output decline. We surmise that another factor is at work here: distance from Europe is in reality related to something else, namely the political situation and bureaucratic traditions. The countries that are farthest from the EU have also been slowest in undertaking and implementing reforms.

Thus the other main culprit is the lack of reform implementation. In all countries the biggest fall in production occurred in the year of price liberalisation: Poland in 1990, Czechoslovakia in 1991, Russia in 1992 and Ukraine in 1994. Price liberalisation changed relative prices dramatically. The production of goods, whose relative prices fell, fell also. This fall should, over time, be offset by the increase in production of goods whose relative price increased. But this increase in production does not occur immediately, hence output falls everywhere. In some countries the increase in production did not take place even after several years because the incentives for shifting resources or for market entry were not there. Johnson, McMillan and Woodruff (1999) asked managers whether they were ready to invest $100 today which would grow to $200 in two years. About 20 per cent of the respondents in Poland, Slovakia and Romania and close to 100 per cent of managers in Russia and the Ukraine would *not* seize this opportunity, presumably because they feared that they would not be able to keep the gain. The lack of property rights is the main difference between

Central Europe and the CIS countries and South-East Europe. All the other explanations evoking a fall in aggregate demand (Berg and Blanchard 1994; Rosati 1994) or a credit crunch (Calvo and Coricelli 1993) are of secondary importance.

A good summary of these arguments (growth and employment) is provided by the evolution of labour productivity reflecting both the change in output and the change in employment. Setting labour productivity in 1989 equal to 100 (see EBRD, 1999: 58), Hungary in 1998 had a labour productivity of 175, or more than twice the Russian level of 65, because excess labour was laid off and production increased. The Czech reticence in laying off labour ranks its labour productivity at 115, below that of Poland (145). Russia's productivity was at the bottom due to the output collapse whilst keeping workers on the payroll. The recovery which started in 1999 has brought some improvement for Russia, but as productivity kept improving at a steady pace in Central Europe as well, this does not change the status of Russia as one of the worst performers.

## 4.2   Stabilisation

Prices were freed early on in all transition countries, but in none was liberalisation initially comprehensive. In most countries price liberalisation was followed by an inflationary surge (see table 4.2). As we argued in chapter 3, the reason was not price liberalisation by itself but a monetary overhang that now could spill over into higher prices. In addition, the absence of normal credit mechanisms meant that monetary policy continued to finance borrowers' needs. In general, policymakers in transition countries had difficulty in understanding or accepting the desirability of budgetary discipline and restrained money supply growth.

The positive lesson that emerged is that stabilisation did not restrain growth – quite the contrary. Only when prices became stabilised did growth resume. Those countries that adopted stabilisation policies early saw growth resume early. Late stabilisers had a deeper and longer output decline.

## 4.3   External liberalisation

External liberalisation covers three related topics: liberalisation of trade and the reorientation of trade from Eastern European partners to Western Europe and the rest of the world; the question of capital account liberalisation; and the exchange regime.

Trade liberalisation has progressed, although tariff and non-tariff trade restrictions are still widely used, particularly in some CIS countries. As shown in table 4.3, Central Europe increased its foreign trade dramatically and achieved a remarkable reorientation of its external trade.

On both accounts Bulgaria, Romania and the CIS countries failed to keep pace. Table 4.3 also lists the total inflow of foreign direct investments for the ten years 1990–9. The lion's share went to the Central European countries. Given the size of CIS countries, inflows have been modest and the trend is stationary. Since about 2000 Russia has also been starting to receive larger inflows. But the flows into Central Europe have kept on increasing as EU membership came closer. On a per-capita basis the difference has thus not really narrowed.

Table 4.3. *Foreign trade and investment*

*Exports in US $, 1999 (1989 = 100)*

| | |
|---|---|
| Bulgaria | 60 |
| Czechoslovakia/Czech Republic | 346 |
| Hungary | 259 |
| Poland | 187 |
| Romania | 105 |
| Baltic States (1992 = 100) | 358 |

*Structure of trade: Central Europe, exports*

| | All | Transition economies | Developed market economies | Developing economies |
|---|---|---|---|---|
| 1999 | 100 | 18.6 | 75.8 | 5.6 |
| 1989 | 100 | 44.4 | 42.6 | 13.0 |

*Structure of trade: CIS countries, exports*

| | | | | |
|---|---|---|---|---|
| 1999 | 100 | 17.4 | 58.0 | 24.6 |
| 1989 | 100 | 26.6 | 41.8 | 31.6 |

*Inflow of foreign direct investment 1990–1999 (in billion US $)*

| | |
|---|---|
| Central Europe | 71.6 |
|    *Czech Republic* | *16.3* |
|    *Hungary* | *19.6* |
|    *Poland* | *20.4* |
| Baltic States | 5.9 |
| CIS | 38.0 |
|    *Russia* | *19.9* |

*Source*: *Economic Survey of Europe*, 2000, No. 1, Geneva: United Nations.

Bulgaria and Romania have, however, seen a dramatic improvement, both relative and absolute.

Most transition economies run current account deficits. Although many Eastern Europeans see this as a disadvantage in the best mercantilist tradition, this is a desirable outcome. The only way a country can import capital to finance accelerated convergence is to run a current account deficit. All in all, the record is excellent on this score for Central Europe and disappointing for the CIS.

## 4.3.1   The choice of exchange rate regime

During the first decade of transition Eastern Europe exhibited a widespread experience with various choices of exchange rate regimes. This makes sense, as the needs of individual countries are not uniform. A small country (with a small exchange market) finds it more attractive to peg its currency to that of a major trading partner and has fewer problems with renouncing monetary sovereignty.

Probably the most interesting experience is Estonia's. When Estonia opted for a currency board many commentators expected the system to collapse within a fortnight. But Estonia managed to stabilise prices and resume growth more rapidly than others. This is, again, a demonstration that quick and courageous decisions, based on strong institutions, pay off. Estonia became a model for others to follow: Lithuania and Bulgaria only opted for a currency board out of desperation to curtail inflation after a collapse of their banking systems. Despite these very unfavourable starting conditions, Bulgaria and Lithuania succeeded in stabilisation.

Most Central European countries pegged their exchange rates to the euro or a basket in recognition of their major trade ties and in the expectation of future membership of the European Union.

The choices for the successor states of the Soviet Union were more complex. Russia remained an important trade partner, but could not deliver stability. Russia itself had a problem, its export revenues depending excessively on the price of oil. Floating was not an attractive option for CIS countries, except for Russia, as exchange markets for most currencies were (and remain) very thin. But even Russia, with its supposedly flexible exchange rate, had to face a serious crisis.

Clearly the lesson is that no single exchange regime is the best choice for every situation. In some cases fixed exchange rates did act as external anchors for price stability. As we have argued above, stabilisation is necessary for growth to resume. In this sense countries opting for stability and using the exchange rate as an anchor did generally better. Of course, such a constraint is of no use if it is not supported by fiscal policy, as demonstrated dramatically by the case of Russia.

A fixed exchange rate is, of course, easier to manage with controls on capital flows. Although no country opted for a two-tier exchange market, as we recommend in chapter 3 (the IMF is categorically opposed to multiple exchange rates), most maintained some controls for some years. The Czech Republic was the most intrepid in liberalising capital flows and faced a serious exchange crisis in May 1997.

As we show in chapter 8, Russia had, de facto, capital mobility in the run-up to the crisis of August 1998. The crisis resulted from a combination of a large fiscal deficit, a weak banking sector, capital flight and the attempt to compensate all this by offering foreign investors treasury bills at astronomical interest rates. Traditionally capital controls served mainly to stem outflows, not inflows. The Russian crisis showed clearly that capital inflows and their sudden withdrawal with changing investors' sentiments are real dangers. Had Russia operated a more flexible exchange rate system it is likely that the rouble would have appreciated before the crisis and would have depreciated as it did, since the fixed rate was not defended for very long. Hence the fixed exchange rate was not the cause of the crisis and flexible rates would not fundamentally have changed the outcome. Free capital flows and flexible exchange rates are not a safe remedy.

The only lesson one can draw is the one we have defended in chapter 3: precipitous liberalisation of capital flows is dangerous. Only when solid macroeconomic stability *and* a robust domestic financial sector are established should the crowning touch, liberalisation of capital flows, follow. The most unproblematic and most gainful part of capital

Table 4.4. *Budgetary subsidies and current transfers to enterprises (% of GDP)*

|  | Czech Republic | Hungary | Poland | Slovak Republic | Russia | Ukraine |
|---|---|---|---|---|---|---|
| Year 2001* | 8.3** | 4.9 | 2.4 | 2.7 | 5.3 | 5.0 |

*Notes*: *If data were available; older data otherwise. **Subsidies to enterprises and financial institutions, including the Czech consolidation agency.
*Source*: EBRD *Transition Report*, 2002.

flows – foreign direct investment – can be obtained, as forcefully demonstrated by China, without full capital account convertibility. Clear and simple rules of law, non-discrimination against foreigners and a sustainable market-based course of economic policy (but no tax favours!) are optimal conditions for attracting foreign investments.

## 4.4   The role of the state

In Western economics there is a consensus on the minimum responsibilities of the state: law and order and safeguard of justice across generations and all segments of society. This includes healthcare, education, physical infrastructure, the pension system, support for the unemployed. Beyond that, there is wide scope for ideology and party-line disagreement. Some very dynamic and successful economies, such as the Scandinavian countries, have an institutional framework that assigns much more than the minimum to the state. Compared to the United States, European states take a greater responsibility in all these domains and do a reasonable job. Education, healthcare and physical infrastructure are not predestined to be better managed in the private sector. They can be mismanaged in either.

In transition countries the state had to reduce its role as entrepreneur and financier. This was necessary, but not sufficient. Private monopolies can be as inefficient, abusive and disrespectful of public interests as state monopolies – particularly when the law is unclear, regulators pliable and politicians cooperative.

The importance of the state (measured by state expenditures as a percentage of GDP) has fallen in all transition countries. This is good news. The bad news is in the details as subsidies and transfers (see table 4.4) remain too high.

Even if one uses a rather restrictive definition, namely including only transfers to enterprises, one sees that subsidies make up a significant percentage of GDP. One of the worst offenders towards the end of the 1990s was the Czech Republic in which the reform of the financial system was botched so that transfers to enterprises, either directly, or indirectly via the consolidation agency, cost over 8 per cent of GDP. Poland (and the Slovak Republic) perform much better in this respect, spending less than one third as much, mainly because the reform of the financial system was carried out more efficiently. But even these latter countries gave their enterprises twice as much as EU-15 member countries do on average (in the EU 15 the average is around 1.3 per cent of GDP). For Russia and Ukraine, subsidies of around 5 per cent of GDP do not seem excessively high. But if one takes into account that in Russia general government expenditure amounted to 36 per cent and federal public spending to about 15–20 per cent of GDP, one sees that subsidies accounted for about 14 per cent of general, and even for more than 25 per cent of federal, expenditure. Furthermore, if credits to SOE are considered as forms of subsidies, the figures would be much higher for countries in which privatisation is still incomplete (e.g. Ukraine).

A number of governments were initially unable to collect sufficient tax revenues. As a result budget deficits were high, endangering price stability. During 1992–3 the average budget deficit in CIS countries was over 16 per cent of GDP, reduced in 1999 to just over 4 per cent. But the situation remained dramatic in countries such as Kazakhstan, which in 1998 had government expenditures of 22 per cent of GDP with a deficit of 8 per cent – comparable to the weakest African countries. To increase the tax base, tax codes should be simplified and rates should be reduced in virtually all countries. Additionally, the state itself must start to honour its obligations to demonstrate payments discipline. Corruption also needs to be reduced. Very low wages, paid irregularly, make state employees easy prey for deals. In Russia a shock therapy was needed but it was not implemented. Only after a traumatic crisis did the government start to collect revenues seriously and to pay its remaining employees on time. See Chapter 5 for more on how a vicious or virtuous circle can magnify the consequences of basic policy choices.

As an aside, we note that federalism turned out to be particularly problematic for transition countries. Czechoslovakia, the Soviet Union and Yugoslavia all exploded. And, as brilliantly demonstrated by Shleifer and Treisman (2000), a major retarding factor for reforms in Russia has been the need to trade off the interests of central and regional governments as dominating stakeholders.

## 4.5   Is the transition over?

A number of studies analyse the prospects of transition economies catching up with developed market economies. Some have concentrated on estimating the time required by transition countries to converge to the Western European level of development using a growth regression approach (Barbone and Zalduendo 1996); Fischer, Sahay and Vegh (1997, 1998) and Fischer and Sahay (2000) assess the 'distance' of the transition countries from Western market economies in terms of macroeconomic indicators such as inflation, budget deficit, etc., whereas Krkoska (1999) examines whether the macroeconomic fluctuations in transition economies are similar to those in Western European economies. The EBRD assesses regularly the progress of reform in each of the transition countries (*Transition Reports*, various years) and provides a quantitative evaluation in a number of important areas (e.g. enterprise reform, market liberalisation, financial and legal institutions).

However, the existing literature takes much richer Western European countries as a model and implicitly assumes that all the characteristics that distinguish transition economies are due to their past as centrally planned economies. This is unlikely to be the case, because many of the indicators according to which transition countries differ from OECD countries are known to be related to the level of development of an economy. In other words one should ask the question: Has central planning under communist rule left a heritage that, even after ten years, differentiates post-communist economies from other countries *with a comparable income per capita?*

The starting points for any transition evaluation are those well-known characteristic traits of centrally planned economies that might have left a mark on economic structures because they could not be changed quickly:

- a marked preference for industry, especially heavy industry and neglect of services;
- very high rates of investment, in both physical and human capital;
- no need for a financial system to allocate savings to investment (done by the plan, usually without assigning a value to time); and
- no need for the legal and institutional framework underpinning a market economy.

This list leaves out many other elements that distinguish a centrally planned economy from a market economy – control over prices, non-market exchange rates and artificial trade patterns to name but three. However, these elements could be, and indeed have been, changed almost immediately and would thus be unlikely to characterise an economy in transition in 2000, ten years later, from a market economy.

The methodology proposed here starts from the observation that most of the potential characteristics of economies in transition are related to the level of development or income per capita.[1] For example, the demand for services tends to increase with income. Richer countries therefore have a larger services sector. More developed economies also have a much denser infrastructure than poorer ones. The same can be said of the financial system, which is much more developed in richer countries. Finally, it is a fact of life that in poorer countries the legal system tends to be underdeveloped, and that the public sector tends to work less efficiently. The main reason for this might simply be that the efficiency of the highly complex market economy of the capitalist world relies on a public sector with a strong human capital base. However, it has also been argued that weak enforcement of property rights impedes growth (Dabla-Norris and Freeman 1999). Which way the causation runs is of no significant concern to the purpose of our analysis.

The results presented below strongly confirm the general observation that most of the elements that might distinguish an economy in transition are related to development. GDP per capita alone (whether measured in PPP or in current $ terms) can explain between 40 and 70 per cent of the variance of the indicators for the legacy of transition in simple cross-section regressions. This suggests a straightforward research strategy. Formerly centrally planned economies can be said to be different if they are systematic outliers in regressions that link indicators such as the importance of industry, energy use, etc. to GDP per capita. (See also EBRD 1999, for a similar approach.)

After presenting the data and methodology in section 5.1, we discuss, in section 5.2, the results for the four characteristics of planned economies mentioned above. In section 5.3 we then perform a fishing expedition by asking what would happen if one were to sift through all countries of the globe armed only with knowledge about the preferences of central planners. If one selected those countries with too much industry, excessive investment, underdeveloped financial systems, etc., would one then end up with transition countries?

Table 4.5. *Regression results*

| | GNP$_{pc}$ PPP | (GNP$_{pc}$)$^2$ | CEEC-8 | SEE | CIS | ASEAN | $R^2$ | Obs |
|---|---|---|---|---|---|---|---|---|
| (1) Industry male employment 97 | 2.06** | −0.10** | 0.53**** | 0.60**** | 0.83**** | −0.16* | 0.68 | 131 |
| | (2.5) | (2.0) | (6.4) | (5.9) | (11.2) | (−1.7) | | |
| (2) Industry female employment 97 | 4.31**** | −0.23**** | 0.85**** | 1.08**** | 1.25**** | 0.37**** | 0.70 | 130 |
| | (5.1) | (−4.6) | (8.3) | (6.9) | (10.9) | (3.3) | | |
| (3) Industry value added % of GDP 97 | 1.46**** | −0.08**** | 0.06 | −0.11 | 0.07 | 0.18** | 0.24 | 120 |
| | (3.0) | (−2.9) | (1.1) | (−0.9) | (0.8) | (2.4) | | |
| (4) Manufacturing value added % of GDP 97 | 1.24** | −0.06** | 0.34*** | 0.22*** | 0.38* | 0.50**** | 0.33 | 110 |
| | (2.4) | (−2.0) | (3.7) | (3.1) | (1.8) | (6.5) | | |
| (5) Commercial energy use p.c. kg of oil equivalent 96 | 0.81**** | | 0.67**** | 0.36 | 0.77*** | −0.04 | 0.76 | 109 |
| | (18.8) | | (6.4) | (1.2) | (3.2) | (−0.3) | | |
| (6) Commercial energy use p.c. kg oil equiv. 96 | −1.64** | 0.14**** | 0.82**** | 0.53* | 0.86**** | 0.03 | 0.79 | 109 |
| | (−2.5) | (3.8) | (6.6) | (1.7) | (3.5) | (0.3) | | |
| (7) Paved roadnet (% of all roads)$^a$ | 1.20**** | | 1.50**** | 1.21**** | 1.57**** | 0.44 | 0.80 | 117 |
| | (12.9) | | (2.8) | (9.5) | (8.5) | (0.9) | | |
| (8) Railnet (km per surface area)$^a$ | 0.71**** | | 1.42**** | 1.34**** | 1.08**** | −0.97**** | 0.73 | 116 |
| | (11.3) | | (11.4) | (11.4) | (4.8) | (−2.8) | | |
| (9) Gross secondary enrolment 96 | 0.58**** | | 0.46**** | 0.46**** | 0.96**** | 0.11 | 0.76 | 119 |
| | (14.5) | | (5.8) | (5.9) | (10.2) | (0.6) | | |

| | | | | | | | |
|---|---|---|---|---|---|---|---|
| (10) Gross tertiary enrolment 96 | 1.03**** | 0.56** | 0.93**** | 1.56**** | 0.13 | 0.81 | 130 |
| | (24.5) | (2.9) | (6.8) | (9.3) | (0.5) | | |
| (11) M2 % GDP 97 | 0.41**** | −0.18 | −0.18 | −0.93**** | 0.29* | 0.55 | 125 |
| | (−10.4) | (−1.3) | (−0.7) | (−6.8) | (1.3) | | |
| (12) Credit to private sector % of GDP 97 | 0.72**** | −0.45** | −0.71* | −1.09**** | 0.65**** | 0.63 | 126 |
| | (13.2) | (−2.6) | (−1.9) | (−4.2) | (2.7) | | |
| (13) Interest rate spread lending – deposit 97 | −0.36**** | 0.04 | 0.61 | 0.66** | −0.64*** | 0.41 | 95 |
| | (−6.7) | (0.3) | (1.3) | (2.9) | (−3.1) | | |
| (14) Corruption (higher value = less corrupt) 98 | 0.38**** | −0.03 | −0.24**** | −0.24 | −0.14 | 0.63 | 80 |
| | (10.7) | (−0.3) | (−5.1) | (−1.5) | (−1.2) | | |
| (15) Euromoney country risk index 97 | 0.38**** | 0.11**** | −0.25* | −0.27*** | 0.2** | 0.77 | 129 |
| | (21.4) | (3.3) | (−1.9) | (−3.0) | (2.1) | | |
| (16) Institutional Investor country risk index 97 | 0.48**** | −0.04 | −0.32** | −0.52*** | 0.32**** | 0.81 | 108 |
| | (18.4) | (−0.6) | (−2.0) | (−3.2) | (4.2) | | |
| (17) ICRG country risk index 97 | 0.12**** | 0.05** | −0.16**** | −0.03** | 0.05** | 0.60 | 103 |
| | (10.1) | (2.5) | (−7.2) | (−2.3) | (2.5) | | |
| (18) Economic Freedom 99 (higher value = less free) | −0.16**** | 0.03 | 0.16**** | 0.18**** | −0.02 | 0.62 | 123 |
| | (−11.4) | (0.6) | (6.4) | (5.3) | (−0.2) | | |

*Notes:* All variables are in logarithms; all standard errors are corrected heteroscedasticity-consistent.

*, **, ***, **** = significant at the 10%, 5%, 1% and 0.1% level, respectively.

[a] Additional explanatory variable: population density.

p.c. = per capita; ICRG = International Composite Country Risk Guide from Political Risk Services.

### 4.5.1   *Data and methodology*

The data were taken from the World Bank Development Indicators database that contains income per capita and a number of structural indicators for 148 countries. In this sample the transition countries mostly fall under the classification 'Middle Income Developing Countries'. To achieve time consistency of the data, per-capita incomes and most of the other indicators refer to the year 1997 or otherwise the latest year available.

Most regressions were run on two transformations of the raw data: first, using the natural logarithm of all variables and, second, using standardised values, i.e. by subtracting the mean and then dividing by the standard deviation. As both sets of results were very similar, only the results using logarithms are reported here. Income per capita can be compared in a common currency (the US $) or in purchasing power parity (PPP) terms. The results presented here are based on GNP per capita in PPP, as this measure is commonly used in cross-section comparisons. The results were again similar using GNP in US-$ terms. This is not surprising, since there is a close correlation between these two measures of development. In a regression of one on the other the $R^2$ is over 96 per cent and the transition countries do not constitute outliers. This is a first indication that their economies are not fundamentally different.[2]

We used simple OLS regressions for a snapshot after transition. The first set of results are reproduced in table 4.5, obtained from the following regression:

$$\text{Indicator}_i = \alpha + \beta\,\text{GNP}_{pci} + \chi(\text{GNP}_{pci})^2 + \phi\,\text{CEEC-8} + \gamma\,\text{SEE}$$
$$+ \eta\,\text{CIS} + \varphi\,\text{ASEAN} + \varepsilon_i, \tag{4.1}$$

with 'i' as the country-subscript, 'Indicator' as the respective variable that is related to per capita income ('$\text{GNP}_{pc}$'), 'CEEC-8', 'SEE', 'CIS' and 'ASEAN' as the country dummies, and '$\varepsilon$' as the error term. All variables – except the dummy variables – are in natural logarithms so that the coefficients can be interpreted as elasticities. The square term of per-capita GNP was added to allow for a non-linear relationship. When the coefficient of the per-capita GNP square term was not significant at the 10 per cent level, this variable was dropped from the equation. Occasionally, the classification of the dummies may disguise underlying country heterogeneity. In order to control for such cases, we supplemented the results from table 4.5 with CEEC-country-specific results by running the following regressions:

$$\text{Indicator}_i = \alpha + \beta\,\text{GNP}_{pci} + \chi(\text{GNP}_{pci})^2 + \nu\,\text{COUNTRY} + \varepsilon_i, \tag{4.2}$$

Specification (4.2) differs from (4.1) only in replacing the four regional dummies by a single dummy named 'COUNTRY', which includes only one transition country in each single regression. All other transition countries are left out of the entire sample, so as to ensure that the benchmark is not distorted by the (allegedly) distorted transition economies. Given that there are 24 transition economies in our sample and 18 regressions in table 4.5, we had to run $18 \times 24 = 432$ regressions to get the coefficients for all transition countries for all indicators examined in table 4.5 alone. The results of this exercise are summarised in the appendix to this chapter, which contains the coefficients of the respective CEEC as well as their heteroscedasticity-consistent *t*-values. Whenever these country-specific results add to the informative value of the dummy coefficients under specification (4.1), they are referred to in the text below.

### 4.5.2    Have command-economy characteristics been washed away?

We are not interested in the performance of individual countries (some results by country are reported in the appendix). We therefore used regional dummies throughout. Four groupings turned out to be useful. Three for transition and one for Asian countries: CEEC-8, encompassing the eight most advanced countries (Czech Republic, Estonia, Hungary, Latvia, Lithuania, Poland, Slovak Republic, and Slovenia), South-East Europe (SEE), including Albania, Bulgaria, Croatia, FYR Macedonia, and Romania, and the CIS countries (Armenia, Azerbaijan, Belarus, Georgia, Kazakhstan, Kyrgyzstan, Moldova, Russia, Tajikistan, Turkmenistan and Ukraine).[3]

The use of three different dummies to treat transition countries as three distinct groups was motivated by the progress they have achieved in reforms towards a market economy. The CEEC-8 countries are clearly the most advanced country group, while the SEE countries have at least started reforms earlier than the CIS countries did. A dummy variable was added for ASEAN countries, which are also widely perceived to have relied heavily on industrial expansion during their development process.[4]

We now turn to the evaluation of the four characteristics of planned economies mentioned above.

#### *The importance of industry*

The preference of central planners for industry suggests the question whether post-communist economies today are still characterised by more industry (and less services) than would be 'normal', given their level of income.[5] One would expect that the share of industry initially increases as a country grows richer, because the workforce shifts out of agriculture into the secondary sector. At high levels of income, when services expand, further increases in income should not lead to more employment in industry, so that the relationship between income and employment in industry should resemble an inverted J. Therefore, the square of income per capita was added to the explanatory variables in the regressions.

The importance of industry in an economy can in principle be measured by the share in employment or in economy-wide value added (GDP). Both indicators were used here.

#### (a)  Employment shares

As for employment shares, the evidence is strong. There is a very close correlation between GNP per capita and the share of industry in employment in the non-linear way described above, but the transition countries clearly do not fit this line. The dummy variables for the three groups of transition countries are positive and highly significant. The point estimates (between 0.5 and 0.8) indicate that the share of industry in employment in transition countries is between one and a half and twice as large as one would expect, given their income.

### (b)  Value added shares

Interestingly, the results are quite different if we look at the share of industry in value added, i.e. GDP. The dummy variables for the three groups of transition countries turn out to be insignificant.[6] It is interesting to note that the dummy for ASEAN becomes significantly positive, which it is not for employment shares.[7]

The results on services are not reported because they represent, as one would expect, a mirror image of the ones for industry: the employment share of services is clearly lower for CIS countries, but much less for the CEEC-8 and SEE. As for the shares in value added, neither dummy is significant.

The difference in the results for shares in employment and GDP suggests that most transition economies still have a problem with structural adjustment. The number of workers in industry is still much higher than necessary and hence their productivity is relatively low, so that the share of industry in GDP is about normal.

The legacy of the preference of central planners for *heavy* industry is harder to measure since it is difficult to define heavy industry precisely and there is very little consistent cross-country data on the composition of industrial output. However, the fact that heavy industry in general is more intensive in energy suggests an indirect way to measure its importance, namely by measuring the energy intensity of the economy.[8] The best indicator available in this respect is commercial energy use (this measure ignores household energy consumption, which is affected by climate). The square of income per capita was again added to the explanatory variables for the reasons outlined above.[9] The square term was highly significant, but the size and significance of the dummies for transition countries was not affected by this addition.

For this indicator the results are unequivocal: in all three groups of transition countries commercial energy usage is much higher than the norm. The three dummy variables are highly significant and the magnitude of the point estimate (around 0.8 for CEEC-8 and CIS) indicates that transition economies consume about twice as much energy per unit of GDP as one would expect.

Could the higher use of energy in transition countries be due to the large industrial sector? This does not seem to be the case. The size and significance of the dummies for the transition countries does not change if the share of industry in value added is included in the regression.[10]

### *Capital investment*

Central planners favoured very high rates of investment, both in physical and human capital.

### (a)  Physical capital

The heavy investment in physical capital might have left a legacy in infrastructure that depreciates very slowly, like roads and rail networks. This is indeed the case. The quality of road network (proxied by the length of all paved roads as a share in surface area)[11] and the extension of the rail network (in km per surface area) are both closely related to income. But the countries in transition obviously constitute outliers in the sense that the dummy variables are highly significant and their point estimates suggest that they have a rail network that is approximately twice as extensive as the norm for countries with similar incomes.

### (b) Human capital

As for human capital, high investment seems to have continued.[12] In regressions with gross secondary and tertiary enrolment ratios the dummies for the transition countries are highly significant and the point estimates indicate again that, given their income levels, countries in transition are characterised by enrolment ratios that are substantially higher than (more than twice as high as) suggested by their development level.[13] In all these cases the dummy for ASEAN countries is not significant, suggesting that investment in infrastructure and human capital was not a particularly strong point of these economies.

### *Financial system*

Under central planning there was no need for a financial system to allocate savings to investment. Everything used to be done by the plan, largely without assigning a value to time. The size of the financial sector is captured by two indicators: the ratio of M2 to GDP (to measure the size of the banking system) and the ratio of credit advanced to the private sector to GDP (to measure the financing available for investment in the private sector).[14]

At first sight, the M2/GDP ratio only partly confirms the impression that transition countries are characterised by less developed financial systems. Only the dummy variable for the CIS countries is very significantly negative,[15] while the other transition dummies are insignificant, but still negative. Closer examination of the country-specific differences reveals that in the case of the CEEC-8 dummy the Czech and the Slovak Republics have a larger than expected banking sector whereas the opposite is true for the others.[16]

The second indicator (credit to the private sector as a percentage of GDP) might be more relevant as it does not include financing of the government. It confirms that the financial systems in CIS countries are clearly less developed than other countries at similar income levels. In this case again, the dummy for the SEE countries is much smaller than that for the CIS, but yet greater than the CEEC-8 dummy.[17] In contrast to the M2/GDP regression, all transition dummies are negatively significant at conventional levels.

The spread between lending and deposit rates may serve as a useful indicator of the *efficiency* of the financial system. In the CIS countries this spread is significantly higher than one would expect, whereas the insignificant results for the other two dummies again hide substantial country-specific differences. As for SEE, a relatively low spread in Albania accounts for this result, while the picture is very mixed among the CEEC-8 countries. Hungary seems to have an efficient financial system compared to its income level, whereas Estonia, Latvia and Slovenia are significantly worse off, and the Czech Republic, Lithuania, Poland and Slovakia appear to fit well into the world pattern.

In sum, even though a few advanced transition countries have established a working financial system, the majority are still relatively backward in this regard, not to mention the CIS and most of the SEE countries, which are even further off the benchmark.

### *Legal and institutional framework*

Under central planning there was no need for the legal and institutional framework underpinning a market economy. Are countries in transition different because they have not yet been able to create the institutional framework for a market economy?[18]

It is often argued that corruption is an important obstacle to FDI and growth and that many countries in transition have a serious corruption problem. Surprisingly, this is not confirmed by the data. It is difficult to measure how widespread and serious corruption is. There exists, however, a widely used indicator, which is based on a systematic survey carried out by the Berlin-based NGO Transparency International.

Corruption is apparently tightly (negatively) related to income. Differences in GDP per capita alone explain 60 per cent of the variability in the corruption index. However, in terms of the dummy variables used, only the SEE countries constitute negative outliers in this relationship. This suggests that corruption is not a problem that is *specifically* worse for the other transition countries. Regarding the result for CIS we note that this comprises Russia (significantly more corrupt) and Belarus (a 'clean' dictatorship within predicted ranges of corruption) turning the overall dummy insignificant. The picture is even more diverse within the CEEC-8 countries: the Czech Republic, Estonia, Latvia and Slovakia seem to be significantly worse off, in sharp contrast to Hungary and Poland, which are positive outliers in the country-specific regression.

How can one measure the quality of the institutional framework? There are several financial institutions that provide indicators of country risk. These indicators provide a measure of the risks faced by foreign investors (that the local government will interfere, for example, with expropriation, or that contracts will not be respected by local partners). Table 4.5 presents the results using the index provided by Institutional Investor (row 16). There is again a very strong correlation with income per capita, but a clear distinction between the three groups of transition countries seems to emerge. The dummy for the Central Europeans is not significant, but it is negative and significant for both the SEE and the CIS dummy, with a greater magnitude associated with the latter.[19]

The indices provided by two other institutions (Euromoney, row 15, and Political Risk Services, row 17) yield slightly different results concerning the CEEC-8 dummy, which enters with a significantly positive sign. As for the Euromoney country risk index, only Slovakia and Slovenia turn out to be within the expected range, while the remaining CEEC-8 countries are all better off. The ICRG (International Composite Country Risk Guide) indicator is only available for a few transition economies.[20]

A similar result is obtained by using the Index of Economic Freedom (Heritage Foundation, row 18), which is supposed to measure the degree to which market forces are free to act on their own. This index is again closely related to income per capita, but the SEE and CIS countries realise values that are statistically worse than expected taking into account even their low level of income.[21] However, this is not the case for the CEEC-8 group.

All in all, there is thus a clear divide between the more advanced countries that constitute the most serious candidates for EU enlargement and the rest of the region, notably the SEE and CIS countries. Certainly for the latter two, transition cannot be said to be over.[22]

Table 4.6. *Overall outliers**

| Lower 5% | Upper 5% |
| --- | --- |
| Burkina Faso | *Armenia* |
| Hong Kong | *Azerbaijan* |
| Ethiopia | *Belarus* |
| Mali | *Bulgaria* |
| | Congo Dem Rep |
| | Cuba |
| | *Georgia* |
| | Guinea-Bissau |
| | *Kazakhstan* |
| | *Russia* |
| | *Tajikistan* |
| | *Turkmenistan* |
| | *Ukraine* |

*Note*: *Given a standard normal distribution, the countries that realise residuals greater than +1.64 (+1.96) or smaller than −1.64 (−1.96) belong to the upper respectively lower 5% (2.5%) of the distribution.

Thus far, we have focused on a sector-by-sector analysis. In the following section, our intention is to derive a summary assessment of the overall location of the CEEC over the indicators presented above and to check whether other countries are similar to the transition countries.

### 4.5.3  A fishing expedition

Although we are well aware of which countries have a history of central planning, our approach could equally well provide a fishing net for a hypothetical visitor from Mars, with no knowledge of earth history, who wants to identify countries with a central planning past. We show that, in order to do so, all this visitor needs are some presumptions about the preferences of central planners, as outlined above.

To make our fishing net, we proceed as follows: we first select a smaller, but representative, set of indicators from each sector[23] (male industry employment, commercial energy use, paved roads, secondary school enrolment, M2 as a share in GDP, interest spread, Euromoney creditworthiness indicator, and the Index of Economic Freedom). We regress these indicators as usual on GNP per capita and – if significant – its square term. After standardising the residuals of each regression (i.e. subtracting the mean and dividing by the standard deviation), we calculate the average of each country's standardised residual across the selected indicators.[24] This average was again standardised to get our final aggregate measure. Given a standard-normal distribution we were then able to identify the outlier countries. Table 4.6 reports those countries in the lower and upper 5 per cent percent of the distribution.

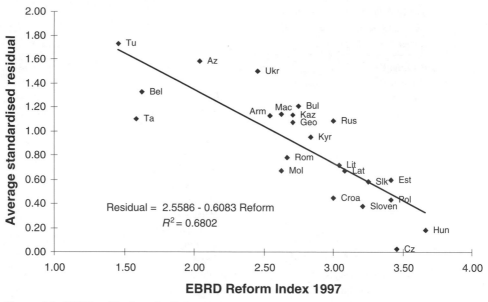

**Figure 4.5** CEEC residuals and reform progress
Source: Own calculation and EBRD (1998).

The countries in the upper percentile are of most interest to us, since they constitute the country group that tends to have more of the central planning characteristics than their development level suggests. The result is telling: the upper 5 per cent – a total of thirteen countries – is largely made up of transition countries (italicised), in particular those that are further behind in reforms, i.e. the SEE and CIS countries. Only three non-transition countries, the Democratic Republic of Congo,[25] Cuba, and Guinea-Bissau, seem to be comparable to these ten transition countries. Notably, two of them are communist states or led by autocratic rule. The probability of such a result (i.e. to find exactly ten formerly centrally planned economies among the thirteen outliers representing the upper percentile) in a random drawing is approximately $2.4 \times 10^{-11}$.

Except for Kyrgyzstan and Moldova, which are known to be more reform-minded, one can thus identify with no prior knowledge the entire CIS from its central planning past.

Considering the transition countries alone, it is interesting to note that the extent of reform efforts is strongly related to the size of the residuals, as is shown in figure 4.5. The more successful a transition country has been in terms of reform policy (measured by the EBRD transition indicator), the more it conforms to the worldwide benchmark.

Hence, this approach – which imposes no a priori judgement on whether the transition countries are different, but starts only with knowledge about the preferences of the socialist planner – corroborates our earlier findings, derived by a priori assuming that the transition countries were different and by therefore assigning dummy variables to them. Some of the transition countries are indeed still easily recognisable merely by looking at the cross-section of all countries in the world in the late 1990s. This implies that the old legacies have persisted, particularly in the less advanced transition countries, which are still far from becoming 'ordinary' market economies.

## 4.6 Conclusions

What can one conclude after more than ten years of continuing reform rhetoric, and in some cases genuine efforts? Our first result is that experience has shown that slow reforms meant, in many cases, just that: slow reforms and no willingness to progress faster after the groundwork had been done. The tortoises did not overtake the hares.

But it seems to us that the most fundamental question is whether transition is over. It is often remarked that the formerly planned economies are not yet up to the standards of the rich West. But we argue that this is not a pertinent observation. Instead one should ask: would it be possible for an economist with no access to time-series data to distinguish the formerly centrally planned economies among the over 130 countries in the world? The answer seems to be yes. Even after ten years, most countries in transition are still characterised by a much higher share of employment in industry and a higher energy use than expected on the basis of their income per capita. They also have a much more extensive physical infrastructure and have a higher proportion of their population in secondary and tertiary education. However, considering indicators that measure the extent to which the institutional framework of a market economy has been put into place leads to more differentiated results. The financial and institutional framework for a market economy clearly is much weaker than one would expect for the CIS and SEE countries, whereas this is not the case for the advanced Central European countries. For some of the latter (i.e. the ten candidates for EU membership minus Bulgaria and Romania) there is even some evidence that their framework is stronger than one would expect given their still relatively low level of income per capita. Significant differences remain, of course, within this group. But on average it seems that the transition is over in Central Europe.

For these countries, ten years were enough to upgrade the economic software, even if the hardware is still recognisable from a different era. However, this raises the question why these countries should still be treated differently from other developing countries with a similar income per capita (e.g. Turkey or Brazil), for example by being served by a special development bank, the EBRD. The countries in the CIS (and some from SEE) are clearly in a different category. They still have problems with the transition towards credible market-based institutions and financial systems. The risk is that they will need another decade to become 'normal' market economies.

# Appendix

Table 4A.1. *Single country dummies and t-values**

| | 1 Indu | 2 Indu | 3 Indu VA | 4 Manu | 6 Energy | 7 Road | 8 Rail | 9 Second | 10 Tertiary | 11 M2% | 12 Credit% | 13 Spread | 14 Corruption | 15 Eurom | 16 InstInv | 17 ICRG | 18 Freedo |
|---|---|---|---|---|---|---|---|---|---|---|---|---|---|---|---|---|---|
| Alb | 0.47 | 0.90 | −0.45 | — | −0.38 | 1.12 | 1.21 | 0.20 | 0.74 | 0.65 | −1.50 | −0.19 | — | −0.55 | −0.78 | −0.18 | 0.12 |
| | *8.80* | *10.30* | *−11.2* | — | *−6.30* | *7.30* | *9.90* | *3.20* | *10.30* | *11.00* | *−17.30* | *−2.20* | — | *−16.50* | *−17.10* | *−9.20* | *7.30* |
| Arm | 0.97 | 1.47 | 0.22 | 0.57 | −0.20 | 1.16 | 1.19 | 0.97 | 0.66 | −1.29 | −1.12 | 1.23 | — | −0.44 | — | — | 0.09 |
| | *17.80* | *16.50* | *5.30* | *9.00* | *−3.20* | *7.90* | *10.00* | *17.40* | *9.70* | *−23.30* | *−13.70* | *15.10* | — | *−14.00* | — | — | *5.50* |
| Az | 0.98 | 1.32 | −0.36 | 0.40 | 1.28 | — | 1.66 | 1.11 | 1.60 | −0.86 | −1.81 | — | — | −0.26 | — | — | 0.29 |
| | *14.70* | *15.00* | *−7.90* | *6.80* | *21.40* | — | *13.00* | *15.30* | *19.40* | *−12.70* | *−18.10* | — | — | *−6.70* | — | — | *15.90* |
| Bel | 0.62 | 0.99 | 0.33 | 0.83 | 0.96 | 0.90 | 1.21 | 0.62 | 1.29 | −1.16 | −1.25 | 0.91 | −0.01 | −0.56 | −0.96 | — | 0.30 |
| | *9.40* | *10.60* | *7.30* | *12.30* | *13.50* | *9.00* | *13.90* | *16.10* | *22.80* | *−23.30* | *−18.00* | *12.60* | *−0.30* | *−24.10* | *−31.20* | — | *17.90* |
| Bul | — | — | −0.17 | 0.15 | 1.25 | 1.35 | 1.53 | 0.56 | 1.45 | −0.55 | −0.71 | 1.66 | −0.23 | −0.21 | −0.41 | −0.18 | 0.20 |
| | — | — | *−3.90* | *2.2* | *18.1* | *12.50* | *16.30* | *13.00* | *24.40* | *−11.00* | *−9.80* | *22.50* | *−5.00* | *−8.20* | *−11.70* | *−13.00* | *12.50* |
| Cro | 0.44 | 0.72 | −0.23 | 0.21 | 0.42 | 1.20 | 1.50 | 0.48 | 0.81 | −0.28 | −0.12 | 0.55 | — | 0.03 | −0.11 | — | — |
| | *6.72* | *7.80* | *−5.14* | *3.10* | *5.90* | *11.50* | *16.2* | *12.70* | *14.40* | *−5.70* | *−0.20* | *7.60* | — | *1.20* | *−3.60* | — | — |
| Cz | **0.54** | **0.76** | — | — | **0.73** | **0.47** | **1.66** | **0.24** | **−0.17** | **0.30** | **0.25** | **0.11** | **−0.10** | **0.05** | — | **0.01** | **−0.21** |
| | **11.7** | **11.10** | — | — | **11.80** | **3.70** | **15.70** | **6.50** | **−2.80** | **5.20** | **3.30** | **1.40** | **−2.50** | **2.70** | — | **1.00** | **−8.80** |
| Est | **0.66** | **0.90** | **−0.12** | **0.04** | **1.39** | **1.17** | **1.20** | **0.70** | **1.18** | **−0.41** | **−0.20** | **0.76** | **−0.35** | **0.09** | **−0.03** | — | **−0.18** |
| | **10.10** | **9.80** | **−2.70** | **0.60** | **19.60** | **11.10** | **13.6** | **18.70** | **21.10** | **−8.10** | **−2.90** | **10.50** | **8.40** | **3.80** | **−1.00** | — | **−10.80** |
| Mac | 0.69 | 1.36 | −0.11 | — | — | 1.13 | 1.29 | 0.48 | 0.83 | — | — | — | — | −0.62 | — | — | 0.16 |
| | *11.7* | *14.60* | *−2.50* | — | — | *9.80* | *13.10* | *9.80* | *13.20* | — | — | — | — | *−21.90* | — | — | *9.40* |
| Geo | 0.90 | 1.15 | −0.18 | 0.31 | −0.54 | 2.04 | 1.44 | 0.96 | 2.12 | — | — | — | — | −0.75 | −0.93 | — | |
| | *16.60* | *13.40* | *−4.40* | *5.20* | *−9.20* | *14.3* | *12.60* | *15.00* | *28.5* | — | — | — | — | *−21.50* | *−19.00* | — | |
| Hun | **0.41** | **0.73** | **0.06** | **0.38** | **0.68** | **1.21** | **1.68** | **0.46** | **0.33** | **−0.13** | **−0.57** | **−0.58** | **0.10** | **0.18** | **−0.11** | **0.05** | **0.08** |
| | **6.64** | **8.50** | **1.30** | **6.00** | **9.90** | **10.90** | **17.30** | **13.40** | **6.00** | **−2.50** | **−8.20** | **−7.80** | **2.50** | **9.10** | **4.40** | **4.90** | **3.90** |
| Kaz | 0.56 | 0.79 | −0.12 | — | 1.33 | 1.68 | 0.88 | 0.74 | 1.29 | −1.31 | −1.52 | — | — | 0.02 | −0.28 | — | — |
| | *9.10* | *8.50* | *−2.80* | — | *19.50* | *8.80* | *6.40* | *16.10* | *21.3* | *−25.70* | *−20.60* | — | — | *0.70* | *−7.80* | — | — |

| Country | 1 | 2 | 3 | 4 | 5 | 6 | 7 | 8 | 9 | 10 | 11 | 12 | 13 | 14 | 15 | 16 | 17 |
|---|---|---|---|---|---|---|---|---|---|---|---|---|---|---|---|---|---|
| Kyr | 0.61 | 1.07 | −0.20 | 0.28 | 0.20 | 1.80 | −0.48 | 0.92 | 0.82 | — | — | 0.12 | — | −0.59 | — | — | 0.21 |
|  | 11.40 | 12.30 | −5.00 | 4.60 | 3.30 | 13.7 | −4.60 | 15.30 | 11.40 | — | — | 1.40 | — | −7.60 | — | — | 12.90 |
| **Lat** | **0.75** | **1.00** | **0.00** | **0.30** | **0.76** | **4.03** | **1.80** | **0.83** | **1.20** | **−0.89** | **−0.38** | **0.30** | **−0.31** | **0.20** | **−0.03** | — | **0.002** |
|  | **11.70** | **10.60** | **0.03** | **4.40** | **10.8** | **38.8** | **20.40** | **14.80** | **20.40** | **−12.40** | **−7.60** | **4.00** | **−6.80** | **8.00** | **−1.00** | — | **0.100** |
| **Lit** | **0.73** | **1.01** | **0.03** | **0.29** | **1.10** | **2.55** | **1.40** | **0.63** | **1.09** | **−1.03** | **−0.80** | **−0.06** | — | **0.17** | **−0.10** | — | **0.06** |
|  | **11.30** | **10.70** | **0.60** | **4.30** | **15.6** | **25.1** | **15.80** | **15.20** | **18.80** | **−14.40** | **−16.10** | **−0.8** | — | **6.80** | **−3.00** | — | **3.70** |
| Mol | 0.98 | 1.58 | 0.32 | 0.85 | 0.91 | 2.10 | 1.95 | 1.19 | 2.02 | −0.55 | −0.20 | −0.02 | — | 0.13 | — | — | −0.03 |
|  | 13.90 | 17.70 | 6.70 | 14.60 | 15.00 | 11.5 | 13.90 | 16.00 | 24.10 | −5.30 | −2.80 | −0.2 | — | 3.20 | — | — | −1.80 |
| **Pol** | **0.51** | **0.50** | **0.20** | — | **0.86** | **1.17** | **1.62** | **0.50** | **0.36** | **−0.72** | **−0.21** | **−0.04** | **0.04** | **0.16** | **0.16** | **0.09** | **0.15** |
|  | **7.90** | **5.70** | **4.40** | — | **12.40** | **10.20** | **16.10** | **14.40** | **6.60** | **−10.50** | **−4.10** | **−0.6** | **1.00** | **7.80** | **5.90** | **8.9** | **7.80** |
| *Rom* | *0.84* | *1.15* | *0.37* | — | *0.89* | *1.09* | *1.54* | *0.52* | *0.76* | — | *−0.65* | — | *−0.23* | *0.02* | *−0.02* | *−0.12* | *0.16* |
|  | *12.90* | *12.20* | *8.10* | — | *12.70* | *9.70* | *15.80* | *12.60* | *13.2* | — | *−12.90* | — | *−5.30* | *1.70* | *−0.70* | *−9.6* | *9.60* |
| Rus | 0.74 | 1.02 | 0.17 | — | 1.61 | 1.23 | 1.10 | 0.63 | 1.34 | −1.15 | −0.82 | 0.81 | −0.45 | 0.02 | −0.24 | −0.03 | 0.23 |
|  | 11.30 | 10.80 | 3.80 | — | 22.90 | 7.30 | 9.00 | 15.30 | 23.20 | −16.30 | −16.40 | 11.10 | −10.40 | 1.00 | −7.30 | −2.50 | 14.00 |
| **Slk** | **0.22** | **0.66** | **0.03** | — | **0.83** | — | **1.49** | **0.35** | **0.08** | **0.03** | **0.33** | **−0.05** | **−0.20** | **−0.02** | **−0.05** | **0.03** | **0.15** |
|  | **3.70** | **8.20** | **0.60** | — | **12.50** | — | **15.10** | **10.20** | **1.40** | **0.40** | **6.20** | **−0.60** | **−5.30** | **−0.80** | **−2.00** | **3.10** | **7.10** |
| **Slv** | **0.47** | **0.83** | **0.21** | **0.49** | **0.35** | **−0.47** | **1.04** | **0.08** | **0.14** | **−0.72** | **−0.38** | **0.37** | — | **0.02** | **−0.45** | — | **0.23** |
|  | **12.2** | **13.00** | **5.10** | **8.30** | **5.80** | **−3.80** | **10.00** | **2.20** | **2.30** | **−9.10** | **−6.20** | **4.40** | — | **0.80** | **−18.40** | — | **9.20** |
| Ta | 0.97 | 1.47 | — | — | 0.44 | 1.24 | 0.29 | 1.31 | 2.05 | — | — | — | — | −0.12 | — | — | 0.19 |
|  | 9.60 | 13.90 | — | — | 6.00 | 7.20 | 2.20 | 15.50 | 22.00 | — | — | — | — | −2.60 | — | — | 9.20 |
| Tu | 0.87 | 0.99 | — | — | 1.83 | — | 1.10 | — | 1.79 | 0.36 | −1.18 | — | — | −0.25 | — | — | 0.26 |
|  | 12.00 | 11.00 | — | — | 29.80 | — | 8.20 | — | 21.10 | 3.50 | −17.00 | — | — | −6.30 | — | — | 13.60 |
| Ukr | 1.04 | 1.46 | 0.35 | −0.81 | 1.74 | 1.81 | 1.86 | 1.07 | 2.08 | −1.9 | −0.82 | 1.27 | — | −0.23 | −0.24 | — | 0.14 |
|  | 19.50 | 16.80 | 8.70 | −13.30 | 29.00 | 12.90 | 16.40 | 17.60 | 28.90 | −21.80 | −14.00 | 14.80 | — | −6.80 | −5.10 | — | 8.90 |

*Note*: For each country, coefficients appear in first line, *t*-values in the second. The dummy coefficients for each country stem from a regression, which contains only the respective transition economy (for which a dummy is defined) plus the rest of the world (without all the other transition countries). Italics indicate SEE countries, bold refers to CEE-8, and the rest is part of the CIS-dummy.

## Notes

1. See also Easterly (1999).
2. The EBRD transition indicators were not used here for a simple reason: they are available only for transition countries and are thus not useful to check whether transition countries are different from other countries with a similar level of development.
3. Owing to lack of sufficient data, Uzbekistan had to be excluded.
4. The ASEAN dummy comprises Indonesia, Laos, Malaysia, Myanmar, Philippines, Singapore, Thailand and Vietnam.
5. This approach rests ultimately on the 'Chenery hypothesis' (Chenery 1960), according to which sectoral growth within an economy is linked to its per-capita income level. For an earlier application to Eastern Europe, but with a focus different from ours, see Döhrn and Heilemann (1991).
6. Unfortunately, the value-added regression shows a comparatively poor overall fit.
7. Somewhat surprisingly, the results concerning the share of manufacturing in value added were different: the dummy variables for both groups of transition countries are large and highly significant. Unfortunately, no employment data are available for manufacturing.
8. It is well documented that the Soviet model of industrialisation, as it had been adopted by all former CMEA countries, leads to excessive energy intensity (see Gray 1995).
9. At high levels of income, i.e. when only services expand, further increases in income should not necessitate more energy, so that the relationship between income and commercial energy use should resemble an inverted J.
10. As one would expect, the share of industry in employment is not significant in predicting commercial energy use. However, it is only in this respect that transition countries are over-industrialised.
11. For similar evidence on the cross-country relationship between road infrastructure and income see Querioz and Gautman (1992) and Ingram and Li (1997). For the rail–income relationship see also Canning (1999).
12. Human capital – measured by school enrolment rates – ranks among the most robust determinants of economic growth according to Levine and Renelt (1992).
13. Beside education, health constitutes an important element of human capital. As several authors have shown (e.g. Pritchett and Summers 1996; Suhrcke 1999) it is also closely related to per-capita income across countries. Running the same regressions as above, but for various health input and output measures, reveals a very similar pattern as for the education variables: all transition dummies suggest a significantly better level of health, mainly because there are significantly more resources devoted to the health sector.
14. The importance of the financial sector for economic growth has been demonstrated by Levine (1997). For a similar approach to ours, see EBRD (1998).
15. The 1997 data used here do not even incorporate the effects of the 1998 crisis in Russia.
16. Apart from Albania, which biases the significance upwards, financial indicators have been available for only two other SEE countries: Bulgaria and Croatia. The results here are broadly similar to those given in EBRD (1999).
17. Qualitatively similar results obtain for indicators measuring capital market development, such as the stock market capitalisation as a share in GDP, where the point estimate of the dummy coefficients is even larger.
18. The role of the institutional framework in determining development prospects has increasingly attracted attention within the framework of the economic growth literature (e.g. Knack and Keefer 1995).
19. Again, the widest intra-dummy differences relate to the CEE-8 countries: Hungary, Lithuania, Slovenia, and Slovakia fare the worst, Estonia and Latvia seem in line with predictions, and Poland appears better than expected.

20. Among the CEE-8 countries Hungary, Poland and Slovakia show a better performance than expected, and the Czech Republic seems to fit well into the predicted pattern. The CIS dummy only contains Russia, and SEE includes Albania, Bulgaria and Romania, all of which are significantly riskier than expected.

21. In the country-specific analysis of the CIS economies, it is surprising to note that Moldova has established a greater degree of freedom than expected. The grouping again hides striking intercountry differences: The Czech Republic and Estonia have a higher degree of freedom, while Hungary, Lithuania, Poland, Slovakia, and Slovenia are less free than predicted, and Latvia is within the 'normal' range.

22. Another indicator of the extent to which reforms have led to a normal market economy environment could be the importance of trade in GDP. The central planners had a preference for trade within their own bloc and tried to minimise dependency on trade with capitalist (i.e. OECD) countries. Whether this regional preference has disappeared is difficult to test with the methodology used here, as one would have to take into account the vicinity of major markets and other 'gravitational' factors. However, Brenton (1999) confirms the judgement that in this respect the transition is over for countries in Central Europe. Gravity equations of the distribution of trade of transition countries indicate that the Central Europeans trade approximately as much with their Western trading partners as one would expect, given income levels and distance. However, this is not the case for countries of the former Soviet Union, which still show a statistically significant bias to trade among themselves more than would be expected from the gravity factors (distance, market size).

23. The results carry over to the entire set of indicators, too.

24. Before doing so, all residuals must be arranged so that a positive residual means a higher actual development level (regarding the respective indicator) than predicted by per capita income. Therefore, the residuals of the interest rate spread and the economic freedom indicators, which are inversely related to per capita income, must be multiplied by minus 1.

25. Which is not exactly 'democratic' in fact.

# 5 Transition: unfinished business

Chapter 4 concluded that transition as a sui generis problem is over in Central Europe. This does not mean, however, that all transition economies are already in a state of bliss. In some, particularly the successor states of the FSU and in South-East Europe, a lot of work still needs to be done to make them prosperous.

In this chapter we do not discuss problems specific to one or a few countries. We focus on one issue that, to varying degrees, applies to all: the task of institution building. Although economists were certainly aware of the need to create markets, laws and regulations and to reform public administration, they underestimated the difficulty of *implementing* the advice offered. If virtually all firms are bankrupt, a bankruptcy law is unhelpful; if property rights are not clearly defined or are not enforceable, banks will not lend. It is, therefore, not surprising that unfinished business mainly concerns those activities where institutional requirements are particularly demanding. The most visible shortcomings of institution building are in the political domain, conditioning shortcomings in the economic domain. Democracy and state institutions have not progressed significantly in many countries. As two insiders of Russian reforms observe (Braguinsky and Yavlinsky 2000): '. . . the economy was not freed from old Soviet-type monopolies; rather these monopolies were freed to pursue their own goals at the expense of the large society, almost without any restraint! Thus, the controls of the planned economy are diminished, but the accountability, legal framework and supremacy of a democratic society have not been established.' The three economic domains where institution building has encountered the most difficulties are corporate governance of privatised firms; collection of tax revenue and creation of a social security net; and emergence of efficient financial intermediation. As privatisation in most countries is more or less complete, we focus on the other tasks still to be accomplished.

Section 1 assesses the importance of democratic decisionmaking in the transition process. Section 2 examines the quality of the government sector as a key condition for growth. Section 3 compares the privatised pension system, as adopted in many transformation countries upon advice from Western institutions, with the pay-as-you-go system. Section 4 looks at the difficulties in creating a monetised economy and proposes a concrete starting point. Section 5 elaborates an approach for dealing with the inter-enterprise debt to get started with hard budget constraints. Section 6 discusses the choices in developing an appropriate financial system.

## 5.1   Political reforms

The transition job consisted in political and institutional reforms, including changes in property rights and a redefinition of the role of the state and of individuals. Table 5.1 includes a democracy indicator and shows that the economically more successful transition countries have also been more successful in creating democratic societies. The less successful countries have not made much progress for reasons exposed in the following quote from Braguinsky and Yavlinsky (2000: 127):

Table 5.1. *Countries in transition: indicators of economic performance, liberalisation, democracy and initial conditions*

| | Average growth 1990–8 | GNP p.c. (US $) 1989 | Liberal index 1990–3 | Liberal index 1994–8 | Democr. Index 1990–3 | Democr. Index 1994–8 | Sec. sch. Enrol. |
|---|---|---|---|---|---|---|---|
| Czech Rep. | −0.36 | 8600 | 0.68 | 0.83 | 0.854 | 0.917 | 89 |
| Slovakia | 0.22 | 7600 | 0.66 | 0.79 | 0.771 | 0.733 | 96 |
| Hungary | −0.41 | 6810 | 0.73 | 0.84 | 0.854 | 0.917 | 81 |
| Poland | 1.98 | 5150 | 0.76 | 0.81 | 0.833 | 0.900 | 83 |
| Slovenia | 0.57 | 9200 | 0.73 | 0.79 | 0.729 | 0.917 | 80 |
| Bulgaria | −4.37 | 5000 | 0.58 | 0.63 | 0.729 | 0.783 | 71 |
| Romania | −2.77 | 3470 | 0.40 | 0.65 | 0.396 | 0.717 | 80 |
| Albania | −0.77 | 1400 | 0.40 | 0.63 | 0.479 | 0.517 | 79 |
| Croatia | −2.43 | 6171 | 0.69 | 0.75 | 0.500 | 0.500 | 80 |
| Macedonia | −5.32 | 3394 | 0.68 | 0.67 | 0.563 | 0.600 | 80 |
| Estonia | −2.68 | 8900 | 0.49 | 0.80 | 0.646 | 0.867 | 92 |
| Latvia | −4.67 | 8590 | 0.40 | 0.72 | 0.625 | 0.850 | 92 |
| Lithuania | −4.08 | 6430 | 0.45 | 0.74 | 0.688 | 0.900 | 78 |
| Russia | −6.14 | 7720 | 0.31 | 0.67 | 0.563 | 0.567 | 92 |
| Ukraine | −10.29 | 5680 | 0.13 | 0.52 | 0.563 | 0.583 | 80 |
| Belarus | −2.43 | 7010 | 0.17 | 0.41 | 0.479 | 0.250 | 92 |
| Moldova | −10.98 | 4670 | 0.26 | 0.62 | 0.375 | 0.567 | 81 |
| Armenia | −7.06 | 5530 | 0.25 | 0.57 | 0.500 | 0.483 | 85 |
| Azerbaijan | −8.04 | 4620 | 0.16 | 0.45 | 0.313 | 0.250 | 83 |
| Georgia | −9.76 | 5590 | 0.23 | 0.55 | 0.354 | 0.483 | 82 |
| Kazakhstan | −5.14 | 5130 | 0.22 | 0.58 | 0.375 | 0.250 | 90 |
| Kyrgyzstan | −4.84 | 3180 | 0.25 | 0.70 | 0.500 | 0.483 | 88 |
| Tajikistan | −8.61 | 3010 | 0.15 | 0.41 | 0.313 | 0.067 | 73 |
| Turkmenistan | −8.32 | 4230 | 0.09 | 0.31 | 0.188 | 0.000 | 70 |
| Uzbekistan | −1.12 | 2740 | 0.16 | 0.54 | 0.208 | 0.050 | 94 |
| **Average** | **−4.31** | **5432** | **0.401** | **0.640** | **0.535** | **0.566** | **83.64** |

*Notes*: GNP per capita in 1989 is in US $ at purchasing power parity as reported by De Melo et al. (1996). Liberalisation index is unweighted mean of the indices constructed by De Melo et al., as extended by Havrylyshyn et al. (1998). The index ranges between zero (no liberalisation) and one (complete liberalisation). Democracy index is average of political rights and civil liberties (reported by the Freedom House), respectively, ranging between zero (no democracy) and one (complete democracy). School enrolment is according to Denizer (1997) and relates to early 1990s.

*Sources*: EBRD *Transition Report* (various issues), De Melo et al. (1996, 1997), Freedom House, World Bank *World Development Report* 1996, *Shell Route Planner*, Fidrmuc (2001).

It is of utmost importance to realise that when a dictatorial socialist state collapses, it is not and cannot be replaced immediately by a constitutional commercial state. Its structures, inherited from those of the socialist state, are being torn apart by segmented parallel economy coalitions and legal property rights . . . become totally exposed and unprotected. Under such a social order, it can hardly be expected that any growth at all can take place . . . The state is weak because there is no economic mechanism functioning, apart from ubiquitous corruption, and this weakness further increases incentives for all kinds of economic activity apart from rent seeking and corruption. The post-totalitarian state is caught in a vicious circle, from which it can be rescued only by a once-and-for-all constitutional arrangement, which will put into place protection of private property and introduce competitive markets, demolishing the structures of the parallel economy.

The analysis is very pertinent, even if the solution fails to be convincing.

Democracy is an important goal in itself. In addition, democratic institutions have checks and balances, protect personal rights and property and limit individual power. For these reasons some economists, such as North (1990, 1993) argue that democracy is a precondition for sustained prosperity. It needs to be recognised, however, that democratic decisionmaking can be slow and geared to the median voter. Barro (1996) stresses the negative implications of excessive income redistribution. Alesina and Drazen (1991) show that efficiency-enhancing reforms may be delayed for distributional reasons. In general, government policies may be excessively influenced by short-term results to improve prospects of re-election.

Table 5.1 shows that the countries that were most successful in establishing democracy were also the most successful in economic liberalisation. Fidrmuc (2001) tested this relationship for causality and concluded that causality runs unambiguously from democracy to liberalisation.

From an equation regressing liberalisation on democracy (with $R^2 = 0.76$) he uses the residuals as a measure of residual liberalisation, that is, beyond the degree caused by democracy. His estimations are reproduced in table 5.2.

The results show that in transition economies democracy has been significant (directly or indirectly via more liberalisation) in positively affecting growth. However, during the initial years, when liberalisation had not progressed enough, democracy was a hindrance to growth. The negative effects mentioned above and greater uncertainty may be the reasons. Also of considerable interest is that residual liberalisation is still statistically significant.

The mystery of the dismal decade in the countries of the FSU is, in fact, not a mystery any longer. These countries have been unable to really change and as long as they retain their inherited, murky spheres of influence, where rights are not defined by law but by the strength of the parties involved, refusing openness, transparency, accountability and equal rights – the basic features of a democratic society – they will not get their economies out of the mud.

## 5.2   Corruption in the public sector

Given the weight of the public sector in a modern economy, its role in setting and implementing the rules of the game, its importance in providing law and order, it is easy to see

Table 5.2. *Democracy and growth*

| Period: Growth rate of: | 1990–8 GDP p.c. | *t*-stat |
|---|---|---|
| Constant | −0.869 | −0.075 |
| Dummy 1994–8 | −9.049 | −2.442 |
| Residual liberalisation | 20.796 | 4.216 |
| Residual liberalisation sqrd | 27.522 | 1.948 |
| Democracy | 19.099 | 3.479 |
| Democracy 1990–3 | −20.015 | −4.709 |
| Dist. fr Brussels (000 km) | −0.112 | −0.204 |
| Sec. school enrolment | 0.111 | 1.889 |
| War dummy | −10.631 | −5.224 |
| War dummy (lagged) | 4.496 | 2.640 |
| 1989 GNP p.c. (log $ 000) | −1.580 | −1.171 |
| Adjusted $R^2$ | 0.771 | |
| Joint sign. liberalisation | 0.000 | |
| Number of observations | 50 | |

*Note*: Estimated by OLS with heteroscedasticity robust *t*-statistics for the 25 countries included in Table 5.1. The indices used in the regressions are the averages for the respective periods.
*Source*: Fidrmuc (2001).

that, for economic efficiency and dynamism, a well-functioning public sector is key. Unfortunately, in many transition economies the quality of the public sector is disappointing and is a major problem for progress.

It would be wrong to believe that public sectors deteriorated everywhere during transition. Even in communist times the inefficiency and corruptness of the administration were already well known, and in some countries the public sector has improved (Central Europe), while in others it has remained unchanged (South-East Europe) and even deteriorated (FSU).

One of the best measures of corruption in transition countries comes from a survey organised jointly by the World Bank and the EBRD. The results from the 1999 and 2002 surveys regarding the frequency and the importance of bribes are summarised in table 5.3. There is a marked difference between the three country groups: the CEEC-8 show clearly lower levels of corruption for both periods than the CIS and the SEE. Both the CEEC-8 and the CIS show some improvement between 1999 and 2002, but the difference has not diminished over this period. On the contrary, the difference in the frequency of firms that report bribing actually increased from 11.7 percentage points in 1999 (35.6 per cent for CIS versus 23.9 for CEEC-8) to 14 percentage points in 2002 (32.5 per cent CIS versus 18.5 for CEEC-8).

The bribe tax as a percentage of annual revenues is on average twice as high for small firms as for large firms; the percentage of firms paying bribes is several times higher for small firms than for large firms; new market entrants are more often required to bribe and at higher rates than established firms; private firms have to bribe more than state-owned firms

Table 5.3. *The frequency and extent of the bribe tax*

| | % of firms making bribes frequently[1] | | Average bribe tax as a % of annual firm revenues[2] | |
|---|---|---|---|---|
| | 1999 | 2002 | 1999 | 2002 |
| CEEC-8 | 23.9 | 18.5 | 1.2 | 0.9 |
| CIS | 35.6 | 32.5 | 2.8 | 2.1 |
| SEE | 34.3 | 28.3 | 1.3 | 1.8 |

*Notes*: Unweighted averages.

[1] Firms were asked to what extent the following statement is true: 'It is common for firms in my line of business to pay some irregular "unofficial payments" to get things done.' Response categories comprised: Always, Usually, Frequently, Sometimes, Seldom, and Never.

[2] Firms were asked what percentage of annual revenues 'firms like yours' make in irregular 'unofficial payments' to public officials. The actual bribe tax as a share of annual revenue was computed on the basis of the midpoint (or the lower end in an open-ended category) of six possible categories listed in the survey: up to 1%; 1–1.99%; 2–9.99%; 10–12%; 13–25%; more than 25%.

*Source*: Own calculations based on Business Environment and Enterprise Performance Survey, EBRD (2002).

to get things done; and the time of managers spent with officials varies from 3 per cent in the Czech Republic to over 12 per cent in Albania (EBRD 2002: 27–31). Under such conditions, market entry and development of small and medium-sized firms – the core of Western economies – are seriously handicapped.

Table 5.4 summarises the performance of governments as perceived by market participants. Firms were asked how problematic nine factors were for the operation and growth of their business. Answers were on a scale ranging from 0 (major obstacle) to 3 (no obstacle). The factors are grouped into four broad sub-categories: microeconomic governance – including taxes and regulations; macroeconomic governance – including policy instability, inflation, exchange rate; physical infrastructure – no sub-categories; and law and order – including judiciary, corruption, street crime, organised crime. The governance index is constructed as the average of the country scores across all nine factors. Here the countries are ranked by their overall score. The first three places are no surprise: Hungary, Slovenia and Estonia. However, the good scores of countries such as Uzbekistan and Armenia also show the limits of this approach: the few surviving firms in these countries might have such low expectations that they give even bad governments good marks. Another problem with this approach is, already noted in chapter 4, that the EBRD ranking does not allow a comparison with established market economies. We now turn to a different approach, which avoids this problem.

Table 5.5 gives the ranking of the groups of countries already used in chapter 4 (CEEC-8; SEE and CIS) by five criteria that are essential for economic efficiency: political instability and violence; government effectiveness; the regulatory burden; rule of law; and graft (see

Table 5.4. *The quality of governance*

| Country | Microeconomic governance | Macroeconomic governance | Physical infrastructure | Law and order | Overall governance index |
|---|---|---|---|---|---|
| Hungary | 0.92 | 1.72 | 2.42 | 2.34 | 1.98 |
| Slovenia | 1.17 | 1.73 | 2.26 | 2.23 | 1.95 |
| Estonia | 1.25 | 1.74 | 2.30 | 2.17 | 1.95 |
| Uzbekistan | 1.40 | 1.44 | 2.11 | 2.16 | 1.83 |
| Armenia | 0.55 | 1.15 | 2.21 | 2.32 | 1.72 |
| Poland | 0.96 | 1.53 | 2.37 | 1.82 | 1.69 |
| Slovak Republic | 0.88 | 1.68 | 2.11 | 1.70 | 1.65 |
| Czech Republic | 0.80 | 1.35 | 1.57 | 1.97 | 1.59 |
| Belarus | 0.67 | 0.77 | 2.18 | 2.25 | 1.57 |
| Lithuania | 0.69 | 1.70 | 2.19 | 1.48 | 1.54 |
| Azerbaijan | 1.02 | 1.59 | 1.73 | 1.56 | 1.53 |
| Croatia | 0.67 | 1.18 | 2.13 | 1.62 | 1.43 |
| Bulgaria | 0.90 | 1.25 | 1.77 | 1.49 | 1.38 |
| Kazakhstan | 0.75 | 0.72 | 1.85 | 1.68 | 1.27 |
| Georgia | 0.67 | 0.93 | 1.78 | 1.47 | 1.24 |
| Ukraine | 0.34 | 0.77 | 1.76 | 1.68 | 1.24 |
| Russia | 0.47 | 0.65 | 1.91 | 1.54 | 1.16 |
| Romania | 0.45 | 0.60 | 1.49 | 1.48 | 1.07 |
| Kyrgyzstan | 0.46 | 0.48 | 1.85 | 0.98 | 0.85 |
| Moldova | 0.52 | 0.35 | 1.42 | 1.10 | 0.82 |

*Source*: *Business Environment and Enterprise Performance Survey*, EBRD (1999).

appendix for individual country data). These rankings were collected by the World Bank and are thus available for all countries, not just transition economies. We chose EU member countries as the most appropriate benchmark because most of the CEEC west of CIS aspire to become members soon (see chapter 9).

A few general points emerge directly from inspection of table 5.5. There is a considerable variance within the EU itself. It is so large that, in all categories, there is at least one CEEC-8 that is better than the worst EU member, but the CEEC-8 average is always worse than the EU average (and better than the CIS average).

This is confirmed for most of the individual categories:

*Political stability and violence*    The difference between the eight EU candidates and the EU-15 itself is minor, but the difference with the CIS is large. This seems to be the area where the CEEC-8 have made most progress.

*Government effectiveness*    The CEEC-8 are about midway between the CIS and the EU-15.

*Regulatory burden*    In terms of averages, the difference between the CEEC-8 and the EU is substantial, but not too large, whereas the CIS is far behind.

*Rule of law*    The CEEC-8 are about halfway between the CIS and the EU-15.

*Graft*    The CEEC-8 are, again, about halfway between the CIS and the EU-15.

Table 5.5. *Quality of governance and the rule of law*

|  | Political instability and violence | Government effectiveness | Regulatory burden | Rule of law | Graft |
|---|---|---|---|---|---|
| CEEC-8 best | 1.25 | 0.67 | 0.85 | 0.83 | 1.02 |
| EU worst | 0.21 | 0.56 | 0.59 | 0.50 | 0.67 |
| EU best | 1.51 | 2.03 | 1.21 | 1.81 | 2.13 |
| CEEC-8 worst | −1.86 | −1.42 | −1.93 | −1.33 | −1.32 |
| EU average | 1.11 | 1.37 | 0.91 | 1.31 | 1.48 |
| CEEC-8 average | 0.78 | 0.36 | 0.50 | 0.45 | 0.36 |
| CIS average | −0.32 | −0.76 | −0.76 | −0.58 | −0.77 |
| Turkey | −0.94 | −0.41 | 0.59 | −0.01 | −0.35 |

*Source:* Own calculations (EU average without Luxembourg) on data from Brunetti et al. (1998).

Also of interest is that the results for Turkey are mostly below the average of CEEC-8, but better than the worst CEEC-8 member.

What makes graft and inefficiency so widespread in Eastern European societies, and especially in the public sector? Boxes 5.1 and 5.2 provide two models to gain some insights. Box 5.1 addresses corruption and shows how a high corruption/low enforcement trap might arise. Box 5.2 turns to a common problem: how to keep bureaucrats under control without making rules too rigid.

Box 5.1 models the frequency of corruption and shows that the difference between heaven and hell can be due to relatively small differences in the enforcement effort. It is, thus, worthwhile to make an effort to provide incentives, controls and the necessary money to pay for the police forces.

What determines the frequency of corruption? From the point of view of an individual official the main factors are the size of the potential bribe, the severity of the punishment if caught and the probability of being caught. These factors play out differently for each individual official, depending on risk aversion and the non-monetary disutility attached to being branded as corrupt. The model shows how these preferences interact with a mechanism that plays out at the macro level, namely the distribution of the enforcement effort over potential cases.

What determines whether hell or heaven will prevail? As equation 5.5 in box 5.1 makes clear, even a country with reasonable prospects can land in hell, in particular if the starting point is bad. A lucky country might have a starting point with the frequency of corruption ($n$) close to zero. Then the effectiveness of any enforcement level ($f$) is high and corruption remains controlled. By contrast, if corruption is widespread then no enforcement effort $f$ will be able to contain corruption over time. Unfortunately, CIS and Balkan countries seem to be close to this situation: the starting point was bad and has become worse during the 1990s. By contrast, some other countries (e.g. the Baltics) had a better starting point and never let the problem get out of control. In Estonia corruption is much less widespread, and those who still take bribes are much more likely to be caught.

Box 5.1   *Multiple equilibria in corruption*

If one orders officials by their preferences one can arrive at a sort of supply function of corruption, which is decreasing in the probability of being caught and punished. Denoting the proportion of officials that accepts bribes by $n$, and the probability of being caught (and punished) by $q$ the function $n(q)$ should have partial derivative $n_q < 0$.

We assume that there is always a (possibly very small) proportion of officials that are not tempted by bribes, even when they are sure that they will not get caught, which we denote by $h$, and the proportion of those without a strong moral fibre is denoted by $c = (1 - h)$. The parameter $h$ describes the sense of duty instilled in the administration by tradition (Prussian or oriental?) or other social factors. The proportion of officials that accept bribes can then be written as:

$$n = c(1 - q), \tag{5.1}$$

which implies that if $q = 1$, corruption (n) is to zero. Nobody will demand or accept bribes as there is no possibility of remaining undetected. If $q = 0$ then the number of corrupt officials is equal to all those 'without a strong moral fibre'.

But what determines the probability of being caught? The probability $q$ that a corrupt official is caught depends on the enforcement effort of the police (or rather the public prosecutor), $f$, and the number of cases that have to be dealt with. The amount of time and effort that can be devoted to each case is equal to $f/n$. The probability of being caught for each individual bureaucrat considering acceptance of a bribe should be proportional to the time the police can devote to each individual case:

$$q = f/n, \quad q = 1 \text{ for } n < f. \tag{5.2}$$

The parameter $q$ thus determines the probability that corruption is detected even if many are corrupt so that the enforcement effort has to be spread very thinly.

Substituting the determinant of $q$ into equation (5.1) yields:

$$n = c(1 - f/n) \tag{5.3}$$

or:

$$n^2 - nc + fc = 0. \tag{5.4}$$

This equation has two solutions:

$$n_{1,2} = 0.5c \pm 0.5(c^2 - 4fc)^{1/2}. \tag{5.5}$$

There are thus two internal equilibria. (The third one is the bliss point of no corruption at all, with $q = 0$, when the police have nothing to do.)

A numerical example might be useful to illustrate the nature of the two equilibria and the influence of the key enforcement effort parameter. Let us assume (heroically?) that

*(cont.)*

**Box 5.1   (*cont.*)**

one half of all officials have such a strong notion of their duty that they will not become corrupt, even if they know with certainty that they will not be caught, i.e. $c = h = 0.5$. Also assume that enforcement effort is low, say $f = 0.045$, implying that if everybody were corrupt the chance of being found out would be only 4.5 per cent (the number was chosen to have a round result). The two equilibria are at $n(\text{high}) = 0.45$ and $n(\text{low}) = 0.05$. When the enforcement effort is low the difference between the two equilibria can thus be very large. In this numerical example, corruption is nine times more frequent in the bad than in the good equilibrium. The same proportion, but inverted, applies to the probability of being caught. In the bad equilibrium corrupt officials are 9 times less likely to be found out than in the good one. In the bad equilibrium nine-tenths (45/50) of the potentially corrupt officials will actually engage in bribetaking whereas in the good equilibrium only 10 per cent (5/50) would do so. As the good equilibrium is unstable in the absence of higher penalties or greater enforcement efforts, eventually society will end up in the bad equilibrium.

How much enforcement effort would be needed to eliminate the potential for two equilibria? Inspection of equation (5.5) shows that for $c = h = 0.5$, $f$ would need to be equal to 0.125 to make the expression under the square root equal to zero. This value for $f$ implies that enforcement would still have to be strong enough to detect 12.5 per cent of all corruption even if everybody is engaged in bribetaking. This implies that the enforcement effort would have to be approximately tripled to get away from the previous case (with $f = 0.045$).

The model says the only way to escape hell is to increase enforcement effort. In reality there is no easy solution and the fight against corruption must be fought on many fronts. An increase in enforcement clearly helps, as does paying public officials enough to make it possible for them to live decently while remaining honest. But experience has shown that a sustained effort is required to change the perception and make the pendulum swing the other way.

But it is not enough to have little corruption. A market economy needs a bureaucracy that enforces laws and regulations in a way that allows the market to work. How can this be achieved? Box 5.2 provides a simple model of the extent of autonomy in decisionmaking by bureaucrats that is consistent with minimising corruption and the social objective of making bureaucrats act responsibly and flexibly, in the interest of efficiency. The model suggests that better education and better pay for civil servants are key to success. Better educated officials can be given more leeway to interpret decisions in a market-conforming way. They are also less likely to use discretion for their own personal advantage as their prospects outside the public sector would also be tarnished by corruption.

In government, as in large private enterprises, the interests of employees and those of the organisation rarely coincide. For that reason all large organisations, and especially

---

### Box 5.2    *How to improve the efficiency of the public sector*

Our operational definition of corruption is the probability, denoted by $D$, that the average bureaucrat deviates from the rulebook. Assume that the baseline is that the bureaucrat just follows the rulebook to the letter. But what if he does not? There are two possibilities: either the discretionary bureaucratic decision is socially desirable and generates a gain, $E$, or the decision is corrupt, leading to a social loss, $C$. The efficient use of discretion has probability $q$, corruption has probability $(1 - q)$.

For government we define as a general objective a social loss function $L$. The social welfare loss function can then be written:

$$L = D[(1 - q)C - qE(D, h)]. \tag{5.6}$$

Policymakers minimise the social cost by choosing the degree of discretion $D$ appropriately.

The social gain due to judicious use of discretion $E$ is written as a positive function of discretion. Certainly, a system without any discretion (i.e. the freedom to make judgements case by case) cannot function well and recalls the most dreadful stories of stoic army behaviour. For example, a tender can be judged on the quality and reputation of the potential supplier, and not only on the basis of quantity, price and whether all forms have been properly filled in. The more a bureaucrat can take into account the qualitative aspects the more likely it becomes that the best supplier is chosen.

Another key variable in determining the efficiency of bureaucratic decisions is the quality of the bureaucrats proxied by their education, the variable $h$ (human capital). With better education, better decisions can be taken. We formalise these arguments as

$$E_D, E_h > 0. \tag{5.7}$$

and assume that the marginal returns to discretion fall ($E_{DD} < 0$. Once a threshold level of discretion is reached the most efficient decision can be taken and more discretion does not add anything), whereas more education increases the marginal returns to discretion ($E_{Dh} > 0$: a better educated bureaucrat can use discretion more efficiently).

$$E_{Dh} > 0 \ E_{DD} < 0. \tag{5.8}$$

The probability $q$ is postulated to depend also on $h$ with

$$q = q(h) \quad \text{with} \quad q_h > 0. \tag{5.9}$$

As better-educated bureaucrats have more to lose, they are less likely to become corrupt. Another interpretation of $h$ is remuneration: a better-educated bureaucrat usually receives a higher pay, hence the opportunity cost increases and the danger of corruption decreases. Similarly, better pay motivates in achieving the social goal $E$.

(*cont.*)

**Box 5.2   (cont.)**

Minimisation of (5.6), using (5.7) and (5.9) yields:

$$\partial L/\partial D = 0 \;=\; [(1-q)C - qE(D,h)] - qDE_D$$
$$= (1-q)C - q[E + DE_D] \tag{5.10}$$

The second-order condition for a minimum is:

$$\partial^2 L/\partial D^2 = -q[2E_D + DE_{DD}] > 0, \tag{5.11}$$

which will be satisfied if $E_{DD}$ is sufficiently large (recall $E_{DD} < 0$).

The first order condition (5.10) shows that for a given probability of corruption $q$ and a given social loss occasioned by corruption $C$, the social gain associated with discretion and its increase with more discretion must be high enough to make discretion worthwhile. If society is already rotten, so that $q \to 0$, or if the cost of corruption is very high, then discretion may need to be limited. But, except for $q = 0$, some discretionary power is always desirable.

At present public sector employees are badly paid in most transition countries and often do not have a good level of education, as the better educated and brightest have left for the fast-growing private sector. This leads us to the question: what is the effect of $h$ on the optimal amount of discretion?

Totally differentiating (5.10) with respect to $D$ and $h$ and then solving for $dD/dh$ gives:

$$\frac{dD}{dh} = -q_h\frac{(C + E + DE_D) - q(E_h + DE_{Dh})}{[2E_D + DE_{DD}]} > 0, \tag{5.12}$$

as the denominator is negative by (5.11).

Two elements contribute to a positive effect of $h$ on $D$:

$q_h > 0$: a better education of bureaucrats makes it more likely that they use discretion in an efficiency-enhancing way;

$E_h + DE_{Dh} > 0$: a better education leads to more efficient decisions (provided there is discretion).

The result is consistent with the real world: rich, well-ordered societies, like Switzerland, can leave their bureaucrats ample room for discretion. By contrast, in poorer countries formal requirements leave very little room for efficiency-enhancing decisions.

As $h$ can also be interpreted in terms of remuneration, it turns out that not paying state employees properly and regularly may be a very detrimental decision. This is exactly what is happening still in a number of transition countries.

bureaucracies, need a code of behaviour and penalties for deviations. The delicate problem is then to provide its agents with enough freedom to take individual decisions within a general set of rules. It is not possible to prescribe in general rules the detailed circumstances for decisions to be taken in all possible cases. Bureaucrats must thus be allowed to make individual judgements in each concrete situation. To fix ideas, we call this freedom to make an individual judgement in a specific case *D*, i.e. the discretionary power of bureaucrats, their freedom to deviate from the rulebook.

This analysis counteracts the fatalistic acceptance of a poor public sector performance in transition countries beset with financial difficulties. Over time, with better training (in which governments should invest more) and better remuneration, civil servants will use discretionary power more responsibly. They may then be given more discretion. A necessary precondition is that the social goals are clearly defined and widely shared by society, thus increasing the probability that discretion is used in a way that enhances social welfare. Only then will it be possible to rely on the discretion of public-sector employees. Unfortunately, this condition is not yet fulfilled in many transition countries (e.g. CIS, the Balkans). But the countries near to EU membership have come close to meeting it and should soon be able to benefit from improving the quality of their public administration. The goal is to evolve from Lenin's maxim '*Doveryai, no proveryai*' ('Confidence is all right, but control is better') to the Prussian maxim of the reform years after the Napoleonic defeat: '*Vertrauen adelt*' ('Trust ennobles').

Two variables in this model are of specific relevance to transition countries: the majority of the civil service came from the old system, which had no tradition of serving the state, and was not resistant to the temptation of bribetaking, especially as the old ideology, which might have provided some moral support, collapsed totally. Moreover, the efficiency of the police and public prosecutors in ferreting out and punishing corruption is often low under the new system with its new laws, which are sometimes contradictory, thus blurring the line between corruption and unavoidable choices among conflicting rules.

## 5.3   Social security: is privatisation the solution?

In most transition economies the government's revenue as a share of GNP has fallen dramatically.[1] Part of the explanation for this is the high share of unrecorded economic activity. But this is not all. The complex and, at times, excessively high taxes encourage evasion. A simplification of tax codes and lower tax rates would increase the tax base. The lack of resources makes it difficult for the government to establish or maintain a social safety net: unemployment compensation, health care and pensions. Western advisers, such as the World Bank, recommend changing the pension system from the traditional pay-as-you-go (PAYG) to a privatised capitalised system. We doubt that this is a promising approach and believe that PAYG should be maintained to ensure a minimum pension, to be topped up with a funded (capitalised) pension scheme.

What are the current problems? Any type of pension insurance in any economic system would face great difficulties if the country's real capital stock and, therefore, its potential for production, suffered such a loss of value in a very short period of time, as was the case in transition economies. In an economy that cannot rely on massive foreign aid all forms of current income, including pensions, can only be paid by the revenue of the existing capital stock, meaning the yield from machines, buildings, and land combined with human labour. If the revenue from the capital stock decreases, then wages, pensions and profits also have to go down. Any one group within such a society can maintain its living standard only at the expense of others.

With a deep general fall in real income, those problems that can currently be observed are to be expected: companies pay their pension contributions either not at all or not on time, because they themselves are faced with such large financial difficulties that workers are happy if they receive at least their wages. As a result, workers do not put any pressure on their companies to pass pension contributions on to the pension system. In Western economies companies unable to pay their pension contributions have to declare bankruptcy. The state in Western countries can compensate and make payments to the unemployed during a recession simply because non-payment in the West is *not* a mass phenomenon, as it is in South-East Europe or in CIS countries.

The burden on the state has also increased greatly in the weaker transition countries because of companies' non-payment, but, in contrast to Western countries, the state has itself responded with non-payment. This has created a situation without a solution: the pension system has become insolvent and would normally have to declare bankruptcy, but it cannot do so, because that would more or less mean the bankruptcy of the entire social system.

It is wrong to attribute the problems resulting from the difficulties of transition to the existing PAYG: problems in the pension system are the result of poor economic developments.

Similar considerations also apply in the case of ageing populations, a demographic trend that is very pronounced in transition countries. Savings put aside today can only be used in the future if sufficient capital returns are then available. If this is not the case because the working population is declining, then the claims have to be reduced. This is the real problem in many transition countries.

When a funded pension system is introduced, as in several transition countries, pensions accumulated before the change would still have to be paid while contributions to the PAYG system from the working population decrease. Such a transition period would last perhaps 20 or 30 years. The state would have to compensate during this time. Pensions would have to be paid by the state, although it would no longer be receiving contributions from companies and workers. The state, therefore, would have to take on additional debt in the amount of the non-existing contributions. This burden on the capital market cannot be avoided. If the state chose to finance pensions by means of higher taxes, a double burden would be placed on the current working population (under Ricardian equivalence equal to the present value of future tax liabilities generated by the indebtedness scenario).

The willingness of the population to change over to a funded system has been low owing to lack of confidence. Viewed as a whole, the transition to a funded system does not lessen the burden on the state in the short run, but increases it instead. The advantages of the new system would only show up in the long run.

A funded system requires, at the minimum, credible, non-corrupt institutions and reliable state administrations just as much as a PAYG system does. If the state does not pay pensions reliably and consistently from the start, a funded system will also not be able to work properly. In such a situation, the state would be whittling away at the contract that implicitly forms the basis of the entire process. The credibility and reliability necessary for the new system has

Table 5.6. *Monetisation in transition countries*

|  | Broad money as % of GDP (end-year, 2001) | Domestic credit to private sector as % of GDP (2001) |
|---|---|---|
| CEEC-8 | 50.0 | 26.6 |
| CIS | 12.7 | 8.1 |
| SEE | 44.3 | 14.7 |
| EU-12 | 68.3 | 108.7 |
| Selected countries: |  |  |
| Bulgaria* | 40.9 | 14.6 |
| Czech Republic | 76.9 | 24.5 |
| Estonia | 42.3 | 27.8 |
| Poland | 44.6 | 18.4 |
| Russia | 17.7 | 14.6 |

*Note*: * Domestic credit for 1999.
*Source*: Own calculations based on EBRD, *Transition Report*, 2002 and ECB data.

to be strengthened by state institutions, not undermined by them. Loss of confidence would be even more damaging if companies did not, from the start, raise wages to the extent that contributions were higher to the new pension funds than for the PAYG system. The planned contributions could then come about only at the expense of the living standard of workers.

The most important aspect is, however, that even a funded system can function only in the presence of high growth, which also presupposes that the population can be confident that capital funds do not serve to enrich only a few managers and bankers. In a PAYG system, the state explicitly promises this according to the intergenerational contract and by means of appropriate economic policy. If future generations are to receive interest on accumulated capital from a funded system, economic policy also has to be successful. Private funds can suffer far greater losses than is usually the case for the state as a whole. The exception is, of course, when these funds invest only in state debt. But in such a case, there is practically no difference between the two systems anyway.

## 5.4　Law and order are required to create a monetised economy

Table 5.6 shows that financial institutions, particularly in CIS countries, are not yet playing the role they play in mature market economies. The negative symptoms are well known: high levels of inter-enterprise credit, the widespread use of money surrogates or often outright barter. This dismal state of affairs is mainly due to a lack of the rule of law. A true financial system can only be created if there is a political willingness to create a transparent economic system. Without such a regime change it will make little sense to deal with the symptoms of the non-cash economy. Table 5.6 shows that the CEEC-8 are close to the euro-area average in terms of broad money (M2) to GDP ratios, but there is a huge gap with the CIS. However, in terms of credit to the private sector all transition countries still perform rather badly.

Only some poor developing countries are as demonetised as the CIS countries. The figures in table 5.6 demonstrate that, particularly in the CIS, the standard transformation functions of banks, i.e. the transformation of maturities, transformation of risks and the transformation of scale (pooling of resources), are either not available at all or have to be provided by non-banks. It is therefore not surprising that the private sector has developed several substitutes for bank money ('deposits') or bank credit. Without the availability of bank deposits or bank credit lines, firms need inter-enterprise credits to bridge gaps between their receipts and their payments. A transferable form of such credits are *veksels*. For firms with a weak bargaining power or a low reputation as debtors, barter is the only solution.

It is obvious that such substitutes are associated with higher transaction costs than operations that are intermediated by the banking system:

- Basic monetary theory shows that barter involves high search and other transaction costs.
- Non-monetary transactions make the whole economic process very untransparent, which has negative implications for tax revenues and for enterprise restructuring.
- Trade relations among enterprises tend to become restricted to established networks that can handle their transactions on a non-monetary basis. This prevents effective competition among firms.
- Without credits from the banking system, firms lack the long-term funds they would need for comprehensive restructuring.
- Governments are not able to tap domestic savings for the financing of deficits and outstanding debts. As a result they have to borrow on international markets with very high spreads.
- Private households often hold their savings in dollar banknotes, forgoing interest incomes. The revenues from seigniorage accrue mainly to the United States and not to the domestic budget.

As this state of affairs has existed now for several years, it is difficult to find easy solutions. In our view the absence of the 'rule of law' has to be regarded as the main cause of the 'non-cash economy'. The fact is that rights are not defined by the law, but simply by power. Bankruptcy, for example, is more a political than a legal question. So is seniority of debt. Property rights are uncertain and difficult to assess. For example, real estate property rights are unclear and cadastres often do not exist. Against what kind of securities and pledges can a bank mitigate its lending risk? In addition to specific risks of the borrower, there is also a rather high systemic uncertainty so that it is perfectly rational for a bank to lend only to 'connected' borrowers. Given these conditions, it is not surprising that banks lend so little. What is amazing is that they lend at all!

In the whole CIS area governments often fail to make payments (for wages, pensions and goods) when they are due. Given this precedent, it is not surprising that private agents do not behave better, especially if they have to make tax payments.[2] In a society with a very weak payments discipline, it is also difficult to enforce a bankruptcy law as the government lacks the moral authority to impose the sanctions that are embedded in the execution of such a law. As a result, the soft-budget constraint, once regarded as the hallmark of the command economy, has been able to survive the first decade of transformation.

This state of affairs has disastrous consequences for the development of a financial system. Banking, more than any other business, relies on trust. The very low levels of bank credit to the private sector reflect the absence of this precondition for banking in all CIS countries. And, as bank deposits are simultaneously created by the process of credit creation, a lack of credits is identical with a lack of bank deposits or money in general.

Of course, this distrust in promises also impairs the reputation of banks. In fact, all CIS countries have seen serious banking crises. As a consequence, most private households prefer to hold their savings in non-interest-bearing dollar notes ('mattress money') instead of depositing them with a domestic bank.

Thus, without establishing a strict payments discipline at all levels of the government and in the private sector, the non-cash economy (or the non-bank economy) will continue. (A strict enforcement of payments would also make it possible to apply bankruptcy laws in consequence.)

Because of the very low wages in the government sector – payment of which is also very often subject to long delays – many government employees are making money through corruption. But if such incomes are not entirely used for consumption (see above), they cannot be invested in the domestic banking system. Thus, all savings out of such incomes have to be held in cash or with foreign banks.

For the case of Russia, Commander and Mumsen (1999) mention two other important causes for the avoidance of banks for payments transactions. First, bank transfers are inefficient and costly for users. Second, Russian banks act as intermediaries for tax collection, and, related to that, the Russian corporate tax system has until recently worked on a cash basis and not on an accrual basis. These factors also created strong incentives to use channels of payment other than the banking system. Gaddy and Ickes (1999) estimate that in 1997 about 40 per cent of tax payments were made in cash.

Each of these contributions to the non-bank economy is by itself very damaging, but in conjunction it is not surprising that they have made the development of a true financial system an almost impossible task. Thus, it will be very difficult to find a comprehensive solution.

## Improving payments discipline

A solution to the problem of payments discipline has to start with the government sector. Only if the government is paying all wages, pensions and bills when they are due will it be in a position to credibly enforce payments discipline in the enterprise sector. Thus, the government would have to make a public declaration that from now on a strict payments discipline will be observed and enforced in all sectors of the economy. Of course, such a declaration must be credible. This requires above all a solution to the *stock problem* of overdue government payments.

This could be solved by the issuance of *special government bonds*. These bonds should be used at their face value for the payment of overdue wages, pensions and bills. The interest rate of these bonds (with a maturity of, say, four to five years) should be considerably lower than the market rate. As a result their market price would be below par. However, if a private agent were to use these bonds for the payment of *overdue* taxes, they would be valued at par, which would be a strong incentive to use these bonds for that purpose. Ideally, this could lead to a clearing of whole chains of overdue payments. This would be the case if a government worker passes bonds to a retail store and if they are transferred to the supplier of a final product, from there to the producers of inputs and eventually to the government. Of course, the whole mechanism will only work if the government announces at the same time that it will come down hard on any enterprise that does not pay its taxes. This would be enhanced by a comprehensive *clearing* of all debts in the enterprise and government sector, as discussed in section 5.

But even a perfect payments discipline would not guarantee a stronger transformation role of the banking system, which is the basis for a mutual growth of bank credits and bank deposits. This problem is addressed in section 6.

## 5.5   Hard budget constraints require a solution to the inter-enterprise debt overhang

The high volume of inter-enterprise debt poses a great problem in CIS countries. Outstanding debt among companies amounts to 30–40 per cent of nominal gross domestic product in CIS countries and many times the value of bank loans to companies. Borrowing among companies does occur in market economies also, but not to the degree that can currently be observed in CIS countries.[3]

### *Causes of the high level of inter-enterprise debt*

In order to evaluate various approaches to solving the problem of inter-enterprise debt, the most important causes have to be identified. In our view these are the severe lack of liquidity in companies, and the lack of incentive structures within state-owned companies.

There is no doubt that companies and individuals have to have a certain amount of money available in order to take care of their economic transactions. The amount of money desired for such transactions depends on the efficiency of the national system of payments and the yields that can be achieved if wealth is invested in other forms.

A perceptible reduction in liquidity took place due to high inflation, following liberalisation. It is reasonable for economic actors to hold as little money as possible with sinking purchasing power. It is, however, problematic that no change occurred even after inflation went down. Owing to the fact that banks are not willing to lend money, individuals and companies have only a very small amount of money available to them.

It is not surprising in such a situation that many companies try to take care of their transactions in such a way that no cash is needed. The simplest way to do this is by trading goods 'on credit', which means that companies temporarily grant credit to each other. A high level of outstanding claims and liabilities between companies emerges almost automatically within a short time. The critical aspect of this problem is that these claims and liabilities usually cannot be balanced out on both sides.

Inter-enterprise debt is a rational reaction from economic subjects to a general lack of liquidity. In a situation where the financial system is collapsing, companies have no other choice than to take on certain functions normally performed by banks: direct credit between companies takes the place of transactions which usually occur via banks. It is obvious that companies are not able to perform such functions efficiently. They are especially overburdened by the responsibility of checking the creditworthiness of other companies as well as by the monitoring of outstanding debt.

## *Clearing using debt–equity swaps*

Such a complex problem can hardly be solved overnight. It requires measures in various areas, including:

- mutual clearing of all outstanding inter-enterprise claims and liabilities,
- rapid privatisation of state-owned companies,
- rapid and sustainable improvement in earnings in the corporate sector, and
- strengthening and restructuring of the entire banking system.

We focus on the first point and propose a model for clearing inter-enterprise debt which is structured in such a way that credit among companies will still be possible. Because increased lending from the banking system cannot be expected in the near future, we consider it important that the mechanism of inter-enterprise credit remains a viable alternative. However, uncontrolled accumulation of claims and liabilities among companies should be avoided.

Comprehensive clearing of existing inter-enterprise debt should form the starting point for any solution. Because companies are not able to do this on their own, it is necessary that the state take on the task of coordinating the appropriate measures. The state's influence should be limited to providing a legal framework for such a process. Public financial means should not be used for paying off any of these balances. Clearing should take place according to the following pattern:

- A state clearing office is set up.
- All companies have to report all outstanding claims until a certain deadline. Claims not reported on time are then considered nullified.
- The state participates in this process by reporting all claims that it has on individual companies. Companies also report their claims that involve the state.
- Each company receives notice of all the claims being made against it. It then has two weeks to report any unjustified claims to the state clearing office. If they do not do so before the deadline, all the claims or liabilities are considered legal.
- In order to prevent the process from being slowed down by creditors that intentionally report unjustified claims or debtors that report justified claims as unjustified, a processing fee ten times the sum of the false claim should be charged in all cases in which claims can be proven incorrect.

The state clearing office can then start with the actual process of clearing. This process is presented in its simplest form in table 5.7. As indicated in the matrix, all claims and liabilities from other companies are first added up. The multilateral balance, which indicates the net position as creditor or debtor, can then be calculated as in table 5.8. During

Table 5.7. *The clearing process*

| Companies' liabilities | Claims from the companies: | | | | |
|---|---|---|---|---|---|
| | A | B | C | D | Total liabilities |
| A | – | 1,200 | 1,400 | 300 | 2,900 |
| B | 1,500 | – | 600 | 1,000 | 3,100 |
| C | 800 | 400 | – | 2,400 | 3,600 |
| D | 2,000 | 1,000 | 500 | – | 3,500 |
| Total claims | 4,300 | 2,600 | 2,500 | 3,700 | 13,100 |

Table 5.8. *Multilateral balances*

| | A | B | C | D |
|---|---|---|---|---|
| Claims | 4,300 | 2,600 | 2,500 | 3,700 |
| Liabilities | 2,900 | 3,100 | 3,600 | 3,500 |
| Multilateral balance (net claims) | +1,400 | −500 | −1,100 | +200 |

the clearing process a very high number of bilateral claims and liabilities is transformed into a far lower number of multilateral claims and liabilities.

Ideally, the clearing process should be organised in such a way that net debtors (companies B and C in our example) make payments to the net creditors (companies A and D) via the state clearing office, which serves as middleman: this should, however, be viewed as a preferred solution only. The financial means received by the state clearing office should be distributed to the various creditor companies according to the share of their claims in the total amount of all net claims. In our example, company A's claims would be 1,400 of total claims of 1,600, or 87.5 per cent of all claims.

It is to be expected that many net debtor companies will not be able to make the appropriate cash payments. This situation has often been solved by the state paying net creditors. Such a move creates the wrong type of incentives, because companies then have no reason to check creditworthiness. The predictable outcome would be uncontrolled growth in inter-enterprise debt once again.

For this reason, we suggest an alternative solution that involves debt–equity swaps, to transform claims into property rights. An investment fund should be created for the management of these claims. Net debtor companies have to pledge shares of their capital to the investment fund according to the extent of their multilateral debt balance. Vice versa, net creditor companies receive shares from this fund according to their claims as a percentage of total claims.

In order to avoid the problem of corruption, the investment fund should be administered by a foreign manager. The manager of the fund has the responsibility of selling all the capital shares in the fund within a certain time period. He has the option of implementing bankruptcy proceedings along the lines of current legislation or selling off existing capital of a company if a company is not slotted for privatisation in the near future. The manager of the fund should also encourage privatisation of companies that can be sold to private investors. The revenue earned from privatisation should then be used to pay off net creditor companies according to their share in total claims.

Outstanding wage payments are a special problem. A political decision has to be made as to whether debtor companies should first pay off their wage debts and then make the necessary payments to the clearing office or vice versa.

Claims and liabilities involving foreign companies or countries should not be included in this clearing process. That would not be feasible for purely administrative reasons. A debtor company should, however, have the opportunity of collecting outstanding foreign claims in order to be able to make the appropriate payments to the clearing office.

### *The incentive structure of the proposed solution*

The incentive structure of the proposed solution can be best illustrated if compared to the two alternatives of annulment of all inter-enterprise debt without compensation and payment of the credit balances between companies by the state.

In the proposed solution companies that have in the past sold more goods to other companies than they have bought receive at least some compensation in the form of shares from the investment fund. In the case of annulment without compensation the problem could arise in the future that goods are sold only in exchange for advanced payment in cash or in direct exchange for other goods. Both situations would be negative. If the state pays off claims, companies would see no problem in granting other companies inter-enterprise credit without checking up on the creditworthiness of their partners.

The proposed solution provides clear sanctions for companies that have in the past taken on liabilities to a large degree: such companies have to hand over part of their equity to the investment fund. Viewed in this context, such a conversion of debt bears a striking resemblance to bankruptcy proceedings. It does however have the advantage of maintaining the existing structure of bilateral claims and liabilities, which prevents the chain reaction that would arise if bankruptcy laws were strictly applied in the current circumstances. In addition, the decision of actually closing down a company or selling it to a new owner is left to the manager of the investment fund. Once again, the incentive structure in such a solution is more favourable than in the case of annulment of all inter-enterprise debt without compensation. A company manager who recklessly accumulates debt to other companies should face the risk of losing control of the company partly or completely as a result. He might, then, act more judiciously.

### 5.6   Which financial system?

Financial markets in CIS countries and in South-East Europe need to be brought up to better standards. This is only possible if the political institutions inspire confidence, and if there is foreign competition. There are thus political preconditions that economists can state, but can do little to bring about. However, it would be useful if reformers had a clear view of where they wanted to go. This clear view was absent in the early 1990s. American and European advisers gave distinctly different recommendations. Now, ten years later, it seems that Europe won the beauty contest.

The question of the optimal configuration of financial markets in Eastern Europe is both a theoretical and an empirical one. The empirical evidence stretches from the more market-based systems of the United States and the United Kingdom, on the one hand, to the more bank-based systems on the European continent.[4] Eastern European countries should not and could not take over any existing system part and parcel, but should build their financial framework by properly adapting an existing Western framework.

The American model, relying on the capital market and on segmented banking, is clearly inappropriate for Eastern Europe at its present stage of development.[5] The political, economic and organisational prerequisites for an efficient capital market exceed by far what is possible in East European countries, as forcefully demonstrated by the CIS countries. Even in Western economies there is only one capital market that comes close to efficiency in terms of completeness, liquidity and safety against abuses, i.e. the US capital market. All other capital markets suffer from a lack of size and of market-friendly, democratic traditions. The UK capital market ranks second, but even successful economies, such as Japan or Germany, have been unable to create efficient capital markets.

The existence of a reasonably efficient, ordinary banking system that collects short-term deposits, handles transfers of funds, furnishes working capital to small and medium-sized businesses and is sufficiently well capitalised to cover ordinary banking risks, such as those embedded in loan portfolios, is what emerging economies need the most. At a low level of development at least, the banking vs. markets debate misses the point. These are not alternatives: banking needs to precede capital markets. Present banking arrangements in most East European countries fail in one or more of these aspects, leading to a substantial circulation of funds outside the formal banking system at wide spreads and high risk.

Until such banking conditions can be met, most East European countries will be disappointed in the results of both their capital market fund-raising and privatisation efforts. They will also be unable to advance to the point where a choice between competing financial systems models can be made. The first priority, therefore, should be to establish a reasonably efficient banking system.

This cannot possibly be accomplished overnight. In the meantime, the basic banking systems need to be reconfigured and fortified as much as possible along West European lines, with strong relationships and monitoring links between banks and industry. Where financial transparency is low and information costs are high, 'insider' status on the part of responsible external monitors is virtually mandatory in order to achieve a viable structure of corporate governance.

In the process the banks urgently need to be regulated so that they can start off in a condition of financial viability. Once a reasonably satisfactory banking system is in place, the choice of models becomes relevant.

We plead for a conservative approach along the lines of the European universal bank model. By having both debt and equity stakes (limited by law to avoid control) in non-financial enterprises, such banks would be in a strong position to force restructuring of enterprises, using both traditional lending sanctions as well as board-level influence. It is arguable whether ordinary control functions exercised either by creditors or by external shareholders are sufficiently up to the task of making unprecedented economic transformations. Indeed, it may be argued that effective privatisations in the absence of a viable equity markets *can only* be carried out in the presence of strong, universal-type bank linkages.

To be sure, these benefits of the European approach need to be weighed against the risk that the financial systems would become highly concentrated – with all financial services provided by a small number of universal banks.[6] It is therefore also important to maintain markets contestable in the emerging banking structures in Eastern Europe. Rather than relying only on legislative means, it is preferable to retain gates open to foreign bank entries. Hungary serves as an example: it has the best-performing banking sector after foreign banks have taken over most national banks. Russia and other CIS countries serve as counter-example: their banks are universal, but virtually unregulated, weakly supervised and often owned by oligarchs. The result is chaos and abuse.

The most important soft spot of universal banking is the potential conflict of interest and the abuse of inside information. For an extensive comparison across different banking structures, see Steinherr and Huveneers (1992, 1993).

Both problems are not unique to universal banks, but are potentially more pronounced. Inside information is an economic advantage that forms the basis of a long-term relationship between bank and client, makes a long-term commitment possible and allows a more precise pricing of risk. It is the necessary condition for banking *tout court* as opposed to ad-hoc deals. Abuse of inside information is difficult to prevent – even with segmented banking. What is needed to reduce this problem is supervision and severe legal punishment.

If one wishes banks to play a role in the remaining privatisation process, in swapping loans for shares, in assisting improvement of corporate governance, then banks need that inside information whether they are universal or not. Because equity holdings and a seat on the company's board improves information, the universal bank is better equipped than others for such tasks.

But some potential conflicts are unique to universal banks. A bank as lender and shareholder may prefer a customer with a less risky strategy to make sure that it recuperates its loans rather than accepting a riskier strategy with a higher expected rate of return in excess of the risk premium (Aoki 1984). But this bias, which may be socially undesirable in mature economies, might be highly desirable in transition countries, beset by all sorts of risks.

Universal banking is both unavoidable and desirable in the context of Eastern Europe. Unavoidable because it is difficult to see how the bad debt overhang could be solved without involving banks themselves through equity swaps and increased participation in the governance of non-financial firms. The need for universal banks derives not only from practical considerations (who else could assure governance?), or temporary constraints (unavailability of a functioning capital market), but also from more basic and general theoretical arguments. For example, Dewatripont and Tirole (1993) show with a principal–agent model that:

- managers should be rewarded by low interference from outsiders when performing well – during times of good performance they should increase borrowing;
- control needs to shift to lenders during difficult times, forcing owners to recapitalise the firm and preventing the firm from gambling on resurrection by restraining its new borrowings.

When a firm has a large number of lenders, there may be an obvious information and incentive problem. It would therefore be better to have a major debt-holder who has access to information and incentives to monitor the firm to appropriate a large share of the gains.

If the firm is a non-bank, the obvious solution is universal banking, as the universal bank typically acts as 'house-bank' (i.e. dominant debt-holder) and has maximal access to information. It plays a role of active shareholder during good times (even infusing a conservative bias into the firm's finances, as the first priority of the bank is to make sure that its credits are repaid) and of active debt-holder during bad times (to recapitalise the borrower).

When banks play a major role in governance of non-banks, governance of banks becomes a key issue. It would be unwise to rely on the disciplinary role of a capital market which will remain in its infancy for some time. A necessary condition would be strict accounting and reporting requirements to make monitoring by shareholders more effective and including clear provisioning rules for problem loans. The main governance function then falls on shareholders and their board of directors. Because the assets of universal banks represent a diversified portfolio they should attract investments by pension and investment funds which cannot build up the same diversification as long as stock markets are underdeveloped. However, because universal banks' corporate governance concerns a significant share of the economy, special precautions are necessary and warranted. For example, the state could retain a minority share and a board seat; a board seat could be reserved for a union representative and another for the central bank;[7] pension and investment funds could receive regulatory incentives to invest in banks and thereby gain board seats. Finally, one directorship could be reserved for a foreign auditing firm having no other relationship with the bank.

## Bank licences: from uniformity to differentiation

We also believe that different classes of bank licences should be issued. The three tiers proposed are:[8]

- Licence A for top of the range banks as measured by their risk-weighted capital ratio and satisfaction of credit exposure norms.
- Licence B for banks satisfying a lower echelon of the same criteria. They would pay higher deposit insurance premiums and may be barred from participation in the payments system, or would be required to hold larger minimum reserves.
- Licence C for banks falling below the criteria set for Licence B. Deposits at such banks would not be insured, lender of last resort facilities would not be available and therefore participation in the payments system would not be possible. Debt of C banks would receive the same risk-weighting as that of non-banks.

This proposal has the disadvantage of not making asset allocation rules and deposit insurance superfluous and also requires acceptance of the universal bank structure. But some very clear advantages also emerge from this tiering of bank licences which (by law) would need to be visibly exposed.

First, it would provide flexibility for the coexistence of differently structured and managed banks. Depositors could opt for riskier or safer deposits – and be remunerated differently – according to their preferences or portfolio needs.

Second, the activity scope of banks would not be constrained by regulations. Of course, if a bank wishes to minimise risk it would, in fact, become a deposit bank. To operate like a universal bank with a substantial share of equity holdings of private corporations, and to enjoy Class A privileges, would require a sound capital base. Perhaps no bank could achieve that in a hard-hit transition country. Then, de facto, there would be a split between safe banks, equivalent essentially to deposit banks, and universal banks, corresponding to low-tier investment banks.

Third, the moral hazard problem would be greatly scaled down by forming more uniform classes. Tier A banks would attach importance to not losing their status and lower-tier banks would try to be upgraded. The risk of the lender of last resort is substantially reduced by not covering Class C banks and depositors would request a risk premium for uninsured deposits at lower-tier banks. Failure of a Class C bank would not generate a run on the overall banking system.

## *Building up securities markets*

As argued in Steinherr and Huveneers (1992), securities markets are underdeveloped in countries where universal banking is firmly implanted, as one is a substitute for the other. It is therefore important to support from the start the development of securities markets with appropriate policies.

Privatisation of SOE and a workable solution for corporate governance contribute to the development of the stock market, although more is required to improve efficiency and rapid growth. Listing requirements, accounting rules, protection of small shareholders, management accountability – all are to be improved in transition economies. Measured by stock market capitalisation in relation to GDP, the most developed stock markets are in the Czech Republic, Hungary and Slovenia. For dollar values, Poland and Russia have the largest stock market capitalisation. Foreign investments play an important role in Central Europe. The weak property rights in Russia are a major repellent to foreign investors.

A fixed income securities market is helpful, and even necessary, in the transition economies. Once the central bank can no longer finance the government deficit, it needs to be financed through the debt market. Similarly, the different debt work-outs, swaps and debt sales require and contribute to the development of securities markets. Banks play a key role in this in order to be able to restructure their asset books. However, as demonstrated by the Russian and Ukrainian crises, this market should not be opened up too early to foreign investors.

Debt markets would also offer an alternative for the allocation of savings to deposits and facilitate convergence to a competitive pricing structure of loans and deposits.

## 5.7   Conclusions

As transition is over in Central Europe, we have focused this chapter on the less successful transition countries. In some of these countries it could well be that the chances of future prosperity were better ten years ago than now. Bad privatisation has created bad corporate governance (chapter 8 gives concrete evidence) and a very unfair and extreme income distribution. Correction is very difficult. The disappointment of a large share of the population with a market economy and the bad reputation of oligarchs and of government officials are difficult to correct and will take a long time. Criminality as engrained and widespread as it is in some countries cannot be easily controlled or reduced. Some seem to have landed in a bad equilibrium.

In many successor states of the FSU, and despite many apparent 'reforms' such as privatisation, the fundamental organisation of society has not changed. It is, therefore, misleading to speak of the failure of reforms. Rather, reforms have not started yet. We showed that in some countries democracy is not yet working and hence the basic rules of a market-based economy do not yet exist. This suits the old nomenklatura, but hurts the interests of the population in these countries terribly.

These are massive problems. We concentrated on two particular aspects, namely two simple models of how corruption (by which we mean bad governance in general) could become rampant and how the reform of the civil service needs to be organised: at first rules would have to be strict and clear so that they could be easily enforced even by a mediocre public administration that is badly paid and trained to think and behave in the old categories. Later, when bureaucrats are better educated, better paid and understand their new role in a market economy, rules can be made more subtle so that they are appropriate for a modern market economy. For the Central European countries this means taking over the *acquis* of the EU, which is complex and thus more difficult to implement, but its implementation is constantly monitored by the EU and it has shown its effectiveness in opening markets and facilitating growth.

We warned against succumbing to the illusion that replacing pay-as-you-go pension schemes by capitalised schemes will be a solution in countries where growth prospects are uncertain, fiscal resources are precarious and confidence in government is lacking.

We then noted that the lack of trust in CIS countries made it impossible to establish a normally working financial sector. Cash intermediation in these countries has reached the level of some African economies. This is both a symptom of the social value of institutions in these countries and a cause of substantial inefficiencies. We suggested that, in order to slowly emerge from this 'bad equilibrium', the public sector must pay its debt and stop behaving arbitrarily. We made a concrete proposal to pay debt and induce tax arrears to be settled.

Because financial intermediation does not and cannot work, given the political situation, firms have developed other ways of overcoming a hard budget constraint. The inter-enterprise lending is, however, viciously biased against newcomers and maintains soft budget constraints. We propose a way of cleaning the slate that requires neither sticks nor carrots (fiscal transfers), but relies on an incentive-compatible clearing and settling.

We concluded with a discussion of the financial sector model that may have the best chances of success. We do not believe that capital markets can be relied upon to effect a large part of financial intermediation, as the institutional requirements are much too high. We propose universal banking, despite the shameful experience with Russian de facto universal banks. With accommodating supervision, pliable regulation and pork-barrel jurisdiction it does not matter which banking system is in place, since anything is then possible. Without a modicum of legal rules and responsible supervision, nothing can be done. We made a concrete proposal to introduce various banking licences in case banking supervision and regulation are taken more seriously. This is just one instance of the general problem of establishing law and order, which remains the core of the unfinished business.

## Appendix

Table 5A.1.  *Quality of governance and rule of law*

| | Political instability and violence | Government effectiveness | Regulatory burden | Rule of Law | Graft |
|---|---|---|---|---|---|
| Bulgaria | 0.43 | −0.81 | 0.52 | −0.15 | −0.56 |
| Czech Republic | 0.81 | 0.59 | 0.57 | 0.54 | 0.38 |
| Estonia | 0.79 | 0.26 | 0.74 | 0.51 | 0.59 |
| Hungary | 1.25 | 0.61 | 0.85 | 0.71 | 0.61 |
| Latvia | 0.46 | 0.07 | 0.51 | 0.15 | −0.26 |
| Lithuania | 0.35 | 0.13 | 0.09 | 0.18 | 0.03 |
| Poland | 0.84 | 0.67 | 0.56 | 0.54 | 0.49 |
| Romania | 0.02 | −0.57 | 0.20 | −0.09 | −0.46 |
| Slovak Republic | 0.65 | −0.03 | 0.17 | 0.13 | 0.03 |
| Slovenia | 1.09 | 0.57 | 0.53 | 0.83 | 1.02 |
| Albania | −1.00 | −0.65 | −0.70 | −0.92 | −0.99 |
| Armenia | −0.45 | −0.65 | −0.57 | −0.15 | −0.80 |
| Azerbaijan | −0.36 | −0.83 | −1.00 | −0.56 | −1.00 |
| Belarus | −0.37 | −0.66 | −1.47 | −0.88 | −0.65 |
| Bosnia & Herzegovina | −1.16 | −1.11 | −1.26 | −1.11 | −0.35 |
| Croatia | 0.41 | 0.15 | 0.24 | 0.15 | −0.46 |
| Georgia | −0.76 | −0.51 | −0.85 | −0.49 | −0.74 |
| Kazakhstan | 0.22 | −0.82 | −0.40 | −0.59 | −0.87 |
| Kyrgyz Republic | 0.32 | −0.58 | −0.76 | −0.47 | −0.76 |
| Macedonia, FYR | −0.40 | −0.58 | −0.31 | −0.26 | −0.52 |
| Moldova | −0.20 | −0.46 | −0.28 | −0.02 | −0.39 |
| Mongolia | 0.37 | 0.02 | 0.17 | 0.04 | −0.15 |
| Russian Federation | −0.69 | −0.59 | −0.30 | −0.72 | −0.62 |
| Tajikistan | −1.86 | −1.42 | −1.52 | −1.33 | −1.32 |
| Turkmenistan | 0.00 | −1.25 | −1.93 | −0.97 | −1.29 |
| Ukraine | −0.24 | −0.89 | −0.72 | −0.71 | −0.89 |
| Uzbekistan | −0.33 | −1.30 | −1.40 | −0.87 | −0.96 |
| Yugoslavia, FR (Serb./Mont.) | −1.42 | −0.95 | −1.54 | −0.81 | −0.99 |
| Turkey | −0.94 | −0.41 | 0.59 | −0.01 | −0.35 |

## Notes

1. Parts of this section are based on concrete field experience reported in Hoffmann et al. (2000).
2. Gaddy and Ickes (1999) show that in Russia the ratio of unpaid taxes was 31 per cent in 1997.
3. Loans between companies in Germany were equal to about 13 per cent of nominal national product (1995). This is just about equal to bank loans to companies. Inter-enterprise borrowing was also below that of bank loans to companies even in the transition economies of Central and Eastern Europe. See Rostowski (1993).
4. A comparison between the two banking systems can be found in Smith and Walter (1993). For a critical evaluation of universal banking in highly developed countries, see Steinherr and Huveneers (1992). Their sceptical views do not pertain, however, to the context of reforming East European countries. Empirical evidence of the contribution of universal banks to growth is contained in Steinherr and Huveneers (1993).
5. Steinherr and Huveneers (1993) set out a detailed comparison of banking systems with market-based systems.
6. At the present time quite the opposite prevails: too many inefficient, undercapitalised banks exist. Nor is there any evidence of excessive market power of universal banks in Western economies. For example, the market share of the five largest banks in Germany is below 15 per cent.
7. This would add to the information of the central bank as supervisory authority and commit the central bank more strongly.
8. Recent US regulations adopt the same approach. See US Treasury (1991).

# Part III

# Extreme cases for reform: scope for disagreements

'Man hat Wirklichkeit gewonnen und Traum verloren.' ('A better sense of reality was gained and dreams were lost.')

(Robert Musil, *Der Mann ohne Eigenschaften*)

# 6 German unification: an example of 'big bang' reform

"I'll pick you up."

From *Die Tageszeitung*, Germany, and World Press Review

E ast Germany used to be considered as the model economy of the socialist bloc. Yet, after unification, little of that economy seemed worth preserving. But the East Germans seemed to be luckier than their eastern neighbours, for reform and reconstruction there would have West German support of a magnitude unavailable to any other former socialist country. Overnight, unification provided the framework and the institutions needed to operate as a market economy and gave access to the financial and managerial resources of West Germany. East Germany thus obtained the necessary legal framework at the stroke of a pen when the unification treaty came into effect on 3 October 1990. Moreover, monetary union (1 July 1990) brought an untrammelled price system, a stable and convertible currency and an efficient capital market. Privatisation was also quickly begun under the management of the Treuhand Agency (THA).

Seen against this backdrop, which combined conditions ideal for a big-bang reform and considerable financial support, East Germany's subsequent vicissitudes are incomprehensible to many. Are the disappointing results due to avoidable policy errors, or was the initial collapse of the East German economy a normal consequence of a big-bang reform that should have been anticipated from the outset? Most observers will acknowledge that the difficulties of restructuring the economy of East Germany may have been underestimated, but they all have their own theories as to the policy errors that may have been made. Although some exaggerated expectations may not have been met, this chapter shows that the East German experience is a lesson for greater realism, and not a demonstration against big bang.

A prime candidate for first place on the miscalculations front is, for many, the German government's decision to start the integration process with monetary union on 1 July 1990. Most German economists had been in favour of fixed or flexible exchange rates between the two German currencies which, it was argued, would have given policymakers more room for manoeuvre and enabled them to keep the two labour markets separate, thus ensuring that wages stayed in tune with the respective productivity levels in the East and the West.

Runner-up for chief culprit is not currency union per se, but the conversion rate chosen which – as also argued by the Bundesbank – was simply set too high. Section 1 comes out against that view.

It was felt by the Bundesbank and by others that currency union could endanger West Germany's inflation record. Equally, reconstruction in the East needed to be financed. Both these facts have repercussions for the external value of the DM, in opposite directions! Higher inflation would weaken the DM in the long run and put its EMS anchor role into question, while reallocation of West German resources to the East would seem to require, according to most economists and at least in the short run, a revaluation. Section 2 sheds light on that question.

As soon as the open-border policy was implemented it became imperative from a political point of view to stem the flow of westbound emigration. Ways had to be found to make it attractive to stay in East Germany. The lure of a brighter future in itself was hardly enough. It was decided to extend West German social security legislation and benefits to all East Germans and to achieve rapid wage convergence. The more radical alternative of redistributing former socialist state property to all East Germans was rejected without further ado. Section 3 explains why that was a mistake.

Financially, the cost of integration has mushroomed, with much more unemployment than was anticipated. Total unemployment in East Germany in 1992 stood at more than twice the level reached at the nadir of the Great Depression in the 1930s. The long-term consequences are analysed in section 4. We end by discussing in section 5 whether convergence to Western incomes has stalled for policy or external reasons.

## 6.1  Currency union

Setting aside the advice of the Bundesbank and the views of most economists, the German government decided to make currency union the starting point of unification. In taking that decision, the historical lesson imparted by the 1948 currency reform – and which is widely regarded as the cornerstone of the post-war economic 'miracle' – proved decisive.

The decision to introduce the DM in the former GDR can be defended on economic grounds, even if the prime motive was political. We argued in the winter of 1989/90 that monetary union would have two main advantages: (i) it would create overnight an efficient capital market that would facilitate international trade and domestic investment, and (ii) it would replace the need for comprehensive price reform.[1] This indeed is what has happened.

### *Currency union creates an instant capital market*

Theoretical considerations suggested already in 1989/90 – and the experience in other reforming countries has confirmed – that the most difficult part of the transformation process would be to create an efficient capital market that can assess investment projects and provide financing to existing and new firms. This was fully achieved by currency union. Firms in the East, many of which are new and small, have access to the federal banking system. Introducing the DM was thus equivalent to immediately creating an efficient capital market, which would otherwise have taken some time to develop. The experiences of other reforming countries show that the lack of well-functioning capital markets was a key obstacle to quick recovery. The West German banking system that 'conquered' the territory of the GDR is providing the bulk of financing for new firms. Moreover, foreign financing of investments is particularly sensitive to a stable monetary framework in the absence of restrictions on capital movements. If the former GDR had retained the Ost Mark it would have had to maintain some capital controls (as in all Central and Eastern European countries), but with the DM as the common currency all capital controls are gone and the financing of trade is no longer a problem. The large current account deficits which East Germany is running (and which could have been expected in 1990) become invisible (like the surplus of, say, Bavaria in the West) and can, in principle, be financed by private capital without any difficulty. (For political reasons a large share is, however, financed by transfers.) With two currencies the current account deficits would have been highly visible, and probably always a cause of concern for policymakers and therefore a source of expectation of exchange rate changes.

The only alternative that would have allowed the new *Länder* to abolish capital controls immediately would have been to adopt a flexible exchange rate for the Ost Mark. This solution would have had the advantage that the exchange rate would have been established in the market and could therefore have reacted to shocks. But given the great uncertainty surrounding the success of the transition to a market economy and eventual monetary unification, the exchange rate might have fluctuated greatly with temporary overshooting. The experience of other reforming socialist countries is telling in this respect. Moreover, under flexible exchange rates the monetary policy of the former GDR's Staatsbank would have been the only anchor for prices and inflationary expectations. Given that it would have taken some time to build up a banking system and establish procedures of monetary control, monetary policy would have been highly uncertain, and over- or undershooting of the exchange rate would probably have been the result. Even in the absence of political considerations, therefore, flexible exchange rates would not have been a desirable alternative to the adoption of the DM as a common currency for a reunited Germany.

## Currency union makes price reform superfluous

Introducing the DM in the new *Länder* (coupled with the elimination of restrictions on trade) had the additional advantage of being equivalent to a comprehensive price reform. Prices needed to be freed anyway, but without the price system of the West prices might have taken longer to find their equilibrium level. By experience, the reforms that have the most immediate effects are the freeing of the price system and *Gewerbefreiheit*, i.e. the freedom to set up a business. What happened after 1990 confirmed what experience in other post-socialist countries suggested anyway, namely that it takes time to privatise. The former state-owned enterprises (SOE) therefore continued to account for the bulk of industrial output for some time. Since these firms were, in many cases, local monopolists, they might have used their power when setting new prices. With the DM as the common currency and open borders, that became impossible.

As predicted, not all prices went immediately to the West German level. Even after the introduction of the DM, prices for non-tradables, i.e. personal services and real estate, continued to be lower in the East.

Before July 1990 it was often argued that the elimination of subsidies would raise price levels, according to some estimates by as much as 30 per cent, and that this would imply a cut in real wages. However, this prediction was never appealing from a theoretical point of view since the savings from the elimination of subsidies can be used to lower taxes and increase direct income transfers. Price reform and the elimination of subsidies should therefore lead to a redistribution of income, but should have little effect on the average level of real incomes. Events immediately following currency union have shown that, on the contrary, price levels in the former GDR have fallen if one compares June 1990 to December 1990, as many goods were overpriced in the GDR.

A fixed exchange rate between two separate currencies would have had a similar effect of equalising prices. But the link would not have been as strong, since the exchange rate might change over time and so allow inflationary pressures to develop in the East, especially since at the outset a tight monetary policy would have been difficult to implement.

The main economic argument against the introduction of the DM in the former GDR is that it would make it difficult to change the real exchange rate if it was too high, because wages cannot be reduced in nominal terms. However, the danger of an overvaluation would not have been avoided even in the absence of monetary union since the newly reformed trade unions would probably have seen through the effects of a devaluation and adjusted their wage demands accordingly.

## Currency union and the choice of conversion rate

In order to implement currency union it is necessary to specify the rates at which current payments and stocks of financial assets are converted. Many have argued that the conversion rate for current payments (wages) was politically imposed and represented an overvaluation. In 1990 we argued that converting wages at much less than 1:1 would mainly have led to inflation without solving the former GDR's competitive problem because Eastern wages were only about one-third of the Western level, and if that discrepancy had persisted a large flow of emigration to the West would have been set in motion. This might have been a necessary adjustment from an economic point of view, but it would have been politically unacceptable. Subsequent events have borne out the view that the conversion rate for current payments would anyway hold only for 'a logical second'. Wages had already increased in July 1990 and the further (substantial) wage increases that have taken place in the ensuing years show that the conversion of wages at less than 1:1 would have anyway been 'corrected' immediately. The initial conversion rate for wages was therefore irrelevant.

There is also indirect empirical evidence in support of this view. If the main reason for East German loss of competitiveness had been an overvalued exchange rate in 1990, then one would expect to see rising unemployment and falling wages. This is the standard adjustment in countries with fixed exchange rates. In East Germany, rising unemployment was, however, accompanied by rising wages in nominal and real terms.

Moreover, and quite regrettably, the objective not only of the labour unions but also of the federal government was rapid convergence of wages in the two parts of Germany. It is this objective rather than monetary union and its terms that has been the reason behind the overvaluation of East German workers.

One of the most contentious aspects of the introduction of the DM in the territory of the former GDR was the rate at which financial assets, especially the savings deposits of East German citizens, were to be converted from Ost Marks into DM. The Bundesbank proposed converting financial assets at 2:1 while providing all East German citizens with a lump sum called *Kopfgeld*.[2] Was this justified? The balance sheet of the consolidated credit system of the GDR in table 6.1 before reunification provides a convenient background for a discussion of the economic impact of the choice of conversion rate for financial assets and liabilities which turned out to be misleading for many people.

Public attention focused for a time on the most important item on the asset side, i.e. 'credit to firms' of 260 bn Ost Marks. This was not warranted, since, in socialist countries

Table 6.1. *Consolidated final balance sheet of the GDR credit system (31.12.1989, in billion Ost Marks)*

| Assets | | Liabilities | |
|---|---|---|---|
| Credit to the domestic sector | 418 | Deposits | 260 |
| of which:    households | *23* | of which:    households | *176* |
| firms | *260* | firms | *60* |
| Claims on external sector | 45 | Foreign liabilities | 162 |
| Other assets | 4 | Cash in circulation | 17 |
| | | Capital and reserves | 28 |
| **Total** | 467 | **Total** | 467 |

like the GDR, there were really only two sectors, households and the government. The latter comprised firms (all government owned) and the 'external' sector (through the government monopoly on foreign trade). The distribution of assets between the state, firms and the external sector was therefore irrelevant and arbitrary under the socialist system.

The fact that the government controlled all firms (which were then taken over by the THA) implies that from an economic point of view it is irrelevant how much firms owe to banks and at what rate this debt is to be converted. If debts had been converted at 1:1 many firms would not have been able to repay them and the government would have had to pay up (or would have received less in firm sales). If firms had been able to service their debt, their privatisation value would have diminished by a corresponding amount and the government would have lost in sales revenues what it received indirectly through the banks in the form of debt-service payments. The rate at which the debt of firms was converted therefore had few economic implications. It determined only what one part of the government sector had to pay the other. Converting the debt of firms at 2:1 did, however, have advantages from an accounting point of view: fewer banks and firms became technically bankrupt. From that point of view, a rate of 3:1 or 4:1 would have been preferable. As it happens, THA frequently had difficulties selling firms with an interesting product line or goods production facilities but also massive debts.[3]

In this situation the main economic impact of the choice of the rate for currency conversion came from the net creditor position of households (vis-à-vis the government sector), This 'exposure' of households was equal to 176 bn GDR marks in savings deposits.[4] Conversion at 2:1 instead of 1:1 did therefore reduce the implicit transfers from the Bundesbank by about 88 bn DM (not taking into account the *Kopfgeld*). The Bundesbank's proposal therefore aroused a storm of protest in the old GDR. Yet the decision was justified on grounds other than distributional equity: it was argued that a conversion of the 176 bn marks in deposits at 1:1 (into DM) would have led to a 'monetary overhang', in the sense that the increase in the DM money supply would have exceeded the increase in money demand coming from the old GDR's economy. But this argument is highly questionable.

The increase in the money supply that follows from conversion at any particular rate can be mechanically calculated from the existing money stock; however, the additional demand for money is difficult to estimate. The difficulties stem from the fact that it was not clear what kind of 'money' was represented by the savings deposits, i.e. whether or not they could be considered equivalent to 'sight' deposits (M1 in technical terms) because they could be cashed without notice. If they were to be viewed as such, then, on the basis of historical ratios in West Germany, the additional demand for DM would have been only about 40 bn and conversion at 4:1 would have been appropriate. If they were to be considered 'true' savings deposits (M3 in technical terms), the additional demand for DM would then have been about 80 bn and conversion at 2:1 would have been appropriate. Finally, if they were to be considered as representing the sum of all financial assets (because no other savings instruments were available in the GDR), households might use them partly to buy other financial assets and even at a conversion rate of 1:1 there would not have been a monetary overhang.

A concern frequently raised was that a more favourable conversion rate for savings accounts would have generated inflationary demand pressures. We did not share this concern, which hindsight demonstrates to be unfounded. The reason for not expecting important inflationary demand pressures from this source was that part of deposits were accumulated to top up the extremely meagre pensions most East Germans could expect. Even though the federal government has increased pensions, many pensioners needed the interest income from their savings for some time. Moreover, savers in the new *Länder* had access to a range of alternative real and financial investments and needed to insure themselves against unemployment. These uncertainties increased their propensity to save, which made it highly unlikely that East German citizens would plunder their savings to go on a spending spree.

Events after unification do not indicate that there was any monetary overhang. Interest rates have risen after unification, rather than fallen, as one would expect from a monetary policy that was temporarily too slack. There was no sign, either, of demand pressures in West Germany originating in savings decumulation in the new *Länder*. As argued below, the separate issue of income transfers is another matter. German unification by itself did not lead to uncontrollable inflationary pressures.

## 6.2 The exchange rate effects of currency union

The external effect of unification was widely expected to result in a real appreciation of the DM for several mutually reinforcing reasons. Some identified the increase in aggregate demand in united Germany as a cause of rising prices for non-tradable goods, and hence the real exchange rate (Artus 1991). Others noted that the increase in demand in the ex-GDR would generate excess demand for West German goods and a real appreciation would be required to redirect German exports to domestic uses (MacKibbin 1990). A study by the IMF (1990) saw real appreciation as a consequence of rapid growth paired with expansionary fiscal policy and restrictive monetary policy.[5] And, finally, from a longer-run perspective, it was noted that the capital–labour ratio of united Germany would fall, and hence its export potential, so that, in the long run, a depreciation would be necessary. Wyplosz (1991) is an exception: using an intertemporal framework he concludes that the real exchange rate change is ambiguous in the short run and a real depreciation is required in the steady state because of the fall in net external assets.[6]

We hold different views about the question whether the DM needed to appreciate in real terms as a consequence of unification (Gros and Steinherr 1991b). To put it provocatively, would anybody expect the US dollar to appreciate if the United States absorbed Cuba?

Some intuition is provided by asking the hypothetical question whether the DM would have appreciated (or been revalued) in real terms within the EMS if the ex-GDR had opted for fixed exchange rates. The two phenomena with an effect on the exchange rate are the shift in the composition of demand in the ex-GDR and the transfer-induced increase in purchasing power to the ex-GDR. The real exchange rate of the DM would only require an appreciation if increased demand for imports in the new *Länder* were biased in favour of West German goods. Even then, given the small size of the GDR and the limited scope for this potential bias, the real appreciation required would be quite small. More importantly, this effect is at least partly offset by the transfer-induced reduction in real income in West Germany, reducing the demand both for tradables and for non-tradables in West Germany.[7] As the price of the latter will need to decrease to clear the market for non-tradables, the DM's real exchange rate is more likely to depreciate.

Thus, when it is recognised that, first, increased demand in the ex-GDR need not be strongly biased in favour of West German goods and against goods from the rest of the world, and that, second, the only clearly bilateral effect between the two Germanys is the transfer, then the presumption of real appreciation of the DM within the EMS becomes much weaker. This is what most people would have expected in the case where the ex-GDR had retained its own currency. A more rigorous demonstration is given in Gros and Steinherr (1995), chapter 10, appendix.

These results are also of relevance in other Eastern European countries with a fixed exchange rate, and one did not expect the DM to appreciate within the EMS when Yugoslavia in 1990 pegged its currency to the DM, and even less so if it had received German transfer payments.

In the following, the essential assumption is that goods that were non-tradable before unification are likely to remain so for some time after unification. It will also be convenient to distinguish between the demand effects that arise in the short run and the supply effects from factor movements that take longer to materialise.

Imagine an EMS composed of two countries: France and Germany. Suddenly demand goes up in one country, Germany. Part of this increase in demand falls on tradable goods, thus reducing the external surplus of Germany, while the remainder goes towards non-tradable goods (whose supply is much less elastic than that of tradables), thus requiring an increase in the relative price of German *non-tradables*. At given nominal wages, an increase in the relative price of German non-tradables (vis-à-vis French non-tradables) requires then an appreciation of the nominal exchange rate of the DM. This is the standard framework that has been used to justify the hypothesis that German unification requires a real appreciation of the DM. The crucial point in this line of reasoning is thus that, at given German wages, the exchange rate of the DM (against the French franc) determines the price of German goods relative to French goods.

This conventional analysis applied to unification is wrong because it does not take into account that unification has had different effects in the two parts of Germany. The key is that their real economies are completely different, even though they use the same currency. It is essential to distinguish between the effects unification has on the demand for non-tradable goods produced in East, on the one hand, and in West Germany, on the other. The relative price of these two goods can alter through changes in wages in East Germany, relative to those in West Germany.

If the standard tradables/non-tradables model is applied to the problem at hand, and if one takes into account the differential impact of unification on West and East Germany, then the conclusion is that no real appreciation of the DM was required. A real appreciation of the DM would have been required only if the demand for *West German* non-tradables had gone up. This in turn can happen only if *West Germans* spend more. It is therefore essential to determine whether unification increased the spending of West Germans.

Although overall demand in Germany had gone up, there was no reason for demand by West Germans to rise (above trend), since West Germans lend or transfer large amounts of purchasing power to East Germany. On the contrary, West Germans know that they will have to pay sooner or later for most of the debt accumulated by the government to rebuild the ex-GDR. The expectation of higher future taxes is the reason that, in general, private savings increase if the government deficit rises.[8] Econometric studies in IMF (1990) indicate that in the short run the increase in private savings is not equal to government dissavings, but still about 30 per cent of additional government dissavings is offset by higher private savings. In the long run the offset rises to almost 100 per cent.

The relative price of East German non-tradables (goods that cannot be traded between, say, Germany and France can presumably also be considered as non-tradables between East and West Germany) will of course have to change. But that relative price can change easily. Indeed, a large jump already occurred through conversion at 1:1 for wages, and further adjustments did take place through wage increases in the territory of the GDR.

The behaviour of prices in West Germany fully bears out our analysis. There is no price index of non-tradables, but there is an index for 'services and repairs' which should account for the bulk of non-tradables. The ratio of the index for 'services and repairs' to the overall consumer price index can thus be taken as a crude approximation of the relative price of non-tradables in West Germany. As there is a productivity bias in favour of tradables, this ratio has a positive time trend, which we estimated with data from 1981 to 1989. The results are shown in table 6.2. The actual price ratio increased much less than its trend value during 1990–3, providing further evidence that demand for non-tradables in West Germany has not increased as a result of unification.

Another framework often used to argue that German unification requires a real appreciation of the DM is one in which the emphasis is on nationally differentiated goods that are tradable. In this approach there would also be a need for a real appreciation of the DM if East Germans (they are the ones who receive the additional purchasing power) have a higher propensity to spend on West German tradables than West Germans do. Although East Germans, at least initially, obviously preferred imported Western goods to their own goods, there is no reason why they should prefer goods from West Germany to goods from Japan or France.

The only way to bring actual data to bear on this question is to use the experience of other European economies of a size comparable to the ex-GDR (e.g. Holland, Belgium). These countries receive about a quarter of all their imports from the Federal Republic. Applying

Table 6.2. *Germany: key data (DM billion)*

|                                                      | 1989  | 1990  | 1991  | 1992  | 1993  |
| ---------------------------------------------------- | ----- | ----- | ----- | ----- | ----- |
| Exports                                              | 640   | 660   | 666   | 671   | **629 |
| Imports                                              | 506   | 556   | 645   | 638   | **568 |
| Trade balance                                        | 134   | 105   | 21    | 33    | 61    |
| Current account                                      | 108   | 75    | −32   | −34   | −33   |
| M1 (Growth rate)                                     | 6.2   | 29.6  | 3.4   | 10.8  | 8.5   |
| M3                                                   | 5.7   | 19.7  | 6.3   | 7.6   | 10.9  |
| Private saving (% of personal income in West Germany) | 13.5  | 14.7  | 14.5  | 13.9  | 13.3  |
| *Prices (1985 = 100)*                                |       |       |       |       |       |
| Overall CPI (only West Germany)                      | 104.2 | 107.0 | 110.7 | 115.2 | 119.9 |
| Services (only West Germany)                         | 109.9 | 112.6 | 116.5 | 122.9 | 130.8 |
| Services/CPI (only West Germany)                     | 105.5 | 105.2 | 105.2 | 106.7 | 109.1 |
| Predicted                                            |       | 106.5 | 107.5 | 108.4 | 109.3 |

*Notes*: Services/CPI $= -1777.38 + 0.947$ (year) $+ 0.00012$ ($t = -6.97$) ($t = 7.37$)
($P = 7.83E - 05$) $R^2$ (adj.) $= 0.87$, $F = 54.34$;
* West and East Germany combined since July 1990; ** break in time series due to statistical revisions.
*Source*: Deutsche Bundesbank, monthly reports and own estimations.

the same percentage to the new *Länder* implies that even if the new *Länder* run a current account deficit of DM 150 bn per annum (as they did in 1991), the additional demand for West German exportables would be only about DM 37 bn (and the reduction in the German current account surplus would be DM 113 bn).[9] The reduction in the current account surplus from DM 108 bn in 1989 to a deficit of DM 32 bn in 1991 is perfectly in line with these back-of-the-envelope computations. Table 6.2 shows that imports jumped in 1991 by DM 90 bn. These additional 'exports' of West Germany represent only about 5 per cent of the overall exports of the Federal Republic of Germany (in 1989, i.e. prior to unification, they totalled DM 640 bn) and their effective supply is not likely to require a large price change.

A different way of looking at the implications of German unification for the EMS is to take into account not only its effects on demand, but to use the standard Heckscher-Ohlin framework, based on factor endowments and movements.[10] The point in this framework is that East Germany starts out with a much lower capital–labour ratio. This should lead to capital flows into East Germany and should also be reflected in the capital intensity of the goods traded by East Germany.[11] However, given that the German capital market is open to the rest of the world, most of the capital will come from the rest of the world (hence the lower external surpluses). As long as the East German economy is in the factor-price equalisation region, movements of goods and factors can equalise prices, and, consequently, there is again no need for a change in the relative price of (West) German exports relative to its imports.

## 6.3   Privatisation

Private ownership as such does not guarantee economic efficiency, nor is it socially desirable per se. More important is the specification of property rights and their enforceability. In former socialist countries two further considerations are crucial: the speed with which ownership rights are distributed and the social acceptability of their distribution in the initial stages.

Germany opted for an approach in which ownership of close to 8,000 firms and *Kombinate* was transferred to a holding company (Treuhandanstalt, THA) whose task consisted of selling them off on the proviso that 'excessive' unemployment should be avoided. THA therefore pursued the dual objective to restructure before privatisation.

An issue that had not been tackled head-on was raised by the implicit social contract of the old GDR. Presumably social ownership of the means of production meant that the state managed productive assets but that these belonged to the people. Even if one rejects this concept, it may not be wise to dismiss the substance of such a social contract completely. Of course, against initial expectations, THA ended up with a net loss covered by the Bonn government, which in addition provides financial transfers to German citizens in the East. But the latter did not obtain extensive ownership of the territory's productive assets and are not able to value transfers as a compensation for the region's sell-out.

On the operational side, THA had great difficulty in making rapid headway towards privatisation. It had been a Herculean task to evaluate 8,000 firms in an environment characterised by profound structural change. Either the job was to be done somewhat superficially or it would take a very long time. Neither option appeared attractive. We therefore strongly believe that an alternative solution should have been given serious consideration.[12] This would have consisted in distributing ownership of the capital stock (state-owned houses and productive assets) to citizens.

To begin with, the ownership of housing could have been transferred to occupants. Rents could have continued to be paid for, say, ten years and considered as instalments towards the acquisition price. They could have been indexed to average wage rates and therefore risen only in line with purchasing power. Houses could have been bought and sold but ownership rights would have to be forfeited in the event of emigration. Instead of following this simple and socially attractive approach, public sector housing was sold.

Second, the same system could have been applied to the agricultural sector, with co-operatives free to split up or stay together.

Third, individual and small firms could have been turned over to their managers and workers, who would have continued to pay taxes and rents to acquire the buildings.

Fourth, most of the *Kombinate*, or holding companies, could have been turned into joint-stock companies. Some would have been sold to non-East German residents when technological modernisation, economies of scale or the acquisition of marketing and management skills could not be achieved in any other way. For the remainder, each *Kombinat* would have issued a number of shares equal to the number of citizens with voting rights. Each citizen would have received one share in each *Kombinat* and hence a highly diversified portfolio of the economy of the former GDR. The value of these shares could not and need not have been known a priori, as they would have been distributed freely. In this way collective ownership would have acquired a concrete meaning, if only at the end of the socialist experience. Such shares would be tradable. Their initial book value might not amount to much, but after restructuring the present value of future earnings could be a multiple for at least some of them. Therefore there is an incentive for holding on to them.

With such widespread share-ownership, all citizens of the former GDR would overnight have become 'capitalists', an objective actively pursued in West Germany – without, however, complete success. Few people invested in stocks in the late 1940s, but those who did have never regretted it, nor would they have regretted staying where they were.

But this option was not retained. Instead, THA was given the mission to restructure and privatise East German firms or, if this was not feasible, to close them down. In effect, therefore, it was responsible for the most important aspect of unification. Although the importance of its task was generally accepted, opinions have varied as to THA's strategy, the speed of the process and, closely related to this, the importance of restructuring first and privatising later. As to the latter, the much-debated question was whether THA could optimally redesign firms or whether that decision already needed to emerge from competitive forces.

One avowed goal was to complete the privatisation process rapidly. Even that goal did not remain unchallenged. The main arguments against rapid privatisation were that it would lead to lower sales revenues owing to the large supply shock[13] and to mass unemployment given that (i) the new private owners would be loath to keep on the supernumerary work-force and (ii) that restructuring starts in earnest after privatisation. High unemployment in East Germany is for a large part the harvest of low productivity, and privatisation merely brings to the surface the widespread inefficiency, which for years was kept hidden through subsidies and price distortions. But the question remains whether a slower pace in selling off industrial assets, or an altogether different approach, would not have mitigated the sharp fall in employment.

Arguments in favour of restructuring prior to privatisation include the difficulty of selling off large conglomerates. It is likewise argued that they need to be split up in order to create a competitive market structure. Neither argument is convincing. If a conglomerate is not profitable, then disintegration could take place via the market. A 'raider' would observe that the value of the sum of parts exceeds the value of the conglomerate and buy it, break it up and sell the parts. International competition and anti-trust law will do the rest. So the only vindication for maintaining the state in an active role is not market failure but the political resolve to control and cushion the social repercussions of the restructuring process.

Thus privatisation in East Germany was designed as a two-stage process. In the first stage, enterprises were spun off conglomerates and transformed into legally independent corporations. This step was completed on 1 July 1991. Supervisory boards were set up during that first stage, providing a vital channel for the transfer of management know-how. By the end of October 1991, about 3,600 business persons from the West sat on such supervisory boards as shareholder representatives and people with Western experience made up 91 per cent of chairs.

The next step was to establish opening balance sheets in DM for these companies. Difficulties arose in evaluating the assets of East German firms. Liabilities included old debts that were not related to firms' performance in the past but were rather the result of political decisions. Since the firms often had higher liquidation values (real estate) than ongoing valuation, case-by-case assessment of the balance sheets and of the potential viability of firms was a necessity. Adjustments had to be made for the liabilities incurred under the old regime (writing-off of the *Altkredite*) in order to provide the minimum equity needed to give potentially profitable enterprises a chance of survival.

When all these time-consuming preparations had been completed, the actual selling could start. By and large, THA opted for inviting public offers. Bidders were asked to produce a business plan complete with investment plans and information on the number of employees to be kept on the payroll. THA then entered into negotiation with the bidders who, if agreement was reached, had to guarantee a certain level of investment and employment. In general, bidding was open to a large group of potential investors both domestic and foreign, individual and corporate. The privatisation process gained momentum in the second half of 1991 and achieved substantial results. By September 1994 about 100,000 out of an initial 4.05 million people were still working in 350 THA enterprises that had not yet been sold.

Most enterprises were sold to investors from West Germany and only about 850 passed into foreign hands. Management buy-outs (MBOs) also played a considerable role, especially in the case of companies with fewer than 500 employees. In support of MBOs, THA pushed through an initiative to promote small and medium-sized enterprises (Initiative Mittelstand) and also promoted management buy-ins (MBI) in order to attract managers with restructuring expertise.

A thorny issue was created by companies that simply could not find a buyer. The danger of an expensive and inefficient subsidy policy for the preservation of obsolete industries was clearly seen. The agency had little option but to close such firms or else provide financial support, usually in the form of bank credit, which meant that, when all is said and done, the federal government was liable for the debts. Since opposition to liquidation was strong in East Germany, and particularly in the affected 'company towns', THA was exposed to strong political pressure and had to delay inevitable decisions or even preserve inefficient structures. But THA resisted this political pressure to some extent and by September 1994 had closed down 3,600 firms while over 8,000 were privatised.[14] Purchasers provided job guarantees for 1.5 million jobs and for investments of over DM 200 bn.[15] By September 1994 sales revenues to THA amounted to DM 65 bn.

To summarise the pros and cons of the THA approach it is useful to have at least an order of magnitude of the costs involved. Much of this cost is contained in the THA opening account for 1 July 1990 in table 6.3 presented in October 1992. At first sight the bottom line result is shocking: the entire net worth of the former GDR is negative and put at minus DM 209 bn.[16] Conceptually, it is not immediately obvious how one can arrive at a negative net worth for an economy that produced enough to give its citizens an average per capita income roughly equal to that of Spain.

Table 6.3. *Opening balance sheet of Treuhandanstalt at 1 July 1990 (DM million)*

| Assets | | Liabilities | | |
|---|---|---|---|---|
| **A. Assets transferred through unification treaty and Treuhand law** | | **A. Provisions** | | |
| I. Corporate shares | 78,909 | I. Restructuring provisions | | 215,296 |
| II. Mining | 1,387 | 1. Financing costs to rebuild net worth | 30,573 | |
| III. Agriculture and forestry | 16,063 | 2. Privatisation | 121,082 | |
| IV. Other | 5,772 | 3. Closures | 44,723 | |
| V. Claims on Treuhand enterprises | 11,844 | 4. Transfer to communal ownership and reprivatisation | 18,918 | |
| | | II. Provisions for ownership claims | | 12,981 |
| | | III. Provisions for value compensation clause | | 14,950 |
| | | IV. Provisions for interest guarantees | | 17,535 |
| | | V. Other | | 6,504 |
| **B. Other assets of Treuhand** | 256 | **B. Liabilities** | | |
| | | I. Bank liabilities | | 39,893 |
| | | 1. Old liabilities | 38,493 | |
| | | 2. Other | 1,400 | |
| | | II. Liabilities to Treuhand enterprises | | 16,363 |
| **C. Negative net worth** | 209,291 | | | |
| **Total** | **323,522** | **Total** | | **323,522** |

Several reasons can be brought forward to explain that negative net worth. First, socialist economies paid very little heed to negative environmental impact. Certain industrial sites would be sold under (West) German law only if cleaned up or suitably restored first.

Second, many firms produced negative value-added (a point emphasised by McKinnon 1991) if assessed at undistorted prices. These firms have become worthless, as have those whose products cannot weather Western competition at any price (or almost – the Trabant motor car epitomises this case).

Third, since the federal government refused to cancel enterprise liabilities, soft loans were transformed into hard loans. THA took over enterprises inclusive of their debts and guaranteed reimbursement. Those who gained in the end were the East German banks, whose loan portfolios were rehabilitated so that they became attractive takeover prospects for West German banks. Bank liabilities to depositors were converted into DM at a rate of either 1:1 or 2:1, whereas assets were mostly converted at 2:1. But they were compensated for that loss so that the banking system faced no difficulties.

The opening statement recognises that additional outlays are necessary to sell firms, some even at negative prices. Loss-making enterprises require financial support until they are sold or closed. Provisions for restructuring and disposing of the assets were put at DM 215 bn, much more than the enterprises' true worth. In addition, THA provided for various legal obligations amounting to DM 51 bn.

DM 45 bn were earmarked for the closure and disposal of enterprises. That was over-optimistic, as the quality of the THA portfolio declined rapidly and as strong regional impacts were already fuelling massive political opposition to closures or layoffs. The THA wound up its operations at the end of 1994 with a total debt in excess of DM 270 bn.

## 6.4  Reconstruction and the decrease in employment

The most striking feature in the restructuring process in East Germany has been the sharp decline in production and employment, a decline far more pronounced than in other former socialist countries. By way of partial compensation East Germany has been spared the monetary instability that has beset other countries on the road to reform.

Yet the fact that production has fallen more drastically in East Germany than elsewhere is not in itself evidence that the 'cold turkey' approach used in Germany is bad. The East German economy completed its overhaul and re-equipped itself both more thoroughly and more speedily than other countries that adopted a more gradual course. Downsizing of employment was much more dramatic in East Germany than in any other transition economy (from 9.89 million employed to 5.75 million in 1998) and investment with West German help has been incomparable.

The share of East German GNP (7.4 per cent) in total German GNP in 1991 was only one-third of the share of the labour force (19.7 per cent), suggesting a productivity level one-third of the West German level. The share of domestic absorption was close to 13 per cent, nearly double the share of GNP, thanks to transfers received. East German private consumption is only a little less than GNP, so that transfers pay for public sector consumption and gross investment. Not a meagre deal. The structure of production is also markedly different. The public sector is more important in the East than in the West, while services and manufacturing are proportionately less important. Manufacturing bears the brunt of the restructuring effort, whereas services were underdeveloped during the years of socialism.

Following economic and monetary union between the two Germanys, industrial production and GDP in the East collapsed when the Eastern industry was exposed overnight to Western competition after years of isolation. Part of the collapse occurred in the first half of 1990 in anticipation of the opening-up of trade and the freedom of Eastern citizens to choose between Western and Eastern goods. It was unprecedented both in comparison with developments in Central and Eastern Europe in the period 1989–91 and with the slump in German industrial production during the Great Depression of the 1930s (Tullio, Steinherr and Buscher 1994). Industrial production in East Germany fell by 28 per cent in 1990 and by a further 30 per cent in 1991. By comparison, the fall in industrial production in Poland, Czechoslovakia and Hungary during this period was only about 25 per cent (see figure 6.1).

Most severe was the decline in the production of investment goods (from a benchmark 100 in 1990 to 48 in 1992), a sector in which the East German industry, like its West German counterpart, had been highly specialised. A prime reason for that decline was the collapse of CMEA exports. Total exports fell by 56 per cent during 1990–1 alone, and three-quarters

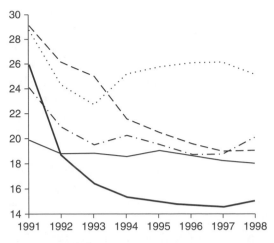

**Figure 6.1** Employment in manufacturing as a percentage of total employment
*Source:* WIIW, German Federal Statistical Office.

of that drop was due to the decline in CMEA trade. That means that about one-third of the fall in industrial production was caused by the decline in export demand and two-thirds by the shift in domestic demand away from home-produced to foreign products.

The collapse of production in East Germany in 1989–91 is unprecedented in peacetime, both in scope and in speed. Despite the rebound in GNP levels in 1992 and 1993, unemployment remains at record levels. Official unemployment increased from 11.7 per cent in 1991 to 15.3 per cent in 1992. These figures exclude a large number of part-time workers, workers temporarily subsidised under government programmes (*Arbeitsbeschaffungsmaßnahmen*) and retraining schemes. If these workers are taken into account, the rate of unemployment increases to about 27 per cent in 1991 and 29 per cent in 1992 (see Table 6.4). If the one million commuters and emigrants to West Germany had stayed, the unemployment rate would have peaked at 37 per cent in 1992. In addition, the retraining programme turned out to be totally inefficient. See Riphahn, Snower and Zimmermann (2000). The main effect was to prolong unemployment compensation claims.

So, while the official rate of unemployment peaked at about the same levels as during the Great Depression, the true unemployment rate reached its nadir at about twice the official level, extensive emigration to West Germany and a spate of early retirements notwithstanding.[17] Despite more generous unemployment subsidies, widespread unemployment – which falls disproportionately on young entrants to the job market – measured against the high hopes raised by reunification has triggered despair and bitterness. The ugly right-wing violence that is staining Germany's post-unification image and straining foreign observers' tolerance may find at least a partial explanation in this fact.

Unification endowed East Germany rapidly with Western institutions. All in all, this was a considerable advantage, but, as illustrated by the high share of public sector consumption of GDP, these institutional transfers also represent high costs. Some of the institutional

Table 6.4. *Employment (millions) and unemployment (% of labour force) in East and West Germany: 1989–92, and in Germany, 1929–32 annual averages)*

| | East | | | West | | Germany | |
| | Employment | Official unemployment | Total unemployment[1] | Employment | Unemployment | Unemployment 1929–32 | |
|---|---|---|---|---|---|---|---|
| 1989 | 9.7 | n.a. | n.a. | 27.6 | 7.6 | 1929 | 5.8 |
| 1990 | 8.9 | 7.3 | n.a. | 28.5 | 6.9 | 1930 | 9.7 |
| 1991 | 7.3 | 11.7 | 26.9 | 29.0 | 6.1 | 1931 | 14.3 |
| 1992 | 6.5 | 15.3 | 28.9 | 29.1 | 6.5 | 1932 | 17.6 |
| 1993 | 6.3 | 15.9 | 23.6 | 28.7 | 8.1 | | |
| 1994 | 6.2 | 14.6 | 21.7 | 28.3 | 9.4 | | |

*Notes*: [1] Includes short-time workers, workers temporarily subsidised by the government (*Arbeitsbeschaffungsmaßnahmen*) and workers involved in retraining programmes.
*Source*: Institut für Konjunkturforschung, *Konjunkturstatistisches* Handbuch, 1933; Sommariva and Tullio (1987); *Jahresgutachten 1993 und 1994 des Sachverständigenrats*.

exports of the ex-FRG are better suited to a mature, rich Western economy and are totally inappropriate for the developing East. It is very unlikely that certain Asian countries would have grown into the tigers they have if they had adopted German labour laws and regulation and had been run by the German bureaucracy.

But arguably the biggest problem has been the political promise of a rapid convergence of living standards. The sharp rise in real wages in the East was to a significant extent to blame for this development on the Eastern labour market. Gross nominal wages in industry rose from 35 per cent of West German levels in July 1990 to 60 per cent by end 1992 and 74 per cent in 1998.

The increase in nominal wages is only one side of the coin. Producers are concerned with real wage costs, that is, gross nominal wages deflated by producers' prices, while workers are eager to increase their real wage income, that is, net wages deflated by consumer prices. The remarkable fact in East Germany is that consumer prices have increased by more than 30 per cent between 1990 and 1992, so that gross real wage income has grown by some 40 per cent (but wage taxation has also increased). Producers had to face higher nominal wages *and* rapidly falling prices for their products (on average by about 40 per cent). The real wage cost has therefore more than tripled between 1990 and 1992.

In order to understand the damaging and unfortunate effects on employment and industrial production of real wage trends in the East, several factors must be borne in mind. First, in post-war West Germany the government has traditionally not interfered with wage bargaining, which it largely considers to be a private matter between workers and company representatives. However, by fixing a quick return to wage parity between East and West Germany as a key policy objective, government has given the wrong signal and seriously interfered with the wage bargaining process. The Bundesbank had made it known that it disagreed. And it was right to do so.[18] Second, Wall or no Wall, wage negotiations in the East have not been comparable to wage negotiations in a market economy, where owner-entrepreneurs have an interest in defending profit margins and their company's value. Corporate governance and hard budget constraints only become operative after privatisation. Third, members of West German trade unions were seconded to the 'inexperienced' trade unions in the East while they were also on the board of the then-state-owned enterprises, so that they were to a great extent 'bargaining' with themselves. Fourth, trade unions in the West had and still have a vested interest in a rapid increase in Eastern wages in order to protect real wages and employment in the West. The same vested interest can be attributed to West German industry, whose prime objective was and is the conquest of maximum market shares in the East.

Curiously enough, the federal government (like West German taxpayers and East German unemployed) has fallen victim to its own 'soft budget constraint'. Most jobs in the East have been at risk. If unemployment benefits are positively related to wages prior to dismissal, workers have an incentive to press for higher wages, even if this increases the likelihood of bankruptcy or accelerates closure. Moreover, if THA has no firm budget constraint and can increase subsidies as losses mount, it has little incentive to resist aggressive wage claims. All the less so when rapid wage convergence is applauded by government.

To be sure, a high wage differential between East and West Germany could have caused a massive outflow of workers from the East. However, the survey conducted by Akerlof et al. (1991) suggests that unemployment is at least as important a factor in triggering emigration as a wide wage differential. Then again, it is not the actual wage differential that causes emigration but rather the expected wage differential (over a number of years) corrected for expected capital gains, which workers in the East could have cashed in if a different privatisation policy had been pursued.

It is clear that the more quickly real wages in East Germany are adjusted to those obtaining in West Germany, the larger will be the annual volume of real investment required to bring labour productivity in the East in line with the higher real wage. The criticism that wages in the East were pulled up too fast must be judged against the scheduled official and private investment effort in the years to come. The investment effort is substantial indeed, but insufficient for a rapid convergence of real GNP per capita.

The speed of adjustment of real wages in the East by itself is unlikely to have much effect on investment (as contrasted to the final level of the capital–output ratio). Investors motivated by low labour costs at any rate will choose other locations in Eastern Europe or Asia, not East Germany. East Germany's attraction for investors is totally different: the availability of a disciplined and highly skilled labour force, a tried and tested West German institutional framework (with all its faults), expected administrative and infrastructure support, and a rich consumer market (the European Union and, for non-tradables, a market in the making). The last argument suggests that investors are attracted by the production of non-tradables, such as real estate, catering, financial services and the like. And indeed, we find that the most impressive investments have been made in the non-tradable goods sector.

Finally, we wish to be very clear on one key point. It is often argued that the terms of the currency union were excessively generous and that the high volume of transfers to East Germany is the price that must be paid. Implicit or explicit in this view are two further judgements. One is that East Germans received a first gift with currency union and a second one in the form of transfers. The other spins a tale of drastic cuts in the competitive position of the East German economy following currency union and maintains that transfers are needed to keep it alive.

This is plain nonsense. We already argued that wage convergence would have occurred anyway, currency union or no, given the institutional integration of labour markets and the government's promises. Furthermore, the overall terms of unification represented no less than the spoliation of the East Germans. The only assets East Germans received were some DM 100 bn on their bank accounts. This is close to DM 6,000 a head. In fact, as we argued in section 6.3, it would have been fair to treat them as owners of the land, buildings and industries in East Germany. The net worth of these real assets is clearly in excess of DM 6,000 per capita.

Another way to ascertain this fact is to use the GNP produced after unification (i.e. after the output shock) and capitalise it. In 1991, East German GNP was DM 193 bn. For a capital–output ratio of 2.5, which is an average value for industrial countries, the value of the capital stock (neglecting non-economically used land) would be close to DM 500 bn, or five times what East Germans received.

Finally, it needs to be stressed that Germany successfully accommodated net immigration flows of over one million a year during 1989–92, mostly from Eastern Europe. Given the scale of the immigration flow, coupled with the fact that it is proving much more difficult to rebuild East Germany than anticipated, the social unrest and violence that have erupted become much more understandable. However, because immigration pressure is unlikely to diminish with the painful restructuring process in the FSU and in some parts of Eastern Europe, a deep-seated change in German immigration policy is called for. Germany needs to become more selective in admitting immigrants and its welcoming policy of social assistance needs to be scaled down. Likewise it should be prepared to integrate its immigrants more easily and help them take their place in the dynamic section of German society.

## 6.5 Convergence and its financing after ten years

Since 1989 transfers from West Germany have amounted to DM 1,700 bn and no decline is in sight, with net transfers of DM 140 bn in 1999. For East Germany the annual transfer in 1999 represents a third of GDP, compared to one-fifth of Italy's Mezzogiorno GDP (Boltho, Carlin and Scramozzino 1996). As a result, Germany's public debt increased from DM 1,039 bn in 1989 to DM 2,700 bn in 1999, despite a special unification tax of 5 per cent in West Germany.

These transfers allowed East Germany to spend much more than it produced. Using the national income identity

$$\text{GDP} = C + I + G + X - M$$
$$= A + X - M,$$

where $C$ = consumption, $I$ = investment, $G$ = government expenditure, $X$ = exports, $M$ = imports, $A$ = absorption, the numbers for 1998 are as follows (in billion DM) (Sinn 2000):

$$436 = 655 - 219.$$

The trade deficit of 50 per cent of GDP is a world record. Independent countries are crisis prone when they maintain a deficit as high as 8 per cent of GDP, as was the case in Mexico or Thailand before they were condemned by financial markets. As long as West Germany continues to pay, there is no problem, but financial constraints may make it difficult to consider the present situation as sustainable.

East Germany's export ratio $(X/Y)$ is about 50 per cent, comparable to that of Austria or Belgium. The import ratio $(M/Y)$ is 100 per cent. By any measure East Germany is as open to foreign trade as any other small economy of the European Union.

The trade account deficit of DM 219 bn is financed mainly by public transfers (DM 141 bn) and capital imports (DM 78 bn) in which public sector borrowings accounted for DM 33 bn. Thus, by 1998, per-capita debt of the East German public sector had surpassed West German levels, although it had started with practically no public debt in 1990 (Seitz 1999).

How are transfers and capital imports being used? Unfortunately, more than 50 per cent of the transfers are for social security and only 12 per cent for infrastructure investment. The remainder represents mainly intergovernmental grants.

Catching up cannot be achieved without an investment boom. Transfers and tax incentives provided the means and the incentives. The share of investment in GDP was between 40 and 50 per cent in East Germany as compared to 20 per cent in West Germany. In per-capita terms it reached 150 per cent of the West German level in 1996 before falling back to 139 per cent in 1998. Whilst very encouraging at first sight, a breakdown of investment into buildings and equipment sobers the positive impression. Per-capita investment in buildings was up to 80 per cent higher than in West Germany (1996) and still 60 per cent higher in 1998. As a result, East German cities are renovated and glittering. Per-capita investment in equipment – the basis for an increased productive base – exceeded West German levels only marginally during 1994–6, and dropped to 90 per cent in 1998.

Figure 6.2 shows that convergence of per-capita output stalled in 1995 at about 60 per cent of West Germany's (and household incomes at 85 per cent). Sinn (2000) offers four complementary explanations for stalled convergence:

- The scaling back of the very generous investment subsidies in 1997, lowering equipment investment.
- The investment subsidies were so large that the cost of capital was negative (estimated by Sinn at −5.1 per cent). As a result, firms overinvested and replaced workers by capital. This should have increased labour productivity. But, in fact, many sectors with a capital–labour ratio higher than in West Germany have much lower labour productivity. One possible reconciliation is excess capacity or, alternatively, overstaffing.
- Dutch disease. East German wages are above labour productivity levels, an equilibrium sustained by transfers. This crowds out the manufacturing sector, exposed to international competition. (In 1998 manufacturing accounted for 15 per cent of total unemployment, down from 26 per cent in 1991.)

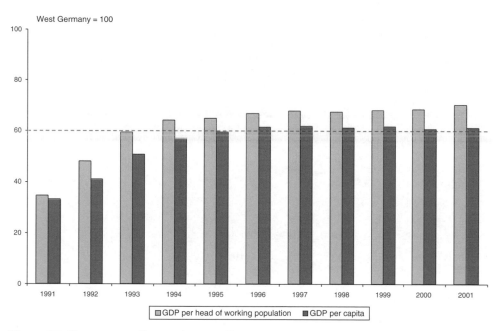

**Figure 6.2** Convergence of per-capita output?

- Mezzogiorno problems. This means that wages in the East are set according to those pre-vailing in the West, as explained above. From 7 per cent of the West German manufacturing average wage in 1990, East German wages increased to 72 per cent of Western levels in 1995 and have remained at that level since. The union goal was to reach 85 per cent of Western levels. This has not happened because firms have left the employers' associations to escape wage agreements. (By 1998, 85 per cent of firms, employing 55 per cent of the workforce, had done so.) Wages in 1998 were higher than in the United States and in most West European countries. Given low productivity in 1998, unit labour costs in East Germany were 20–30 per cent higher than in West Germany.

To summarise, figure 6.3 depicts the remarkable increase in labour productivity, a record among transition economies. High wage costs and low capital costs favoured employment destruction (as was shown in figure 6.1), another record. As a result, in comparison to neighbouring transition countries, the initial decline in GDP was most pronounced in East Germany with a recovery that falls short of Poland's.

A puzzle remains: the fact that some of the manufacturing sectors with a capital stock per worker in excess of West German levels have labour productivity levels much lower than in West Germany. Klodt (1999) established a negative correlation between relative labour productivity and relative capital intensities. However, Quehenberger (2000) shows, with a Cobb–Douglas production function and using panel data, that capital intensity has had a positive effect on labour productivity and that capital returns were positive on average (but much lower than in West Germany).

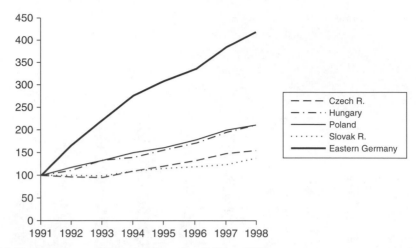

**Figure 6.3** Productivity growth in manufacturing (1991 = 100)
*Source:* EBRD, German Federal Statistical Office.

## 6.6   Conclusions

Investment, output and employment growth have all declined in East Germany during 1995–2000. In the East, output per capita is stuck at about 60 per cent of the Western level. Is this the end of convergence?

It certainly is the certification of an inappropriate economic policy. Transfers and investment subsidies combined with excessive wages are no basis for sustained growth. Some of the policy mistakes can be corrected, others probably not for lack of political will.

It was a mistake to take away all real assets and compensate East Germans with quick wage convergence. Although it is now too late for a major policy measure, as privatisation is completed, more limited initiatives are still possible. As proposed by Sinn (2000), in exchange for wage moderation employees could be compensated with company shares.

Transfers produce a Dutch-disease effect and should be reduced. This includes remaining investment subsidies. A striking example of the misallocation of resources produced by massive and discriminatory subsidies is housing. For new construction the subsidy is twice that offered for renovation of existing real estate. In 2000 more than a million dwellings were unoccupied. New subsidies are now demanded to reduce the existing stock of housing.

In the view of most economists, the most dramatic policy mistakes were made in the labour market. A return to full employment without major policy changes is unlikely. Most important of all is a liberalisation of the labour market, including the reduction of social assistance, which in effect sustains a lower limit on wages. Instead of subsidising inactivity, a subsidy could be created for working. A concrete example would be the US-earned income tax credit. For details on a subsidy for *additional jobs*, see Gros and Steinherr (1995, chapter 10). For other proposals replacing investment subsidies with some form of employment subsidies, see various contributions in Riphahn, Snower and Zimmermann (2000).

It is unlikely that reforms targeted at East Germany alone will achieve much. Absolute growth of the East German economy has certainly been slowed down by the lacklustre performance of West Germany (which has helped convergence, however). Therefore, supply-side reforms in West Germany would be helpful as well.

East Germany also demonstrates the relevance of the endogenous growth model. According to the neo-classical growth model, available labour skills in East Germany should attract an increasing share of investments in Germany. But that investment is in competition with lower labour costs in the rest of the world and much of Germany's investments occur outside Germany. However, only part of that foreign investment is explained by differences in labour costs. West German industry invests in West Germany for scale and external effects and in the United States for the same reasons. Even in East Germany there is a distinct differentiation between the already historically more successful south and the less advanced north. If the endogenous growth model is more relevant than the neo-classical model, then the growth prospects of Eastern Germany depend on its inclusion in a dynamic growth pole. Enlargement of the European Union will thus present the eastern part of Germany with the challenge of overcoming its cost disadvantages and benefiting from rapid growth by new EU members.

## Notes

1. See Gros and Steinherr (1990).
2. The amount finally agreed varied between 2,000 and 6,000 DM, depending on age.
3. Dornbusch and Wolf (1992) consider the failure to start off with a clean slate by cancelling enterprise debt as an important mistake.
4. The exact exposure of households is 176 bn plus 17 bn cash minus 23 bn of real-estate credit.
5. This study is correct in its predictions but it attributes appreciation not to currency union and reconstruction per se but to the predicted policy mix. Independently of that, it is interesting to assess the exchange rate effects of integration per se.
6. Hughes Hallett and Ma (1994), using the IMF's Multimod multi-country model, conclude that '. . . as a result of unification the DM appreciates and then depreciates more than it otherwise would have done'. The medium-term depreciation by 1997–8 would be stronger than the initial appreciation.
7. If East Germans have the same marginal propensity to save and spend on West German and on non-German goods as do West Germans (assumptions which seem close to reality), then the intra-German transfer has no external effect other than via non-tradable goods prices. See Dornbusch (1980), chapter 3. The massive net transfer starting in 1990 contributed therefore to a real depreciation of the DM.
8. This argument does not assume 'full Ricardian equivalence' and that therefore all future taxes are immediately taken into account by consumers. All it implies is that the German public is very well aware of the future burden on the public finances over the coming years. This public awareness, coupled with higher interest rates dampened expenditure in West Germany.
9. These crude calculations do not take into account the import content of West German exports into the GDR, which has been estimated to be as high as 40 per cent, implying that each DM of exports from West to East Germany reduces the current account surplus by 0.4 DM. However, preliminary calculations suggest that this effect is more or less offset by the fact that exports from the rest of the Community (and EFTA) contain imports from the FRG.
10. The demand-side story takes place implicitly at given factor endowments.

11. Perfect, i.e. instantaneous, mobility of both factors would, of course, lead to instant equalisation of the capital–labour ratio. However, since movements of both factors involve adjustment costs, the capital–labour ratio will not be equalised immediately.

12. This view is also shared by Dornbusch and Wolf (1992): 'In both the treatment of property rights and the cancellation of debts, the Germans' unwillingness to look forward and let bygones be bygones was a grave mistake.'

13. Sinn and Sinn (1991) argue that in a once-and-for-all auction of all THA assets the clearing price could approach zero under conditions of imperfect information.

14. THA sold more firms than they had received owing to the split-up of many *Kombinate* into smaller units.

15. Investment and employment pledges turned out to be valueless in the economic downturn of 1993. Frequently the new owners requested additional financial support from THA to compensate for adverse conditions. Fraud had also turned out to be a problem. Some deals about to be closed fell through after demand forecasts were revised. One example is Daimler-Benz's decision to put plans for a DM 1.5 bn truck plant on ice because of higher production costs than initially forecast and because of a downward revision of demand. Other, more labour-intensive activities were rechannelled to Central European countries where labour costs are much lower than in East Germany.

16. In 1989, Hans Modrow, the last communist leader of the GDR, put his country's net worth at DM 1.5 trillion. In 1990, his CDU successor, Lothar de Maizière, revised this estimate to the lower value of DM 880 billion. After unification, Detlev Rohwedder, the first head of THA, gave an estimate of DM 600 billion for the assets on his books. In 1991 he had to admit that assets and liabilities would balance each other. The opening balance sheet net worth of THA of minus DM 209 billion still falls short of the net worth of minus DM 270 billion in September 1994.

17. Arguably, any such comparison between production and employment cutbacks in the ex-GDR following unification and other historic periods needs to be qualified. The Great Depression was chiefly a result of shrinking demand, whereas the problem in the ex-GDR is one of fundamental structural change. In this respect a comparison with reconstruction after the Second World War is closer to the mark, yet still not directly comparable. After the Second World War the economy had to rebuild its capital stock, but it did not have to catch up with a 20–30-year technological headstart, nor did it have to adjust to an entirely new institutional and motivational set-up. On the positive side, Marshall Aid for West Germany amounted to much less than the current transfers to East Germany.

18. The Bundesbank has at times in the post-war period indirectly pursued income policies by threatening an interest rate increase if wage negotiations should have a negative impact on inflation, or by postponing interest rate cuts until wage negotiations had been completed. After unification, the Bundesbank increased interest rates and made a reversal of its policy contingent (i) on a reduction in the federal fiscal deficit; and (ii) on moderation of wage increases in both parts of Germany.

# 7    The disintegration of
#        the Soviet Union

Reprinted by permission: Tribune Media Services

Before 1990 nobody would have ventured to suggest that the Soviet Union might disappear. When it did in 1991 most observers saw it as a historical accident. We argued in Gros and Steinherr (1991a), written before the split, that the explosion was unavoidable and, in economic terms at least, desirable.

It is, in fact, interesting to observe that socialist states with a federal structure – the Soviet Union, Yugoslavia and Czechoslovakia – split up during transition. There are strong reasons for this dramatic failure. First, all three federations were composed of different ethnic groups with a history of painful conflicts. Adversity was reinforced in the Soviet Union and Yugoslavia by religious differences. Second, the Soviet Union and Yugoslavia were artificial, imperial creations. As argued in chapter 1, the Soviet Union just pursued Russian imperialism by adding the Baltic states, transferred entire ethnicities and subjugated dissonant people or countries, such as the Ukraine. Togetherness was maintained only by brute force in all three federations. Third, none of the three federations provided a harmonious balance of rights and responsibilities between the centre and the states of the federation. The federal structure was a paper construction, a Potemkin façade. All the power was with a Communist Party that had a monolithic structure. States of the federations had little real autonomy. Fourth, in market-based federations, such as Germany or the United States, income redistribution is achieved through budgetary transfers. Rich states keep most of their revenue, but support less prosperous states. This did not happen in socialist federations, although differences in income were very large. For example, average income in Slovenia, the richest state of Yugoslavia, was more than seven times the average income in Kosovo, the poorest region. Instead, especially in the Soviet Union, a major source of transferring income was the underpricing of energy. For importing states, whether poor or rich, this was a gift! The oil-producing areas paid for it (or rather, lost revenues), thus feeling robbed of what belonged to them. Planning, not basic economic considerations, decided where investments were to be made. Factories were not established in states whose population was distrusted or politically disliked. Therefore, in addition to political and nationalistic problems, these federations were not efficient economic arrangements.

It is not, therefore, surprising that once the risk of immediate military repression faded away, rich as well as poor states with different ethnic populations gave high priority to independence. The split-up of the Soviet Union was dramatic, but generally peaceful, and the Czech–Slovak divorce was an example of wisdom and elegance. But hatred ran deep in Yugoslavia, as can be seen from the ensuing wars. Conflicts in the Caucasus resulted in local wars and high noon is still not in sight.

This chapter analyses the economic aspects of the disintegration of the biggest socialist federation, the Soviet Union (FSU). Opinions about it are usually of two extremes. One maintains that the economic links between the former Soviet republics were artificially created by central planners. The intensity of inter-republican trade should, therefore, not have been a constraint on the newly independent states, which should have introduced national currencies immediately in 1992. The opposite extreme (and one prevalent among Western official institutions until 1991–2), argued that the former Soviet republics were so tightly integrated that they should have stayed together in the Soviet economic sphere for some time even after they became politically independent.

The analysis of this chapter suggests that both extremes were wrong and that serious policy mistakes were made. If separation had been managed carefully, taking into account both the trade structures inherited and their likely future evolution, the economic costs of the collapse of the FSU could have been mitigated. The immediate breakdown of intra-CIS trade could have been avoided and even Russia's output decline would have been less severe.

Section 1 opens with a brief description of the starting point, namely the high degree of integration and the massive transfers from Russia that were implicit in the old pricing system. A closer look in section 2 at inter-republican trade within the FSU leads to two apparently conflicting conclusions. If one accepts the limited degree of openness of the FSU to the rest of the world, inter-republican trade had a structure similar to that of trade among market economies. However, the level of inter-republican trade was clearly far above what one would expect if trade with the rest of the world had been free. This suggests that, while inter-republican trade had its own logic under the old system, it was condemned to become marginal after opening up.

Section 3 shows that, once reforms had started, it did not make sense to keep the former Soviet republics together in an economic and monetary union. Section 4 then turns to the monetary aspects and asks whether the FSU really had, during its last years of existence, 'the worst monetary constitution one can imagine'. It also shows that the strange rouble zone that survived until late 1993 cannot be considered a cause of inflation, as has often been argued. Section 5 turns to a missed opportunity: that of the multilateral clearing system that had been agreed among ten CIS states, but was never implemented.

## 7.1 The starting point

### *The centre vanishes*

The FSU was a centralised state in which all power came from one structure, namely the Communist Party. Formally speaking, however, the Union was a federal structure based on fifteen constituent republics. The population that lived in the different republics maintained a separate identity in terms of language and culture throughout the Soviet period.

We are concerned here with the economic aspects of the process of disintegration. Most of this chapter is devoted to an analysis of the events that followed the dissolution of the Soviet Union. In this section, we discuss in particular the interplay between disintegration and economic reform during the years that preceded the onset of serious reforms in Russia at the beginning of 1992.

The formal dissolution of the FSU in late 1991 was only the final act of a gradual process that had started much earlier and that evolved differently from one republic to another. One common feature, however, was that the republican structures, which had hitherto been practically irrelevant, were suddenly filled with life through the initiatives of the local population and political elites. This process first occurred in the Baltic and Caucasian states, where there still existed the memory of a separate statehood. Subsequently, however, it spread to most other republics, including Russia.

As the policy of glasnost advanced, the republican structures became more active and, starting in 1989–90, they felt strong enough to deal with economic reform, which constituted after all the central issue of that period. The two processes of disintegration and economic reform thus became intertwined.

Even a brief look at the history of attempted reforms in the FSU shows there was no shortage of plans. In 1990 alone, no fewer than four major reform programmes were discussed at the highest political level. Despite some differences in emphasis, they all agreed on three goals: a market economy, stabilisation of the economy and the need to maintain an economic and monetary union for the territory of the Soviet Union.

However, none of these programmes could be implemented because of the 'war of laws' that was being waged at the same time. One republic after the other passed a declaration of sovereignty stating that its laws took precedence over Union laws, whereas the Union government insisted that Union law took precedence. Since at that stage the Union government under Gorbachev did not want, or rather did not dare, to use force, the reforms could be implemented only after agreement on a new Union Treaty had been reached that would define the respective powers of the republics and the Union. An agreement was reached in May 1991, but when it was about to be put into force the attempted August putsch set in motion a chain of events that led within four months to the demise of the Soviet Union.

The increasing regional disintegration was thus the main reason why the reform plans of 1990 and 1991 were not implemented. Moreover, the loss of control of the Union government over the budgets of the republics was an important factor for the large public sector deficit that destabilised the Soviet economy. Many Western observers and the Union government argued therefore that a disintegration of the Soviet Union into a number of independent economic units that competed against each other should have been avoided even in the face of the demands for total independence advanced by some republics as early as 1990.

The war of laws paralysed economic policy, damaging the reform process. However, this does not imply that a centralised approach to economic reform would necessarily have been superior to competition in reform (see Gros and Steinherr 1991a).

In economic terms the fundamental point is that any sub-unit that is part of a larger area with distorted prices can gain by implementing reforms on its own and allowing its inhabitants to trade freely at 'true' market prices. It was often alleged in 1990–1 that price reform had to be implemented at the Union level because otherwise differences in prices would lead consumers to buy where the goods are cheapest.

For example, if any republic had implemented a complete price reform (a partial reform might not be beneficial because of 'second-best' considerations), abolishing all subsidies and taxes, its price structure would have been different from that of the rest of the Union. Residents of other republics would then certainly have come to 'plunder' shops for those goods that had become cheaper in that particular republic. However, this 'plunder' would have been desirable since all these goods would have been sold at their marginal cost of production, and an increase in demand can only lead to an increase in the surplus of domestic producers. Given the Soviet habit of taxing many consumer goods viewed as 'luxuries', the producers of a large range of consumer goods would have benefited. Similarly, consumers of the republic that initiated a reform in isolation would have gained by buying goods such as bread and other staple commodities in the rest of the Union at the old subsidised prices.

However, all this 'arbitrage' is the essence of a market economy and should thus have been viewed not as a cost, but as a gain in efficiency. Moreover, price reform would also have acted on the supply side. Entrepreneurs in a republic that was the first to implement fundamental reforms would therefore gain by being able to satisfy a pent-up demand for diversified products coming from the entire union area. While a reaction in supply is not immediate (as the subsequent experience of the reform process showed), any supply response would have increased the benefits from reform.

In an uncoordinated reform process those republics that were slow to reform thus lost because residents of the republic that initiated reforms then bought more union goods priced below cost. This had the advantage that it was an incentive to implement reforms in the remainder of the Union as well.

Competition in reform thus had advantages. The real problem with an uncoordinated reform process was a political one. The response to unilateral price reform in some republics turned out to be border controls to suppress commodity arbitrage. These border controls contributed to the collapse of intra-FSU trade and were in themselves costly. However, the task of an enlightened Union government would have been to maintain open borders and thus allow competitive pressures to act at least within the borders of the union.

The reaction to the price reform undertaken unilaterally by Russia in January of 1992 shows that the economic mechanism was very powerful. The other smaller republics could not really contemplate closing their borders to Russia and not following its lead. This sort of competition in reform should have been allowed earlier on. China offers an example of regional structures that compete in reforms in which each province emulates the most successful, and usually most open, provinces to improve the standard of living of the local population (see Qian and Roland 1994).

In the area of macroeconomics, however, competition can be dangerous because negative externalities can arise quite easily. This is apparent in the monetary sphere: it is not possible to have one currency and several competing central banks. Each central bank has an incentive to create as much money as possible because the inflationary consequences are borne by everyone whereas the benefits remain with the home country. This was the central problem during the Soviet Union's last year of existence. It is discussed at some length in section 4, since it was at the root of the developments in 1992–3. In the monetary sphere, it is thus clear that competition within one currency area is dangerous.

In the fiscal area, a similar danger existed. Indeed, a central aspect of the power struggle between the Union and the republics concerned the distribution of expenditures and taxes. Despite the formal federal structure of the FSU, there was no organised fiscal decentralisation. Only the Union was empowered to levy taxes, but in practice much of public sector revenues (enterprises and wage taxes) fell increasingly under the control of the republican authorities. The latter were obviously tempted to keep the revenues for themselves while holding the Union government responsible for the payment of subsidies and the provision of public goods. The result was a growing deficit of the Union government whereas the republican budgets remained balanced until 1991, when all controls were lifted. The deficit of the Union government was, of course, not unavoidable. If the Union government had given macroeconomic stabilisation the priority, it could have slashed subsidies and balanced the budget. However, Gorbachev either did not realise this or felt that he was politically too weak to do this. Qian and Roland (1994) show that a well-organised fiscal decentralisation can actually be beneficial as long as there is a clear will at the centre to stabilise.

We therefore conclude that competition in economic reform would have been beneficial, but that a poorly defined macroeconomic system in which different levels of power compete can lead to disaster. The Soviet Union was in the worst of all worlds during its last years of existence: no competition in reform, but macroeconomic destabilisation.

Was this unavoidable? If Gorbachev had wanted to create a market economy, he should have allowed the republics much greater freedom early on in structural reforms (elimination of price controls, privatisation, etc.), in exchange for stricter controls on the macroeconomic side. As this fundamental choice was not made, the reform process never got off the ground in 1990–1, and the macroeconomic destabilisation that had occurred in the meantime made the structural reforms that started in the newly independent states in early 1992 much more difficult.

## *Economic relations among the Soviet republics*

As long as the FSU was one country, it was only natural that the constituent parts of this economic space were tightly integrated. The high degree of integration became a problem only when the local population, acting through the republican structures, asked first for more autonomy and finally for total independence. The desire for independence was in most cases politically motivated, especially in the case of the Baltics, but this conflict between political aspirations for full independence contrasted initially with the existence of a common economic space.

Just how tightly the fifteen republics were integrated is shown in table 7.1. For the smaller ones, trade with other republics accounted for one-half of output, and, even for Russia, inter-republican trade was more important than international trade. Moreover, as most trade had gone through Moscow, the smaller republics traded up to eight times as intensively with the rest of the FSU as with the outside world. This extraordinary degree of integration was the reason why it was often argued that the republics could not survive on their own.

Another reason was that the Soviet pricing system implied very large transfers from the producers of underpriced raw materials (mainly in Russia) to the producers of overpriced manufactured goods. Table 7.2 shows the trade balance individual republics would have had if all goods, or at least energy, had been priced at world market levels. This table shows that the smaller industrialised republics would have had trade deficits up to one-third of the value of their production (NMP). For the Central Asian states, this implicit subsidy came on top of direct transfers from the Union budget. For Lithuania or Tajikistan the situation was comparable to the situation of the new *Länder* in unified Germany.

It was already clear, even before the Soviet Union was dissolved, that the old pattern of inter-republican trade and subsidies within the former Soviet Union could not be sustained in the emerging new environment of fifteen independent states with market-based economies,

Table 7.1. *Soviet republics: trade with the USSR and the rest of the world, 1988*

|  | Trade as % of GNP* | | | |
|  | Total | Domestic | Foreign | Population (millions) |
| --- | --- | --- | --- | --- |
| USSR total | 30 | 21 | 8 | 284.5 |
| Russia | 22 | 13 | 9 | 146.5 |
| Ukraine | 34 | 27 | 7 | 51.4 |
| Belarus | 52 | 45 | 7 | 10.1 |
| Uzbekistan | 40 | 34 | 5 | 19.6 |
| Kazakhstan | 34 | 29 | 4 | 16.5 |
| Kyrgyzstan | 46 | 40 | 5 | 4.2 |
| Tajikistan | 44 | 38 | 6 | 5.0 |
| Turkmenistan | 42 | 38 | 4 | 3.5 |
| Armenia | 54 | 48 | 5 | 3.5 |
| Georgia | 44 | 38 | 5 | 5.3 |
| Azerbaijan | 41 | 35 | 5 | 6.9 |
| Lithuania | 55 | 47 | 7 | 3.7 |
| Moldova | 52 | 46 | 6 | 4.2 |
| Latvia | 54 | 47 | 7 | 2.7 |
| Estonia | 59 | 50 | 8 | 1.6 |

*Note*: * Assuming the same GNP–NMP ratio as for the USSR as a whole.
*Source*: *Statistical Year Book of the Soviet Union*, 1990.

and fifteen different currencies. It was also clear then that most republics would, in the long run, dramatically increase their trade with the rest of the world.

The following section quantifies the shift towards world trade that could be expected in the long run and estimates to what extent the inter-republican trade pattern under the old system was similar to what one would expect from the experience of market economies.

## 7.2   Trade patterns: past and future

### *Explaining past inter-republican trade patterns*

All of the former republics, with the possible exception of Russia, were fairly open economies. It was therefore vital for them to have an idea of how their foreign trade would evolve in the future. Most Western economists and most of the new policymakers agreed at the start of the disintegration process that in the long run there had to be a radical reorientation in trade, away from inter-republican trade and towards more trade with the West. But by how much and how quickly?

As shown in table 7.1, under the old regime inter-republican trade was several times larger than international trade (i.e. trade with the former Comecon area and the West together). It was already clear before the FSU collapsed that this had to change. But was all intra-FSU trade condemned to disappear?

Table 7.2. *Soviet republics: inter-republican trade account, 1988*

| | Trade account as % of NMP | |
| --- | --- | --- |
| | At world prices* | Only energy at world prices** |
| Russia | 6.5 | 3.5 |
| Ukraine | −3.5 | −3.7 |
| Belarus | 1.9 | 7.3 |
| Uzbekistan | −24.2 | −20.7 |
| Kazakhstan | −23.2 | −22.3 |
| Kyrgyzstan | −18.4 | −14.1 |
| Tajikistan | −31.8 | −26.9 |
| Turkmenistan | −3.7 | 8.4 |
| Armenia | −3.2 | 6.0 |
| Georgia | −16.1 | 2.1 |
| Azerbaijan | 10.2 | 20.8 |
| Lithuania | −35.4 | −19.5 |
| Moldova | −20.1 | 4.0 |
| Latvia | −24.1 | −8.9 |
| Estonia | −28.2 | −9.7 |

*Notes*: * Trade account adjusted for total world import prices means that
trade was evaluated at world market prices. In practice this means that the
values of trade of all branches were adjusted by a conversion factor equal to
the world import price/inter-republican price.
** Trade account with only energy evaluated at world prices, because it was
not always easy to determine the world market price for other goods.
*Source*: Bofinger and Gros (1992).

The approach used here to provide an answer to this question is the standard 'gravity equation' which starts from the idea that the amount of bilateral trade between two countries is determined by their size and the distance between them. The larger the two countries, in terms of income and population, the more trade there should be between them. The greater the distance, the less trade one should observe. Box 7.1 provides a more detailed description of the gravity approach.

The existing estimates of this gravity approach show that it explains trade patterns among market economies quite well. The three variables (income, population and distance) together with dummy variables for other factors (such as whether or not the two countries have a common frontier, participate in a preferential trade agreement or share a common language) usually explain well over half of the overall variance of the geographical distribution of trade.

Gros and Dautrebande (1992b) follow this approach using data about the matrix of bilateral trade between all the fifteen former republics. They explain the amount of bilateral trade (of all possible 210 combinations) as a function of the NMP of the two partners, the distance between them (and their areas as a further proxy variable for distance). These variables explain over 90 per cent of the variability in the geographical distribution of

**Box 7.1   The gravity model**

The gravity model explains the geographical distribution of the bilateral trade of a given country (or region) with its different trading partners. It is usually estimated on cross-section data referring to a single year or an average of several years.

The model describes the trade flow, say exports, from a particular country $i$ to another country $j$. Exports from country $i$ are assumed to depend on national income in $i$ (as proxy variable for the supply of exportables) and national income in $j$ (as proxy variable for the demand for $i$'s exportables in country $j$).

Per-capita output is sometimes also used to take into account the fact that a country with a higher income per capita trades more intensively (has more exports and imports) than a poorer country. Similar arguments apply if one estimates the distribution of imports: national income of the home country represents demand, and national income of the foreign country represents supply.

Most of the other variables used in the estimation of the gravity approach reflect transport costs and other obstacles to trade. The most obvious factor here is distance, which should have a negative effect on trade. The area of the importing or exporting country should also have a negative effect because it stands for the transport cost from the hinterland to the economic centre. A related variable is adjacency, that is, the presence (or absence) of a common border that should affect trade positively.

The equation estimated here is therefore:

$$
\begin{aligned}
\text{Ln (exports from i to j)} = {} & a \times \ln \text{(distance between } i \text{ and } j) \\
& + b \times \text{(adjacency: dummy)} \\
& + c \times \ln \text{(NMP of } i) \\
& + d \times \ln \text{(NMP of } j) \\
& + e \times \ln \text{(per capita NMP of } i) \\
& + f \times \ln \text{(per capita NMP of } j) \\
& + g \times \ln \text{(area of } i) \\
& + h \times \ln \text{(area of } j).
\end{aligned}
$$

The same equation was estimated for imports of country $i$ from country $j$. Data for the complete $15 \times 15$ matrix of inter-republican trade for 1987 (the most recent year available) were then used to estimate this type of equation. See Gros and Dautrebande (1992b) for details.

inter-republican trade. Moreover, the parameter estimates for the elasticities of trade with respect to income and distance are quite similar to the ones found in other studies of the gravity approach, which used data from market economies. This is surprising, since it implies that the Soviet planning system led to a geographical distribution of trade that was similar to the one typical for market economies.

A comparison with the results for market economies is even more revealing of the good fit of the gravity approach for intra-FSU trade. This is done in table 7.3, which

Table 7.3. *Estimates of inter-republican trade compared to studies of market economies*

| Explanatory variables | Inter-republican trade | H&P, 21 middle-income LDCs | W&W, 76 market economies | Aitken, 12 European countries |
|---|---|---|---|---|
| constant | −10.48 (−7.9) | −9.54 (−5.7) | −12.49 (34.2) | 1.07 |
| ln(dist $ij$) | −0.39 (−6.3) | −1.56 (−16.4) | −0.75 (22.3) | −0.35 (2.74) |
| border | 0.59 (3.1) | 1.15 (4.0) | 0.78 (3.3) | 0.89 (4.41) |
| ln(GDP$i$) | 1.01 (19.1) | 0.86 (13.7) | 0.79 | 0.72 |
| ln(GDP/pop $i$) | 0.32 (2.7) | 1.05 (5.5) | 0.38 | 0.33 |
| ln(area $i$) | −0.11 (−3.0) | 20.01 (20.2) | | |
| ln(GDP$j$) | 0.69 (13.2) | 0.93 (23.3) | 0.80 | 0.54 |
| ln(GDP/pop $j$) | −0.06 (−0.5) | 0.22 (3.3) | 0.22 | 0.15 |
| ln(area $j$) | 0.16 (4.4) | −0.18 (−6.5) | | |
| Other variables – trade integration – dummies – Linder effect | | 0.08 (0.9) | | |
| $R^2$ | 0.92 | – | 0.7 | 0.87 |
| S.E. | 0.47 | 1.67 | – | 0.22 |
| Observations | 210 | 420 | 4320 | 132 |

compares our results for inter-republican exports to three other widely known estimates: Aitken (1973), Havrylyshyn and Pritchett (H&P) (1991), and Wang and Winters (W&W) (1991).[1]

The basic message of table 7.3 is that the intra-FSU trade is explained remarkably well by the gravity approach. First of all, the fit of the inter-republican equation is better than that of the two recent estimates, H&P and W&W. Only the estimate for Europe in the 1960s has a better standard error, but its adjusted $R^2$ is still lower. While one should not put too much emphasis on these indicators of the overall fit, it is clear that the economic variables used here explain the distribution of inter-republican trade remarkably well.

A comparison of the point estimates of the different coefficients for the main explanatory variables also reveals more similarities than differences,[2] which suggests that the distribution of inter-republican trade was governed by similar considerations.[3]

Given that the gravity equation performs so well for inter-republican trade (in some respects better than for trade among market economies), the size of the parameter that shows the relationship between trade and distance becomes the key to the argument that intra-FSU trade was not driven by the market and should hence disappear as soon as possible. The implicit argument has often been that the planners set up enterprises in remote areas without regard for transaction costs.

Table 7.3 shows for inter-republican trade an elasticity of trade with respect to distance of around −0.4, which is close to those found for European market economies[4] (i.e. Aitken 1973, who finds −0.35), but this does not necessarily indicate that Soviet planners took

Table 7.4. *The importance of transport and communications*

| Share of transport and communications in: | FSU (1985) | European Union (1987) |
| --- | --- | --- |
| NMP (Gross value added) | 6.1 | 6.5 |
| Employment | 7.2 | 6.2 |

*Source*: IMF et al. (1991), Lipton and Sachs (1992) and Eurostat, *National Accounts*, detailed tables by branches.

transport costs adequately into account. Given the logarithmic formulation, this question cannot really be answered on the basis of the coefficients of the gravity equations. If transport costs were on average twice as high in the FSU as in Europe, this would just show up in the constant.

Another, very simple, piece of evidence, however, suggests that transport costs were not excessive: in the FSU about 6 per cent of national income (NMP) was devoted to the sector 'Transport and communications'. This is almost exactly equal to the share of this sector in the European economy (measured by gross value added). Since one could argue that, given the distorted pricing system in the Soviet Union, NMP shares cannot really be compared to shares in value added at market prices in the West, one can compare shares of employment. However, the share of total employment in this sector in the FSU was also similar to that of the EU, as shown in table 7.4.[5]

## *Anticipating the shift in trade*

How could have one have anticipated the shift in trade patterns in 1992? This could have and has been done quite easily. One could start by using parameter estimates from the studies on the geographical distribution of international trade of market economies already mentioned above.[6] A prediction of the future distribution of trade of a given former Soviet republic, say Ukraine, can then be obtained by multiplying these parameter estimates with the actual values of the income and the population of Ukraine (and those of all its potential trading partners) and the distances between Ukraine and its trading partners. (See box 7.2 for details.)

This exercise yields estimates of the shift in the direction of trade that the former Soviet republics will experience in the long run. The same method was also used in Baldwin (1994), Wang and Winters (1991) and Havrylyshyn and Pritchett (1991) to predict the future trade patterns of the Central European countries.

To apply this approach to the former republics only requires data about income, population and distances. The latter two variables can be measured easily, but to guess the income per capita of the former republics in the long run was more difficult. We assumed back then a per-capita income of $2,500 for Russia. This was above the actual value for 1993–4, but close to the average during the late 1990s (see box 7.2).

*Box 7.2   Predicting future trade flows*

We use here the parameter estimates of three estimates of the gravity model for market economies. Two represent recent work with data from the 1980s and the third is a classic study referring to Europe in the 1960s. As will be shown below, all three sets of parameter estimates yield quite similar predictions for the future trade pattern of the former republics. The three studies used are again: Wang and Winters (1991), Havrylyshyn and Pritchett (1991) and Aitken (1973). See table 7.3 for the parameter estimates obtained by these studies.

To form predictions about the future trade patterns of the former republics, we combine the parameter estimates with the independent variables, which are distance, population and some economic data. The former do not change a lot over time. The only economic input needed to calculate the future trade of the former republics is national income (GDP). Estimates of the income of the FSU were always unreliable and the experience with Central Europe has shown that most Western estimates (especially those made by the CIA) were on the high side. We therefore use a low estimate of $2,500 for the entire Soviet Union, which should be a reasonable minimum as argued in Gros and Steinherr (1991a). This figure is also close to, but still above, the GDP per capita of Russia in 1994, the third full year with a market economy. Since the per-capita income in Russia is, according to official Soviet figures for 1987, approximately equal to the average for the entire old Soviet Union, we assumed that Russia has a GDP per capita of $2,500. GDP per capita for all the other former republics was then calculated by multiplying the $2,500 with the ratio NMP per capita of the republic concerned over NMP per capita of Russia. Multiplying the per-capita figures by population then yields the total GDP for each republic.

As before, the distance between two regions is calculated as the straight-line distance between the two economic centres (usually the capitals) of the regions. The adjacency dummy equals 2 if the two countries share a common border; otherwise, it equals 1.

In the case of Russia, it is difficult to maintain the assumption that the capital is the main economic centre for trade. In other words, the distance between Alma Ata and Moscow might not be the relevant factor for predicting trade between Russia and Kazakhstan since Kazakhstan would naturally trade more with western Siberia than with the Moscow region. Moreover, for trade between Japan and Russia, the distance between Vladivostok and Tokyo should be more relevant than the distance between Moscow and Tokyo. Russia was therefore divided into six regions with the following centres: former Leningrad, Moscow, Volgograd, former Sverdlovsk, Novosibirsk and Vladivostok. Each region was assigned a total income equal to its share in the total population of Russia.

Using the parameter estimates of table 7.3, we then calculate the potential exports of the former Soviet republics (fourteen countries plus the six regions of Russia) to the other republics and to eight other countries or regions: the EU-12, Scandinavia, Japan, Germany, United States, Central Europe (Czech Republic, Slovak Republic, Hungary,

Poland, Romania, Bulgaria, Yugoslavia (Serbia)), China and India. These countries and regions accounted for 89 per cent of Soviet exports in 1989.

A number of authors have used the gravity equation to predict not only trade shares, but also the actual level of trade (e.g. in billions of US dollars). However, it has not been recognised that the figures for the predicted exports are strongly influenced by the constant in the estimation of the three studies used here. This constant is usually not precisely estimated; it represents the joint effect of all the factors that affect trade (exports) proportionally and does not affect distribution. In Havrylyshyn and Pritchett (1991), the standard error surrounding the point estimate of the constant exceeds 1.5; this implies that even a one standard error band of confidence around the predictions for the absolute values is plus or minus 3. Since this is in logarithmic terms, this implies that the upper bound is 20 times as large as the lower bound. The predictions for the trade flows in absolute dollar terms are therefore not reliable.

We therefore concentrate here on the *relative distribution* of the predicted exports in percentage terms over the main economic regions taken into account.

Table 7.5 summarises the outcome of this exercise. The main result is that most of the international trade of the former republics will be (in the long run, but was not yet in 2000) with the West and not with other former republics. The reason for this is that in gravity equations the most important determinant of the distribution of trade is income. The income of the entire FSU (all the former republics together) is less than one-tenth that of the European Union. This size effect is not offset by a strong distance effect for the western former republics, for which trade with the EU will thus become several times as important as trade with the other former republics.

Given its large market size and relative proximity, the EU emerges thus as the dominant trading partner of all former republics. The United States is further away than the EU and its market is slightly smaller; it is therefore not surprising that it is predicted to trade (and actually does) much less with the former republics.

Table 7.5 presents the predicted percentage distribution of the overall international trade for the average of all former republics, indicated by the FSU and Russia separately, using the mean of the predictions that one obtains based on the parameter estimates of the three studies mentioned above. Gros and Dautrebande (1992b) show that the predictions one obtains from each of these three different studies are very similar.[7]

The gravity model predicted already in 1992 that the share of trade with the other former republics would have to drop dramatically. In the past the ratio of international trade to inter-republican trade was 1:4. Table 7.5 suggests that, in a world where market relations dominate, this ratio might be the other way round, that is, closer to 4:1. The mean of the three predictions is that the (average) former republic should conduct only 15.3 per cent of its trade with the FSU. Moreover, the non-Russian former republics will only conduct 7.3 per cent of their trade with Russia. It is unlikely that in the long run Russia will be able to dominate its neighbours in economic terms as it does at present.

Table 7.5. *Predicted trade patterns of former republics*

| % of total trade with: | EU-15 | Japan | US | FSU | Central Europe | Russia |
|---|---|---|---|---|---|---|
| Average | | | | | | |
| FSU-Republic | 45.6 | 17.4 | 12.2 | 15.3 | 7.4 | 7.3 |
| Russia | 45.9 | 24.9 | 13.7 | 7.5 | 5.4 | – |
| Actual trade pattern in 1996 | | | | | | |
| Ukraine | 19.0 | 1.0 | 3.4 | 52.5 | 10.8 | 40.5 |
| Russia | 36.2 | 2.2 | 5.2 | 30.8 | 5.8 | – |

The share of the EU-15 is always estimated at around 50 per cent and that of the countries of Central Europe is between 6 and 8 per cent for the average of all former republics and between 4 and 7.5 per cent for Russia. By the early 1990s it was thus clear that the collapse of trade with Central Europe that had already taken place was unlikely to be reversed in the future, and that the EU would emerge as the dominant trading partner for Russia and most of the other former republics.

To what extent have the predictions based on the gravity model been borne out? It is well known that trade between the FSU and the former Comecon collapsed, and trade among former republics also fell sharply. But has the equilibrium been reached?

Table 7.5 gives the geographical distribution of trade for the two largest former republics: Russia and Ukraine. Trade patterns have adjusted a lot, but have not yet reached the long-run equilibrium predicted by the gravity approach. For example, over half of Ukraine's trade is still with the FSU, three times as much as predicted. By contrast, the share of the EU in Ukrainian trade is less than half (about 20 per cent) of what is predicted (over 40 per cent). This suggests that in Ukraine foreign trade has not really been reformed (and there has been little progress since 1996, the year to which these data refer). The case of Russia is more difficult to analyse since gas and oil, which form a large part of Russian exports, are bound to particular markets because of the way the pipelines were built. Moreover, for Russia by the mid-1990s there was still a large difference between trade recorded in international statistics and overall trade recorded by the national accounts. This difference results probably from barter, itself an indication of a lack of reforms. What is known about the geographical distribution of trade thus reflects only about two-thirds of the total for Russia. For this part, it seems that the adjustment towards a normal trade pattern is more advanced than for Ukraine, as the EU is now the largest trading partner of Russia, accounting for more than a third, not that far from the 45 per cent predicted by the gravity approach. But trade with FSU countries also remains important, at 30 per cent of the total (four times what is predicted by the gravity approach). By contrast, actual trade with Central Europe is almost exactly equal to potential.

It needs hardly to be emphasised that this reorientation of trade has occurred naturally and does not call for any specific policy actions. But it should lead policymakers in the CIS to pay more attention to their trade relations with the EU.

## 7.3   Should the CIS form an economic and monetary union?

Economic integration can bring large economic benefits. For the European Union, economic arguments have been one of the main motors of the integration process (see Commission of the European Communities, 1988 and 1990a). Do the same arguments apply to the former Soviet Union and justify the attempts to preserve or create a CIS economic space? We discuss this issue separately for monetary and trade matters.

### A 'CIS customs union'?

Exports and imports within the CIS are now subject to a variety of restrictions. In 1992–3 most of them were in the form of quantitative limitations instead of tariffs since many of the peripheral CIS countries were much slower in their reform effort than Russia. This has changed; trade is now subject to ordinary tariffs, contradictory VAT rules, on occasions growth limits and – this is the most serious part – the whim of customs officials. All barriers to trade have economic costs and these restrictions certainly contributed to the decline in inter-republican trade that has intensified the disruption of production. A policy of free trade pursued by all former republics unilaterally represents the optimal scenario from a general point of view. While this was politically impossible, an acceptable 'second-best' alternative might have been to keep the CIS together in a customs union. Should the CIS countries have formed a customs union or should they still consider this possibility?

The standard analysis of customs unions shows that the benefits from joining a customs union are primarily a function of (1) the degree of protectionism practised by the union, (2) the size of the union, and (3) the regional distribution of trade.

1. If the external trade policy of a potential CIS customs union were close to free trade all member states should participate, since they would then have virtually free trade with the entire world. However, this is not a likely outcome because Russia would certainly dominate any customs union and has a restrictive policy on imports. The smaller CIS countries are much more likely to keep a liberal trade policy stance on their own because in most cases they do not have domestic products to protect. The other CIS members would therefore be better off conducting their own liberal commercial policy: inside a CIS customs union they would import more high-cost products from the other republics (so-called 'trade diversion').
2. The size of the customs union is also an important factor because the larger the customs union, the more likely it is that it contains the lowest-cost producers of most goods. Therefore this aspect does not favour a potential CIS customs union because, in economic terms, the FSU is quite small. The value of the output produced by all fifteen former republics is less than one-tenth that of the EU.
3. The most fundamental reason for believing that the FSU is not an attractive trading bloc is that in the long run inter-republican trade will drastically decline in importance. It does not make sense to create a customs union with a group of countries that do not trade intensively with each other.

In a sense, a CIS customs union would be similar to the several customs unions (and other preferential trading areas) between the poorer countries of Latin America. These regional agreements have never really worked for the same reason: trade among the members is usually only a small fraction of overall trade. In the case of the CIS one has to add some practical problems that have impeded the implementation of the numerous treaties and agreements concluded during the early 1990s to create a customs union in the CIS. A first issue that was never really resolved centred around the decisionmaking mechanism for setting the tariffs for the Union. Russia was not really ready to subordinate its own tariff structure to majority voting in some sort of customs council and the other CIS states were not willing to abdicate the determination of their external tariff policy entirely to Russia. Ensuring a proper redistribution of the tariff proceeds also turned out to be difficult to organise.

Finally, until 1994, Russia insisted that any free trade or customs union agreement in the CIS should exclude export tariffs. The background to this curious demand for asymmetry was that Russia wanted to keep domestic energy prices low through export tariffs on oil and gas, but was not willing to let Russian oil producers supply the other CIS countries with large amounts of oil and gas at a fraction of the world market price.

These political difficulties came on top of the fact that sectoral interests were determining trade policy more and more in Russia and pushing it in a direction that was too different from that of the other CIS countries. This is why a customs union was not created, despite a treaty to this effect that had been signed and ratified in due form.

## The former Soviet Union as an optimal currency area?

Would the CIS countries benefit economically from having a common currency? The 'optimal currency area' literature says that countries should form a monetary union if (1) they trade intensively among themselves, (2) asymmetric shocks will be minor, (3) the monetary union will deliver price stability and (4) a national fiscal policy cannot threaten the common monetary policy stance. These points are discussed in a medium-run perspective to put the specific problems that dominated the events of 1992–3 into a broader framework.

### Trade links

The first criterion in deciding whether or not a country should be part of a monetary union is the importance of trade within the potential currency area. It was shown above that in the past trade links were very intense, but that the future should bring a completely different trade pattern. The likely reorientation of trade is thus a first argument against a monetary union.

One might argue that the Baltic states (and some other smaller CIS countries) are too small to be viable currency areas on their own. What should they do? Section 2 has already shown that there will be (and has been) a redirection of trade. The Baltics already have a geographical trade pattern that resembles that of Finland. They would gain more from joining the European Economic and Monetary Union (EMU) than from remaining in the rouble area. Estonia has already effectively done this through the currency board arrangement that links its currency to the DM.

For the larger republics, inter-republican trade was less important in relation to output (see table 7.1; for Ukraine it was under 30 per cent, comparable to the ratio for France, which has approximately the same population) so that the economic argument against a separate national currency is weaker. The larger republics may therefore represent viable currency areas of their own.

### Asymmetric shocks

The main advantage of a separate currency is that exchange-rate changes can facilitate the adjustment to nationally differentiated shocks. The classic argument goes like this: imagine a country that is hit by an adverse shock to its balance of payments and that would need a real depreciation in order to restore external balance. If the country is part of a monetary union, the only way this real depreciation can be achieved is by a fall in domestic wages and prices (relative to those in the rest of the currency area). In the face of an external shock, the exchange rate is a useful adjustment tool because a fall in wages and prices is often difficult to achieve and always takes some time, whereas the exchange rate can be moved instantaneously.

In the case of the FSU, this argument has been particularly relevant for several reasons. In the short run, the reform process in itself already provides a source for large regionally differentiated shocks because price reform (especially energy price reform) leads to large changes in relative prices and therefore to an important redistribution of income, given the high degree of specialisation of many republics and regions. For example, wages in Ukraine fell to less than a third of the Russian level in real terms, even after Ukraine achieved the same level of stabilisation as Russia in 1994. Given that Ukraine imports most of its energy the direction of movement in relative wages was not surprising, but the extraordinary size would have been difficult to predict, given that under the Soviet regime wages were at about the same level. Belarus experienced a similar real depreciation. Figure 7.2 in section 4 (page 214) provides more evidence on the evolution of relative wages in the CIS. Moreover, the overall reform process proceeded at different speeds in the different former republics.

In the longer run, one large source of asymmetric shocks will remain. Because the value of the Russian rouble will be determined by the world market price for oil and gas, the rouble will become essentially a 'petro' currency. Given that Russia (together with Kazakhstan and Azerbaijan) accounts for most energy exports of the FSU, changes in the world market price for oil would thus constitute a major source of asymmetric shocks.

### Price stability

The most important consideration concerning a monetary union is that a common currency also implies a common inflation rate. This could be achieved through maintaining the rouble as a common currency or through an EMS type of fixed exchange-rate system with the rouble providing the anchor, like the DM in the EMS. Could a link to the rouble assure price stability in either case? This has clearly not been the case so far and it is not likely that in the future the rouble will be a very stable currency. However, there is also little reason to believe that national currencies will be more stable than the Russian rouble, so this argument seems to cut both ways. Except for the Baltics and Kyrgyzstan, all former republics adopted even more inflationary policies than Russia when they were forced to introduce their own currencies. Again one has to consider all the options. For the Western former republics an alternative that could provide some price stability would be a link to the euro. In the short run this would have been too tight a policy constraint for most former republics, but now that the euro is the single currency of the enlarged Community, it would provide a stable anchor.

### Financing budget deficits

The decisive factor that destroyed all attempts to maintain the rouble as the common currency was, however, different from the optimum currency area considerations discussed so far. In the early years of the reform process the government could finance deficits only by printing money, since markets for public debt instruments simply did not exist. A common currency therefore implies also a common fiscal policy, at least during the transition period. There were enormous differences in the degree to which governments were willing and able to withstand the multiple pressures for social safety nets and subsidies to uncompetitive industries. At one extreme is Estonia, where a balanced budget was seen as crucial for the survival of the country, and at the other end is Ukraine, where a weak government tried to spend its way out of the structural problems.

The sharp difference between the short and the long run that has come up repeatedly in this section suggests one conclusion. Even under the best of circumstances, most of the former republics would anyway sooner or later have found that it was in their interest to establish a national currency. The real question is therefore how the disintegration of the rouble zone should have been organised. The optimal solution would have been a stable and convertible rouble to serve for some time as a common currency. As soon as the banking systems in the other CIS countries had developed enough to allow for normal international banking relationships, these countries should have introduced their own national currencies one by one: currencies that would also have been convertible and stable. However, this did not happen. The rouble was semi-stabilised only after two years, and in the meantime trade among CIS countries collapsed as the normal payment channels were disrupted. The following section analyses what actually happened and why it did not conform to this prescription.

## 7.4   The 'worst monetary constitution one can imagine'?

The seeds for the dissolution of the (Soviet) rouble zone were already sown some time before the dissolution of the Soviet Union. The rouble zone started to crumble once the Central Bank (Gosbank) of the Soviet Union started to lose control over its head offices located in the fifteen republics.

The Gosbank was organised, like all institutions of the Soviet Union, formally along federal lines. There were thus national head offices in all fifteen republics. As long as the

---

**Box 7.3    From Soviet to Russian banknotes**

Soviet banknotes carried inscriptions in all the fourteen official languages of the FSU. In the course of 1992 the Russian mint began to substitute the old 'Soviet' designs on banknotes. In a first step, the translation of the face value (1, 3, 5, etc. roubles) in all fourteen official languages of the FSU was suppressed, and the only 'language' used on banknotes was Russian. But until mid-1992 these banknotes still carried the heading 'State Bank of the USSR' and conserved the old 'Soviet' symbols. The next step came with rouble notes without 'Soviet' symbols (i.e. without Lenin's face and the hammer and sickle), which bore the mark 'issued by the Central Bank of Russia'. These banknotes circulated for some time in the eleven former Soviet republics that did not introduce a national currency until the end of 1993, despite the fact that they are clearly 'Russian' and not 'Soviet' or 'CIS'. The old Soviet cash was gradually taken out of circulation in 1992–3 as the old, lower-denomination, banknotes became useless because of inflation. The final step came when the CBR announced, in July of 1993, that pre-1992 banknotes would no longer be accepted in Russia after September and that Russia would no longer deliver any cash to the other republics unless they sign a treaty to subordinate their monetary and fiscal policies to that of Russia. This completed the creation of the 'Russian' rouble.

---

party controlled everything, this did not really matter. Things changed when, during 1991, the Union Gosbank lost control over its republican branches. When the different republics declared their sovereignty, the head offices of the Gosbank became 'central' banks on their own, which were supposed to be free of control from the Union.

There were thus fifteen 'independent' central banks,[8] with the self-declared authority to create money in a single currency area. This situation was not tenable because each 'national central' bank had an incentive to give its clientele (state-owned enterprises, republican governments) as much credit as possible. The consequences in terms of greater inflationary pressures would be borne by the entire Union. There was thus a clear free-rider problem, which was most acute in the case of the smaller republics. For example, if the central bank of a republic that initially accounted for 5 per cent of the total credit supply (and 5 per cent of the total income of the FSU) doubles the credit to its own government, total Union credit increases only by 5 per cent. A small republic could thus assume that even huge rates of domestic credit expansion would have virtually no inflationary consequences for itself. This is why it was often said that in 1991 the Soviet Union had 'the worst monetary constitution one can imagine'.[9] As will be shown below, however, the Union authorities could have controlled the situation as long as they avoided expansionary fiscal policies and controlled the printing press.

At the end of 1991, the Soviet Union ceased to exist.[10] All the national central banks that emerged from the republican head offices of the Gosbank continued to give credit in roubles. But, despite a very serious cash shortage, they dared not print additional 'Soviet' roubles and all printing presses were located in Russia (see box 7.3 for the story of banknote designs in Russia). The Baltic republics and Ukraine announced immediately that they would introduce their own currency as quickly as possible. In fact this did not happen right away: Estonia started the process in late June 1992 and Ukraine followed only in November. However, these countries did start immediately to print substitute roubles (so-called coupons).

In the meantime most of the former Soviet republics were thus in the strange situation that they still used the 'Soviet' rouble and their central banks continued to grant credit in roubles. Thus, the free-rider problem continued in 1992. The main change with respect to 1991 was that after price liberalisation, excessive credit expansion could (and did) show up quickly in higher prices. In a sense the free-rider problem became even more acute than before, since the states that intended to introduce their own currency anyway had no concern at all for a stable purchasing power of the rouble.

The situation was different for Russia. Since Russia considered itself to be the successor state to the dissolved USSR, it wanted to keep the rouble. Gaidar's government pledged to stabilise the economy with a tight monetary and fiscal policy in Russia. It recognised quickly, however, that it could never succeed if the central banks of the other countries from the FSU could continue to issue credit in roubles. One solution would have been a monetary reform, that is, simply to introduce officially a Russian rouble. However, this path was not used for political reasons.

The problem for Russian policymakers was therefore how to isolate Russia from the perceived inflationary impact of rouble credits originating from other countries in the CIS. (Below we show that in reality there was no threat.) The solution adopted was to impose controls on cross-border movements of bank accounts.[11] The Central Bank of Russia (CBR) decreed that all bank transfers to and from other former Soviet republics would have to pass through special correspondent accounts held by its headquarters in Moscow. The idea underlying this move was simple: if the CBR could ensure that there were no *net* movements of funds between Russia and the other former Soviet republics, higher credits in these countries could no longer affect the money supply in Russia. In this way Russia would be able to stabilise the rouble. In effect this measure was equivalent to the introduction of a Russian non-cash rouble.

The correspondent account system was imposed by the CBR over the space of six months (January–July 1992). Transfers to and from the Baltics were immediately controlled starting in January 1992. But for the rest of the FSU, the system started working only after 1 July 1992. Before that date, all payments from CIS countries were automatically credited in the Russian banking system and the CBR was informed only ex-post facto of the balance of outgoing and incoming payments. Box 7.4 provides a chronology of the evolution of the correspondent system and the dissolution of the rouble zone.

The correspondent account system worked as follows: imagine that an enterprise in Ukraine wished to pay an enterprise in Russia for a delivery of oil. It would send a 'payment order' to its local bank that in turn transmitted the corresponding transfer order to the National Bank of Ukraine. In Kiev all transfer orders towards Russia (i.e. requests to transfer funds to pay for imports from Russia) were collected and sent periodically in large sacks to the 'international computing centre' in Moscow. This organisation, part of the CBR, also collected all the payment orders coming from Russian enterprises wanting to pay for Russian imports. All payments from Ukraine (i.e. Ukrainian imports from Russia) were

---

***Box 7.4   Chronology of the dissolution of the rouble zone***

**1992**

| | |
|---|---|
| January | All former republics still use the (Soviet) rouble, correspondent account system created but, except for Baltics, all payments from other former republics are automatically credited in Russia. |
| May | Agreement on the creation of a joint Central Bank council for the CIS (never implemented). |
| June | Estonia is the first former republic to introduce national currency (kroon); agrees to return old Soviet roubles to Russia. |
| July | Limits on balance on correspondent accounts introduced by Russia after a large Russian surplus has been accumulated and Ukraine decides on a huge credit emission. To facilitate introduction of the new system, overdrafts in the form of 'technical credits' are given. |
| September | Agreement on the creation of an Interstate Bank at Bishkek (Kyrgyzstan). Negotiations on details start. |
| Aug.–Nov. | Technical credits exhausted, the CBR blocks correspondent accounts and processes payments from other former republics on a selective basis. |
| November | Ukraine formally de-links 'coupons' from rouble. |

**1993**

| | |
|---|---|
| January | Agreement on Interstate Bank signed (not implemented). |
| Jan.–June | Credits on the correspondent accounts in principle no longer available from the CBR. Other countries can run a deficit only if the Russian government provides explicit government-to-government credits. Existing credit balances are transformed into official debt and indexed on the dollar. |
| July | The CBR decides suddenly to withdraw all old 'Soviet' (i.e. pre-1992) banknotes from circulation by September and announces that it will deliver new banknotes only to those former republics that subordinate their monetary and fiscal policy totally to that of Russia by signing an agreement on a monetary union. Many CIS countries initially declare their intention to join the monetary union. |
| Sept.–Nov. | End of rouble zone. When the other CIS countries see the fine print on the monetary union proposal, all decide to introduce a national currency. |

---

booked on the liability side of the correspondent account of Ukraine, and Russian imports from Ukraine were put on the asset side. The net payments were supposed to be balanced over time.

In theory the nature of the correspondent accounts system changed radically in July 1992 when the CBR decreed that the correspondent account would have to balance. However, the CBR gave each CIS country, including Ukraine, a line of credit at the start of the new system (1 July 1992) to allow them time to adjust. In principle, each republic thus knew the maximum amount of debt it could accumulate and should thus have taken measures to reduce its deficit when it came close to its limit. However, the limits were not taken seriously because each CIS state hoped to obtain additional credits once the initial one had been exhausted. They counted on the pressure of Russian exporters on the CBR to pay (sometimes for deliveries already made). In some cases policymakers did not comprehend why the Russians should be allowed to block a payment order that had been properly filled in and sent to Moscow. This explains why the initial credit lines were used up quite quickly. Ukraine had from the beginning a negative balance (or deficit) so that its debt towards Russia was growing all the time. Within two or three months, many former Soviet republics had already reached their limit. At that point the CBR started to get tough. For each republic that had exhausted its credit line, it processed each day only an amount of payments for imports of that republic equal to the amount of the payment orders for exports coming from the republic concerned.

There is considerable anecdotal evidence that the deficits of Ukraine, for example, did not reflect an excess of Ukrainian imports over its exports to Russia, but capital flight from Ukraine where interest rates were even lower than in Russia, despite even stronger inflationary pressures. However, this cannot be verified since no reliable customs data for the trade between Russia and Ukraine exist for this period.

## The rouble zone in 1992–3: a recipe for inflation or a disciplinary device?

There were nine CIS countries that kept the rouble (a 'generic' rouble as opposed to a well-defined national rouble or the Russian rouble) as their currency during 1992 and most of 1993. However, this 'rouble zone' was not a unified currency area. Households in these countries used Russian banknotes, but domestic transactions in non-cash form were denominated in roubles (without any specification) and transfers through bank accounts to and from Russia had to go through 'correspondent accounts' and were subject to a variety of regulations and delays.

Since the official correspondent accounts were often blocked, it was very difficult for enterprises outside Russia to pay their Russian suppliers, even if they were in principle ready to pay a premium. This was one of the reasons why during 1992–3 commercial banks were again allowed (gradually) to have direct correspondent accounts with commercial banks in other countries. These only semi-regulated transactions between commercial banks developed into an informal market for 'national' roubles, that is, roubles in bank accounts in any one of these countries. The roubles outside Russia were usually worth less than the Russian rouble, that is, in a bank account in Russia. In this sense, the CIS countries that used the rouble in 1992–3 already had 'quasi' national currencies.

This ill-defined situation satisfied neither the Russian government nor the other CIS states. The Russian political system was itself divided. Some political forces, notably in the conservative parliament, wanted to save at least part of the former empire. In that view, the preservation of a unified rouble zone was an indispensable part of that strategy. The more reformist elements of the government, however, preferred a clean solution. They demanded that the other CIS countries either introduce their own currencies or give up all their monetary independence.

The other CIS countries were constantly torn between two considerations: on the one hand they wanted to have an independent monetary policy; but, on the other, they also wanted to reap the advantages of staying in the rouble zone. These advantages were important: as a part of the rouble zone they could, in principle, have a slice of the cheap credit distributed by the CBR. Moreover, at least in 1992–3, the Russian government linked the price of oil to the currency issue. Countries within the rouble zone were charged a price in roubles that was close to the domestic Russian price. Other countries had, in principle, to pay the world market price, which was two to five times higher. Given that imports of oil accounted for a very large proportion of their national income,[12] the second point was the crucial one.

During the first half of 1992, international efforts to help Russia concentrated on a rouble stabilisation fund of potentially $6 billion. It was widely perceived, however, that it would not be possible to stabilise the rouble unless a clear arrangement for the rouble zone was found. In early 1992, the other CIS countries were not willing to introduce national currencies for the motives mentioned above. Under pressure from the IMF[13] and the Russian government, most CIS countries thus signed in May 1992 an agreement on a joint central bank council that would determine credit expansion for the entire area and take decisions on all relevant monetary policy instruments (interest rates, minimum reserves, foreign exchange interventions, etc.). However, that agreement was never implemented. That there was never any intention to do so is clear from the fact that one article stipulated that the decisions of the joint central bank council would be binding only on those members that agreed to be bound.

The key issue that made an agreement on a joint central bank impossible was the voting power to be attributed to each state. Russia insisted, for obvious reasons, on a formula that linked voting power to size or economic strength. The CIS states were not willing to give up even a small part of their sovereignty, so recently acquired, and insisted on the principle of 'one state, one vote', as in the Maastricht Treaty for European Economic and Monetary Union.

The failure of the joint central bank project was one of the reasons for the introduction of the limits on the correspondent accounts between central banks in July 1992. However, as Russia continued to deliver oil at below world market prices and extend credit to the rouble zone during 1992 and early 1993, the CIS states in Central Asia and Belarus succeeded for a while in having their cake and eating it too.

A central question was whether the existence of a 'quasi-rouble zone' made it impossible to stabilise the (Russian) rouble. As mentioned above, the IMF and the Russian government took the position that the introduction of a real national currency in the other CIS countries was a precondition for an effective stabilisation programme for the (Russian) rouble.

In contrast, we argue that the use of the rouble by other countries cannot really have been an obstacle for the stabilisation of the Russian rouble. On the contrary, the rouble zone was rather a 'disciplinary device' for the other CIS countries, forcing them to subordinate their national monetary policies to that of the CBR, because the other CIS countries were constrained by the Russian monopoly on rouble banknotes and by the fact that, since July 1992, interstate credit had been limited.

The proposition that control over the printing press allowed Russia to guarantee price stability follows immediately, if one accepts the view that the price level can be controlled as long as there is a well-defined demand for cash in real terms (see Fama 1990). This argument simply says that if the government determines the nominal quantity of any good for which there is a well-defined demand in real terms, it also indirectly determines the price level.

However, one can also make the argument in terms of the more conventional premise that the price level is determined by the supply of 'money'. The latter is usually defined as the sum of cash and deposits with the *domestic* banking system. Through the usual system of requested reserves, the central bank can ensure that the domestic banking system can expand its deposit base (if and) only if the central bank increases the monetary base. Control over the monetary base thus implies control over inflation. This is the standard framework used in macroeconomic textbooks (see, e.g., Dornbusch and Fischer 1981).

That the rouble zone cannot have been a major source of inflation in Russia is evidenced by the fact that it was comparable to a currency board. However, it was a special currency arrangement because of the separation between the cash and the non-cash circuits. These two aspects are now discussed in turn. See also Box 7.5.

### The use of the rouble as a currency board arrangement

In most respects the relationship between the rouble zone countries and Russia was not much different from that of Estonia vis-à-vis Germany. Estonia opted for a currency board arrangement when it introduced a national currency. Estonian kroons could from the start be exchanged at a rate of 8:1 against the DM. Belarus was a good example of a rouble zone country. It issued banknotes, the so-called 'hares', that were perfect substitutes for Russian roubles at the rate of 10:1.

The Central Banks of Estonia and Belarus were in principle free to grant as much credit to their national economic agents (government or private sector) as they wanted. These credits could have been denominated in roubles, kroon or theoretically even DM. The argument that rouble credits granted by the Central Bank of Belarus created inflation in Russia must ultimately rest on the idea that rouble credits originating from the Central Bank of Belarus led to an increase in the monetary base in Russia. The same should hold true for DM credits issued by the Central Bank of Estonia. However, nobody would seriously claim that when the Central Bank of Estonia granted credits, German monetary policy or, more precisely, the assets and liabilities of the Bundesbank would be affected. The following step-by-step analysis shows why such a claim cannot be made.

Imagine that the Central Bank of Estonia gives credits in DM (the equivalent of the Central Bank of Belarus issuing credits in roubles). As long as these credits are given only to Estonian enterprises and banks there will obviously be no impact on money supply (and demand) in Germany. But Estonian economic agents might use the credit to buy goods and services in Germany. The German exporter, presumably, wants to be paid with something that can be used to pay for the costs in Germany. The Estonian importer cannot pay in cash, but can only give the German exporter a claim in DM on the Estonian Central Bank. The

---

*Box 7.5    Cash versus non-cash*

Up to this point, we have shown that operations of other CIS countries should have no impact on the money supply in Russia. This is indeed the case for fully fledged market economies in which all agents can exchange unlimited amounts of cash into non-cash on a 1:1 basis, as in Estonia after the introduction of the kroon. However, this was not the case in the CIS in 1992–3. This separation of the cash and non-cash circuits played a central role in giving national central banks outside Russia some room for manoeuvre. The dual standard of cash and non-cash should, in principle, have been eliminated with the radical reforms undertaken by the Russian government in early 1992. However, in contrast to other reforming countries in Central Europe, this did not happen in Russia.

As mentioned, non-cash payments between Russia and the other CIS countries had to go through so-called 'correspondent' accounts between the CBR and other national central banks. However, from July 1992 the CBR tended to block payments through these accounts whenever the partner country in question had a deficit that exceeded certain limits. The currency board-type mechanism, which relies entirely on bank transfers, therefore does not work in the CIS. Would cash transactions be a substitute?

Until 1994 it was difficult to convert non-cash into cash in most CIS countries. This was crucial for interstate transactions as well. If it had been possible to exchange un-limited amounts of local non-cash into cash, enterprises (and households) could have just converted their local bank accounts into cash and sent the cash by plane to Moscow (or somewhere else in Russia) to pay their Russian suppliers.[*] In this case 'excess' credit creation by other CIS countries would have had to be covered by reserves of (Russian) cash. However, these countries did not have substantial reserves of (Russian) cash since most of them received only enough cash from Russia to keep their local economies supplied with currency to effect transactions.

The separation of the cash and non-cash circuits outside Russia was thus necessary to safeguard some independence for the national central banks. As shown, any national central bank that guaranteed to exchange its liabilities at 1:1 into (Russian) roubles (in the form of banknotes) would de facto become a mere currency board. But how much autonomy did the separation between cash and non-cash give national central banks in Central Asia and the Caucasus?

The crucial point here is that the separation of the two monetary circuits was not perfect. The explicit and implicit restrictions on the conversion of non-cash into cash varied from country to country so that it is difficult to make generalisations. However, there were some restrictions in all countries and cash traded at a premium over non-cash most of the time.

How can this premium arise? Imagine that a local central bank issues too much credit (by definition in non-cash form). If this credit is given to enterprises to pay wages, the central bank cannot really refuse to hand out the same amount in cash almost

---

[*] Straight cash deals between enterprises are forbidden in Russia. But the cash could have been deposited into a Russian bank account first.

*(cont.)*

*Box 7.5   (cont.)*

immediately, since in most CIS countries enterprises have the 'right' to demand cash to pay their workers. The local central bank will thus not be able to engineer a local credit expansion to pay wages if it does not have enough Russian cash. In this respect it has to behave like a currency board or it will not be able to provide enterprises with enough cash to pay wages, and cash will then become more valuable than non-cash.

Of course, it is possible that the credit from the local central bank is given to enterprises for payment to other enterprises, so that the local central bank does not have to hand out any cash right away. However, the credit ends up being used either to pay wages or to pay for imports. In the latter case either the national central bank will be asked to provide dollars (for hard currency imports) or, if the additional imports come from Russia, more payment orders will be sent to the CBR, which, once a certain limit has been attained, will not accept them. Once the bilateral correspondent account with the CBR is blocked, the local authorities will have to ration imports. This implies that, within the country where the credit expansion took place, the premium of cash over non-cash will increase because enterprises will demand more cash to make payments to Russia.

The premium of cash over non-cash should thus be an indicator of the degree to which credit expansion outside Russia has been larger than inside it. Anecdotal evidence suggests that this premium has rarely exceeded 30 to 50 per cent. The exchange rate for cash roubles on which more systematic data are available never deviated more than about 10–15 per cent from the rate in Moscow. This partial evidence suggests that in 1992–3 the national central banks in other former Soviet republics did not really try to have an independent monetary policy. The common cash rouble has thus probably imposed some discipline on the non-Russian rouble zone countries during this period.

German exporter will then ask the Estonian Central Bank to provide DM funds through a bank account in Germany. The Estonian Central Bank can do this only if it has foreign exchange reserves. In this case the Estonian Central Bank can thus extend credit only to the extent that it has foreign exchange reserves, that is, if it follows the rules of the currency board.[14]

The analogy between the currency board of Estonia (using the DM) and that of Belarus (using the rouble in 1992–3) is not perfect because the Estonians knew that they would never obtain any credit from the Bundesbank if they were to run a deficit on their external accounts. Belarus did receive substantial credits from Russia and was thus able to cover its large deficits. However, this policy was not inherent in the rouble zone arrangement; it constituted a deliberate policy choice of the Russian government. If the Russian government (and the CBR) had simply refused to give any credits to the other CIS countries (for example in the context of a tough rouble stabilisation programme) there could have been no inflationary pressure coming from the other rouble zone countries. In reality the Russian government chose to extend large credits, domestically and towards some CIS countries, but this does not imply that the rouble zone arrangement per se was inflationary.

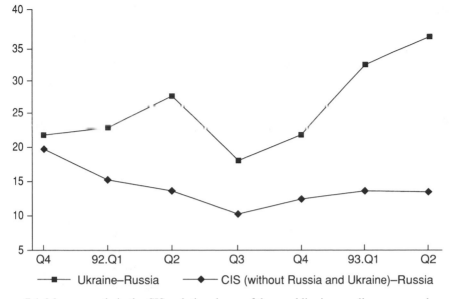

**Figure 7.1** Money supply in the CIS: relative shares of the republics in overall money supply

## The evidence

The view that the use of a common rouble in a number of CIS states was inflationary and destabilised monetary policy in Russia implies that monetary policy in the other CIS states was even more expansionary than in Russia. This can be checked by looking at the monetary aggregates in the CIS relative to those for Russia. The only aggregate for which one can obtain a comparable series is M3. Figure 7.1 therefore shows the ratio CIS Russia for M3. Since Ukraine left the rouble zone earlier than the others, and since Ukraine already had a parallel currency in the form of coupons in 1992, figure 7.1 shows two lines: one is the ratio of Ukrainian M3 to Russian M3, the other is the ratio of the sum of the M3s of all the other CIS states that used the rouble to Russian M3. Even a superficial look at the data suggests that the policies in the rest of the CIS (excluding Ukraine) were not more expansionary than in Russia since the ratio actually declines somewhat in 1992. Only in late 1993, when the rouble zone was dissolved, did most CIS states embark on a really inflationary policy. Ukraine is different since its inflationary path had already started by the end of 1992. But even in this case there is no evidence that in early 1992 Ukrainian monetary policy was worse than that of Russia.

Another way to test whether the other CIS states had a highly inflationary policy on the back of the common rouble is to look at the behaviour of wages. If policies in the rest of the CIS had been too expansionary, wages should have risen relative to those in Russia. However, this was also clearly not the case, as shown in figure 7.2, which again shows two lines. One shows wages in Ukraine as a percentage of those in Russia and the other shows the (unweighted) average wage in the rest of the CIS, again as a percentage of wages in Russia. Since wages in the rest of the CIS were already lower than in Russia before the

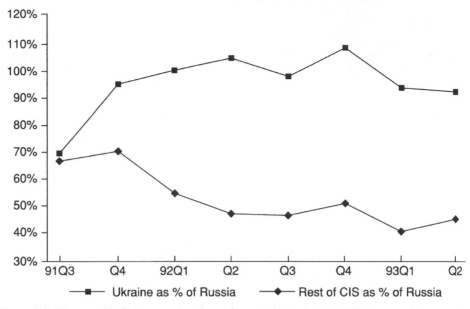

**Figure 7.2** Wages and inflation: a comparison of nominal wages in the CIS

reforms started, one should compare the 1992 and 1993 data with the data from the end of 1991. However, even on this basis, one cannot see a tendency of wages in the CIS to increase relative to those of Russia. By the end of 1991, wages in the CIS (without Ukraine) were about two-thirds of Russian wages. By mid-1993, they had fallen to about a half. It is interesting to note that the process of wage dispersion had started much earlier. In 1985 wages in the eight Soviet republics considered here (Armenia, Azerbaijan, Belarus, Kazakhstan, Kyrgyzstan, Moldova, Tajikistan, Uzbekistan) stood at 93 per cent of the Russian level, by 1990 they were at 84 per cent and by the last quarter of 1991 they had fallen to 70 per cent. This development might have been one additional reason for the increasing dissatisfaction with the 'Union' during that period.

The Ukrainian data show some slight increase in 1992 relative to the baseline at the end of 1991, but it is so small, about 10 per cent, that it cannot have had a strong impact. The really inflationary policies in Ukraine come much later. But the fact that Ukrainian wages (in karbovanetz) reached 200 per cent of the Russian level is completely irrelevant for Russian monetary policy, coming as it did one year after the formal break with the rouble in the third quarter of 1992.

The data on money supplies and wages are, of course, the outcome of a general equilibrium game under the rules explained above. However, the argument made here is that this game should lead to the result found here: a roughly similar rate of monetary expansion because of the currency-board nature of the rouble zone. Given that the linkages were not perfect, one would expect monetary expansion to be somewhat *higher* outside Russia if these countries had more inflation. In 1991–2 the opposite was true; monetary expansion was somewhat *lower* outside Russia.

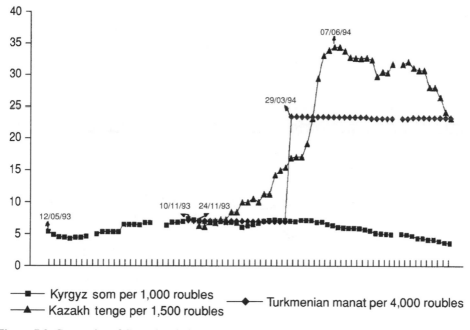

**Figure 7.3** Currencies of Central-Asiatic republics of the FSU, 12/05/93–21/10/94

There is thus no compelling evidence that the other CIS states that used the common rouble pursued a more inflationary policy than Russia and thus created additional inflation there. The badly defined rouble zone that existed in 1992–3 cannot be held responsible for inflation in Russia during that period.

Quite to the contrary, the rouble zone, as long as it lasted, exerted a disciplinary effect on the peripheral countries. This can be seen from figures 7.3 and 7.4, which show the evolution of six of the new national currencies against the rouble during 1993–4. Figure 7.4 shows the rouble exchange rate of the three Western former Soviet republics: Belarus (rubel), Ukraine (karbovanets) and Moldova (lei). It is apparent that all three of these currencies started to depreciate against the rouble (itself not a very hard currency even during the temporary stabilisation of 1993) as soon as they were created. The Belarussian rouble started out at 1:1, but reached over 25 to the Russian rouble late in 1994; the Ukrainian karbovanet also started off at 1:1 and fell to over 10. These two currencies thus depreciated by 2,500 and 1,000 per cent, respectively (always vis-à-vis the Russian rouble). The Moldavian lei did marginally better with a depreciation over this period of 'only' about 500 per cent.

The exchange rates of the three Central Asian currencies depicted in figure 7.3 are also instructive because they show three completely different approaches. The straight line corresponds to the Turkmenian manat that was officially pegged to the Russian rouble, but had to be devalued by 500 per cent in one step in March 1994, because domestic inflationary pressures were too great. The continuing straight line after the depreciation does not indicate a radical stabilisation programme, but shows the lack of reforms in that

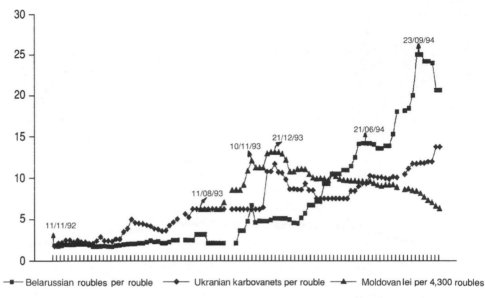

**Figure 7.4** Currencies of Belarus, Ukraine and Moldova, 11/11/92–21/10/94

country, which in principle should be very rich, given its huge reserves of natural gas. The official exchange rate of the manat is about as important as the official exchange rates of the Soviet rouble under the old regime. The almost stable line at the bottom of the picture shows the market-determined exchange rate of the Kyrgyz som, which could be stabilised because the government embarked on a radical reform and stabilisation programme. The Kyrgyz programme succeeded, not only because it received strong support from the IMF, but also because the authorities were really determined to stabilise the economy. The Kazakh authorities did not succeed, although this large country has enormous reserves of natural resources. Continuing large fiscal deficits could only be financed by printing money, which explains why the Kazakh tenge depreciated initially by over 700 per cent.

The theoretical argument that the rouble zone was a currency board for the other CIS countries applies a fortiori also to the situation that existed during the last days of the Soviet Union. The only difference was that the Union government controlled, at least until early 1991, the printing presses and was thus in a similar position to Russia in 1992–3. It was often thought then that the Union government could not stabilise the Soviet rouble since it could not control the republican branches of the Gosbank that had declared themselves to be independent central banks. However, this is also contradicted by the facts. The main cause of destabilisation during the last years of the FSU was the deficit of the Union, not deficits of the republics. It is true that part of the fiscal problems of the Union government were caused by the republics that withheld revenues. But the larger part of the deficit of the Union came from an *increase* in expenditure, not a fall in tax revenues. Moreover, a Union government determined to stabilise the economy could have slashed expenditure whenever the republics (including Russia) used their increasing political powers to obtain a larger slice of the tax cake. The root cause of increasing inflationary pressures during the last days of the Soviet Union was thus not the 'worst monetary constitution one can imagine', but a lack of resolve by the Union government to balance its budget.

The important conclusion emerging from this analysis is that the existence of an ill-defined rouble zone cannot have been one of the major causes of inflation in Russia. This implies that, contrary to what was argued all throughout 1992 by the IMF and others (e.g. Sachs 1994), the creation of true national currencies in all CIS countries was not a precondition for stabilisation in Russia and should thus not have been regarded as a precondition for granting the rouble stabilisation fund that was much discussed in 1992–3, but never disbursed.

Another implication of this analysis is that, even in 1991, the Union government under Gorbachev could have stabilised the (Soviet) rouble if it had maintained strict control over the printing press, which would have been possible if it had balanced the Union budget.

We now turn to the missed opportunity of 1992–3, namely, the failed attempt to create a multilateral clearing system to offset the bilateralism of the correspondent accounts.

## 7.5   An opportunity missed: the Interstate Bank

The system of bilateral correspondent accounts incited each participant to aim for a bilateral balance, since it was not possible to offset a surplus with one country against a deficit with another country. This section describes the damage done by bilateralism and the potential gain from overcoming this constraint through the creation of a multilateral payments mechanism incorporated in the Interstate Bank.

### *The gains from multilateralism*

How important was the absence of multilateral clearing in the CIS? This is a difficult question to answer because one has to compare two hypothetical situations: full multilateralism versus strict bilateral balancing as implicit in the correspondent account system.

It is not possible to say what level of trade would have taken place in 1992–3 if all payment relations had been on a multilateral basis. However, an indication of the orders of magnitude can be obtained from the data on inter-republican trade flows in the FSU. For example, the correlation coefficient between the balances calculated on the 1987 data and the actual outcome during the first quarter of 1993 is 0.8, if one values the 1987 trade flows at world market prices.

One way to assess the impact of bilateralism is to assume that all CIS countries want to achieve a precise balance in all their bilateral relationships and that the supply of exports is given in the short run. Under this hypothesis the amount of trade is determined mechanically by the lower values of either exports or imports. A second approach, used in Kaplan and Schleiminger (1989) to assess the European Payment Union (EPU), just compares the sum of the absolute value of the bilateral balances to the sum of the overall, multilateral balances. Both approaches are pursued in box 7.6.

Box 7.6 suggests that the Interstate Bank (IB) would have made it much easier to sustain a volume of trade worth 4 per cent of the NMP of the 'peripheral' CIS members and about 3 per cent on average for the entire CIS, including Russia, using the second approach. Russia

---

**Box 7.6   *Quantifying the losses from bilateralism***

*The effects of strict bilateral balancing*

If one imposes a strict bilateral balancing requirement, one also eliminates the structural deficit of the rest of the CIS vis-à-vis Russia. However, this deficit was anyway not sustainable. Its elimination should thus not be regarded as a consequence of bilateral balancing, but rather as an unavoidable adjustment process.

One way to eliminate the influence of the structural surplus of Russia is to eliminate Russia from the trade matrix. If this is done, strict bilateral balancing implies that trade (among the ten remaining CIS countries) goes down by about 30 per cent. This is still about 4 per cent of the combined NMP of this group of ten states. This result is interesting since it shows that the potential gain from a multilateral payments mechanism that does not involve Russia would be substantial. But in this case the benefits for Russia are, by definition, equal to zero.

Another way to eliminate the influence of the Russian structural surplus is to assume that Russia has an overall balance with the other ten countries and that this balance is achieved through a reduction in Russian exports that is the same in proportional terms for all surpluses. One can then compare the hypothetical strict bilateral balancing to this other hypothetical situation, which requires only overall balancing (for Russia). This yields the result that strict bilateral balancing reduces trade by about 3.3 per cent of the overall NMP of the CIS. However, the gains are very unevenly distributed: for Russia the gain is only 1.5 per cent of NMP, for the other ten CIS countries the gain is, on average, 6.5 per cent of NMP.

*Overall imbalances versus bilateral imbalances*

This approach just looks at the sum of the (absolute value of the) imbalances in trade. Under bilateralism the bilateral imbalances 'matter' while under multilateralism only the overall (or multilateral balance) 'matters'. 'Matters' in this context means that deficits have to be financed so that the imbalances determine the need for reserves. If one uses this approach, there is no longer a problem with the Russian surplus since one looks only at the difference between the two sums, which does not imply anything for the overall Russian position. Using the same data source as above, this yields the following result: the sum of the absolute value of the bilateral imbalances was 83.6 billion roubles while the sum of the multilateral imbalances was 65.9 billion roubles. The ratio of these two numbers is about 1.3 and the difference is equivalent to about 3 per cent of the combined NMP of the CIS.

---

would have gained much less in relative terms: about 1.5 per cent of GDP using the first approach. In relative terms this result is not surprising, since Russia has a surplus with most CIS countries. Of course, these numbers just indicate an order of magnitude. In 1992–3 both the numerator (trade) and the denominator (NMP) had contracted strongly in real terms for other reasons. It is thus difficult to know what would have been the situation if an efficient multilateral clearing system had existed then.

Are these potential 'gains' large? In ordinary circumstances a gain of several percentage points of GDP would be considered very large. For example, the gains that were expected from the internal market programme of the EU are of a similar order of magnitude. However, the CIS countries were not in ordinary circumstances. The transition process and policy errors had already caused output to drop by more than 20 per cent. The bilateral nature of the system that emerged in 1992–3 can thus not have been responsible for most of the output decline that actually occurred and the creation of a multilateral system would not have been sufficient to reverse the decline. But eliminating one-fourth or one-fifth of the overall decline would still have been a substantial contribution.

Another way to measure the potential importance of a multilateral mechanism for the CIS, relative to the European experience, is to look at the experience of the European Payments Union (EPU) that was created after the Second World War. The EPU is the standard by which all plans to create a payments union for Eastern Europe have been measured (see Eichengreen 1993 and Gros 1993). Most analyses of the EPU emphasise one important difference: the EPU covered a large proportion of world trade as all European countries (plus their overseas dependencies) participated in the system. It is thus in a certain sense unfair to use the EPU as a yardstick. However, the result is still interesting. For the first year of its operations, 1950–1, clearing under the EPU, that is, the difference between the sum of the bilateral and the multilateral imbalances, was equivalent to about 1 per cent of the GDP of EPU member countries at that time, much less than the potential for the CIS identified so far. The reduction in trade that would have come with strict bilateral balancing (relative to unrestricted multilateral trade) would have been about 20 per cent, the same as for the CIS.

The estimates of the gain from multilateralism presented here are based on past intra-FSU trade data. This trade was expected to diminish sharply in the long run. The results based on 1987 data thus overstate the importance of intra-FSU trade in the long run, and some adjustment towards the long run had already taken place by 1992. The real question is, however, whether this adjustment takes place gradually within an environment in which firms choose to shift their exports in response to market forces, or whether entire markets are suddenly cut off by the lack of a multilateral payment system. Even if one assumes that the shift away from the old trade patterns would anyway have led 'naturally' to a reduction of intra-FSU trade by 50 per cent (within one year!), the potential contribution of a multilateral clearing system would still have been significant. In terms of percentage of GDP, this could have been even more important than the EPU.

There is, however, some evidence suggesting that the estimates based on 1987 data underestimate the economic costs of the breakdown of intra-CIS trade. An analysis of the output decline across a number of Russian industries suggests that the decline in intra-FSU trade had a significant impact on the output decline. Duchene and Gros (1994) regress the output decline in a number of products/sectors of the Russian economy against a number of sectoral indicators, such as the share of oil input, the share of output going to the military, the increase in profitability resulting from a switch to world market prices, to name only the most important. Most of these indicators are not significantly correlated with the decline in output in 1990–2. However, there is one indicator that shows a robust and significant relationship: the share of gross output going to other republics. The estimated coefficient is about 0.35 to 0.39. Since, in 1990, 18 per cent on average of output went to the rest of the FSU, it implies that a reduction in intra-FSU trade by 50 per cent could explain a fall in output in Russia of about 3 per cent. The actual decline in intra-FSU trade was probably much larger, but this is impossible to document. While this is only a fraction of the overall drop in output in Russia, it is still a substantial cost that might have been avoided or mitigated. For the other FSU countries the cost must have been much higher since their economies depended much more on intra-FSU trade. Not all of this decline was due to bilateralism, but since the Interstate Bank would also have improved the intra-CIS payments system in general, it should have helped to avoid a considerable part of this decline in trade.

## The Interstate Bank

The treaty on the creation of the Interstate Bank (IB) was signed in January 1993. This institution was planned to run a multilateral payments system for the CIS. It would thus have overcome the bilateralism of the correspondent accounts with the positive effects mentioned above.

However, the IB never started to operate. What were the reasons for this failure to implement an agreement that promised sizeable economic gains? There are two main reasons that should be kept in mind, because they have implications for future efforts to arrange cooperation between CIS states.

The first symptomatic reason for the failure of the IB project was a typical collective action problem: no particular CIS state had an incentive to take the initiative (and possibly incur some political costs) to push for the creation of the IB because most of the benefits would anyway accrue to all the other states. The (narrowly defined) self-interest of Russia was anyway not served by the creation of a multilateral system because the power of Russia could be brought to bear much more effectively on a bilateral basis.

The second symptomatic reason for the failure of the IB project lies in the nature of the public service in Russia and elsewhere in the CIS. Lower and middle-ranking officials do not always carry out decisions taken at the top, especially if these decisions run counter to their own interests. This lack of discipline, coupled with a pervasive corruption, was actually the main reason for the overall failure of stabilisation in Russia. The creation of the IB would have severely limited the discretionary power of some officials at the CBR to decide which transfers to other CIS states should go through. This is the main reason why the CBR in particular showed little interest in setting up the IB.

Finally, there was, and still is, a deep-seated tendency in many CIS countries to wait for Russia to take the initiative. However, Russia never took the necessary steps to set up the Interstate Bank because there was no strong political motive to do so – Russian leaders felt, correctly, that Russia did not need such an institution since it ran a surplus with all CIS countries. Finally, there was considerable opposition from some of the radical reformers in the Russian government against any official payments mechanism. The basic reason for this opposition was that the IB would lead to more pressure on Russia to extend cheap credit. This was basically a political judgement since the charter of the IB explicitly excluded any further credit. The overall argument, strongly supported by the IMF, was that convertibility is 'first best' and, in the view of the IMF, attainable immediately, so that there was no need to discuss anything else!

An additional reason the IB was not created is that it has proven extremely difficult to create any type of public institution in Russia. Given that the gain for Russia would have been small, a weak opposition was sufficient to stop all the practical steps that were needed to set up the IB.

## 7.6   Conclusions

In some ways, the story of the dissolution of the FSU is one of missed opportunities. During the last years of the Soviet Union, the adoption of strict macroeconomic policies at the Union level, combined with a substantial devolution of powers to the republics to foster competition in economic reforms, would have allowed the reforms to start much earlier and would have diminished the transitional costs.

The main reason why these opportunities were missed is that extreme and simplistic positions determined the debate about economic relations among the FSU states. On the one side, it was argued that the currency separation should have been faster, because the ill-defined rouble zone that existed in 1992–3 was inflationary, and that the collapse of intra-FSU trade was desirable because that trade had not been driven by the market. On the other, it was argued that, because of the high degree of integration of the economies of the former Soviet republics, a common currency should be maintained to preserve the existing trade links.

These two extreme positions do not stand up to close analysis. While the level of inter-republican trade was clearly excessive, it did have its own logic. It is therefore not surprising that the collapse of this trade contributed to the decline of production even in Russia. The problems of the disorganised rouble zone of 1992–3 came mainly from inconsistencies in Russia's policies. One cannot argue that expansionary policies in the other CIS states under-mined Russia's attempt to stabilise when wage increases and rates of monetary expansion were lower outside Russia.

The economic analysis thus reveals that the separation was inevitable; attempts to maintain an economic and monetary union were doomed from the start. However, the speed with which the existing trade links were disrupted made the process of separation very costly for all the countries that were once Soviet republics. This adds to the other reasons, discussed in chapter 4, for the dismal first decade of independence with a 'market'-based economy.

## Notes

1. Aitken (1973) uses annual data for a sample of seven EFTA and the five original EC countries (Belgium-Luxembourg counts as one for this purpose). His results do not vary from year to year; we compare ours with his 1967 results. H&P have two different samples with the data averaged over 1980–2. We use their results for a group of 21 countries for the comparison below. W&W have the largest sample, 76 countries, and also average their data (over 1984–6).

These comparators used roughly the same explanatory variables; however, in some cases income and population were only used separately, not in the combination income and income per capita (i.e. income/population). We decided therefore to rearrange the coefficients to make them comparable. Whenever we did this we do not report the *t*-statistics, as they are no longer applicable. The overall fit of the equation and the coefficient estimates of the other variables are obviously not affected by this procedure.

2. An anomaly appears in the coefficients of area, which should have a negative sign because they represent transport costs within the country. For the home country, $i$, our coefficient is consistent with this presupposition (and the findings of the comparators), but for the partner region, $j$, we find a significant positive sign. This is puzzling.

3. The most important explanatory variable is always income. For the elasticity of trade with respect to the income of the home country (country $i$) our coefficients are similar to those obtained for market economies.

   However, the coefficients regarding the influence of per-capita output reveal some important differences: while we have a similar result to W&W (around 0.3), H&P find a value of 1 for the home country $i$. For the partner country $j$, the comparators find a significant coefficient, equal to 0.22 in H&P and W&W and 0.15 in Aitken, whereas we find a negative sign; but our coefficient is not significant.

4. The other two studies find a much higher elasticity: H&P find $(-1.56)$ and W&W find $(-0.75)$. However the difference between our results and the two recent estimates could be due to the fact that the latter include a number of maritime distances. This is not the case in inter-republican trade and in the sample of European countries used by Aitken where most trade is via land (or river).

5. In 1987 the sum of the value added of inland transport services, maritime and direct transport services, auxiliary transport services plus communication services, was 201.9 bn ecu, compared to a total value added (GDP) of 3,320 bn ecu. These same sectors employed 6.3 million workers out of a total European workforce of 106.5 million.

6. It is worth emphasising that this approach deals only with the *geographical distribution of the volume* of trade. It has nothing to say about the product composition of trade, nor about bilateral (or even overall) balances.

7. The results from the estimations of the old intra-Soviet Union trade are not used here, because it might be objected that this would perpetuate Soviet trade patterns. This objection is groundless because the parameter estimates are similar. Hence it does not really matter which set of parameter estimates one uses.

8. Initially these so-called central banks consisted of little more than a president with a secretary. Even in Ukraine, the largest republic after Russia, the headquarters of the NBU numbered only a dozen employees in February 1992.

9. This dictum is commonly attributed to Stanley Fischer.

10. After the attempted August 1991 coup, a treaty on an economic and monetary union to be composed of twelve former republics was concluded and signed by some at Alma Ata. This treaty was never implemented and became irrelevant when the CIS was created in December 1991. The economist Gregory Yavlinsky who had been nominated Prime Minister of the Union after the failed putsch, was then succeeded, as Prime Minister of Russia, by a proponent of the 'Russia first' approach, Yegor Gaidar.

11. Controls on the movements of bank accounts (i.e. non-cash in the Soviet terminology) are in principle not sufficient, since the other CIS countries could print substitute roubles (in the form of coupons, etc.); not that rouble banknotes could come back to Russia, but this effect had to be limited. Once all rouble notes had concentrated on Russia there could be no further inflationary effect for Russia from the printing of coupons and other rouble substitutes in other countries of the FSU. Since the cash that was held outside Russia at the beginning of 1992 accounted probably

for more than 50 per cent of the total 'Soviet cash', substitute roubles could be responsible for, at most, a doubling of the cash component of the monetary base in Russia. Viewed against the almost tenfold increase of cash (in Russia) during 1992 this effect could never have been the main cause of inflation. Moreover, later events showed that Soviet roubles were held in considerable quantities outside Russia.

12. For many CIS countries the value of the oil imported from Russia would have been larger than their entire GDP if world market prices had been applied.

13. Representatives of the IMF have repeatedly denied that they put any pressure on the other CIS countries. They maintain that the IMF had only asked them to choose between a common central bank and a national currency. However, from the point of view of the Central Asian countries it was out of the question to introduce a national currency in 1992. This is why the IMF was perceived as putting pressure to sign an agreement on a joint central bank.

14. In case the German exporter does not insist on being paid immediately (or if a German bank is willing to provide an export credit) Germany exports capital. However, in this case the fact that the Estonian central bank issues credits in DM (as opposed to kroons) is irrelevant. German economic agents will extend this credit anyway only if they expect that they will be repaid in the future. An inflationary impact in Germany could arise only if the Bundesbank provided an implicit bailout guarantee for German banks that lend to foreigners in DM, so that the German monetary base increases automatically when there is a default by foreign borrowers. Of course, if German banks extended credits at highly negative real interest rates the German authorities would intervene and try to stop these gifts to foreigners. However, this is a different question that has nothing to do with the control of inflation in Germany.

# 8  Russia: after a lost decade the phoenix rises from the ashes?

Evaluating Russia is not straightforward – and has never been. In 1925, Keynes summed up his impression of the new economic system as follows:

> The economic system of Russia has undergone such rapid changes that it is impossible to obtain a precise and accurate account of it . . . Almost everything one can say about the country is true and false at the same time.

Keynes's statement remains valid today. Judgements on the effectiveness of the reforms in Russia from international institutions, academics and the press have ranged across the entire spectrum from very optimistic to extremely pessimistic. The best example of Russo-mania remains probably Layard and Parker's (1996) title *The Coming Russian Boom*. This boom had a rather short life, but predictions of descent into hyperinflationary chaos and disintegration after the crisis of 1998 proved equally wide of the mark. It is thus not easy to provide an overall judgement of the reforms in Russia as already anticipated by Keynes seventy-five years earlier. Hence, this chapter does not pretend to provide a comprehensive overview of developments in Russia over the last decade. Instead it concentrates on the most salient features of the reform process in Russia, often comparing them to what happened in Central Europe (especially Russia's largest Slav brother, Poland) in order to find some general features that can help in understanding how the Russian economy works in general, and where it might be going in the future.

In 2000 the verdict on 'ten years of transition' in Russia seemed clear: a lost decade.[1] A comparison with Poland is instructive. At the end of the previous decade, the 1980s, Poland was in such a deep crisis that widespread famine was feared and many in the West had given up hope. By contrast the Soviet Union while also visibly under strain, was still functioning and had a very strong natural-resource base. Ten years later the perspective was completely different: Poland was growing vigorously whereas the Soviet Union had become only a distant memory and the economy of Russia had almost collapsed in 1998 under the weight of its foreign debt after a currency crisis. The comparison with Poland illustrates what difference a decade can make in terms of real income. Setting the GDP of Poland and Russia for 1988 equal to 100, Poland reached almost 120 by the end of the millennium. A cumulative increase of 20 per cent over ten years might not be impressive, but it is quite an achievement compared with Russia, which recorded a *fall* in income of almost 50 per cent over the same period. This means that the Polish reform delivered more than double the results of the Russian in the space of a decade.

How did Russia get into such a mess? At the outset the position of the Soviet Union, and in particular that of the Russian republic, looked much the stronger: it had vast resources of oil, gas and other minerals and could count on a very large military–industrial complex. The fundamental reason must be that the similarity in the official reform rhetoric often masked a quite different reality, and that Russia made the crucial mistake of relying too heavily on fickle international capital markets.

A few years after Russia had been written off by the West it seemed to have risen phoenix-like from the ashes: robust growth combined with internal political stability had transformed Russia into an anchor for a volatile region. How could this happen? We argue that in several instances there were self-reinforcing mechanisms at work which implied that small shocks could have very large effects.

The structure of this chapter is as follows: after describing the developments that led to the reform process in 1992, section 2 analyses the circumstances of the 'big-bang' price liberalisation of January 1992. The main conclusion here is that the very large size of the jump in prices, which was politically costly for the reformers, could have been anticipated. Moreover, the benefits of price liberalisation did not become apparent as quickly as in other reforming economies because local and regional price controls persisted for some time and there was no immediate reaction from the supply side because of the desolate state of the agricultural sector.

External liberalisation, discussed in section 3, was another area where it should have been possible to achieve results quickly. A closer look shows, however, that substantial distortions remained, at least until the end of 1993. The verdict on privatisation is also mixed (section 4). While privatisation proceeded quickly on paper, it did not lead to efficiency until firms faced a clear budget constraint. The mistakes committed in both areas had negative budgetary effects, which contributed, perhaps decisively, to the delay of stabilisation for a number of years, as discussed in section 5. Stabilisation was finally achieved, but it was built initially on weak foundations, namely foreign capital. The speculative attack of August 1998 proved so damaging because huge capital flight had left the government with a foreign debt it could not service unless it received continuously fresh capital.

One common thread that emerges from this analysis is the large discrepancy between appearance and reality. During the early years, the actions of the Russian government had little to do with their official programmes. When this is combined with the virtual absence of market institutions and enforcement mechanisms for private sector contracts, one can begin to see why the reform process has had only partial success.

Section 6 touches briefly on the question 'Who lost Russia?', much discussed during the 1990s. While Russia was not lost in the end, it still lost a decade. If the real question is why stabilisation was not achieved in 1992–3 despite large official aid flows, the answer has two parts: Russia is to blame because, given the massive subsidies to imports, most of the aid that was actually delivered, namely trade credits, had a negative impact. More of that sort of aid would have made matters worse. However, even given the (wrong) policies pursued by Russia, the right sort of aid, namely direct subsidies to the budget, could have increased the chances of achieving stabilisation. It takes two to tango (meaning, in this case, to produce a failure): more aid for the reformers would have been desirable, but if the reformers had been smarter in using the aid that was available, they could have achieved stabilisation at a much earlier date.

The reader should be warned from the outset that any accurate analysis of the Russian economy is made extremely difficult by the absence of reliable statistical data. Prices (foreign exchange rates, commodity prices, etc.) can be measured without great difficulty and are regularly recorded in the Russian business press. But serious problems arise for variables that require calculations and adjustments or are based on data from many different sources. The problems are most severe on the external side. To give just one example: the estimates for Russian imports based on customs data and those based on national accounts differ by as much as 50 per cent. The corresponding estimates of the trade surplus for example, in 1996, were therefore also very different: 38 billion versus 17 billion US dollars. We do not wish to go as far as Ericson and Ickes (2000), who claim that Russia's economy is only 'virtual'. But there is an element of truth: the impression of the Russian economy one gets from official statistics resembles sometimes the façades of happy villages set up by Prince Potemkin in the eighteenth century to impress his empress.

## 8.1   Setting the stage

### *Preliminaries*

This section provides a brief description of the political developments that led to the late start of the reform process in 1992. It is not widely appreciated that the partial reforms before 1992 were important because they set the stage for what happened later.

The Russian state in its present form is young, since it emerged only in December 1991 from the ruins of the Soviet Union. The beginning of the reforms in January 1992 thus coincided with the creation of a new state. The main reason that fundamental reforms started so late was that Mikhail Gorbachev persisted in his belief that socialism was superior to capitalism. As long as Gorbachev was the head of the Soviet Union (as First Party Secretary of the CPSU and later as President of the Soviet Union), no real reforms were possible.

The movement towards reforms acquired momentum only when Boris Yeltsin, then only President of the RSFSR (Russian Soviet Federated Socialist Republic), acquired more effective power than the Union government under Gorbachev by standing up publicly to the attempted putsch in August of 1991. Immediately after the failed putsch, it still seemed that it would be possible to keep the Soviet Union together, at least as an economic and monetary union. That would have implied that reforms would have to take place at the Union level. In the last three months of 1991, however, the Union government rapidly lost most of its influence and the republics became the only real power centres. Moreover, most republics were not willing to contemplate radical reforms, whereas the leadership of the Russian republic, which had inherited most of the reformist elements of the Union government, was determined to act as quickly as possible. Nevertheless, the Russian government did not really have the legal and political means to proceed on its own as long as the Soviet Union continued to exist. The creation of the Commonwealth of Independent States (CIS) and the dissolution of the Soviet Union in December 1991 finally gave Russia the chance to start real reforms.

When the Gaidar government came to power in Russia at the end of 1991, it proposed to implement a package of radical reform and stabilisation measures. The intention then was certainly to effect a 'big bang' in Russia, even if these words might not have been used. Two years later, the leading reformers (Deputy Prime Minister Yegor Gaidar and Finance Minister Boris Fyodorov) left government and explained to the Western press that Russia's problem was not that it had undergone shock therapy, but that, on the contrary, there had been no shock at all (and by implication, no therapy). What went wrong? Before addressing this question it is useful to take into account the background of numerous reform plans developed while the Soviet Union was decaying.

## Background: failed reform plans in the last years of the Soviet Union

January 1992 certainly opened with a 'big bang' in the form of 300 per cent price rises in the first days of that month. This indicated that a very serious disequilibrium had built up during the previous regime. In order to understand why it had come to that point, it is useful to consider briefly the last years of the Soviet period.

The 'big bang' that was supposed to take place in Russia in January 1992 came after a long period during which a number of competing reform plans had been discussed, but nothing much had been done. Indeed, reform projects enjoyed a long tradition in the Soviet economy. The system of central planning never worked satisfactorily, even to the standards of its creators, and was therefore overhauled from time to time – since the Second World War, in 1957, 1965, and 1975. On top of that, the currency was changed in 1947 and 1961. None of these reforms, however, was supposed to change the nature of the system. Similarly, the various partial (and mini-) reforms attempted between 1985 and 1989 were also directed at increasing the efficiency of the existing system of central planning.

The partial and piecemeal reforms up to 1989 undermined the central planning system. This led to a deterioration of the economic situation because the plan could no longer be fully enforced and most of the non-state economic activities thrived on the distorted pricing system still in use. The 1987 law that gave enterprises a modest degree of financial autonomy can be viewed as the end of the strict planning period because enterprises could now evade constraints imposed from the 'centre' by initiating their own operations. This law loosened financial discipline and was thus the beginning of a considerable acceleration in the growth of the monetary overhang as documented in section 2 below. But this law also increased the incentive to export to the West, which initiated a shift in the export structure of the FSU that predates the collapse of the CMEA. Section 3 below shows that the shift in exports towards Western markets was already well advanced by 1991, so that the (partial) trade liberalisation of 1992 did not have a strong effect on trade patterns.

The general weakening of central control led in 1989–90 to the widespread admission that the entire system of central planning had to be abandoned. During the summer of 1990, three competing comprehensive reform plans for the transition to a market economy were presented to the Supreme Soviet of the Union, which was to adopt the necessary legislation. The Supreme Soviet, however, refused to approve any of the three plans. Instead, it gave President Gorbachev broad emergency powers and authorised him to present a plan of his own. The compromise plan presented by the president, called 'Basic Guidelines for the Stabilisation of the National Economy and the Transition to a Market Economy', was then approved by a large majority on 19 October 1990.

The president's guidelines, which were more general and political than the other three plans, became the official programme of the Union government, but their implementation was checked by the constitutional crisis that developed between the Union and the republics.[2] The economic situation continued to deteriorate. Prices had to be increased and a clumsy attempt by the Ryshkov government in April 1991 to confiscate large-denomination notes was a complete failure. In May 1991 the Union government again presented a vague outline of a reform plan, concentrating on macroeconomic stabilisation.

The four major plans that dominated the discussion in 1990–1 all agreed on three final goals: a market economy, stabilisation, and the preservation of the Soviet Union as a unified economic space. Furthermore, all of these plans contained most of the necessary elements outlined in part II of this book.[3]

None of these programmes could be implemented, however, as long as President Gorbachev did not really believe in a market economy. Moreover, even timid reform measures were impossible as long as there persisted the 'war of laws', under which each republic passed a declaration of sovereignty stating that its laws would take precedence over Union law, whereas the Union government insisted that Union law would take precedence. The implementation of reforms would have required an agreement (in effect, a new Union treaty) that defined the powers of the republics and the Union. Such an agreement was reached in May 1991, but the aborted coup of August of that year set in motion a chain of events that led to the dissolution of the Soviet Union.

Towards the end of 1991, it became clear that only the nascent Russian state would be able to implement reforms. The Russian President Yeltsin then created a government with a group of economists, led by Yegor Gaidar, which was charged with the elaboration and implementation of a comprehensive reform plan. Since this new team was installed only late in 1991, and since the political environment was changing quickly, it is not surprising that the plan was elaborated in detail only in early 1992, i.e. after its key element, namely price liberalisation, had already been implemented. However, given that the deterioration of the economy accelerated with the overall breakdown of authority, the Russian government did not really have a choice.

## 8.2   Price liberalisation with a 'big bang'

### *The first disappointment*

The liberalisation of prices that occurred in early 1992 was thus inevitable, given the accelerating loss of control of the government, rather than a deliberate choice that could have been avoided. The most outstanding feature of price liberalisation in Russia is the size of the jump in the price level that occurred almost instantaneously. At the end of January 1992, the consumer price level was almost four times higher than at the end of December 1991 (an increase of 280 per cent). Industrial producer prices increased by 100 percentage points more. But even if one is only concerned with consumer prices, the Russian experience is extreme when compared with those of other reforming economies.

It is difficult to decide whether the entire impact of price reform should come within the first month or whether it takes longer for the monetary overhang to be eliminated. Table 8.1 shows what happened during the first month and the first quarter after price reform or price liberalisation. The table shows the percentage increase in both prices and money (cash in circulation) to segregate the impact of price reform from that of an expansionary monetary policy that might also have had an influence on prices. It is apparent that for the first month,

Table 8.1. *The impact of price liberalisation*

| Country/(month of price reform) | Percentage increase in the PPI after price reform | |
|---|---|---|
| | in 1st month | in 1st quarter |
| FSU (4/91) | 52 (7.3) | 71 (21.7) |
| Russia (1/92) | 296 (13.6) | 518 (42.9) |
| Poland (8/89) | 40 | n.a. |
| Poland (10/89) | 55 (18.3) | 124 (63.4) |
| Poland (1/90) | 80 (12.4) | 115 (91.5) |
| Czechoslovakia (1/91) | 26 | 41 |
| Bulgaria (1/91) | 123 | n.a. |

*Note*: The figures in parentheses represent the percentage increase in money over the same period, where money is defined as cash in circulation (where data were available). *Source*: Koen and Philips (1993) and IMF, *International Financial Statistics*, various issues.

the increase in money is so small compared with that of the price level that one can neglect its impact. However, after one quarter, the potential influence of monetary policy, while still small in most cases, can no longer be neglected.

Table 8.1 presents data for three distinct periods in Poland, two of which were a combination of partial price liberalisation and administrative price increases under the last communist government. These episodes represent a key to understanding what happened in Russia, as argued below. The data show clearly that Russia had by far the highest price jump among the group of four economies with rapid price liberalisation. The second highest increase was about 120 per cent in Bulgaria. By contrast, in Poland it was 'only' 80 per cent during the first month of final price liberalisation in January of 1990, which is usually considered to be the Polish 'big bang'. If one considers the first quarter following price liberalisation, the difference is even larger: in Russia, prices increased by 518 per cent, almost five times more than in Poland, where the increase during the first three months of 1990 was 115 per cent.

The extent of the price increase in Russia surprised the government (and most observers), although by the end of 1991, the ratio of free to controlled prices had reached multiples of five (Koen and Phillips 1993). For example, the IMF had calculated before the reforms took place that a jump in the price level of around 50 per cent would be sufficient to eliminate the monetary overhang (see IMF et al. 1991 and Cottarelli and Blejer 1992).

Gros and Steinherr (1995) argue that, with a better analysis of the historical data on money supplies and a closer examination of the Polish experience, the size of the jump in prices could have been anticipated to a large extent. The basic argument is that in Russia price liberalisation merely allowed the velocity of circulation of cash to return to the value it had in the 1960s, i.e. before the accumulation of the monetary overhang. The headline jump in prices on 1 January 1990 in Poland that is commonly associated with the start of reforms there was much smaller, but it was not sufficiently appreciated that a large part of the monetary overhang had already been eliminated in Poland under the communist regime during 1989. In Poland the total increase in prices over the five-month period that starts with the partial price liberalisation in August 1989, and ends just before the final price liberalisation in January 1990, was 400 per cent, whereas the increase in the money supply during the same period was 123 per cent; real money had thus already halved. By contrast, the price increase of about 120 per cent in the FSU between April and December 1991, before the price liberalisation of 1992, did not really dent the monetary overhang since the money supply had increased by about the same amount (110 per cent) (Gros and Steinherr 1995).

The Solidarność government thus inherited a much better starting position than the Gaidar team in Russia because a large part of the monetary overhang had already been eliminated.[4] This explains why the price increase in January 1990 turned out to be 'moderate' in Poland, at least in comparison with Russia.

The much larger than expected price increase in Russia was not just an embarrassment for economists; it also constituted a severe setback for all the other reform measures that were planned for 1992. The extreme and sudden increase in prices gave a lot of ammunition to the conservative opponents of Yeltsin who came to dominate the Russian parliament, which then effectively blocked many reforms until the crisis of September–October 1993.[5]

## *The political economy of price liberalisation in Russia*

The perceived fall in living standards that came with price liberalisation became a major argument against further reforms. Part of the popular discontent with the reformers was undoubtedly due to the fact that, as consumer prices rose almost fourfold in January 1992, measured real wages were cut to about one-third of their (measured) end-of-1991 level. The anti-reformist camp obviously seized this apparent fall in real wages as the best proof that the reforms were 'misguided' or 'hasty'. In other countries, notably Poland, similar arguments had also been used, but the size of the price increase in Russia meant that, given that wages did not rise along with prices in January 1992, measured real wages also fell by much more in Russia than in other reforming economies.

On impact (i.e. comparing December 1991 to January 1992), measured real wages fell in Russia to about one-third of their previous level, more than in Poland, where measured real wages fell to about one-half, and in Czechoslovakia, where they fell by only 20 per cent. However, it is by now generally accepted that these reductions in real wages were mostly a statistical artefact – in the last years, sometimes months, of the socialist system workers obtained large increases in nominal wages with which they were unable to buy anything since production was already declining. This had been particularly pronounced during the last days of the Soviet Union.

It is thus clear that one cannot compare wages deflated by the price level immediately before and after price reforms. A more appropriate comparison would use a base year in which shortages were minimal. Koen and Phillips (1993) argue that 1987 represents a good base year. If one thus compares real wages in 1992 to their level in 1987 the result is quite different. In 1992, real wages stabilised after an initial strong dip at about 20 per cent below the measured 1987 level. Most of the huge cuts in measured real wages that one finds when looking at the first months thus disappear if a more appropriate base period is used.

The drop in real wages in Russia, using 1987 as the base period, was similar to the one that occurred in the Central European countries. However, this should be viewed as an anomaly. In principle there should have been a stronger recovery of real wages in Russia than in other transforming countries because, with the dissolution first of Comecon and later of the Soviet Union, Russia no longer had to subsidise the other countries and republics with cheap energy and raw materials. The latter did not happen immediately, but by the end of 1993 even most former Soviet republics were charged world market prices for energy deliveries (although most 'paid' initially only in arrears). Russia thus reaped a considerable terms-of-trade gain. By contrast, the Central European countries had to accept a terms-of-trade loss. Hence real wages should have been able to increase during 1992 and 1993 in Russia; however, if anything, they have declined even further continuously along with production.

In Russia price liberalisation, while inevitable given the lack of effective control of the government over the economy, could not become popular given the continuing fall in production. The immediate gains from price liberalisation can only be small as price liberalisation per se does not affect the size of the overall cake to be distributed – only its distribution. In Poland a flexible agricultural sector increased immediately the supply of food, but this was not possible in the unreformed Soviet-type agriculture of Russia. Moreover, Polish enterprises quickly switched production to new products and markets (in the West). This quick change was the result of external competition since privatisation took much longer to implement. The Russian reformers were, of course, aware of the need for external liberalisation, which was part of their platform. However, the next section will show that in this area reality was quite different from perception and serious errors were made.

It is sometimes argued that external liberalisation should be less important for a large country such as Russia. But the Russian economy is as open to trade as the Polish economy. The ratio of trade (average of exports and imports) to GDP is around 25 per cent for both economies (in Russia it varies much more with the exchange rate of the rouble).

## 8.3   External liberalisation

### *Liberalisation of international trade*

Full external liberalisation can in principle be achieved with the stroke of a pen. However, this was not the case in Russia in 1992. In most evaluations of the Russian reforms, it is stressed that imports were almost completely liberalised, in the sense that in January 1992 quantitative restrictions were abolished and only in July was a flat import tariff of 5 per cent levied. The problem with the policy on imports was not trade barriers, but in a sense the opposite, namely the huge budgetary subsidies given to state trading organisations that paid only a fraction of the world market price for their imports. During 1992, these subsidies amounted to over 10 per cent of GDP. As shown in Gros and Steinherr (1995), the distortions caused by these subsidies led to welfare losses of possibly up to 10 per cent of

GDP. Fortunately, these import subsidies were reduced considerably in the course of 1992 and completely phased out in 1993 (Konovalov 1994).

However, even more serious problems arose on the export side as the initially very liberal stance on imports contrasted starkly with the regime that was retained for exports of raw materials and energy which had to be controlled because domestic prices of these goods had not been liberalised. The government evidently feared that most of the large industrial enterprises would go bankrupt if they had to pay world market prices for energy and other raw material inputs. The reasons for this decision are not important for this section. What matters is that these products accounted for about 75 per cent of all Russian exports. In view of the 'Lerner symmetry theorem' (Lerner 1936), which states that an export tariff is equivalent to an import tariff, one cannot speak of trade liberalisation if most exports are subject to restrictions.

The maintenance of restrictions on the exports side was necessitated by the price controls on energy (and other raw materials) that continued in 1992 and 1993. (See appendix 8.1 on the importance of raw materials for the Russian economy.) Although the official prices of oil, gas and electricity were increased from time to time, their dollar equivalents did not always come close to the world market price. The ratio of domestic price to world price was thus highly variable for these goods, but the domestic price was typically only a fraction of the world market price, as shown in Gros and Steinherr (1995).

It is difficult to find the precise reason for the price difference for each product as there is not always an explicit export tax and/or export quota that could account for it. Instead of going through the official records of export regulations, one can simply use the proportional price differential as a crude approximation of the (ad valorem) export tariff that is equivalent to the export restrictions that were actually applied. This approximation is not exact since it neglects transport costs and exchange-rate fluctuations that make it difficult to determine the exact world price compared to the price quoted on the Russian commodity exchanges. However, the orders of magnitude that this exercise yields are revealing.

Gros and Steinherr (1995) calculate that the implicit export tax on energy-related products must have exceeded 100 per cent most of the time. Since energy alone accounted for 50 per cent of overall exports and since for other raw materials (like aluminium, which accounted for another 25 per cent of exports) a similar differential between domestic and world market prices existed, about 75 per cent of all exports were thus implicitly taxed at this rate. In view of the equivalence between export and import tariffs mentioned above, one can only conclude that the liberalisation of Russian trade in 1992 was partial, at best.[6] Exports picked up only after the 1998 crisis. As we will argue below, this was due not only to the real devaluation that took place then, but was even more a consequence of the fact that hard budget constraints were imposed for the first time after this crisis.

## Fiscal consequences of porous borders

It proved impossible for the Russian government to enforce the official restrictions on raw material exports. The main reason was that initially Russia did not have a customs service along its borders with other former Soviet republics. The huge difference between the domestic Russian price and the world market price for oil and other raw materials meant that large gains could be made by transporting these commodities to other former republics and then re-exporting them for hard currency. On top of that must be factored the notorious corruption of the Russian civil service, which was exposed to extraordinary temptations. The price difference on a simple shipment of 20,000 litres of fuel on a single truck would be worth $2,000, several times the annual salary of a Russian customs official.

How much in potential government revenue was lost? This is difficult to estimate precisely, since the official tariffs changed over time. However, a crude calculation can indicate the order of magnitude: in 1992 Russia exported about $20 bn worth of energy products and other raw materials. Given that the implicit export tariff was about 100 per cent, the Russian government should have been able to collect at least $10 bn (50 per cent of export sales at world market prices) in tariff revenues from these exports. At the average 1992 exchange rate of about 250 roubles to the dollar, the loss of revenue was thus equivalent to 2.5 trillion roubles. This should be compared to total government revenues of about 5.3 trillion roubles and an official deficit of 650 billion roubles (3.3 per cent of revised GDP). The official 1992 budget deficit could thus have been easily covered from this source, which alone would have increased government revenues by 50 per cent. This is of course a very crude calculation. But it serves to indicate the order of magnitude of the problem. Revenue losses of a similar, but somewhat smaller magnitude could be calculated for subsequent years as well. This loss of tariff revenues persisted for quite some time. The IMF (see Gray 1998) calculated for 1995 that only about one half of the revenue the government could expect from the oil and gas sector was actually collected. For 1998 the EBRD reports a ratio of tariff revenues to imports of about 7 per cent, whereas the official average tariff rate was over 15 per cent.

Who obtained the revenues the government lost? This is impossible to determine precisely; most went presumably to producers and agents in energy trade. A significant part was also given away directly as the government granted many exemptions to particular regions or producers.

## Export performance

'The proof of the pudding is in the eating.' The proof of a substantial liberalisation of foreign trade is the strong growth in exports and imports. On this account the picture is mixed, but compatible with the view that trade liberalisation came on later when (implicit and explicit) export restrictions were abolished. There are no reliable trade data for the years surrounding the break-up of the Soviet Union. Russian export statistics suggest that the exports of Russia were flat in 1992 and 1993, but jumped by almost 70 per cent between 1993 and 1999. This delayed reaction is quite different from the Polish experience. Polish exports increased considerably during the first year of reforms as even state-owned enterprises were not blind to the profit opportunities that arose when wages were only about $100 per month.[7] Since most of Russia's exports are raw materials, the supply of which does not react strongly to wages and the real exchange rate, one should perhaps look at exports of manufacturing goods only. However, as documented in Gros and Steinherr (1995), exports of manufactured goods from Russia also did not react to the official trade liberalisation and the low dollar wages.

It is often argued that a major achievement of the liberalisation of foreign trade was a redirection of trade away from the 'bad' trade with the socialist economies and less-developed countries that did not pay for their imports of Soviet weaponry, towards 'good' trade with Western economies based on market principles. However, as documented in Gros and Steinherr (1995), this redirection of trade had already started much earlier. Between 1986 (when the law on the partial financial liberalisation of enterprises mentioned above began to take effect) and 1991, the share of CMEA fell by a half, from about 40 to 20 per cent of overall exports. During the same period, the share of market economies approximately doubled, from about 30 to 60 per cent. By 1991, the adjustment was thus complete. In a sense this should not be surprising since the CMEA had ceased to exist by then. However, subsequent developments are more surprising in that, after 1992, the share of industrialised countries in Russian exports fell strongly and the share of the CIS countries, which for some time continued to represent 'soft' markets (with frequent barter and payment problems) increased again.

A more thorough analysis on the basis of the gravity model that takes into account market size and distance, presented in Brenton (1999), comes to a similar result: the geographical distribution of Russian exports does not correspond to the pattern one would expect if Russia were a fully fledged market economy. For example, the share of the EU-15 in Russian exports should be 42 per cent, but is only about 33 per cent. Conversely the share of other CIS countries (the 'soft' markets) is still close to 20 per cent, whereas one would expect that, given the small size of these economies, its equilibrium share should only be about 6 per cent when the transition is complete.

### The foreign exchange market

Progress was quicker on the issue of convertibility, which can also be achieved with the stroke of a pen (as long as the exchange rate is not fixed), since all that the government has to do is to allow anyone to buy or sell foreign currency without restrictions. Full current account convertibility was not permitted immediately, but in July 1992 the various exchange rates were unified and anyone with an import contract could then participate in the increasingly frequent auctions for foreign exchange. This implied that, from July 1992 onwards, the rouble was convertible for current account transactions. Given the laxity of controls, one could even argue that de facto convertibility also extended to capital account transactions. A large degree of capital account convertibility was officially permitted when, in the summer of 1993, non-residents were allowed to open rouble accounts, which they could also use for investment purposes.

Gros and Steinherr (1995) document that the foreign exchange market became quickly efficient in the technical sense by testing the so-called 'weak' form of market efficiency (which implies that information on past prices cannot be used to predict future prices). Formal tests of market efficiency indicate that the foreign exchange market in Russia was efficient almost from the start. Efficiency means in this context that the exchange rate did not follow any predictable pattern in general. This finding shows not only that financial markets adjusted quickly to the new environment, but also that, de facto, capital mobility existed early on. However, the crucial importance of de facto capital mobility became apparent only much later, during the collapse of the rouble in the summer of 1998.

## 8.4  Privatisation

Privatisation provides another illustration of the discrepancy between reformist rhetoric and reality. The privatisation process in Russia was extremely controversial from the beginning, and even today it is difficult to arrive at a final judgement. With hindsight three facts stand out:

(1)  Most of the Russian economy is now in private hands. This aspect is underlined by the defenders of the Yeltsin regime (see for example Boycko et al. 1996).

The negative aspects that dominated the political atmosphere are:

(2)  The most valuable state assets were given away to a small group of politically well-connected 'oligarchs'.
(3)  The Russian population remains convinced the entire process was totally corrupt.

Privatisation proceeded essentially in two steps: first the voucher approach was used for the bulk of industry, which consisted mostly of large enterprises of dubious profitability.[8] The energy sector, plus some other natural resource-based industries, which constituted the only profitable parts of the Russian economy, were later handed over to a small group of politically highly visible individuals, collectively called 'oligarchs' because of their wealth and their prominent role in engineering the re-election of President Yeltsin in 1996.

The formal privatisation process began in 1992 and was supposed to be a 'big bang' via the voucher approach. Each citizen was to be issued a voucher, which could be used to bid for shares in the thousands of enterprises that were on the initial privatisation list. However, the entire process became immediately bogged down in political infighting, which forced the government to allow insiders (workers and management) to acquire control (51 per cent) at extremely low prices. This option was used in 80 per cent of the cases. In most instances it was thus impossible for outsiders to acquire control with the vouchers.

Once the insiders had been appeased, mass privatisation proceeded relatively quickly and by the end of 1995 the process was essentially completed, with the bulk of Russia's industry no longer owned by the state. But insider control had become even stronger as managers and workers had actually increased their shareholdings at auctions and in most cases less than 25 per cent of share capital had been bought with the vouchers.

The relatively quick completion of the mass privatisation process (about two years) shows that insiders were eager to have their de facto control legalised. But the evolution of the value of the vouchers gives a better indication of the economic significance of mass privatisation in Russia.[9] The price initially was around $10; it then fluctuated within a narrow range with the political debate, rising when the fortunes of the reformers rose, and falling when the old timers seemed to get the upper hand. Towards the end of the process it settled down to $7–8. The value of the vouchers thus remained always a fraction of an average monthly wage. No wonder that the 'millions of owners' were not much impressed. This was not just due to the fact that Soviet-type industries are not worth a lot. In the Czech Republic the vouchers were worth several monthly salaries.[10]

That voucher privatisation was equivalent to a giveaway can be seen in another perspective: at about $7–8 per voucher the total value of the vouchers was about $1 bn (given that about 140 million of them were issued). This is about as much as the government raised in the loans for shares deal described below.

Enterprises that were deemed to be important for the 'national interest' were excluded from this first wave. This included most oil, gas and other natural resource-based companies (such as the world's biggest nickel mine), which were the only profitable ones and were supposed to be sold for cash. However the cash sales proceeded only slowly and the budget remained chronically in deficit. In late 1995 the cash-strapped government therefore accepted a proposal from major banks to pledge controlling stakes in twelve of the most profitable mineral resource-based enterprises as security on loans equivalent to about $1 billion. The loans were not repaid and the banks became owners of these enterprises. See Box 8.1.

The result of mass privatisation plus the shares for loans deal was that by about 1996 most of the Russian economy was no longer under state control and the reformers claimed victory. However, the process had alienated the overwhelming majority of the population and made the entire reform process very unpopular. Moreover, there were no sizeable economic gains to show. Despite stabilisation, the economy continued to contract for several years. Restructuring did start in some cases, but it remained painfully slow and was confined to a minority of enterprises so that the overall gains in productivity were generally modest. All this sparked a heated debate about what had gone wrong. Should privatisation have been postponed? Or should it have been done differently?

The key point one has to keep in mind in this debate is that already by 1992 the government was no longer able to control the managers in nominally state-owned enterprises. Hence it seemed to make sense to accept reality and allow managers to become also de jure owners. The counterargument starts from the same point: If privatisation just ratified the de facto control of insiders, why bother? Why should the reformers expend precious political capital and time for this goal? The key argument in favour of privatisation (see e.g. Shleifer and Treisman 2000) remains that privatisation made the de facto property right of managers tradable and would thus open the door to a more efficient allocation of resources. After all, the Coase theorem implies that an efficient allocation of resources can be achieved whatever the initial distribution of property rights. However, the Coase theorem can work only if transaction costs are negligible. This was definitely not the case in Russia, especially not during the rowdy period of the distribution of state assets.

A straightforward application of the Coase theorem would say that a more efficient allocation of resources can be achieved through takeovers. The value of the firm under an entrenched but inefficient management must be smaller than with an efficient outside management. To put it more crudely: Western experts familiar with world markets and modern technology should be able to increase the value of enterprises that had been mismanaged by

---

### Box 8.1    Loans for shares

Faced with the disappointing revenues generated by cash auctions, the government changed its privatisation strategy in late 1995. To finance the growing budget deficit government contracted loans for about $1 billion against the collateral of shares owned by the state in twelve profitable enterprises in the energy and other natural resource industries. The contracts granted banks the right to sell the shares in case of non-repayment of the credits and keep 30 per cent of the capital gains. Several features of this deal were curious:

- The tendering of the loan contracts clearly favoured certain banks connected to government.
- The loan amount was so large that the chances of repaying within the agreement's 9-month term were from the outset close to zero. Hence the real decision was to provide some selected banks with strategic shareholdings in the most profitable industries. And the timing was impeccable: loans matured just before the presidential election!
- The market value of the shares was much higher than the loan amount. Hence the 'winning' lenders stood a good chance of making large gains if government defaulted.
- But lending banks were contractually forced to auction off the shares and could only keep 30 per cent of the capital gain. How to get round these obligations?
- After the deadline passed in September 1996, banks began selling off the shares held in trust. They served both as organisers and bidders, and larger bids from outsiders were often disqualified on technical grounds. In most cases the trustholders themselves, or an affiliated company, bought the stock – at a price that limited the capital gain.
- The result of this scheme was the creation of conglomerates headed by an 'oligarch'. In recognition of the loans-for-shares deal, they supported Yeltsin in the 1996 election.
- Banks involved in the scheme stopped seeing an interest in maintaining high inflation. High inflation would have reduced the real value of the credits the government owed them and would have made it easier for the government to repay the loans. Once the shares were acquired, the new industrial conglomerates were also interested in reducing inflation as they planned to sell off some of the shares to foreign investors. And foreign investors are put off by uncontrolled inflation.

See Shleifer and Treisman (2000).

---

communist apparatchiks. The former should thus be able to buy out the latter. Privatisation should have made this possible. The expectations were that foreign capital would just buy out insiders, assume control and increase efficiency.

However, reality was quite different. Property rights, even when formalised on paper (shares), proved impossible to enforce and trade. The best illustration of this came when (naïve?) foreign investors tried to turn up at a crucial shareholder meeting of a very large and valuable mine located deep in Siberia. The legal representatives of these important shareholders were met by armed thugs, who prevented them from attending the meeting, at which a discretionary increase in capital was ratified, which transformed the foreign share holding into an insignificant minority stake.

While this is an extreme example, it does illustrate a general tendency: the ability of entrenched management to resist any encroachment on their de facto rights. Under these conditions formal privatisation meant very little.

Another key element that was missing in Russia was a hard budget constraint. The example of Poland shows that managers of state-owned enterprises, who are essentially on their own because the government can no longer control their day-to-day decisions, will re-structure their enterprises if that is the only way to ensure their own survival. By contrast, in Russia all enterprises faced rather soft budget constraints. The central bank distributed huge amounts of 'directed' credit at interest rates much below the rate of inflation and the price of energy remained controlled. These subsidies distorted incentives so much not only because of their sheer size, but even more so because of their discretionary nature. There were no clear rules for the distribution of the 'directed' credits, which remained largely under the control of middle-level officials. Moreover, payments discipline was not uniformly enforced, so that many enterprises could just refuse to pay for energy deliveries, to pay taxes or to service even the cheap directed credits.

The continuing availability of huge subsidies on essentially discretionary terms implied that, in Russia, the success of a manager would be measured by the amount of subsidised credit or cheap energy the enterprise received, rather than the ability to find new markets or reduce costs. As managers of private enterprises were in the same situation, privatisation did not really matter. All managers in Russia had become 'rent seekers'.

Soft budgets survived for some time. Directed credits were eliminated early on. But that meant little so long as political connections determined which debts had to be paid and who got cheap energy. These sources of implicit subsidies were brought under control only years later, when the Putin administration started to enforce existing laws and regulations. Privatisation only became really effective at this point. It is not surprising that this also marks the point at which growth finally started.

To sum up: privatisation was more difficult in Russia because of the weakness of the state and the huge discrepancy between the very profitable energy sector and the vast system of loss-making heavy industry, which occupied the bulk of the labour force. Privatisation did not lead initially to appreciable gains in economic efficiency, given that it just ratified the de facto control of managers over enterprises, and given that enforcement of property rights was so weak that it was generally impossible to unseat entrenched insiders. These – initially – small economic gains must be set against the huge political cost of privatisation making the reforms so unpopular in Russia.

In this sense privatisation was a failure in Russia. However, it was inevitable, as everywhere, so the only question is whether the political cost might have been lower if it had been postponed or implemented differently. Maybe the reformers had no better option, given the extreme weakness of the state. We would argue, however, that this extreme weakness of enforcement institutions should not be taken as a given. The entire transition process, not just privatisation, might have had much more success if the reformers had concentrated on strengthening institutions and worked on the details of implementation,

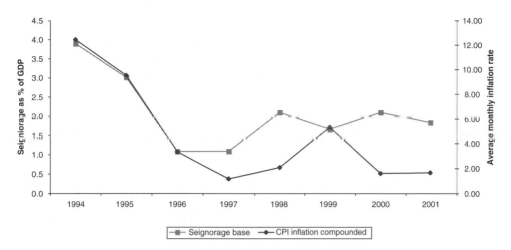

**Figure 8.1** Inflation and seigniorage

rather than squandering their limited political capital in pushing through ambitious paper schemes. Privatisation would have been less corrupt and thus less unpopular if it had come at a time when property rights could actually have been enforced. It would then have also yielded much larger revenues for the state budget.[11]

## 8.5 Macroeconomic instability

The reforms in Russia began with an increase in the price level of 280 per cent at the beginning of 1992. This was not the end of the story, however. Prices continued to increase at two-digit levels and the *monthly* average for the year excluding January was close to 20 per cent; the average for 1993 was similar. Average inflation fell below the one-digit level (always on a monthly basis) only in early 1994. Stabilisation took thus several years, much longer than in Central Europe, where inflation never took off. (See figure 8.1 for the evolution of the inflation rate). In this section we discuss three specific aspects of macroeconomic instability in Russia: the fiscal aspects of inflation; multiple equilibria in capital markets and the ability to service foreign debt; and how Russian banks captured regulators.

### *Inflationary finance*

The ultimate cause of high inflation is almost always a large fiscal deficit that is financed by the central bank. Russia is no exception to this rule, but its fiscal accounts are such a mess that it is impossible to document the underlying deficit.[12] Reported figures for the fiscal deficit during 1992 range from official Russian figures of 4.8 per cent of GDP, to IMF estimates of 7 per cent and private sector estimates of over 9 per cent. All these estimates leave out the import subsidies of 15 per cent of GDP that were discussed above. In the case of Russia one can therefore use just two statistics: cash in circulation (or more comprehensively, the monetary base, from the balance sheet of the CBR) and credits from the IMF. The first

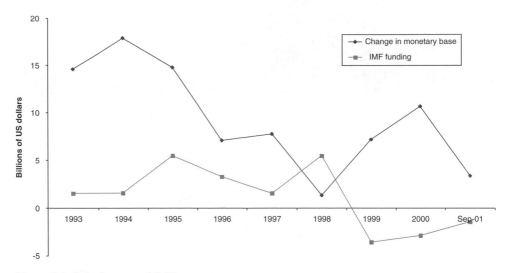

**Figure 8.2**  Seigniorage and IMF support

gives an indication of monetary financing (seigniorage); the second gives an indication of the amount of foreign aid that contributes to non-inflationary financing of the deficit.

Printing money obviously creates inflation. The very close link between inflation and seigniorage can be seen in figure 8.1, which shows both inflation and seigniorage (the increase in the monetary base) as a percentage of GDP. Seigniorage amounted to over 10 per cent of GDP during the early 1990s, but fell to little above 1 per cent during 1996 and 1997 before picking up again in 1998. The pick-up in seigniorage in 1998 came mainly during the second half. During the first half of this year the monetary base actually contracted. During this latter period the Russian government was thus able to finance its (continuing) deficit through non-inflationary means, and this led to the reduction in inflation. It is interesting to note that after the crisis seigniorage remained relatively high while inflation remained moderate. At first sight one would have expected the opposite: the crisis should have shown the population how unstable the rouble could be and this should have led to a reduction in cash holdings, thus reducing seigniorage. But seigniorage remained high, probably because Russians had learned to trust their banks even less than their central bank. They thus preferred to keep rouble cash to keeping bank deposits, which had never been a very efficient instrument for transactions and had turned out to be an even riskier savings vehicle than cash (see below for a closer analysis of the (mis-)behaviour of Russian banks during the crisis).

Where did the non-inflationary finance that allowed the temporary stabilisation of 1997–8 come from? At the start of the reforms it was expected that the West would support the reformers decisively. However, support of Russia through the IMF came rather late. Figure 8.2 shows the two sources of financing for the budget (IMF lending and increases in the monetary base) in billions of US dollars. It is apparent that during the first two years of the reforms IMF lending was negligible (around $1 bn) compared with monetary financing of over $10 bn. This changed only later, basically during 1995–6 when IMF lending rose to almost $3 bn per year. However, it remained always modest compared to the scale of monetary financing at the start of the transition, as can be seen from figure 8.2. After the crisis Russia did not receive new funding for some time while continuing to service its IMF debt. The financial contribution of the IMF to the post-1998 stabilisation was thus actually negative. This shows once again that the key to lasting stabilisation cannot be external financing, but the imposition of hard budget constraints at home.

## *Multiple equilibria?*

It was access to private capital that allowed the Russian government to finance its deficits through non-inflationary means on a grand scale. However, this exposed the government to the vagaries of capital markets, and, given the openness of the capital account, this also meant that Russia was exposed to sudden withdrawals of foreign capital, in other words, to speculative attacks.[13] In 1997, nearly 30 per cent of the federal budget deficit was financed from foreign sources and in early 1998 this proportion was even increasing. When this flow stopped abruptly during the summer of 1998 the currency collapsed and the government declared a unilateral 'moratorium' on foreign debt service. In effect, Russia went into default.

Was the sudden collapse of stabilisation in 1998 just the result of a speculative attack? The literature on speculative attacks emphasises that under certain conditions highly indebted countries can fall into a low-credibility trap. This occurs when a government is judged not to be credible by financial markets. It then has to pay a risk premium in terms of higher interest rates. The higher debt service burden that results, if inflation is kept low, makes it even more likely that the authorities will abandon the attempt to stabilise and try to reduce the real value of the debt through a surprise inflation. This further increases the risk premium demanded by financial markets, possibly leading to a spiral of increasing interest rates until the government caves in.

However, the debt trap is not the only equilibrium. The same country could also end up with low interest rates if it can start a virtuous circle of high credibility and low interest rates. All that is needed to reach this equilibrium is that markets think a priori that the government will be tough on inflation. It will then pay lower interest rates and thus have, at the same inflation rate, a lower debt service burden to carry. This in turn could validate the initial assumption. Hence there could be two equilibria in financial markets and a mere shift in expectations leading to the bad equilibrium would have to be validated even by a hard-nosed government. Of course, a country without debt does not face the threat of the bad equilibrium because an increase in interest rates would not affect its expenditure. Two equilibria become possible only when there is enough public debt to make debt service an important part of overall public expenditure.

The experience of Russia provides a good illustration of both equilibria. After basic stabilisation was achieved, large capital inflows allowed the government to finance a continuing fiscal deficit at lower interest rates. At first the real ex-post interest was very high, but this did not matter much since the stock of debt was minuscule. As low inflation persisted, nominal interest rates fell throughout 1996 and into early 1997. At interest rates of around 20 per cent (p.a.) the Russian government was able to service its debt. This was the good equilibrium. But in the meantime the debt to GDP ratio kept increasing and with the onset of the financial crisis in Asia capital flows to emerging markets in general fell dramatically. Investors could also see that the Russian government would not be able to service its debt at much higher interest rates (and still keep inflation under control). The CBR could not really tighten monetary policy because raising interest rates increases the fiscal deficit even further. This was the bad equilibrium. When foreign capital stopped coming in, the Russian government could not service its debt and could no longer support the exchange rate, which fell precipitously from about 6 to 24 roubles per dollar.

The August 1998 crisis led to a new increase in inflation (for a brief period above 100 per cent at an annual rate) and thus threatened the hard-won stabilisation. However, Russia did not collapse: the lesson that hyperinflation has very high social and political costs had been learned even by the new/old leadership, including the President of the Central Bank of Russia, Mr Gerashenko, who had presided over the inflationary early 1990s.[14]

However, the difficulties of Russia in servicing its foreign debt were not only due to the interplay between market expectations and interest rates. Another factor magnified the crisis. This magnification came from the possibility (not widely appreciated) that the interplay between the real exchange rate and the ability of the government to service its foreign debt might also contain two equilibria – even in the absence of the interaction between expectations and interest rates emphasised so far. A basic formal framework is illustrated with a rudimentary model in appendix 8.2.

The nature of the two equilibria can best be understood by concentrating on the question how many dollars (or euros) the Russian government can obtain at a given ability to tax the domestic economy. At a low real exchange rate (a strong currency) exports are low, but the government can obtain enough tax revenues to service foreign debt because the non-tradables part of the economy is valued highly in terms of international purchasing power (wages are high in dollar terms). At a more depreciated exchange rate exports would be higher, but the non-tradables part of the economy would also be worth much less (dollar wages are then much lower). This mechanism seems to have played out in the aftermath of the 1998 crisis. As the rouble plunged, the tax revenues of the government in dollar terms also plunged and the government was no longer able to service its debt. During 2000 the reverse mechanism came into play. As the real exchange rate recovered (also thanks to higher oil prices, see below) it became easier for the government to service its debt (and the prices of Russian euro bonds rose dramatically).

One can thus see that, in the case of Russia, more than one self-reinforcing mechanism first tended to make the situation look good, and then magnified the crisis to the point that for a time Russia seemed 'lost'. After the crisis the mechanism went again into reverse, allowing, for a time, Russian financial markets to become a 'safe haven' among emerging markets (see below).

### *Beware of Russian banks!*

Everything about Russia is special, but its banking sector is even more special than the rest of the economy. All transition countries had problems with the banking system. Regulating enterprises that produce money is difficult everywhere, but it became almost impossible in Russia in a general gold rush. In Central Europe, commercial banks emerged under a regulatory framework inspired by the EU model and with an administration that at least tried to impose some control. By contrast, Russian banking emerged without any solid foundations. Capital requirements for a banking licence were very low (one could open a bank with several hundreds of thousands of dollars) and bank supervision was non-existent. Enterprises were allowed to create their own house or 'pocket' bank. Within a few years some 2,500 banks sprang up. By 1998 1,476 banks had survived, of which only 29 (2 per cent) were foreign owned. In Hungary, by contrast, there were 40 banks in 1998, of which 27 (67 per cent) were foreign owned. The fencing of the Russian banking market to foreign competition was constantly justified, at least officially, by the argument that this was an 'infant' industry.

Banks in Russia did not undertake boring 'normal banking' operations, that is, the mobilisation of savings for lending to enterprises. (This remained the task of Sberbank, which continued to be government owned. More precisely, the banking regulator, the Central Bank of Russia, holds 61 per cent of the capital. What would be totally unacceptable in countries concerned about institutional controls, is standard in Russia.). Bank credit to the private sector amounted to only 8.7 per cent of GDP in 1997, compared to 23.4 per cent in Hungary or 44 per cent in Slovakia. But even this figure is to be interpreted with care as 'connected' lending was practised on a large scale (to the industrial group to which the bank belonged and to individuals of that group), often leading to outright transfers comparable to asset-stripping observed in the enterprise sector. Russian banks concentrated on making quick money, i.e. short-term speculation and on transferring capital abroad. By one estimate, quoted by Shleifer and Treisman (2000: 55) the financial sector thereby earned 8 per cent of GDP in 1992. How was it possible to extract such a large rent from deposits? How was it possible to maintain deeply negative real rates of interest? Several factors reinforced each other. One was lack of competition, as the banking sector only became organised in 1992. But government helped by keeping foreign banks out until 1995. Second, Sberbank held about two-thirds of deposits and its owner (the government) fixed deposit rates. Third, tax policy created another incentive to keep deposit rates low. For taxable income, banks could only write off interest paid up to the central bank discount rate plus 3 per cent. If they paid higher deposit rates their margin would shrink and they would pay taxes on net revenue not received.

Bank supervision was notoriously 'accommodating' until 1995. Some regulatory tightening reduced the number of banks by about a thousand. But by 1998 there was still no bankruptcy legislation applicable to banking institutions. Capital increases required by regulation after 1995 were often achieved by accounting tricks, such as funds borrowed from the bank itself (Snoy 2000).

At first sight, Russian banks were well capitalised. According to CBR reports capital adequacy ratios (for which the minimum standard BIS requirement is 8 per cent) increased from 20 per cent in 1995 to 25 per cent in 1997. However, this solidity is highly misleading: 30–40 per cent of assets were claims on government (80 per cent of which were investments in state securities) with a zero-risk weighting. Loans to the private sector were of poor quality. In July 1998 the CBR estimated that 6 per cent of total loans were 'overdue'. The

Table 8.2.  *Russian banks with large forward contracts on 1 July 1998*

|  | Forward contracts (R bn) | % of assets |
|---|---|---|
| Inkombank | 169.2 | 469.9 |
| National Reserve | 99.4 | 944.4 |
| MDM-Bank | 84.6 | 4,656.8 |
| Unibest | 77.6 | 3,709.2 |
| Tokobank | 66.9 | 871.7 |
| ONEKSIM-bank | 47.3 | 197.9 |
| Sberbank | 39.5 | 19.7 |
| SBS-Agro | 31.2 | 115.8 |
| Avtobank | 26.8 | 303.2 |
| Gazprombank | 25.7 | 189.5 |
| Menatep | 24.2 | 131.5 |
| Vneshtorgbank | 24.1 | 132.9 |
| Mezhkombank | 23.6 | 690.5 |
| Rossiski Kredit | 22.0 | 113.8 |
| Metkombank | 19.2 | 2,000.0 |

*Source*: *Profile* magazine.

OECD (1997) put the proportion of bad loans around 30 per cent in 1996–7, expecting this share to grow over time. Hence, the banking system's capital base would have disappeared under Western accounting rigour.

On the liabilities side, deposits represented only 49 per cent in 1997 for the entire banking system and only 30 per cent on average if Sberbank is excluded. Banks sought refinancing in foreign currencies. By mid-1998 commercial banks were highly unbalanced, with $20 bn of liabilities and only $12 bn of foreign assets. This foreign exchange exposure was then multiplied by forward commitments, as shown in table 8.2. No Western supervision would have tolerated such a risk exposure. In the crisis the presumed liquidity of banks – mainly treasury paper – evaporated.

Some banks represented the most powerful industrial groups, others the most influential oligarchs. It is, therefore, not surprising that banks were among the most favourably treated interest groups. Boycko et al. (1996) argued that they had to be 'compensated' to bring them on-board and make stabilisation possible. The argument goes as follows: banks benefited outrageously from inflation in several ways. They could refinance at the central bank at negative real interest rates, remunerate deposits at negative real interest rates, and were notoriously slow in effecting payments, thereby earning the float (a form of inflation tax). Assets were invested in foreign currency to gain from the rouble's depreciation.

The compensation for lost inflation gains took two forms. One compensation was provided with the launch of the treasury bill market, which allowed banks to avoid the trouble of assessing the credit risk of private sector borrowers and, instead, earn a fat margin on a tradable claim on the lowest risk in Russia, the government. Figure 8.3 shows the returns. The other form of compensation was the infamous 'loans for shares' deal of 1995–6, which

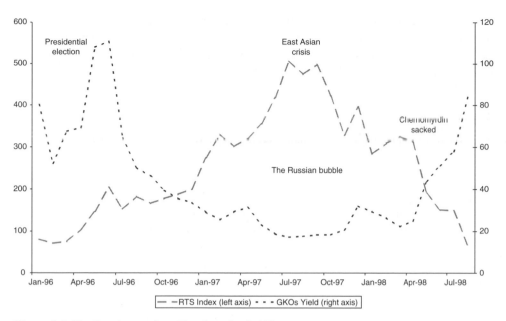

**Figure 8.3** The Russian stock and bond market bubble

for a pittance turned banks into the major strategic owners of Russia's most important enterprises, including the media. This deal also served to win the banks' support for the privatisation programme.

Much applauded by international observers was the opening of the treasury-bill market to foreigners, although prudence would have suggested otherwise. As we have argued in Gros and Steinherr (1995), it is safer, and not costly in forgone growth to delay capital account convertibility. In 1998 when foreign investors became concerned about Russia's ability to service the rapidly growing debt and keep the rouble's exchange rate at 6 to the dollar, they covered their rouble exposure. Counterparts were Russian banks. As shown in table 8.2, Russian banks acted like any borrower that never intends to pay back. To give just a few examples: MDM-Bank and Unibest had foreign exchange forward contracts equivalent to 4,000 per cent (40 times!) of all assets and some 50,000 per cent (500 times!) of their capital. Generally accepted prudential ratios would restrict any large exposure to less than 25 per cent of capital. The fact that Russian banks bet their capital several times over raises two questions: first, about the role of the supervisor and, second, about how banks got off the hook when disaster struck.

The supervision of banks is the responsibility of the Central Bank of Russia (CBR), which is formally accountable to parliament (the Duma) and not to government. De facto, however, parliament cannot be sufficiently informed about the details and was thus easily 'captured' by banks with their large pockets. The same happened to the CBR and to the administration, where low-paid civil servants had strong incentives to look after the interests of those they are supposed to govern and supervise. This explains why there was no real supervision of banking in Russia for the first ten years of the transition.

The same situation is also responsible for the most egregious case of regulatory capture seen anywhere, namely the unwinding of the huge forward commitments documented above. The reason no central bank in the world would have tolerated the commitments of table 8.2 is that a devaluation as small as 20 or even 10 per cent would have wiped out the capital of most of the banks in table 8.2. But the devaluation of September 1998 was several times larger than this, as the price of the dollar (in terms of Russian roubles) went up by more than 300 per cent.

Foreigners had correctly perceived that the strong rouble policy that had led to the temporary stabilisation could not be sustained forever and many hedged their Russian investments via forward contracts concluded with Russian counterparties. Banks usually trust each other because they assume that they are all strictly regulated and that the risk that they cannot live up to their commitment is minimal. But too few realised that Russian banks are different. Forward contracts in Russia contained an exceptionally high counterparty risk. Forwards concluded before August 1998 on a three-month basis had prices of R7.50 to R8.50, compared to a spot price of R6. But when the devaluation came, the dollar went up to R20. The Russian banks that had sold the forward contracts should thus all have been bankrupt. In reality, most of them survived. How?

A first escape was that derivative contracts commonly include a *force majeure* clause that permits the parties to the contract to terminate the contracts without performance if an event occurs that has a pervasive effect on markets and makes performance of all contracts impossible without enormous losses to the contractual parties. Russian banks and securities houses apparently exercised this *force majeure* clause and refused to honour the derivatives contracts they had sold to customers wishing to hedge the currency risk on their Russian treasury bonds.

But more important were some other, less acceptable practices. On days when large amounts of forward contracts matured, Russian banks delayed selling orders for the rouble in the spot market to drive the rouble price up and make execution cheaper. For example, on 15 September 1998, the rouble appreciated from R20.80 to the dollar the week before to R8.67 and went back to R16 the following week. Russian counterparties reduced their forward execution liabilities to close to nothing (Steinherr 2000b).

Some foreigners thought that they could avoid the counterparty risk by hedging at Moscow Interbank Currency Exchange (MICEX). They were mistaken. At the peak of Russia's financial crisis on 26 August, Russia's market regulator, the Federal Securities Commission, suspended trading on MICEX. For foreign exchange contracts MICEX ordered the settlement of all open positions on the exchange rate prevailing before suspension, destroying the value of these contracts. Regulators were clearly 'captured' by the major bank interests.

This capture can also be seen by the fact that during the first three weeks of August 1998 the CBR provided R33 bn rouble loans to banks, slightly more than the first transfer of IMF assistance of $4.8 billion (equivalent then to about R30 bn). All this money immediately left Russia, depleting further the reserves of the CBR and thereby forcing the devaluation of 17 August.

The Russian financial crisis was thus also the result of government capture, and therefore soft supervision and soft budget constraints. Banks were private, but the institutional framework that disciplines a market economy was lacking and the public institutions were essentially at their service. In the end some banks went bankrupt, but only because the government stopped servicing its debt and owners stripped them of any cash still available.

## 8.6    Could the West have helped more effectively?

The evolution of the Russian economy is closely followed in the Western press and, starting in 1992–3, the G-7 economic summits devoted a lot of their time to discussion and debate on how to help Russia. In 1999 Russia was even included in this club of the major economic powers. From all this, one could gain the impression that the Russian economy is somehow important for the global economy. This would be completely wrong. That Russia is important for non-economic reasons may be obvious, but it is not widely appreciated how small the Russian economy really is. Translated at market exchange rates, the Russian GDP oscillates around $250–350 billion, depending on the exchange rate. This puts Russia in the same league as Brazil.

It is often argued that one cannot translate the Russian GDP at the market exchange rate and that one should use a purchasing power exchange rate to measure the Russian economy. The debate about the appropriate purchasing power exchange rate is really beside the point, since the numbers mentioned above only serve to measure the weight of Russia in the world economy; they have little to say about just how poor the Russian population is. To measure the latter, one would indeed have had to apply a purchasing power corrected exchange rate. But in order to avoid this argument one can also measure the weight of Russia by its international trade. Even from this point of view, Russia is small: its exports are at about $80 bn (statistically recorded, imports much less), about the same as Sweden, less than Mexico. In terms of exports of manufactured goods, Russia is much smaller than either of these two countries (and somewhat smaller even than Poland).

Despite its small size, the Russian crisis of 1998 did have a strong impact on the world economy. In this sense all the attention devoted to Russia turned out to be justified. However, the impact of the Russian crisis on the world economy came through financial markets and not through the short-lived collapse of Russian imports (which implied a fall in demand of about $20 to 30 billion, a negligible sum compared with the volume of world trade). It is ironic that the political attention devoted to Russia during the two crucial periods 1992–3 and August 1998 is in inverse proportion to the economic impact on the West. During the early reform period it was perceived to be politically very important that the reforms in Russia succeed, but the economic impact of success or failure would have been negligible. In 1998 the impact on the Western economy was much stronger, but politically Russia had been written off.

### *1992–3: the wrong form of aid?*

The debate about aid to Russia during 1992–3 became sterile: Western officials pointed to the large amount of aid actually delivered (over 10 per cent of GDP and 40 per cent of imports in 1992), whereas the critics pointed out that this was the wrong kind of aid and that the Russian government did not receive what it needed most, namely direct budgetary support (Lipton and Sachs 1992). Gros and Steinherr (1995) show that both sides were right (and wrong) if one analyses more closely the economic mechanisms at work during the early period of incomplete reforms.

The basic point is that the critics of Western aid policy towards Russia during 1992–3 were even more right than they suspected, since the credits to finance Russian imports did actually harm the Russian economy because the Russian government subsidised imports at that time. If Russia had adopted different policies (taxing imports instead of subsidising them), it could have used these credits to stabilise the economy. The basic argument (explained in more detail in Gros and Steinherr 1995) is a straightforward application of standard welfare theory in a second-best situation.

Regarding the welfare from emergency credit, one has to start from the fact that credits to finance imports do not constitute a gift; they have to be repaid at some point in the future. Consumers in an economy that does not have access to (private)[15] world capital markets gain from such credit because it allows them to smooth consumption. Emergency credits should thus increase welfare of the recipients, even though they have to be repaid. But this is necessarily the case only if there are no distortions in the receiving economy. If the government subsidises imports, additional credits magnify the losses from an existing distortion. One then has to set the gain from consumption smoothing against the standard welfare losses from the import subsidies applied by the Russian government during 1992.

Gros and Steinherr (1995) present a small model that can be calibrated to the data which suggests that the net effect of the emergency assistance to Russia in 1992 was probably negative, resulting in a welfare loss, equivalent to anywhere between 1 and 7 per cent of GDP for 1992. Welfare losses of this magnitude, of course, are not a desirable result of foreign aid.

One can certainly discuss the details of the calculations based on such a crude model, but the central point is quite clear: the export credits lavished on Russia in 1992 probably helped to reduce the welfare of the average Russian citizen. This was not the fault of the West, since the cause of this unintended effect was the underpricing of imports through massive subsidies operated by the Russian government. But this example shows that sometimes helping a severely distorted economy can have unintended negative side-effects.

But why did the West accept the bad policies of the Russian government? It should have taxed imports. In this way it would have avoided the welfare losses and the resulting receipts would have allowed it to stabilise the economy much earlier.

These considerations show that both the West and the Russian government are to blame for the fact that the substantial assistance given during the early reform period did not lead to a quick stabilisation. Stabilisation started much later, not only because of the impressive efforts of the new finance minister Fyodorov to cut credit emission, but also because the environment for aid changed: import subsidies had been abolished and import tariffs were gradually introduced so that the declining amounts of import credits did have a positive effect. Moreover, some limited amounts of the 'right' type of aid were slowly forthcoming.

The West also lost an opportunity in the sense that, even given the bad policies pursued by the Russian government, a moderate amount of the right aid, namely budgetary assistance to the government, could have helped to achieve stabilisation. How large should direct assistance to the government have been in order to achieve stabilisation? The proper criterion should be the level of support from the West that would have allowed the authorities to avoid creating too much money. It was argued above that the relevant part of seigniorage was worth about 2,000 billion roubles; approximately $8 bn at the average 1992 exchange rate. Buying stabilisation this way would have been more expensive in 1993, when the increase in cash in circulation was worth about $12 bn. But this would still have been less than the export credits that were given in 1992. This is not surprising: providing a country of 140 million people with international purchasing power is an expensive proposition, but providing the government with internal purchasing power to cover its deficit is cheap if the real exchange rate is low.

## *The crisis of 1998*

Stabilisation thus eventually came to Russia, even if somewhat late. The 'right' form of aid (from this point of view IMF credits) also came late, perhaps so late that it had again unintended perverse effects. A good indicator of external official balance-of-payments assistance is the amount of fund credit because an IMF programme is usually a condition for other institutions, notably the World Bank. Most of the assistance from the IMF came only during 1995, helping to achieve stabilisation. But there was again a catch, which was not immediately visible. At first sight the stabilisation of 1994–5 was impressive. Starting from early 1995 the nominal exchange rate was held constant. Inflation continued, but at a much lower rate, so that the appreciation of the real exchange rate seemed tolerable, especially as the current account remained in surplus. The real (CPI-based) exchange rate against the dollar appreciated by 60 per cent during May–December 1995, but only by 5 per cent in 1996 and 4 per cent in 1997.

Then came the collapse of the exchange rate in August 1998 and inflation started to accelerate again. We discussed above the view that the disaster of 1998 can be seen as a manifestation of vicious circles involving financial markets and the ability of the Russian government to service its debt. But even a vicious circle needs to start somewhere. Were the external accounts of Russia in such a bad state that they could justify a speculative attack? The answer must be a resounding no if one looks at the overall external accounts of Russia. It is not widely recognised that despite the real appreciation mentioned above Russia did not have a current account deficit before the crisis.

Table 8.3 displays some of the relevant data. It shows that the cumulative current account surplus over the five-year period up to 1998 was actually about $30 bn. However, despite continuing current account surpluses, the external debt of Russia kept on increasing, by about $35 bn. The figures indicating a current account surplus imply that, if one can trust this data (from the IMF), Russian economic agents were accumulating until 1998 claims on the rest of the world worth about $30 bn. At the same time the liabilities of the Russian government were increasing instead of falling. This is the classic constellation of capital

Table 8.3. *Factors influencing Russian foreign debt ($ bn)*

| Russian external accounts | 1994–8 | 1999 | 2000 | 2001 | 1994–2001 |
|---|---|---|---|---|---|
| Current account | 30.4 | 24.7 | 46.4 | 35.1 | 136.6 |
| Capital account | 0.4 | −0.3 | 10.7 | −9.4 | 1.4 |
| Financial account | −76.8 | −19.1 | −33.8 | −5.4 | −135.1 |
| Net errors and omissions | −26.4 | −7.0 | −9.4 | −9.0 | −51.8 |
| Increase in foreign debt | 35.1 | −10.2 | −17.3 | −10.3 | −2.7 |
| *Capital flight* | *65.5* | *14.5* | *29.1* | *24.8* | *133.9* |

*Source*: IMF, Joint BIS-WB-IMF tables on external debt, Russian Central Bank.

flight: residents do not trust their own government and transfer everything they can abroad while the government is left the task of servicing the mounting foreign debt.

The sum of the cumulative current surplus and the increase in foreign debt could be called capital flight. (As the foreign exchange reserves of the CBR did not change over this period they are neglected here. See Dooley (2000) for a model and different estimate of capital flight.) According to our estimates it amounted to $65 bn over the five-year period up to end 1998. This was the key problem facing Russian policymakers then: they were left servicing an ever-increasing debt while their own citizens accumulated huge assets abroad. According to official statistics a large part of foreign direct investment in Russia came from Cyprus during the late 1990s. Most of this capital was presumably owned by Russian citizens. According to newspaper reports a large fraction of the eurobonds issued by the Russian government were owned by Russian citizens (via their offshore investment vehicles).

It is often argued that IMF funding until 1998 was useless because it ended up financing capital flight. This is likely, although it is not possible to say what would have happened in the absence of IMF lending. But it is also clear that the little over $14 bn from the IMF during this period could at most have financed a small part of the total capital flight that took place. Table 8.3 shows that one can trace part of the capital flight, not through ordinary capital account transactions, but through the 'financial account' and 'errors and omissions'.

The positive aspect of the 1998 crisis was that this marked the beginning of the first period in which the Russian government really faced a hard budget constraint. As IMF and foreign funds were cut off for a time, the only way out was either to cut spending and increase revenues or to revert to printing enormous amounts of money. As the costs of the latter option were clear from the 1992–3 experience, successive Russian governments were forced to undertake the arduous task of actually enforcing some discipline on taxpayers.

Table 8.3 shows that after 1998 foreign debt at least started to decline. After three years it was down by $37 bn. However, this does not mean that capital flight stopped. The main change with respect to the pre-crisis situation was that the current account surplus became astronomical, reaching almost 20 per cent of GDP.

The last column of table 8.3 shows what happened over a longer period, i.e. between 1994 and 2001: the cumulative current account surplus of Russia reached $130 bn over these eight years (equivalent to about $1,000 per capita). But its external debt was almost unchanged (increasing until 1998 and then declining). This means that over almost a decade of being a net capital exporter, Russia (or rather the Russian government) ended up with about the same external debt as before. If there had been no capital flight, Russia would have had no external debt left by the end of this period as the cumulative current account ($130 bn) was almost equal to the debt level at the beginning of the period (also around $120–130 bn). It is understandable that, in these circumstances, the Russian population became somewhat disenchanted with its political and economic elite.

## 8.7   Conclusions

The particular aspects of ten years of transition in Russia that have been highlighted in this chapter suggest that a closer analysis quite often reveals a significant gap between perception and reality. The specific instances discussed here (price and external trade liberalisation, privatisation and stabilisation) show that most economic policy measures were at first implemented only partially and thus contained internal contradictions. Over time, however, the initial shortcomings were slowly made up for. In a certain sense one can therefore conclude that the 'big bang' lasted for rather a long time in Russia. The most serious mistakes of the reformers were not to have increased energy prices and not to have eliminated import subsidies immediately. Later on, their freedom to manoeuvre was less and further reforms became more difficult. The next mistake was to rely excessively on foreign financing of continuing fiscal deficits, which in effect allowed Russian citizens to accumulate huge assets abroad while the government had to service an ever-increasing foreign debt.

Russia thus did not have ten years of reform, but rather ten years of transition. The old system had already started to disintegrate before 1992 and a critical analysis of the policies actually implemented under the initial 'big bang' (as opposed to the policy announced) shows that they had serious negative welfare effects. This can explain why the constituency for real reforms was initially rather weak. However, since most of the initial errors were slowly corrected, the welfare gains from the elimination of import subsidies and the reduction of export controls were probably dimly perceived by the population at large, and this might be the main reason that the reforms never stopped. But as the initial errors were corrected the country was putting its stability in the hands of international capital markets by a combination of excessive opening of financial markets, imprudent fiscal policy and a corrupt banking system. This mixture proved almost lethal when private capital inflows suddenly stopped and a classic currency plus banking crisis followed.

But the lesson that reforms and stabilisation improve the economy and pay off politically in the long run was not lost on the political system. This is the key reason Russia did not descend into hyperinflation and disintegration after August 1998. One can therefore expect for the near future a continuation of the slow progress that has been the hallmark of developments in Russia so far.

The Russophoria of 1996–7 and the over-reaction of financial markets to the crisis of 1998–9 illustrate the tendency to exaggerate developments in Russia in both directions. We discussed models that imply that sometimes small shifts in fundamentals and expectations can lead to large differences in outcome. But financial markets are not the only area in which large swings can be set in motion by small events. In the case of Russia, similar self-reinforcing mechanisms might have played a role in other areas as well, e.g. law enforcement, as we demonstrated in chapter 5. If nobody obeys the laws the police will be overwhelmed and will not be able to follow up most cases effectively. As a consequence people have little incentive to obey the law. They know that the probability that they will be caught is close to zero. (Although private enforcement mechanisms, which are usually much more convincing, might spring up.) A different equilibrium would be the Swiss (or Estonian?) one, in which most people obey the law so that there are few infringement cases, which can all be followed up effectively so that people will hesitate to transgress.

What does all this imply for the future? It suggests that the approach championed by President Putin, namely to strengthen the administrative machinery and start vigorously enforcing existing legislation, might lead to a change of regime: once the authorities succeed in limiting the frequency of malfeasance they could start a snowball effect towards the better equilibrium. During the year 2000 something like this seems to have started in the area of tax collection. The new Russian administration was able to increase considerably federal tax collection relative to GDP (from about 10 per cent in 1999 to about 17 per cent in 2000, some additional tax revenues being due to a shift from the regional to the federal level) without increasing tax rates. As more and more people actually pay their taxes, the tax police can concentrate its efforts on fewer cases so that it becomes easier to enforce a tax code, which had until then often remained a dead letter.

The recovery from the 1998 crisis was of course aided by the rebound in the price of energy. Russia watchers do not agree on the relative contribution to the recovery of reforms (or better implementation of laws) and higher energy prices (see appendix 8.2 for more details).

The key question remains a longer-term one: Will the positive developments continue until Russia becomes a 'normal' country? Will the rebound from the 1998 crisis, which started so spectacularly, prove to be the start of a period of solid long-term growth? This is impossible to predict at the start of the second decade of transition. But a quote from the noted economist already cited in the opening seems appropriate – and mildly encouraging:

> If one is to make any generalisation in present conditions, it must be this – that at a low level
> of efficiency the system does function and possesses elements of permanence.     J.M. Keynes

## Appendix 8.1     The importance of raw materials for the Russian economy

A few numbers can illustrate the importance of energy for the Russian economy. In 1998 the total production of tradable energy (i.e. forms of energy that can be easily sold on the world market such as oil and natural gas) amounted to about 800 mtoe (millions of tonnes of oil equivalent), with a world market value of about $80 bn even at the low oil price of that year (compared to only 200 mtoe for Mexico, worth about $20 bn). At the start of the transition Russia appeared to have such solid economic foundations because at that time its tradable energy production was even more important, about 1,000 mtoe, worth over $100 bn.

Natural resources must be taken into account under three aspects:

(1) *The level of income* The large endowment, especially of energy which can be sold easily on the world market, should make Russia rich. To calculate the contribution of the energy sector to GDP (i.e. national value added) one has to deduct the cost of production from the gross value of energy production. As most of the infrastructure for extraction and transport already existed in Russia at the end of the 1980s, the current marginal cost of extraction must be small, probably only around 20 per cent of the value of production. This would imply that oil and gas contributed about $64 bn to a total GDP of only around $170 bn in 1998. Oil and gas alone thus contributed over 30 per cent to Russian GDP. (Russia has other sources of energy, for example it also produces significant amounts of coal. But it is generally agreed that most mines are not covering their costs, so this activity does not contribute to value added. Nuclear power and hydroelectricity are quantitatively much less important: about 50 mtoe p.a., less than 10 per cent of the total primary energy consumption.)

The importance of all natural resources in Russia is even greater than suggested by these numbers if one takes into account other forms of mineral wealth: diamonds, metallic ores, etc.

(2) *Economic implications of natural resource endowment.* To economists it is clear that a large endowment of natural resources that are cheap to exploit can increase the level of GDP, but has no direct implications for the growth rate. There are, however, political-economic reasons to suggest that a lot of natural resources can actually be detrimental for growth. That natural resources are so important for Russia must actually be one of the reasons why the transition was more difficult. Even in the most open and free-market economies of the world the government always controls access to natural resources. Managing access to the national wealth in an efficient way is already difficult in well-organised societies. But it proved impossible in a country like Russia in which the old power structure (the Communist Party) had fallen apart before a new one could be put in place. Leite and Weidmann (1999) show that an abundance of natural resources tends to increase corruption and stymie growth. Russia thus became the classic 'rent-seeking society'.

(3) *Recovery from the 1998 crisis.* It has been suggested that the recovery from the 1998 crisis was to a large extent due to a recovery of oil prices, and not of the policies followed by the Putin administration.

Raw materials in general, and energy products in particular, dominate Russian exports (energy products account for roughly 66 per cent of total exports). This raises the question of how exposed the Russian economy remains to changes in world market energy prices. This issue has been studied recently, applying standard statistical techniques (VAR and cointegration techniques), see Rautava (2002).

Rautava (2002) finds that output (GDP) depends on the levels of both the real rouble exchange rate and oil prices. More specifically, a permanent 10 per cent real appreciation of the rouble is associated with a 2.4 per cent drop in GDP. A 10 per cent permanent rise of the international oil prices would translate into a 2.2 per cent higher GDP level. These two results confirm standard economic thinking: a more appreciated exchange rate makes imports cheaper and reduces net exports, hence lowering GDP.

Rautava (2002) also finds that a permanent 1 per cent rise in GDP is associated with a 2.7 per cent boost to central government fiscal revenues, although the output elasticity of revenues appears sensitive to the estimation period. Moreover, a 10 per cent permanent hike in oil prices would also positively affect federal real revenues by 3 per cent of GDP in the long run. This demonstrates that the Russian fiscal position greatly depends on oil prices, and fiscal crises could be aggravated, if not triggered, by rapid swings in international energy markets. The low price of oil in 1998 was certainly one of the factors behind the crisis.

It is interesting to note that coefficient estimates presented above appear relatively stable over time. In particular, Rautava concludes that the data do not support the view that Russian output has become any less dependent on the real rouble exchange rate or oil prices after the 1998 crisis. These results thus do not suggest that the reform efforts by Putin's administration have decreased Russia's dependency on oil price developments.

Rautava's results imply that the effects of oil prices on output may be balanced by respective movements in the real exchange rate. Thus, if a rise in oil prices leads to an appreciation of the rouble in real terms, the overall effect on GDP could be slightly negative, depending on the oil-price elasticity of the rouble.

These estimates suggest that it would be possible for a doubling in oil prices (ceteris paribus for the real exchange rate) to increase GDP by roughly 20 per cent. This could explain what was observed between 1998 and 2000, when petroleum prices shot up more than 110 per cent over the two-year period. But at the same time the rouble appreciated considerably in real terms (at least if one starts from the trough immediately after the crisis hit; comparing 1997 to 2002 the rouble actually underwent a real depreciation). There has been some correlation between the oil price and the real exchange rate (correlation coefficient of 40 per cent) in Russia over the past decade. Hence it remains difficult to determine whether the recovery from the 1998 crisis was due mainly to luck (the increase in oil prices), or to good policy choices.

## Appendix 8.2    Debt service capacity and the real exchange rate

The aim of the following model is to describe the impact of changes in the real exchange rate on the ability of a government to service its foreign debt when tax revenues come at least partially from the taxation of the non-tradables sector. This implies that the real depreciation that might be needed to cure a current account deficit makes it also more difficult for the government to service its foreign debt.

For simplicity it is initially assumed that the government is credit-constrained. This eliminates interesting intertemporal considerations, but experience has shown that access to foreign capital is usually no longer available during crisis episodes, i.e. when large devaluations are enforced by the market. Furthermore, it is assumed that the domestic private sector does not have access to the international capital market so that all foreign debt is government debt. Again, this seems appropriate when considering the Russian crisis of 1998. Even in the case of the Asian economies this assumption would not be very far from reality as it turned out that, de facto, governments had to take over the foreign debt run up by their financial sectors.

The starting point is an equation that links tax revenues to economy-wide value added (GDP), taking into account that income is composed of tradables and non-tradables. The first building block is the (probably realistic) assumption that the tax revenues available for debt service, measured in international prices, cannot exceed a certain proportion, $\tau$, of GDP. This limit of the ability of the government to raise taxes could be political or simply administrative. In Russia both factors conspired to make $\tau$ rather low. Total federal tax revenues never exceeded 20 per cent of GDP in Russia. The amount needed to service foreign debt is given by $RB$ ($B$ is the level of debt, $R$ is the international interest rate, which is given to the small country). Measuring everything in terms of tradables debt service capacity can be expressed by:

$$\text{tax revenues} = \tau(Ne_t^{-1} + X_t) = RB_t, \tag{8A.1}$$

where $e$ is the exchange rate (amount of non-tradables for one unit of tradables) and $N$ stands for the production (equals consumption) of non-tradables.

The model is in real terms. Nominal wages in domestic currency are normalised to one. For convenience it is assumed that labour is the only factor of production. Non-tradables are produced under constant economies of scale ($L_N = N$) so that the price of non-tradables in domestic currency is equal to the wage rate. The international price of tradables is constant. The real exchange rate thus represents also the inverse of the wage rate in international currency.

The supply of exports, $X_t$, is determined by the exchange rate:

$$X_t = \gamma e_t. \tag{8A.2}$$

This supply function can be motivated by a simple quadratic production function (or rather labour requirements function) of the form: $L_X = X^2/2\gamma$, where $L_X$ is the amount of labour used in the production of exports). In the case of Russia one would assume that the short-run elasticity of supply of exports is rather low as it is given essentially by the oil and gas fields that are already in production.

With full employment there is a link between the level of non-tradables production and exports:

$$L_N = 1 - L_X = 1 - X^2/2\gamma, \tag{8A.3}$$

where the overall labour supply has been normalised to one.

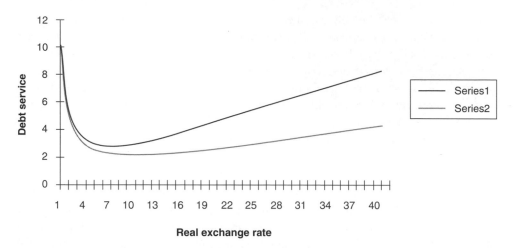

**Figure 8A.1** Debt service capacity and the real exchange rate
Series 1: $\gamma = 4$, Series 2: $\gamma = 2$.

Inserting equations (8A.2) and (8A.3) into (8A.1) yields, after some straightforward simplifications:[16]

$$RB_t = \tau(e_t^{-1} + \gamma e_t/2) \tag{8A.4}$$

This equation can have two solutions, depending on the parameter configuration. The solutions for the exchange rate that satisfy the constraint (8A.4) could be found by rewriting it as a standard quadratic equation. But it is more convenient to analyse the RHS of equation (8A.4) as a function of the exchange rate (the LHS is just a constant). Figure 8A.1 plots two examples of the values for the debt service that result from two different parameter configurations. It is apparent that the slope of the function given by the RHS of equation (8A.4) is negative for small value of $e$, and tends towards minus infinity at the origin. For large values of $e$ the slope tends towards $\gamma$.

The minimum of the RHS of equation (8A.4) is at the point $e = (2/\gamma)^{1/2}$. There will thus be two solutions to equation (8A.4) as long as the minimum debt service capacity (at any given tax rate) is smaller than the actual debt service obligations:

$$\tau(2\gamma)^{1/2} < RB_t. \tag{8A.5}$$

A low value of $\gamma$, i.e. the elasticity of supply of exportables, a low value of $\tau$, the ability to levy taxes, or a high debt service requirement, would thus make it more likely that there are two equilibria. Russia seems to fulfil all three conditions.

The nature of the two equilibria can best be understood by considering the terms within the brackets on the RHS of equation (8A.4), which represent the value of GDP in terms of tradables. At a low real exchange rate (a strong currency) exports are low, but the government can obtain enough tax revenues to service foreign debt because the non-tradables part of the economy is valued highly in terms of international purchasing power. At a more depreciated exchange rate exports would be higher, but the non-tradables part of the economy would also be worth much less.

It is possible to relax the initial assumption that the government is credit constrained and consider issues of debt accumulation. It is clear that the two equilibria for the exchange rate cannot both ensure external balance. For any period foreign debt is fixed, but it will not be constant over time unless the current account is balanced. Given that the difference between exports and imports (denoted by $M$) is equal to the trade balance, the accumulation of foreign debt is determined by:

$$B_{t+1} = B_t(1 + R) - X_t + M_t = B_t(1 + R) - X - \gamma e_t + M_t, \tag{8A.6}$$

where $x$ is a catch-all constant that could stand for any exogenous element in exports (e.g. an oil or gas well that produces without any labour input). Alternatively, $x$ could represent any other foreign exchange income that is independent of the exchange rate, e.g. unilateral transfers. The current account is then given by $x + \gamma e - M - B_t R$.

The model can then be closed by determining the demand for imports via the usual Cobb–Doublas utility function, which leads to a direct link between imports and exports of the form:

$$\alpha e_t M_t = (1 - \alpha)N_t. \tag{8A.7}$$

The assumption of constant expenditure shares is not compatible with the experience of Russia and other countries undergoing large devaluations. But it can be shown that a more general formulation under which the share of tradables in expenditure would rise after a devaluation would not change the nature of the solution.

Using the labour market equilibrium, the current account can then be written as a function of the exchange rate, and the accumulation of foreign debt would be governed by:

$$\begin{aligned} B_{t+1} &= B_t(1 + R) - x - \gamma e + [(1 - \alpha)/\alpha][1 - (e_t \gamma)^2/2\gamma)]e_t^{-1} \\ &= [(1 - \alpha)/\alpha]e_t^{-1} - x - [(1 + \alpha)/2\alpha]\gamma e. \end{aligned} \tag{8A.8}$$

Inserting one of the solutions to equation (8A.4) would then yield a non-linear difference equation for the stock of foreign debt, $B_t$.

Inspection of equation (8A.8) shows that a higher value of $e$, i.e. a more depreciated exchange rate, reduces the current account balance and makes it more likely that a deficit results. The dynamics induced by the two equilibria for the debt service could thus be quite different. At the higher (more depreciated) exchange rate net exports will be higher so that foreign debt could decline. In terms of figure 8A.1 this would tend to lower the horizontal line, so that the next-period exchange rate could also be lower (more appreciated). This process would stop when the horizontal line, indicating the debt servicing capacity of the country is just tangent to the LHS of equation (8A.4). By contrast, at the second equilibrium, i.e. the one with a stronger exchange rate (fewer non-tradables are needed for one unit of tradables), the current account could be in deficit. Debt would thus increase period after period. This process would actually accelerate as long as the economy remained in this equilibrium, since in this case the real exchange rate would continue to appreciate and the current account deficit would widen with each period.

## Notes

1. The term '*decada perdida*' was also applied in Latin America to the 1980s. The worst performance there was that of Argentina, with a fall in GDP per capita of 'only' 20 per cent between 1980 and 1990.
2. A law establishing a two-tier banking system and an independent central bank was approved on 1 November 1990, and survived the subsequent upheavals not only in Russia, but also in most other former Soviet republics.
3. For a comparison of various reform plans, see Commission of the European Communities (1990b). There were important differences between the reform plans in the emphasis given to these goals and the speed with which they were to be attained. In general, the government programmes put more emphasis on macroeconomic stabilisation than on liberalisation, and they insisted, for obvious reasons, on more powers for the Union.
4. A prominent expert on Eastern European economies is widely quoted as saying that 'the best thing the Communist government could do for Poland was to increase prices and then resign'.
5. The new parliament that was elected in December 1993 after the violent confrontation between the old Supreme Soviet and President Yeltsin, however, was not much different; this was the main reason why most of the reformers (especially Gaidar and the finance minister Fyodorov) preferred to leave government in early 1994.
6. It is also interesting to note that the domestic price of wheat (of which Russia is a net importer) stabilised at 54 per cent of the world market price after the wheat market was liberalised at the end of 1993.
7. The export boom went hand in hand with a boom of imports from the industrialised countries. As foreign financing became more widely available, imports increased by more than exports and most Central European countries developed a trade deficit. But this development has nothing to do with the overall expansion of trade generated by trade liberalisation.
8. We leave aside small-scale privatisation, which was implemented quickly and posed, as usual, few problems.
9. It is symptomatic that most accounts of reforms in Russia neglect even to mention the evolution of the value of the vouchers. Instead they concentrate on the number of enterprises privatised.
10. President Yeltsin defended privatisation in 1992 by stating that 'Russia needs millions of owners, rather than a handful of millionaires'. He was right on the needs of Russia, but the outcome of his policies was exactly the opposite.
11. See Davis et al. (2000) for a comparative study of the fiscal impact of privatisation.
12. For a thorough analysis of fiscal policy in Russia see Lopez-Claros and Alexashenko (1998).
13. See Komulainen (1999) for a survey of the currency crisis theories and the application to the Russian case.
14. See Gaidar (1999) and Havrylyshyn and Wolf (1999).
15. There was a need for official credits because private lenders were not willing to extend credit to Russia in 1992–3 (on the contrary, they even asked for reimbursement of old debts coming due). In this situation the only way to maintain imports until exports picked up was to use official credits.
16. Using the labour requirement function $L_X = X^2/2\gamma$, the terms in brackets in equation (8.1) becomes: $((1-e^2\gamma^2/2\gamma)e_t^{-1} + \gamma e_t)$.

# Part IV

## The new Europe from the Atlantic to the Urals

'The one absolute certain way of bringing this nation to ruin, of preventing all possibility of its continuing to be a nation at all, would be to permit it to become a tangle of squabbling nationalities.'

Theodore Roosevelt (1915)

# 9 From transition to integration: joining the EU

The collapse of socialism in Eastern Europe transformed the economic and politic parameters of the European continent. Creating market economies was not the only hope that arose after the liberating events of 1989–90. Indeed, the basis for any analysis of the future of the transition countries must be that most of the countries west of the FSU made their choice early on: they wanted to join the European Union (EU). Since it was not possible for them to join the EU immediately, a transitional arrangement for trade was created in the early 1990s. Section 1 describes the transitional arrangements and section 2 provides a theoretical framework for judging their utility as a bridge to EU membership.

The EU is much more than a free trade area.[1] If it were only that, the case for joining the EU rather than opting for worldwide free trade would be greatly weakened. The EU offers an integrated single market underpinned by a single currency – with free movement of capital and labour – supported by institutions that make the single market work and provide an indispensable common regulatory framework plus a solid monetary policy. How does this affect the choice of the applicant countries? The strength of this institutional framework makes membership particularly attractive for countries that have had only a decade to build market institutions, or, in some cases, simply did not exist before 1990.

Enlargement to the east has been described as a political imperative, but a closer examination of the economic aspect reveals that the issue is quite complex and that not every Eastern European country should join. Section 3 clads the discussion around the question of the optimum size of the EU. The main parameters retained for this discussion are the structure of the economies concerned, the goals of the EU and the capacity of institutions to make decisions.

It is natural that the CEEC want to join the rich man's club in Europe. Joining the club will not make them automatically rich as well, but will it at least make them a bit richer? And will the incumbents, the EU-15, benefit too, or will they have to pay for this big Eastern enlargement? In sections 4 to 6 we sharpen our understanding of the costs and benefits of enlargement. Section 4 shows how the CEEC measure up against the EU-15. Section 5 concentrates on one issue that has dominated discussions in the EU, namely the budgetary cost of enlargement. Finally, section 6 provides some realistic estimates of the welfare gains from enlargement. ('Realistic' because the benefits from joining the EU looked gigantic when the transition countries were still at the beginning of their transformation process. Now that the transition is more or less accomplished in most CEEC the benefits of EU membership are perceived to be much smaller than suggested by some early estimates. Even so, they remain substantial.) Section 7 concludes with an outlook.

## 9.1   European trade initiatives during the 1990s

The single most important trade initiative for the transition economies were the so-called 'Europe Agreements' (EA) between the EU on the one side and the former Czechoslovakia, Hungary and Poland on the other, signed in December 1991. Bulgaria and Romania followed a year later.[2] With some lag the three Baltic countries and Slovenia also signed, so that by the mid-1990s all the ten applicants for EU membership had an EA.

Table 9.1. *Exports of countries in Central and Eastern Europe to the OECD*

|  | 1988 | | 1992 | | |
|---|---|---|---|---|---|
|  | Total ($ million) | OECD share (%) | Total ($ million) | OECD share (%) | EU* share (%) |
| Bulgaria | 683 | 31.9 | 1466 | 56.5 | 44.8 |
| CSFR | 4992 | 34.1 | 7950 | 64.5 | 60.0 |
| Hungary | 3786 | 38.1 | 7517 | 70.2 | 64.1 |
| Poland | 6160 | 45.9 | 9729 | 69.2 | 64.3 |
| Romania | 4712 | 36.9 | 2111 | 47.2 | 38.0 |
| ex-USSR | 21539 | 51.8 | 29305 | 60.0 | 51.2 |

*Note*: * Includes Switzerland and Norway.
*Source*: IMF trade statistics.

These EAs were clearly critical for the recovery of the Central European countries during the early 1990s since, as table 9.1 shows, the EU (which, in trade matters de facto represents via the European Economic Area (EEA) also Switzerland and Norway) by then already accounted for over 60 per cent of the overall foreign trade of Poland, Hungary and Czechoslovakia. Trade with the EEA in turn accounted for 80–90 per cent of the trade of CEEC with the industrialised world. This table also shows the increase in exports by CEEC to the Western world (approximated here by the OECD area) since the end of socialist rule. The growth of exports is remarkable and illustrates the speed at which structural changes took place.

The EAs (see box 9.1 for details) aimed to further the integration of CEEC with the EU by providing steps towards the free movement of goods, services and factors, establishing a framework for political dialogue, harmonising legislation, cooperating on science and technology, and providing for financial assistance and technical cooperation from the EU in a number of areas. The key was, however, that these agreements explicitly recognised from the start the ultimate goal of joining the EU.

The EU has also concluded Partnership and Cooperation Agreements with Russia and some other Western CIS countries (Moldova, Ukraine). However, these agreements do not go much beyond the mutual granting of 'most favoured nation' status and do not imply a significant trade liberalisation by the EU. Most importantly they clearly do not imply a promise of future membership.

The promise of membership was made both more explicit and subject to conditions when, at the Copenhagen EU summit in June 1993, the associated CEEC were offered the clear perspective of EU membership upon fulfilment of a number of general economic and political conditions. Economic conditions include, among others, the 'capacity to cope with competitive pressure and market forces within the Union'. No date was set for formally revising the progress made towards meeting these criteria, but the multilateral political dialogue and consultation were institutionally strengthened.

---

**Box 9.1    *Europe Agreements***

The EAs established a (bilateral) free trade area for trade in goods between the EU and the respective partners within a period of up to ten years. The provisions of the Agreements were asymmetric: the period for phasing out import restrictions was usually much shorter for the EU than for the CEEC partner. For most products the EAs allowed free entry into the EU from the start. For certain 'sensitive products', which included coal, iron and steel, some chemicals, furniture, leather goods, footwear, glass, clothing and textiles, a maximum of five years (six years for products included in the Multifibre Agreements) was stipulated in separate protocols for the elimination of tariffs and/or quotas by the EU. The sensitive items scheduled for slower liberalisation accounted for up to half of the exports of the partner countries at the time the EAs were concluded.

Trade in agriculture remained excluded from free trade, but some reductions in customs tariffs for a number of agricultural products, generally within a set quota, were granted. As membership became a more concrete prospect the EU concluded in 2000 special agreements covering agricultural trade, providing substantial further liberalisation.

The EAs also contained some additional procedural and institutional provisions, in particular a consultative mechanism regarding contingent protection (in addition to the usual GATT procedures). Thus, anti-dumping action and temporary safeguards for handicapped industries are permitted only after a thirty-day period during which the Association Council – supplied with the relevant information – attempts to find an acceptable alternative or the exporter takes steps to overcome the difficulties, for example through price adjustments or voluntary export restraints (VERs). For a transitory period countervailing duty (CVD) action was also permitted in the case of state aid to exporting industries and both parties provided the information needed for the relevant calculations upon request. Lastly, the partner country (but not the EU) may, within certain limits and with a set timeframe for elimination, introduce protection for infant industries or sectors undergoing restructuring.

---

The EAs were initially severely criticised by liberal economists on several counts. First, 'sensitive' goods such as agricultural products, steel products, textiles and leather products were to remain protected in the EU for some time. This was a major drawback for Eastern European countries, which are particularly competitive in these products. However, after 1995, trade in manufacturing products was further liberalised, so this was mainly a transitional problem.

Second, the Union is pursuing a 'hub-and-spoke' approach (Baldwin 1994) by negotiating bilaterally. This biases competition in favour of the Union as long as CEEC do not pursue free trade among themselves. It could also discourage investments in the East to serve the entire region. Although only a temporary disadvantage (until Union membership), the dynamics of locational accumulation are such that a permanent disadvantage may result from the initial situation (Krugman 1991a). Empirically, however, this argument may not be as important as it sounds. For CEEC the most important decision is to get access to the 'hub'; trade with other CEEC is not that important, as demonstrated in chapter 11.

Third, those countries not enjoying an EA are obviously disadvantaged. And because the ultimate goal of an EA is Union membership, not all Eastern countries can obtain one. The Union's approach should be based on two concentric circles: one of future Union members (including the Balkans, see chapter 10) and another that includes the rest of Eastern Europe with a free trade arrangement.

Fourth, it was alleged that the safeguard clauses contained contingent protectionism, in the sense that a surge of CEEC exports in any particular sector might lead to a response by the EU. This might deter investment in export-oriented activities. But, as the high growth rates of exports from CEEC show, this protectionism must have remained truly contingent. It cannot have had a strong impact on trade flows or FDI.

Were these criticisms of the EAs valid? A look at the numbers is useful to check how trade has actually developed. During the 1990s countries with EAs have had impressive growth rates of exports to the West and the EU. Did the remaining protectionism of the EU stifle an even better performance? This is a difficult question, but a tentative answer can be found by using the gravity model.

Brenton and Kendall (1994) estimate such a model with 1992 data. The details of the results are presented in box 9.2. They find, not surprisingly, that trade between EU members is about 60 per cent larger than would be expected on the basis of distance and income alone, but that trade between the EU and the five EFTA countries in 1992 was already about normal. These results have been confirmed by other studies as well; hence the equation shows entirely typical results. However, if a so-called 'dummy' variable for east–west trade (i.e. trade between EU members and CEEC) is included, this variable carries a significant *positive* coefficient. The estimated value of the 'excess east–west trade' variable is 0.23, as shown in box 9.2. This implies that trade between the CEEC of this sample and the EU is about 23 per cent *larger* than would be expected on the basis of geography and income alone. Hence it is difficult to argue that the EU has been over-protectionist; if this had been the case overall trade would have been reduced.[3]

As an aside, we note that box 9.2 also shows that the higher than expected east–west trade is heavily skewed. Trade between Germany and CEEC is about 100 per cent higher than would be expected on the basis of distance and income alone, whereas trade between the rest of the EU and the CEEC is about normal. (This might also explain why Germany attaches so much more importance to a pro-Eastern Europe policy of the EU.) The special trade pattern of Germany can be explained by the fact that German industry specialises in the investment goods needed for the new industries emerging in the CEEC.

All in all there is no indication that the EU has been protectionist against imports from the transition economies. On the contrary, all the data from trade suggest that by 1992 trade had already re-oriented itself towards its natural pattern.

## 9.2 Joining the EU versus free trade with the rest of the world

The previous section showed that the EAs have virtually established free trade. So why bother joining the EU? The major economic argument against joining the EU is that free

## Box 9.2    Estimates of the gravity model, 1992

This box presents some of the technical details of the results found by Brenton and Kendall (1994). They used 600 observations of bilateral trade flows for estimation of the following cross-section equation:

$$\ln T_{xm} = \alpha + \beta_1 \ln GDP_x + \beta_2 \ln POP_x + \beta_3 \ln GDP_m + \beta_4 \ln POP_m$$
$$+ \beta_5 \ln DIST_{xm} + \Sigma \gamma_k D_{kxm} + u_{xm},$$

where

$T_{xm}$ is the value of the trade flow from country $x$ (exporter) to country $m$ (importer)
$GDP_i$ is the Gross Domestic Product of country $i$, ($x$ or $m$)
$POP_i$ is the population of country $i$, ($x$ or $m$)
$DIST_{xm}$ is the distance between countries $x$ and $m$
$D_{kxm}$ are dummy variables representing the adjacency of $x$ and $m$ (ADJ) and preference relationships between $x$ and $m$
$\alpha$, $\beta_i$ and $\gamma_k$ are parameters to be estimated
$u_{xm}$ is the error term

*Estimates of the gravity model using data for 25 countries for 1992*

|               | A              | B              | C              |
|---------------|----------------|----------------|----------------|
| Constant      | 1.38 (4.80)    | 0.92 (2.60)    | 1.03 (2.97)    |
| $GDP_x$       | 1.01 (27.75)   | 1.05 (25.93)   | 1.03 (26.11)   |
| $POP_x$       | −0.24 (−4.99)  | −0.28 (−5.50)  | −0.28 (−5.53)  |
| $GDP_m$       | 0.89 (24.61)   | 0.94 (23.11)   | 0.92 (23.26)   |
| $POP_m$       | −0.14 (−2.98)  | −0.19 (−3.65)  | −0.19 (−3.70)  |
| DIST          | −0.64 (−16.11) | −0.61 (−14.61) | −0.60 (−14.68) |
| ADJ           | 0.75 (6.86)    | 0.78 (7.11)    | 0.74 (6.74)    |
| EUEFTA        | 0.52 (5.63)    | 0.57 (6.02)    | 0.57 (6.09)    |
| CEEC          | 1.38 (7.72)    | 1.63 (7.81)    | 1.60 (4.76)    |
| EU12CEEC      |                | 0.23 (2.26)    |                |
| EU11CEEC      |                |                | 0.11 (1.06)    |
| GERCEEC       |                |                | 1.06 (4.76)    |
| $R^2$ adj     | 0.87           | 0.87           | 0.88           |
| $F$           | 520.03         | 466.06         | 432.90         |
| S.E.          | 0.73           | 0.72           | 0.71           |

*Source*: Brenton and Kendall (1994).

The dummy variables not previously specified are: EUEFTA: equal to one when both countries are members of either the EU or EFTA (to represent the EEA); EU12CEEC: equal to one if one of two trading partners is in the EU-12 and the other is one of the CEEC; EU11CEEC: equal to one when one of the two trading partners is in the EU-12 and is not Germany and the other is one of the CEEC; GERCEEC: equal to one for trade between Germany and the CEEC.

The $R^2$ shows that the equations can account for more than 85 per cent of the variance of the over 600 bilateral trade flows within this group of twenty-five countries.

trade with the entire world is preferable to free trade restricted to a geographic area. Why then are the CEEC set on joining the EU and why is the EU ready to accept at least some of these applicants? The major reason is that for these countries the EU accounts for 80–90 per cent of all trade with the wealthier part of the world[4] (and 60–70 per cent of overall trade). Free trade with the EU thus means, effectively, free trade with the only market that really counts for the CEEC.

However, there is an additional reason why integration with the EU brings economic gains. The EU offers far more than free trade. It offers the elimination of border controls and a framework that ensures the durability of its free trade, backed by legal provisions and institutional support. And it offers free movement for capital and labour, coordination of economic policies and a treaty for economic and monetary union. It also offers financial support to accelerate convergence and enhance cohesion and it operates sectoral economic policies, such as the CAP, scientific development, development aid, etc.

Finally, the prospect of EU membership is a strong incentive to establish rapidly an institutional framework that promotes growth. It would be wrong to believe that the CEEC seek membership mainly for the financial advantages, although we will show that they will be substantial. The policy and institutional framework of the EU offers much more than financial incentives, which may have to be revised at any rate before integrating new members.[5]

Theoretically, the CEEC could complement the EA with a policy of unilateral free trade against all other countries. In this way they could be certain that the EA does not lead to trade diversion (i.e. that they import goods from the EU that are produced with higher costs, but are cheaper than products from third countries because they are not subject to tariffs). However, it must be remembered that no country has ever adopted free trade with the entire world, although regional efforts abound. Some are successful, such as the EEA (European Economic Area comprised of the EU and EFTA) and NAFTA (North American Free Trade Area), others less so, such as various past efforts in Africa and Latin America.

Why do countries wish to form or join preferential trade areas despite the warning lights of theory? One argument is that the political economy of free trade is not favourable. From a public choice point of view the interests of producers are better organised than those of consumers (who are the main beneficiaries) and (some) producers lose from free trade. If governmental policy is conditioned by group pressure then unilateral free trade is not the optimal public choice outcome. A preferential trade area (PTA) provides visible advantages for exporters as quid pro quo for higher imports and makes it more attractive for producers as a social group.

A second argument is that a PTA guards against the risk of more protectionist policies of trading partners in the future. And as a PTA usually regroups the most important trading partners[6] this insurance can be worth more than the loss from trade diversion. Moreover, when the most important ex-ante trading parties are in the PTA then trade creation dominates, so there is a net gain. The additional gains from free trade with the rest of the world may then be marginal.

Third, PTAs may serve as building blocks rather than stumbling blocks for global free trade. When the EC was formed the average external tariff was reduced from 13 per cent in 1958 to 10.4 per cent in 1968 and 6.6 per cent after the Kennedy round (Sapir 1992).[7] Since 1958 the Community of Six has evolved into a European Economic Area comprising eighteen countries and forming the largest free trade area in the world, with supplementary agreements allowing the free entry of goods from a large group of Mediterranean and ACP countries.

Fourth, in PTA it is possible to push integration beyond trade: free movement of factors of production; coordination of associated policies such as those concerning external trade; product standardisation and certification, etc. But there is also a risk: the Common Agricultural Policy (CAP) is an example of a policy that negates free trade, causes massive trade diversion and was negotiated as a complement (and side-payment) to the free trade arrangement of the EU.

Finally, whilst a small country on its own has little weight in trade negotiations and cannot affect world prices, a larger block of countries can more easily defend its interests and may even turn the terms of trade to its advantage.[8] This advantage is, of course, only one side of the coin: the other is the temptation to become more protectionist (witness the concern expressed about 'fortress Europe').

Having established the second-best economic rationale for a PTA (free global trade remaining first-best), it should be obvious that every PTA needs to be examined for its welfare potential and that not all would make economic sense.[9] Does it make sense for CEEC to join the EEA? Consider first some general arguments.

The chances of gaining from joining a PTA increase (i) the higher the tariffs of the newcomer and the lower the tariffs of the PTA; (ii) the larger the PTA (a free trade area comprising the whole world is global free trade); and (iii) the more competitive the existing (but the more complementary the potential) trade structure of the newcomer with that of the PTA.

How do these arguments stand up against prospective CEEC membership in the EU? On argument (i) the external tariffs of the EU are low, indeed lower than those of most Eastern European countries. The EU is a very large trading area, so argument (ii) also favours EU membership. The last argument, (iii), is more difficult to judge since little is known about the potential trading structure of the CEEC once they have joined.

How about the existing trade structure? How does one measure similarity in the product structure of trade between two countries? A widely used indicator of similarity in trade structures is a coefficient that relates the differences between the shares of different products in exports.[10] This indicator can range between a value of 100, which indicates that the country concerned exports the same goods that are also prevalent in EU trade (as we take always

Table 9.2. *Trade similarity coefficients*

| | With respect to: | | | With respect to: | |
|---|---|---|---|---|---|
| | Intra-EU | Extra-EU | | Intra-EU | Extra-EU |
| **Small CEE countries*** | | | **Visegrad countries** | | |
| Estonia | 25 | 30 | Poland | 44 | 41 |
| Latvia | 16 | 20 | Czech Rep. | 53 | 43 |
| Lithuania | 19 | 22 | Slovakia | 44 | 35 |
| Romania | 27 | 29 | Hungary | 48 | 46 |
| Bulgaria | 27 | 29 | Slovenia | 47 | 36 |
| *Average* | *23* | *26* | *Average* | *47* | *40* |
| Turkey | 28 | 30 | | | |
| **Small euro area countries** | | | **Large EU countries** | | |
| Greece | 29 | 28 | Germany | 80 | 54 |
| Finland | 38 | 31 | France | 79 | 55 |
| Austria | 61 | 46 | Italy | 66 | 50 |
| Ireland | 38 | 35 | United Kingdom | 74 | 64 |
| Portugal | 47 | 40 | Spain | 65 | 45 |
| *Average* | *43* | *36* | *Average* | *73* | *54* |

*Source*: Own calculations based on Eurostat data for 2000.

the EU as the comparator), and 0, which would indicate that the country concerned exports products that are of little or no importance in EU trade. A value of close to zero indicates that there is no relationship between the product composition of national exports to the EU and that of intra-EU trade (we also provide the numbers for the comparison of national exports to the EU with extra-EU trade). In this case the potential for asymmetric shocks should be large. The raw values of this indicator are reported in table 9.2, with respect to both intra-EU and extra-EU trade. For reasons that will become clear below, the candidates and the control groups from the EU have been grouped under two somewhat different headings in this table.

Table 9.2 suggests that there are two groups among the candidates that differ considerably in the degree to which the product structure of trade is close to that of EU trade. We comment mainly on the coefficients relating to intra-EU trade, because the issue at hand is whether the candidates, once inside the EU, would be affected by shocks differently from the rest of the EU. The results using extra-EU trade as the benchmark would be similar.

It is apparent that the values of the similarity index are rather low for the three Baltic and the two Balkan countries. The similarity indicators are clearly below 30 per cent in this group. By contrast, among the Visegrad countries (to which we added Slovenia), which are either richer (Slovenia) or larger in economic terms (Poland, Czech Republic) the indicator is substantially higher, generally above 45 per cent. In order to provide a benchmark this table also reports the same indicator for five small and five large EU countries. The values for some of the smaller euro area members are actually below those of the Visegrad countries, and much below those of the larger EU member countries.

That the trade similarity indicators are lower for smaller countries should not be surprising as it is likely that smaller countries do not produce and export all the 1,200[11] products in the four-digit classification used here. Moreover, the low values for Portugal and the Balkan countries suggest that poorer countries have a lower trade similarity indicator than richer ones at the same size. The first conjecture can actually be documented by a simple regression analysis, which shows that indeed size (measured by total exports) is a very important determinant of the trade similarity indicator. The evidence is more mixed for the correlation between the level of development (measured by GDP per capita) and the similarity in trade structures.

How do the candidates fit into this relationship? The regression results reported in Box 9.3 suggest that the product composition of their exports to the EU is actually considerably more similar to intra-EU trade than one would expect given their size and income per capita.

All in all it thus appears that the Visegrad countries and Slovenia do not differ much in their potential for asymmetric shocks from the smaller euro-area member countries. If anything they seem to be somewhat more integrated in trade terms. By contrast the Baltic and Balkan countries fit less. For the Baltic countries the differences in trade structure might mainly be due to their small size, which implies that they have to specialise in a narrow range of products. For the Balkan countries the lack of reforms probably plays a role, a suspicion confirmed by a comparison of the 1998 data with 1993 data. For the Visegrad countries, the trade similarity index has increased between 5 and 10 percentage points, whereas it has actually fallen slightly for the two Balkan countries.

The results presented in box 9.3 are also interesting from another point of view. To join the EU does not mean only joining a trading area. It also potentially means joining a monetary union – and all the candidate countries have declared their intention to do so as quickly as possible. One key prerequisite of a monetary union is usually held to be that the trade structures of the participating countries are sufficiently similar to make large asymmetric shocks unlikely. Exchange rate adjustments are a useful policy instrument if a shock hits only one country. In that case it will usually be quicker to change the exchange rate than to wait for wages and prices to adjust.

The finding that the structure of trade of Central European countries with the EU is not too dissimilar from intra-EU trade implies that countries like Slovenia and the Czech and Slovak Republics are less likely to be subject to asymmetric shocks than poorer member countries such as Greece and Portugal.

What does trade theory suggest for the further trade intensity and structure of the EU with the CEEC? A by now widely accepted synthesis of the traditional comparative advantage view and the modern view of trade based on economies of scale and product differentiation (see Helpman and Krugman 1985) states that there will be intense intra-industry trade between highly developed countries (e.g. within the EU-15). At the same time there might be intensive inter-industry trade between countries with different capital–labour ratios (e.g. between the EU-15 and the CEEC-10). There should be little trade, however, between countries with a similar capital–labour ratio that are not developed enough to specialise in the industrial goods exchanged among the group of rich countries.[12] Thus, trade between developed countries consists of the exchange of differentiated industrial goods produced

---

### Box 9.3  What explains trade similarity?

We report the results of a simple cross-section regression with the trade similarity index as the dependent variable and three explanatory variables:

level of development (measured by the natural logarithm of GDP per capita in euro)
size (measured by the natural logarithm of total exports in US dollars)
a dummy variable with a value of one for the ten candidates and zero for EU members.

| Regression statistics | | (dependent variable: trade similarity index) | | |
|---|---|---|---|---|
| Adjusted $R^2$ | 0.85 | | | |
| S.E. | 7.37 | | | |
| Obs. | 24 | | | |
| Explanatory variables | Coefficients | S.E. | $t$-stat | $P$-value |
| Intercept | −37.8 | 32.4 | −1.2 | 0.257 |
| Ln GDP/cap | 4.2 | 3.5 | 1.2 | 0.250 |
| Ln total exports | 12.0 | 1.5 | 8.3 | 0.000 |
| dummy CEEC | 13.9 | 6.3 | 2.2 | 0.039 |

*Source*: Own calculations. N.B. 24 observations from EU15-Lux + candidates 10.

The results indicate that the last two explanatory variables are highly significant. Since the explanatory variables are in natural logarithm the point estimates of the slope coefficients can be interpreted in a straightforward manner. The point estimate for the dummy variable implies that the candidate countries have, on average, a trade similarity index that is about 14 percentage points higher than one would expect given their size and income per capita. The coefficient on GDP per capita is positive, as one would expect, but not significant. This result might be due to the fact that most of the candidate countries have a low GDP per capita, so that the CEEC dummy is correlated with this variable. However, this problem of colinearity suggests that income per capita is not a major determinant of trade similarity. The structure of production in the Visegrad countries is atypical for their income level, probably became of their industrial history and the delocalisation of production from EU countries.

---

with economies of scale but similar capital intensities, whereas the trade between rich countries with high capital–labour ratios and less-developed countries with low capital–labour ratios consists of an exchange of products with different capital–labour ratios.

We have shown that the CEEC already sell most of their exports to the EU. For them the case is clear. However, for the FSU trade with the outside world in general and with the EU in particular was far less important. Will this change? Chapter 7 showed, on the basis of a gravity model, that in the future the 'average' CIS country will conduct about 50 per cent of all trade with the EU, the EU's importance increasing the further west a country is located.

We have argued so far that the trade patterns of established market economies imply that the countries on the western edge of the FSU will in the future trade much more with Western Europe than with each other. This argument is valid only if the trade links created in the past can be changed. Although Krugman (1991a) suggests that historical accidents may have a permanent impact on trade, it appears from recent experience (see table 9.1) that reformed former socialist countries in Central Europe did redirect their trade flows very rapidly.

## 9.3   The optimal size of the European Union

If the EU were only a PTA then the determination of the optimal size of the EU would be relatively easy: it should be as large as possible. And, indeed, the negotiations that led to the creation of the EEA were definitely easier than those that characterise any EU enlargement. The question is, therefore, is this expansion in some sense desirable for the citizens of the EU? If so, where should the EU's border be drawn?

Trade theory is of little help in determining the optimal size of the EU, because the EU is much more than a PTA. As some subgroups of members are more homogeneous than the group of all present fifteen members in terms of economic structure and policy preferences, a two-speed integration has been applied, which is a way of saying that the entire EU is not necessarily the optimal size for EMU, or for other advances in integration, such as external ('European intervention force') and internal ('Schengen Agreement') security. This is one of the reasons why 'widening' (i.e. admitting new members) is seen as an alternative to 'deepening'. Experience has shown that widening does not necessarily impede deepening. But this can continue only if the new members satisfy conditions more demanding than those imposed on some present members, such as Greece and Portugal. Only by being more demanding can it be ensured that EU expansion is positive for the incumbents as well. This applies to all the various political economy dimensions of the EU (factor mobility, social policy, CAP, structural funds, monetary integration).

It would be helpful if newcomers had political preferences close to those of the EU, taking into account that membership is likely to make preferences more convergent. On that basis Austria was and Hungary will be more readily admitted than Turkey or Bulgaria. Furthermore, the newcomer should show evidence of an aspiration to become a member of the European family – as is the case of the Visegrad countries – and not be absorbed by internecine struggles. To fit into the EU the whole political apparatus of the newcomer must conform to European institutions: democracy, human rights and a decentralised economic structure must be firmly established; otherwise the country could not operate within the political, legal and institutional framework of the EU. All this is summarised in the Copenhagen criteria:

- Stability of institutions, guaranteeing democracy, the rule of law, human rights and respect for and protection of minorities.
- The existence of a functioning market economy, as well as the capacity to cope with competitive pressures and market forces within the Union.
- The ability to take on the obligations of membership, including adherence to the aims of political, economic and monetary union.

But even if the candidates fulfil these criteria, can and should they be admitted before institutional and financial reforms and adaptations of the EU institutions have been undertaken? Certain institutions and features lose their 'optimality' when EU membership is extrapolated from fifteen to twenty-five members or more. Moreover, current beneficiaries of EU funds fear the redistributive effects of enlargement and are often less supportive of expansion than are net contributors.

Apart from financial questions, the EU needs to make difficult institutional adjustments. For example, in the Community of Six it was not too problematic to accept all four member languages. When the EC expanded to twelve members, nine languages were certainly no longer optimal, let alone eleven languages for fifteen members. Without a choice of core language(s) for the EU, any expansion will rebuild a Tower of Babel as the number of possible combinations of $n$ languages is equal to $n(n-1)/2$. An EU-30 with twenty-five languages would require 600 interpreters at every full meeting!

An expanding EU is necessarily becoming more diverse. Therefore it is only desirable to expand if decisionmaking can be made easier in other ways. One reform goal embodied in the European Convention of 2003 consists in moving to majority voting. Other goals concern the reform of the political and administrative institutions of the EU (as it is not possible simply to add directorates to create room for additional staff from new members) and the redistribution of decisionmaking power to the European Parliament, to fill the 'democracy gap' between the Council and the Commission. Some of these features are captured in a theoretical model in Box 9.4.

In the end it is therefore the level of union (how deeply integrated?) and its decisionmaking capacity (e.g. federation or confederation) that are decisive for the optimal size of the EU. The more ambitious the ultimate goal, the more restrictive is its optimal size. The more a potential member differs in political and economic structure and maturity, the less compelling is membership.

What are the practical implications? EU members are aware of the fact that the optimal size depends on the internal organisation of the Union. But agreement of reforms has proved difficult. The first attempt to prepare for enlargement, at nine, ended in failure became it involved only governments fighting for their national interests. The second attempt, using a different approach (the Convention), went much further.

So far, the message for enlargement has been that the next wave will take in the most successful transition economies. The door remains open for the countries in South-East Europe, but the time is not yet ripe, as they have not yet been successful enough in reforming their political and economic structures. The EU has remained silent on the subject of the countries of the FSU, other than the Baltic states. In principle, this door is not closed either, at least for some of the countries of the Western FSU. For example, if Ukraine had been as successful in reforms as Poland (which would have been difficult, but not impossible), it would probably now be a member of the first wave. In other words, there seems to be no politically acceptable argument for the EU to refuse membership to a European country that clearly fulfils the 'Copenhagen Criteria'.

At the other end of the spectrum, the Asian and Caucasian countries of the FSU are, for reasons of geography, sociology and structural diversity, not acceptable candidates. And

### Box 9.4    *The optimum size of a club*

Clubs are associations in the pursuit of a well-defined common interest. Their optimum size is neither one individual, nor humankind (with its diverse tastes). To find the optimum size of a club, the benefits and costs of increasing membership need to be defined. In the following it is assumed that membership benefits are a *private* good and not a *public* good.

Starting from a small number of members, benefits to incumbents will initially rise with increasing membership but eventually start to decline as congestion becomes dominant (congestion implies that not only the benefit of a new member declines, but that of existing members as well). Similarly, the cost to incumbents of an additional member declines initially, but will increase eventually. Increasing marginal costs are also the result of congestion and the increasing difficulty of finding agreement among more numerous members with more heterogeneous preferences. Costs will also increase more than proportionately for the freedom of each additional member to express its political viewpoint, independent of size.

The optimum club size (M*) is given by the equality of marginal benefits and costs of incumbents, who are the decisionmakers for new admissions, as shown in figure 9.1. Institutional changes can affect both benefits and costs. For example, replacing unanimity decision rules by majority voting will shift the marginal cost curve downward so that optimal size increases.

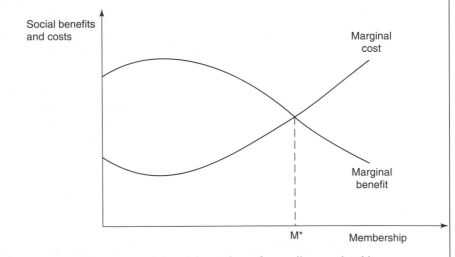

**Figure 9.1** Costs and benefits to existing club members of expanding membership
*Source:* De Benedictis and Padoan (1994).

Assuming that the European Union of fifteen members is close to the optimal level M*, or even above it, with its present institutional set-up, does this mean that CEEC could not be gainfully integrated into the European Union?

In figure 9.2 it is assumed that the present EU of fifteen members (M0) is already larger than optimum membership M* with its presentinstitutional arrangements. If M0

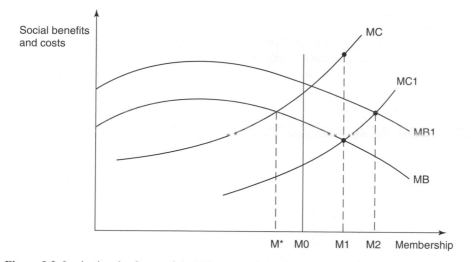

**Figure 9.2** Institutional reforms of the EU as a condition for enlargement to the east

were to the left of M* there would be scope for enlargement, but M0 is to the right of M*, so enlargement requires institutional reforms (such as majority decisions, reform of the CAP, which would be desirable even without enlargement). Enlargement to M1 without institutional reforms would increase the welfare cost as measured by the vertical distance between MC and MB at M0 to the one at M1. Reforms shift the marginal cost curve MC down to MC1. If those reforms were substantial enough, enlargement to M1 would be optimal. Some of these reforms, such as to the CAP, would not only decrease costs but would also increase benefits, shifting the MB curve to MB1, thereby making a greater enlargement to M2 desirable. For a given reform programme, expansion of optimal membership may not be enough to accommodate all membership candidates. Only those with marginal benefit in excess of marginal cost should be admitted. Further enlargement makes sense only if either the countries that are refused membership reform themselves to increase the marginal gain above the marginal cost of the EU, or further EU reforms are carried out. These examples illustrate that optimal enlargement depends on policies both in candidate countries *and* in the EU.

One concern about EU enlargement is that deepening integration might be made more difficult. It is often argued that enlargement of the euro area to include structurally weaker East European countries is likely to make deepening even more difficult. Figure 9.3 illustrates this argument.

The horizontal axis in figure 9.3 measures the depth of integration (e.g. adoption of the euro, participation in the Schengen area or the common foreign and security policy). For the EU of fifteen members the optimal depth of integration might be D*15. The actual level is presumably lower, at D15, so there is scope for more deepening. Adding new members may shift the marginal benefit curve upwards, although this gain may be small, at least in economic terms as the ten candidates together account for less than

(*cont.*)

### Box 9.4   (cont.)

5 per cent of the GDP of the incumbent fifteen. For simplicity, figure 9.3 assumes that the marginal benefit curve to incumbents remains unchanged. The cost, however, is bound to increase. The optimum level of depth of integration is therefore reduced from D*15 to D*20. In this sense it can be argued that enlargement is likely to require a trade-off in terms of deepening.

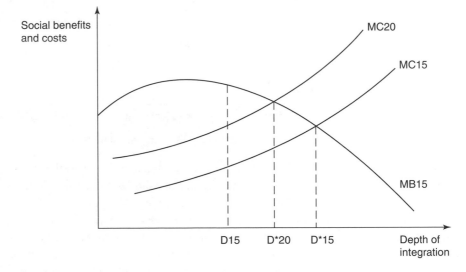

**Figure 9.3**  Deepening integration in an enlarged EU

Of course, D*20 is not necessarily to the right of D15. If it is, then further gainful deepening is still possible. If it were to the left of D15 then the current level of depth of integration would already be excessive for an enlarged union.

Russia? We would argue that Russia is too large geographically, and potentially too big politically, to become a member of the EU (even if it wanted to, which is unlikely). It would destabilise the balance of powers within the EU, even if economically there would be convergence. The open-door policy is thus to be limited to Belarus, Ukraine and Moldova. As things look at present, they may be part of a third wave in a generation or two. But all countries of the FSU should immediately be offered a special relationship, comprising a free-trade area.

## 9.4   What is special about the Eastern enlargement?

The main reason why the Eastern enlargement is expected to create problems for the EU is that the new members from CEEC are poor and agricultural. Since the EU spends mainly on poor regions and on farmers this seems to imply that enlargement would necessarily overburden the EU budget. However, a closer look reveals that the budgetary issue has been overblown.

Table 9.3. *Size of the eastern enlargement compared with previous expansions*

|  | Population | GDP (in euros) | Trade |
|---|---|---|---|
| UK + DK + IRL as % of EC-6 | 33.5 | 27.9 | 13.1 |
| Spain + Portugal as % of EC-10 | 17.5 | 8.3 | 4.7 |
| CEEC-10 as % of EU-15 (2000) | 28.0 | 4.1 | 10.9 |
| Turkey as % of EU-15 (2000) | 17.0 | 2.4 | 1.9 |
| Turkey as % of EU-25 (2000) | 13.2 | 2.3 | 1.7 |

*Source*: Own calculations using EU and EBRD data.

We should clarify, *en passant*, that the level of income per capita is not a criterion for membership. Accession means that the new members have the capacity to implement the *acquis communautaire* and to participate in EMU. A poor country with a well-functioning public sector, capable of implementing the *acquis* and conducting sensible macroeconomic policies, and so able to participate in EMU, is likely to grow fast and will cause much less problems than a country with a higher income whose administration cannot really provide a level playing field for the economy by implementing EU rules and regulations properly and that is stagnating because of inappropriate macroeconomic policies (e.g. Greece, until recently).

Tables 9.3 and 9.4 check whether this enlargement is different from others because the applicants are poor and agricultural. It is often argued that the Eastern enlargement is unprecedented in terms of the increase in population and other measures. However, this is not the case if one considers the size of the countries that joined during previous enlargements, relative to the size of the EC they joined.

This enlargement is thus significant in terms of population because the new members (CEEC-10) would increase the population of the EU by over one quarter (the increase is equivalent to the increase in the German population due to unification). However, by most economic measures the candidate countries are negligible, even if one assumes that their economies will grow rapidly. Table 9.3 also shows that in terms of GDP, evaluated at current exchange rates, the ten accession countries combined account for less than 5 per cent of the EU's GDP. This corresponds roughly to the weight of the Netherlands in the EU-15. We have also added two rows that evaluate the relative weight of Turkey, whose economy has some similarities with the CEEC-10 and which is a longtime candidate for membership (although its prospects of ever joining the EU are still uncertain).

It is often argued that this enlargement is special, because the candidates are much poorer than the present EU-15. This is especially true in respect of GDP measured at market exchange rates, where the CEEC-8 reach barely 21 per cent of the EU average as shown in column 1 of table 9.4. A better and more widely used indicator of living standard is GDP per capita at PPS (purchasing power standards), shown in column 2. On this account the CEEC-8 group looks a bit better, but remains, on average, clearly below 50 per cent of the EU-15 average. This is still about 15 percentage points lower than the values for Portugal

Table 9.4. *Accession countries: structural indicators (2000)*

| | Per capita GDP in euro (% of EU average) | Per capita GDP at PPS (% of EU average) | Share of industry in GDP (%) | Share of agriculture in GDP (%) | Employment in agriculture (% of total civilian employment) | Employment in industry (% of total civilian employment) | Degree of openness (exports plus imports of goods and services, as % of GDP) | Openness: Exports to EU (% of total exports) |
|---|---|---|---|---|---|---|---|---|
| Czech Rep. | 24 | 60 | 33 | 4 | 5 | 30 | 147 | 69 |
| Hungary | 22 | 52 | 28 | 5 | 7 | 27 | 129 | 75 |
| Poland | 20 | 39 | 28 | 4 | 19 | 24 | 69 | 70 |
| *CEEC-3 (average)* | *22* | *50* | *30* | *4* | *10* | *27* | *115* | *71* |
| Slovak Rep. | 17 | 48 | 29 | 5 | 7 | 29 | 150 | 59 |
| Slovenia | 44 | 72 | 31 | 3 | 10 | 32 | 122 | 64 |
| Estonia | 17 | 38 | 22 | 6 | 7 | 27 | 196 | 77 |
| Latvia | 15 | 29 | 19 | 5 | 14 | 20 | 100 | 65 |
| Lithuania | 15 | 29 | 26 | 8 | 18 | 21 | 97 | 48 |
| *CEEC-8 (average)* | *22* | *46* | *27* | *5* | *11* | *26* | *126* | *66* |

| | | | | | | | | |
|---|---|---|---|---|---|---|---|---|
| Bulgaria | 24 | 7 | 24 | 15 | 24 | 26 | 23 | 51 |
| Romania | 27 | 8 | 31 | 13 | 43 | 22 | 74 | 64 |
| Turkey | 29 | 14 | 23 | 15 | 35 | 18 | 55 | 52 |
| *1990–1 data* | | | | | | | | |
| Portugal | 61.0 | 37.1 | 31 | 5 | 18 | 34 | 68 | 80 |
| Spain | 76.5 | 68.8 | 17 | 4 | 11 | 33 | 56 | 65 |
| Italy | 101.9 | 101.1 | 31 | 4 | 9 | 32 | 46 | 53 |
| Greece | 59.4 | 43.3 | 15 | 14 | 21 | 24 | 41 | 62 |
| *Club Med* | | | | | | | | |
| *(average)* | *75* | *63* | *24* | *7* | *15* | *31* | *53* | *65* |

*Notes:* The data on employment for Bulgaria are for 1998. For Greece the data are for 1993 (except for the share of agriculture in CDP which are for 1992).
*Source: ECB Monthly Report,* February 2000; European Commission, 2001 Regular Reports, Statistical Annex of European Economy and 'The agricultural situation in the EU 1994 Report'.

and Greece at the beginning of the 1990s (several years after their accession to the then EC and eight years before their participation in the euro area).

The candidates are thus poor, but do they also have different economies? The answer seems to be no, since in terms of broad indicators of economic structure it is difficult to find strong systematic differences between the candidates and the poorer member countries. At around 5 per cent the share of agriculture in GDP (i.e. value added) is already rather low in the CEEC-8 group, but clearly higher in the two laggards Bulgaria and Romania.

The shares of industry in GDP are also not notably different from some current member countries. The fundamental reason why it is so difficult to make any firm judgement about systematic differences in economic structure is that there are large differences even among the present EU members. For example, in terms of the share of industry in GDP the range is large even in the group of so-called 'Club Med'[13] countries. In both Portugal and Italy the share of industry is rather high, at around 30 per cent of GDP. This cannot be considered a sign of a high (or low) level of development, since Italy's GDP per capita is slightly above the EU average and Portugal (with Greece) is the poorest member country. By contrast, industry is much less important in Spain and Greece, providing only around 15 per cent of GDP. As three of these countries are already successful members of the euro area there is apparently a very large range of economic structures that are compatible with membership of the EU and of EMU. On the basis of the limited data that are available, it appears that the candidate countries do not fall outside this range.

In terms of employment the differences in economic structures would appear to be larger, particularly with respect to Romania, Bulgaria and Poland, where a huge part of the labour force is officially employed in agriculture. However, while this will undoubtedly create social problems in these countries and problems for the Common Agricultural Policy, it is less relevant for the issue of EMU membership since value-added in this sector is a small part of GDP.

Moreover, one cannot avoid questioning the reliability of the data and of the definitions used for identifying farmers, particularly concerning Poland and Romania. In the former communist countries many who are classified as farmers exercise this activity only on a part-time basis and it appears that their average age is close to 60, so that their numbers will, anyway, be shrinking rapidly over the coming years. A comparison with Club Med is again instructive. The 1991 data for employment in industry and agriculture in Portugal, shown in table 9.4, are almost the same as for Poland in 1998. Thus the concerns regarding the large share of employment in agriculture for the candidates are overstated.

In considering the cost of enlargement, the most important country is therefore Poland, with the largest population and an economic structure that resembles that of Portugal a decade ago. The other five to seven small countries that might join before 2005 are already highly industrialised, and in this sense similar to the existing EU members. Bulgaria and Romania are clearly in a different category.

The difference in economic structure is thus manageable. More of a problem would be the other two specificities of the enlargement: the high number of countries and their low income. In an EU-25 there will be a majority of poor countries that could use their majority to resist 'rich country' policies and to obtain larger income transfers. At the very least they could block integration deepening or reforms of the CAP. For this reason it is important that a reform of the decisionmaking processes be carried out before enlargement.

## 9.5   The cost of enlargement

More than 90 per cent of the budgetary costs of enlargement (as seen from the incumbent EU-15) fall on two policy instruments: Structural Funds and the Common Agricultural Policy.

### Structural Funds

The EU spends at present each year about 25–30 billion euros on poor regions through the various 'Structural Funds' (the Regional Fund, the Social Fund, the Agricultural Fund) and the Cohesion Fund to promote 'Economic and Social Cohesion'. This sum amounts to approximately 0.5 per cent of EU GDP and roughly one-third of the overall EU budget. The budget available in this area is usually fixed for six-year periods in advance (1994–2000, 2000–6, etc.). The total amounts available and the distribution over different funds and countries are determined essentially by political horse-trading. The current six-year period will end in 2006 and should thus cover the first years of the enlarged EU.

About 70 per cent of all Structural Funds spending is allocated to assistance of the so-called 'Objective 1' regions, i.e. regions,[14] not countries, with a GDP per capita *measured at purchasing power parity* (PPP) below 75 per cent of the EU average.[15] The qualification 'at PPP' is important because the GDP of poorer countries is in general much higher if valued at PPP than if valued at current exchange rates, since their prices of non-tradables (mainly services) are usually much lower. Within the EU-15 it is a rule of thumb that a country or region will reach 75 per cent of the EU average GDP measured at PPP if its income measured at current exchange rates reaches about 60 per cent of the EU average. But for the CEEC, the difference is much larger. For example, the GDP per capita of the Czech Republic in 1998 was less than 25 per cent of the EU average measured at current exchange rates, but about 60 per cent of the EU average measured at PPP. As can be seen from the second column in table 9.4, this puts the Czech Republic 'only' seven years behind Portugal, whose GDP per capita at PPP stood in 1991 at only 61 per cent of the EU average (then comprising only twelve members). Portugal has in the meantime caught up partially and its GDP per capita is above 75 per cent of the EU average. There is thus some reason to believe that a country like the Czech Republic should be able to come closer to the threshold of eligibility for Structural Funds by the time it enters.

The accession of poorer countries will have the effect of lowering the EU average, possibly by as much as 5 percentage points.[16] This makes it even more likely that at least some of the new members will not stay below the threshold of 75 per cent of the EU average, thus further reducing the pressure on expenditure.

At present all of Portugal and Greece, most of Spain, the south of Italy and the new eastern *Länder* of Germany are the regions that benefit most from Objective 1 status.[17] The poorest regions (Greece, Portugal) receive around 300 euro per head each year.[18] Those countries with regions that are only marginally below the 75 per cent threshold will, of course, fiercely resist any cuts if their regions exceed the threshold merely because the EU average falls.

As shown above, all CEEC candidates for membership are currently so poor that they will all qualify for Objective 1 status. With their combined population of about 100 million an extension of the present policy on cohesion would cost about 30 billion euros per annum. Although this would represent less than 0.5 per cent of the EU's GDP it might be impossible to finance because the EU budget is now already close to its ceiling of 1.27 per cent of GDP. This ceiling has been accepted by successive European Councils as binding, and has also been applied for the period 2000–6. It would thus appear at first sight that enlargement would be impossible before 2006 unless the ceiling on spending is lifted or other spending is cut. Both solutions would be politically rather awkward.

This conundrum of how to stick to the promise of membership without busting the budget forced the EU institutions to find a solution, the 'Berlin compromise', which was ratified at the 1999 meeting of the European Council in Berlin. With this agreement it became possible to finance enlargement under the 1.27 per cent ceiling. The key decision was to limit the maximum amount of Structural Funds a country could receive to 4 per cent of its GDP. As many applicants still have a GDP below 4,000 euros per capita, their maximum entitlement would be only around 160 euros per capita, or a total of 16 billion euros if all of them joined immediately. Further 'savings' could be obtained because the Structural Funds would have to be phased in gradually and because not all ten CEEC candidates become members before 2005. While these savings are temporary, they have relieved the pressure on the EU to reorganise its financing mechanism and expenditure policies.

How generous is a transfer limited to 4 per cent of GDP? Quite generous, when compared with the famous generosity of the Marshall Plan, which represented 2 per cent of GDP for recipient countries for a period of four years. Structural Funds are capped until 2006 at double that value and represent only one instrument of aid. As long as regions remain below the 75 per cent limit, they can obtain support without a time constraint. By any reasonable standard, Structural Funds are to be considered as very generous, probably too generous, given their lack of effectiveness. In a startling document (*European Economy* 1996) the EU Commission comes to the conclusion that the Structural Funds make no significant contribution to the convergence of the target regions.

Table 9.5 summarises the Berlin compromise. The compromise covers the period until 2006 and postpones the real issues. As it is likely that a number of countries will have joined the EU by that date, the debate on the cost of enlargement has effectively been short-circuited. The new members that join in 2004 will have to accept lower transfers for a couple of years. But they will certainly not be willing to accept such an outcome for the next planning period, i.e. 2006–12. Moreover, the limitation of Structural Funds to 4 per cent of GDP means that, initially at least, the burden placed by the new members on the EU budget will increase as their income grows. The 4 per cent limit amounts to only around 160 euros per capita at the present GDP levels, but this figure will quickly rise if there is strong growth in the CEEC (see Box 6.5 for a more detailed explanation). After 2006 the expanded EU of twenty-five members will simply have to confront the alternative

Table 9.5. *The Berlin compromise (all figures in bn euros at 2000 prices)*

|  | 2000 | 2006 |
|---|---|---|
| Total for EU-15 | 89.6 | 89.3 |
| As % of GDP of EU-15 | 1.13 | 0.97 |
| Available for accession |  | 14.2 |
| *Agriculture* |  | *3.4* |
| *Other expenditure* |  | *10.8* |
| Overall ceiling | 89.6 | 103.5 |
| Ceiling as % of GDP | 1.13 | 1.13 |
| Margin (%) | 0.14 | 0.14 |
| Own resources ceiling (%) | 1.27 | 1.27 |

*Source*: Berlin Council, Conclusions of the Presidency.

between reducing expenditure somewhere else or going through the ceiling of 1.27 per cent of GDP for the EU budget. We can thus expect a series of rowdy late-night sessions of the European Council on this issue. For now there is a third option: the 4 per cent limit will remain in force for quite some time. In terms of efficiency, this is an attractive solution.

There is another consideration that is usually overlooked in the discussions about the cost of enlargement. This is simply that one should look not only at the budgetary cost of a new member state today, but also at its potential future contribution once it has caught up.

In other words one should look at the net present value of present and future Structural Funds and contributions to the EU budget. It is apparent that this requires a view on how quickly the new EU members can catch up to the EU average (and eventually surpass it?). Given the high human capital endowment and the relatively good institutional framework these countries have, as documented in chapter 4, the prospects for a rapid catch-up should be good. Moreover, as discussed below, EU membership should itself be a powerful boost to growth in the CEEC, which constitute small open economies. The experience within the old EU-15 is also encouraging, as it has been amply demonstrated that there is a long-run tendency for GDP per capita to converge across countries (but not necessarily across regions within countries).

So how quickly could the new members from CEEC converge? Assuming that they follow the pattern found in the literature on convergence, convergence typically proceeds at around 3 per cent per annum (meaning that poorer countries can make up each year around 3 per cent of the difference in GDP per capita between them and the most advanced economies). If this rate of convergence is assumed to hold for the new members it would imply that most of them would need a generation to achieve even partial convergence. Even were the CEECs able to converge somewhat faster (say at 4 per cent), this would still be much worse than the EU's star performer, Ireland.

## *Box 9.5  Less to the needy?*

### *The relationship between income and the cost of enlargement*

The ceiling of 4 per cent of GDP for the Structural Funds has an interesting implication: it implies that enlargement becomes more expensive the more the applicants grow. The current average GDP per capita of the EU-15 is about 20,000 euros. All regions with less than 15,000 can thus qualify for structural funds. At 4 per cent of GDP a region (or country) could thus theoretically receive a maximum of 600 euros per capita, although a further ceiling of 400 euros in terms of the absolute amount was also introduced to reduce the potential burden. The cost of enlargement will at first increase as the GDP of the new members grows, and then reach a plateau. If one takes into account that the contribution to the EU budget each member has to pay is about 1 per cent of GDP, this implies that the net cost of enlargement to the EU budget first increases and then falls as the applicants grow richer.

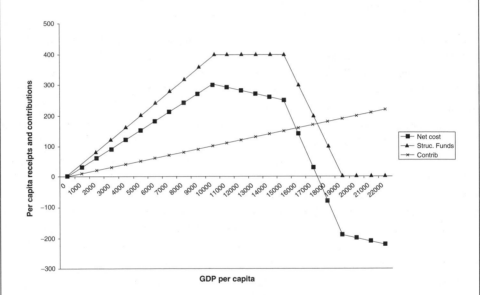

**Figure 9.4** Structural Funds and contributions to EU budget

Figure 9.4 provides an illustration of the relationship between the GDP per capita of a country (or region) and the net transfers it should obtain from the EU budget. The key assumptions are: Structural Funds are limited to 4 per cent of GDP, up to a maximum of 400 euros, which is reached when GDP per capita reaches 10,000 euros. Between this figure and 15,000 euros the Structural Funds are limited to 400 euros. As the EU average equals about 20,000 euros Structural Fund eligibility should cease beyond 15,000 euros. In reality this does not happen abruptly, and it is assumed that they decline from 400 to zero between 15,000 and 19,000 euros in GDP per capita. Contributions to the EU budget are assumed constant at 1 per cent of GDP.

Table 9.6. *The cost of enlargement in present value terms*

| Starting point for GDP (per capita as % of EU-15) | Speed of convergence | | |
|---|---|---|---|
| | Normal: 3% | Fast: 4% | No convergence |
| 20% | 8.7% | 6.3% | 4.1% |
| 40% | 9.2% | 5.9% | 13.0% |
| 60% | 2.0% | −0.5% | 18.3% |

*Source*: Own calculations.

Once a convergence pattern has been chosen, one can extrapolate the evolution of GDP per capita of the new members into the future, apply the existing rules for Structural Funds and contributions to the EU budget, and finally discount all future flows back to the present. The results are shown in table 9.6 for three convergence hypotheses (normal, fast and no convergence) and three starting values in terms of GDP per capita (20, 40 and 60 per cent of the EU average). All the entries refer to the net present value of the per-capita cost to the EU budget of a new member as a percentage of annual EU-15 GDP per capita.

A first point emerges immediately from comparison along the first column: a very poor country (starting GDP per capita of 20 per cent) can actually cost somewhat less, even in present value terms, than a 'middle' poor country (starting GDP per capita of 40 per cent). This is due to the limitation of Structural Funds receipts to 4 per cent of GDP as mentioned above. The effect of this comes through even more clearly in the last column, in which it is assumed that the country concerned does not converge at all. A country with a very low GDP per capita (e.g. Bulgaria) will cost less than a similar-sized country with a much higher income (e.g. the Czech Republic). If the Bulgarian GDP per capita were to stagnate at only around 2,000 euros, each Bulgarian would continue to cost the EU budget only 60 euros per annum (= 4 per cent Structural Funds minus 1 per cent contribution). By contrast, each Czech citizen might cost the EU budget three times as much, i.e. around 180 euros, because Czech GDP per capita is at around 6,000 euros, three times that of Bulgaria. The last column shows that once all flows are discounted back to the present a stagnant Bulgaria would cost (on a per-capita basis) each EU citizen about 4 per cent of its annual GDP, whereas a Czech citizen (stagnating at 40 per cent of EU GDP) would end up costing almost 13 per cent of the annual GDP of an average EU-15 citizen.

A second point emerges by looking at the last row. It shows that the worst case for the EU budget is a relatively well-off country that does not grow. A country that is stuck at 60 per cent of GDP per capita would cost twice as much as a poorer country that converges, if only at normal speed. A country that converges quickly, and starts at 60 per cent of the EU average, could even, on a present-value basis, bring more than it costs initially.

## *Agriculture*

Many politicians fear, and economists hope, that enlargement would bankrupt the Common Agricultural Policy (CAP). The hopes of economists are based on the fact that the CAP constitutes a jungle of market distortions with an insurmountable defence against real reforms. For the politicians supporting the CAP the fears are based essentially on two numbers. The agricultural area of the ten applicants represents more than 40 per cent of the total in the present EU-15, and their over 9.5 million farmers outnumber the 8 million farmers of the EU.

Moreover, the climate and soil of these countries favour the production of wheat, beef and milk, which already cause problems in the EU because of the large surpluses that have to be financed by the CAP. Given these numbers, it is not surprising that it has been predicted that enlargement necessitates a fundamental reform of the CAP or would otherwise bankrupt the EU.

A closer look at the situation reveals again that the problem is not so dramatic, and certainly not so simple. Lumping all applicants together is especially misleading in this case. In terms of the number of farmers, over 70 per cent of the 'problem' comes actually from just two countries: Poland and Romania. They are home to more than 7 million of the total of 9.5 million farmers for all the ten countries. The other countries have generally a much lower proportion of their overall workforce in agriculture.

While the CEEC have a large agricultural workforce and a lot of arable land, their productivity is still rather low. Most analyses of the issue concentrate on the difference in physical productivity (in quantity terms, tonnes of wheat per hectare, litres of milk per cow, etc.), or yield differentials. Yield differentials between EU and eastern countries are large: for cereals the difference is about 50 per cent, less for oilseeds, but somewhat more for milk. The difference is highest for sugar. But this is one commodity whose production in Europe would be close to zero without the CAP.

The yield differentials are already at present smaller for the more developed CEEC, such as the Czech and Slovak Republics, Hungary and Slovenia. As their production is thus unlikely to increase greatly these countries should represent only the 'usual' problems for the CAP. The key country in terms of agriculture is Poland, whose farming sector is very fragmented and much less efficient.

These differentials in agricultural productivity are presumably due to a lack of know-how (human capital) and a lower use of inputs, such as fertilisers. It is feared that when the CEEC join the EU their farmers will obtain much higher prices and would therefore use more inputs to increase yields so that the yield differential will be rapidly reduced, i.e. that production will expand once these countries have joined the EU and benefit from the CAP. In the meantime transfer of know-how should take place through direct investment and better access of Central European farmers to the latest technologies and best practices in the EU. However, there are two reasons to doubt that accession to the EU will lead to a large increase in production.

First, prices and costs have already converged to a large extent before accession. Farm-gate prices might have been much lower during the initial under-valuation of the CEEC currencies (see Knaster 1997). The basic reason is that prices follow domestic cost inflation instead of world market prices because there was in any case little trade in these raw commodities. (There is, however, a great deal of trade in other products and highly processed food.) The input prices for farmers and the shadow price for their time went up with the overall price and wage level. Accession to the EU might thus mean a further increase in both prices and costs, with a much smaller increase in the incentive to increase production than is commonly assumed.

Second, the main reason for the extremely low productivity of Polish agriculture is that most of the land is parcelled into small pieces. The average holding is only about five hectares versus about fifteen hectares in Hungary, the Czech Republic and the EU.[19] The experience of other countries suggests that such a dispersed holding pattern inhibits productivity growth. The real problem for an enlarged EU might thus not be so much excess supply coming from the new member countries as the plight of 3 million Polish farmers. It remains to be seen whether this will be considered a problem that Poland has to solve on its own or whether EU money will be mobilised in the name of European 'solidarity'.

Even if it were possible to predict the increase in production following accession it is not straightforward to calculate the budgetary cost of a hypothetical extension of the current CAP regime to an enlarged EU because one has to take into account many factors: some commodities (e.g. grain) serve as an input for other products (beef), consumption will increase, world market prices can change and it is difficult to estimate the reaction of production to higher prices. Estimates of the cost vary from 6 to 37 billion euros p.a., depending mainly on the assumed elasticity of output. Moreover, as explained in box 9.6, there is the contentious issue of whether CEEC farmers should receive the same compensatory payments currently doled out to their EU colleagues.

A better estimate of the cost of enlargement in the field of agriculture can be obtained by using a simple economic approach. Instead of concentrating on tonnes of wheat produced, we concentrate on the value-added produced in this sector. For the EU the total value-added of the agricultural sector is about 200 billion euros, which compares to about 15 billion euros for the CEEC-10. This corresponds roughly to the difference in overall GDP and is thus not too surprising. About 40 billion euros from the EU budget are spent on farmers, which amounts to about 20 per cent of their value-added. (Total agricultural subsidies are much larger because member states also spend a lot on this sector.) The Berlin compromise foresees only about 3 billion euros per annum being spent on the agriculture of the countries that will join. This group of countries produces about two-thirds of the output of the entire CEEC-10 group, or 10 billion euros. While a figure of 3 billion euros for eight countries might appear meagre, it would constitute a higher percentage of value-added (30 per cent) than for the current EU-15. Moreover, 3 billion euros for 6 million farmers would amount to about 500 euros per head, which is a significant fraction of the overall income of farmers (whether part time or not) in the CEEC. (Of course it is much less than the average of about 6,000 euros of EU transfers per farmer in the EU-15.)

We have so far concentrated on the impact enlargement would have on the budget of the EU given the current state of the CAP. The most important effect of enlargement might, however, be elsewhere. Once a number of Central European countries with still relatively large agricultural sectors join and have a vote in the Council of Ministers, the power of the agricultural lobby may well increase such that further reforms of the CAP become

---

*Box 9.6    The CAP: problem child of the EU*

The commitments underwritten by the EU in the context of the WTO agreement on agriculture will anyway increase the pressure on the CAP even without enlargement. The WTO agreement contains a phasing out of export subsidies, which implies that domestic EU prices will have to be brought down to world market levels. If the EU sticks to this commitment enlargement should not place a large burden on the EU agricultural budget. One alternative would be to keep prices up but stick to the self-imposed growth limit for spending on agriculture (at most 74 per cent of GDP growth). This limit could then be obeyed only at the cost of more bureaucratic management of farming through mandatory set-aside rules, production quotas, etc. This would clearly lead to large inefficiencies and it would anyway be impossible to control the output of 3 million small Polish farmers.

The CAP has moved towards lower guaranteed prices, which are made acceptable to farmers by giving them so-called 'compensatory payments' that top up their income. Ideally, at the end of this process internal EU prices would be equal to world market prices and the EU would no longer have to subsidise exports if production still were to exceed domestic consumption. This is more efficient from an economic point of view because it implies that farmers face the correct price, but it can increase the direct budgetary burden because under the old system consumers paid part of the transfer to farmers through higher prices. Since households in Central Europe are poorer and spend a much larger proportion of their income on food (about 30 per cent compared to 20 per cent for the EU-15) they would certainly favour paying lower prices for food. The additional budgetary cost through compensatory payments would be borne by European taxpayers, i.e. mostly inhabitants of the present EU-15 who will account for over 90 per cent of the GDP of the enlarged Union and hence also for over 90 per cent of the contributions to the EU budget.

Enlargement will make it necessary to rethink the system of 'compensatory payments'. It is difficult to counter the argument that farmers in Central Europe need not be 'compensated' for price cuts they never experienced. But it is also difficult to have a supposedly common agricultural policy that distributes large payments to only a part of the Union.

At the European Council meeting of Copenhagen during which the financial deals for enlargement were finalised a compromise was also found for the compensatory payments. As this is only a question of redistribution there could be no efficient solution, just a compromise that everybody could accept. After much last-minute posturing even the Poles (and all the other candidates) settled in the end for initial payments of only 25 per cent of the EU-15 level for their farmers, with an agreement that this percentage should rise to 100 over the next 10 years.

This compromise saved the CAP for the day, but the proper solution would have been to 're-nationalise' one aspect of agricultural policy, namely income support for farmers. This is basically part of social policy, which will anyway remain in national hands for the time being.[20] The CAP would then not be abolished, only its economically most inefficient aspects would disappear. The CAP would still be needed to provide the food safety regulations indispensable to the functioning of a common market in food and it may stabilise prices around a fluctuating world market level. But it would no longer be an obstacle to enlargement or world trade.

impossible. It cannot even be ruled out that some reforms will be rolled back. The Polish government, for example, might argue that prices for wheat and milk must be increased to save millions of Polish farmers from misery.[21]

The only defence against the demands that are certain to arise for more spending on agriculture is a strict overall ceiling on the agricultural budget. This has already been agreed upon with the commitment of the European Council to limit any increase in spending for agriculture to less than 80 per cent of the increase in nominal EU GDP. This is not a very strong constraint. Over the next decade EU GDP might increase by about 50 per cent (in nominal terms). With this limit CAP spending could increase a lot, but by less than 40 per cent, implying a decline of about 10 per cent as a share of GDP – a modest, but useful, step in the right direction. The Central European candidate countries should thus be asked during the enlargement negotiations to agree explicitly to a continuation of this ceiling on overall agricultural spending.

The threat of enlargement was not sufficient to force the EU-15 to consider a real reform of the CAP. As discussed above, they preferred even in late 2002, at the last European Council which dealt with enlargement, to find a messy compromise rather than to consider reforms. However, pressure was also building up from the major trading partners of the EU in the World Trade Organisation (WTO), and the next round of talks on further trade liberalisation. The rules of international trade require all countries to 'de-couple' support for agriculture (as for other industries) from production. Further steps in that direction were finally agreed in 2003, thus providing another respite for the CAP and probably reducing the cost of enlargement.

## 9.6  Benefits of enlargement

The public discussion in the EU-15 about the budgetary cost of enlargement sometimes obscures the fact that enlargement should bring economic benefits. How large will they be? Should they be a key consideration for the CEEC or should those countries join mainly for other reasons, e.g. to protect themselves against Russia? This question is difficult to answer because everything depends on the alternative. For example, if one were to assume that the Czech Republic could become a sort of Switzerland if it did not join the EU one would conclude that membership does not bring this country any appreciable economic benefits. For its neighbour, the Slovak Republic, one might have to assume instead that the country would go back into the orbit of Russia and stop its reforms if it did not have the alternative of becoming a member of the EU. These are admittedly extreme examples, but they are useful to highlight the general problem underlying all attempts at measuring the welfare benefits of enlargement. A further reason why it is difficult to quantify the economic effects of enlargement is that it affects all aspects of the economy.

One approach is to zero in on one key aspect and simplify as much as possible. This is done in the appendix, where we concentrate on one basic tenet of economics, namely that integration between different economies should actually lead to more economic gains than integration between similar economies. This idea can be illustrated in a simple model, which formalises the most basic set-up in which two separate economies with different capital–labour ratios become totally integrated. One can then compare income before and after integration. This simple standard model shows that world GDP increases with integration as capital moves from a region with relatively low marginal capital productivity (the EU-15) to a region with relatively high marginal capital productivity (the CEEC). However, this is not the main result. The main result is that the increase in world GDP is higher the greater the difference in capital–labour ratios prior to integration. The model also shows that the gain does not go only to the CEEC. The present EU-15 also benefit and their gain is also an increasing function of the initial difference in capital–labour ratios.

How large are the gains? An illustrative calibration, which replicates approximately current income differentials, suggests that the gain for the EU-15 should be modest, about 1 per cent of income, versus a 50 per cent gain for the CEEC. The calculations also show the importance of distinguishing between GNP and GDP when assessing growth in the CEEC. The GDP of the CEEC might increase by over 100 per cent when they import massive amounts of capital. But the increase in GNP (which determines purchasing power for consumption) is much lower because the returns to the capital go to the lender, i.e. the EU-15. These numbers cannot be taken to show the welfare gains from enlargement as a lot of integration can take place even without membership in the EU, but they show the potential gain from economic integration between very different economies. Even if trade integration were already yielding four-fifths of this potential (because most formal trade barriers have already been eliminated), the benefits from enlargement would still be substantial.

Another approach to dealing with the complexity of the issue is to use a so-called 'computable general equilibrium' model taking into account the interactions between trade, labour markets and investment via the capital markets, to mention only the most important elements of this type of model. This is done by Baldwin, François and Portes (1997). They assume in a first 'conservative scenario' that the main effect of EU membership is to reduce the cost of trading between the ten associated states and the EU by 10 per cent and to eliminate trade barriers for agricultural products.[22] The first element is the key to their results. The 10 per cent reduction in trading costs reduces total costs by 2.5 per cent since in their model the starting level of the cost of trading across borders is 25 per cent of the transaction value. With membership this is supposed to go down to 22.5 per cent. They find that under this scenario real income in the candidate states would increase by about 1.5 per cent[23] and only 0.2 per cent in the EU. The small impact on the EU is understandable if one takes into account that exports to the associated states account for about 2 per cent of the GDP of the EU-15. However, one would expect the impact on the CEEC to be much larger because their trade with the EU-15 accounts for up to 25 per cent of their GDP.

A gain of 1.5 per cent for the candidate states seems very conservative, given the estimates that have been made of the benefits from integration within the 'old' member states. Enlargement implies essentially an extension of the internal market and monetary union.[24] The benefits of these two integration projects for the EU-15 membership have been estimated and could be used as a guide. Recent estimates of the transactions cost savings from the introduction of the euro are in the neighbourhood of 1 per cent of GDP (see also chapter 7 in Gros and Thygesen 1999). It is more difficult to estimate the gain from participation

Table 9.7. *Measurable benefits to the CEEC-10 from EU membership (discounted at 5% p.a.; % of EU-15 GDP, 2001)*

| | |
|---|---|
| Common currency | 1.0–1.3 |
| Internal market | 4.4–6.0 |
| Total | 5.4–7.3 |

*Source*: Own calculations based on estimates for the EU-15 of the gains from a common currency and an internal market.

in the internal market. CEC (1988) found that this should yield welfare benefits of between 2.5 and 4.5 per cent of EU GDP. Could this estimate be used for the candidates as well? Several arguments would indicate that the benefits for the CEEC should be at the larger end of this range, or even higher. The key consideration is that all the CEEC are very small economies, which should thus benefit more from the additional competition fostered by the internal market than the larger and more diversified EU economies. Moreover, integration and market opening in the EU has proceeded well beyond the sectors considered in the initial '1992' programme.

Even if these elements are ignored, any estimate of the welfare gains for the CEEC is bound to be higher than that for the EU-15 since intra-EU trade accounts for about 15 per cent of EU-15 GDP, whereas trade with the EU-15 accounts on average for well over 20 per cent of the GDP of the CEEC. The benefits for the new members should thus be at least one-third higher: 4.4–6.0 per cent of GDP for participation in the internal market and 1.3 per cent for using the common currency. Table 9.7 summarises these back-of-the-envelope calculations, which lead to the result that EU membership should yield a measurable benefit of between 5.4 and 7.3 per cent of GDP for the CEEC.[25]

These measurable gains are already sizeable, but much larger gains can be obtained by assuming that membership transforms conditions under which the associated countries have access to the world capital market. At present, interest rates in the associated countries are much higher than those in the EU, even for countries that have a strong reputation for price stability, such as the Czech Republic, or a currency board, such as Estonia. For other countries, e.g. Poland, the domestic real interest rate is even higher.

Where does this risk premium come from? Baldwin et al. (1997) argue that the current risk premium on interest rates in the associated states is due not to monetary factors, but to uncertainty about the future of reforms. The crucial assumption is then that only membership can dissipate the doubts in the minds of investors and reduce this risk. Countries that are not allowed to become members would not be able to assure investors about the durability of their reform programmes. The size of the reduction in the risk premium that would come with enlargement is difficult to pinpoint. Baldwin et al. (1997) use Portugal as an example and argue that accession to the EU would imply a reduction in the risk premium of about 15 per cent (i.e. the interest rate would drop from, say, 14 per cent – with 5 per cent risk-free interest plus 9 per cent risk premium – to 12.65 per cent). The result under this scenario is that real income in the associated states might increase by 10 per cent or more! This at first sight astonishing result is actually not too surprising given that the models of capital accumulation used by economists imply that the long-term capital stock is extremely sensitive to changes in the real interest rate. Box 9.7 provides the basic model behind these calculations.

What are the implications of these very large potential gains from membership arising from a reduction in the risk premium? A first point to note is that this approach assumes that investors will only upgrade the new members and not downgrade the existing ones. While this is possible, it could also be argued that the new equilibrium of political forces within the enlarged Union will make economically sound policies less likely (see the discussion about 'power politics' in agriculture above). The loss to the EU from a slight increase in its risk premium could easily exceed the gains of new members on account of a lower risk premium for them. Moreover, the quantification of the gain in the risk premium must remain arbitrary as the risk premium in the absence of accession cannot be observed. A more fundamental objection concerns the difference between GDP (production) and GNP (closer to consumption potential). As the imported capital has to be remunerated the increase in welfare is much smaller than the increase in GDP.

The reduction in the risk premium on imported capital might thus not be the most important advantage of EU membership. However, these illustrative calculations of the potential gains from membership are useful because they highlight one important aspect. There are certain gains from joining the internal market and EMU that can be quantified. In our view these gains should be in the neighbourhood of 5 per cent for the CEEC-10, which are all very open economies. But the potentially more important gains are not quantifiable: they come from joining an area that embodies through internal market rules the principles of open competition in the largest market of the world and that promotes sound macroeconomic policies within the context of EMU. This framework for sound policies should favour growth through various channels and might ultimately raise income by even more than 10 per cent. But one has to admit that this is not a judgement that can be proven with scientific methods.

Another useful lesson from these estimates is that the welfare gains for the EU are also real, although much smaller in terms of the EU-15 GDP. Expansion to the east would increase trading opportunities for the EU-15. The CEEC account for less than 5 per cent of the EU GDP but about 10–15 per cent of the EU's external trade. Assuming the gain from the internal market is about 4–5 per cent of EU-15 GDP, the gain to present EU members from the inclusion of the ten CEEC in the internal market and the euro zone should thus be about 0.4–0.5 per cent of GDP, or about 25 billion euros p.a. This alone would be about the same as the total budgetary cost. Moreover, the gains for the EU can only grow over time as the economies of the new member states grow along with their trade. Their share in the overall external trade of the EU has already doubled since 1990 and on current trends it could well double again by 2005–6. At that point the estimated benefit would be twice as large as it appears from today's point of view. However, the budgetary costs would not increase proportionally. It is thus likely that the economic benefits of enlargement to the EU-15 will soon outweigh the costs even more clearly than they do today.

---

**Box 9.7 The neo-classical growth model**

The standard 'neo-classical' theory of growth is based on a model in which firms produce one (possibly composite) product with capital and labour under constant returns to scale and perfect competition. Given an exogenous labour supply the long-run equilibrium is reached when the marginal productivity of capital is equal to the real interest rate fixed in the world capital market. This can be illustrated using a diagram that relates the capital stock (per capita) on the horizontal axis to output (per capita) on the vertical axis.

The curve $F(k)$ shows how much output per capita, $y_t$, can be produced given the per capita capital stock. The functional form most often used is:

$$F(k_t) = A k_t^\alpha, \tag{9.1}$$

where $\alpha$ denotes the elasticity of output with respect to capital and $A$ is a productivity parameter ($(1-\alpha)$ is the share of labour in national income). The long-run level of output is determined by the condition that the marginal product of capital has to equal the cost of capital, which in turn is equal to the rate of interest, $r$. This corresponds to the point of tangency between a straight line (whose slope is given by the interest rate) and the production function $F(k)$. This point of tangency determines the steady-state capital stock denoted by $k_{ss}$. Formally, it is determined by the condition:

$$F_k(k_{ss}) = r = \alpha A k_{ss}^{\alpha-1} \quad or \quad k_{ss} = (r/\alpha A)^{1/(\alpha-1)}. \tag{9.2}$$

The steady-state level of output per capita can be calculated by using this result in the production function

$$F(k_{ss}) = A(r/\alpha A)^{\alpha/(\alpha-1)} \quad or \quad y_{ss} = F(k_{ss}) = (r/\alpha)^{\alpha/(\alpha-1)} A^{1/(1-\alpha)}. \tag{9.3}$$

It is apparent that this framework explains only the *level* of steady-state income (per capita). Continuing *growth* is possible in this framework only if productivity grows. (Growth in the labour force leads only to growth in total output, but does not affect income per capita.)

The key result in equation (9.3) is that if $A$ increases by 1 per cent per capita output increases by $1/(1-\alpha)$ per cent. Since $1/(1-\alpha)$ must exceed one it is also called the 'multiplier' (of steady-state output with respect to a change in productivity). Setting the elasticity of output with respect to capital, $\alpha$, equal to one-half corresponds to a multiplier of two $[1/(1 - 0.5) = 2]$. For a broad concept of capital, including human capital, $\alpha = 0.5$ is conservative.

Savings in transactions costs should be broadly equivalent to an increase in overall productivity since without these transaction costs output can increase by 1 per cent with the same inputs. This model thus implies that the total output gain should be about double the initial reduction in transaction costs.

Equation (9.3) also implies that any change in the interest rate, $r$, will be 'magnified' by the factor $\alpha/(\alpha-1)$. With $\alpha = 0.5$ this factor is equal to one. It follows that a 10 per cent change in the interest rate should lead to a 10 per cent change in output in the long run. A reduction of interest rates by 10 per cent does not necessarily imply very low rates. It could be obtained if the real interest rate to be paid on business investment were to fall from 5 to 4.5 per cent (or from 10 to 9 per cent).

## 9.7  Conclusions

The EU had already recognised by 1992 the 'European vocation' of the CEEC and indicated that membership negotiations could start with ten of these countries. These negotiations turned out to take much longer than initially hoped for. It took twelve years to finalise formal membership for the first group of eight CEECs. But this does not mean that in the meantime integration was put on hold. During the 1990s the European Agreements gradually abolished barriers to trade in industrial goods and trade expanded manifold over the decade. Later, when membership negotiations were so well advanced that the end was in sight, capital started to flow abundantly to the prospective new members.

A decade after liberalisation from central planning the transition period has thus ended in most of Central and Eastern Europe.

Joining the EU is certainly a positive step for the CEEC, but does that mean that the EU should encompass all of Europe? What is the optimal size of the EU? It does depend, most of all, on how successful the Union itself is in adapting its decisionmaking institutions and its financial programmes. To make membership, especially membership in EMU, viable for all concerned, everybody needs to adjust. The current members need to welcome migrants and the Central Europeans need to converge in social, political and economic terms. History and present performance suggest that most of the candidates will meet this challenge. The same applies probably to most EU-15 countries. Those that refuse to adapt, those that do not reform sclerotic labour market institutions, will fall behind.

Because the EU is more, much more, than a free trade area, its optimal size is not the world. For the foreseeable future the countries of the FSU will not fit into the EU, and other institutional arrangements, such as a free trade arrangement, need to be found for them. The EU would also be well advised to assist in improved financial intermediation. Russia and other CIS countries no longer need financial aid. They need assistance, or rather incentives, to make better use of their own resources.

Many observers sense that this enlargement is different from all previous ones. This is true, but not simply because these countries are poor or have different economic structures. We pointed out that economic theory suggests that integration is actually more beneficial the greater the differences in endowment. The fact that the new members are so much poorer is thus not only a potential source of tensions, but also a source of potential economic benefits.

Whatever the economic benefits, the combination of increased diversity and much larger numbers of members means that enlargement requires a major effort from the EU to reform its decisionmaking capacity. With the reform process started by the Convention on the Future of Europe, established in 2001–2, there is reason to be optimistic. But the history of European integration over the last fifty years suggests that progress is often uneven and temporary setbacks occur.

The costs of enlargement, which have occupied such an important place in the discussions among the EU-15, are significant, but manageable. CAP reform, including reform of compensatory payments, and national responsibility would go a long way to ironing out the biggest difficulties and some steps have already been taken. Anyway, the large number of small and not very productive Polish farmers will soon find out that the CAP will not be manna from heaven. It would also be useful to insist on a more rigorous implementation of structural policies, restricting benefits to those countries that fully fulfil conditions. At any rate the EU transfers are such that they make the Marshall Plan look modest.

The benefits from EU accession for the candidate countries are very substantial and independent of financial transfers, while EU incumbents' benefits are second order in economic terms. The fact that the gains to CEEC are large without the transfers suggests that both parties should de-emphasise the transfer aspect. It would be regrettable if accession countries were excessively focused on the bonus (transfers) rather than on the real benefits of EU membership – which are integration in a vast market and the graduation from 'transition' countries.

## Appendix: Diversity and the gains from integration

It is often argued that enlargement towards the east is more difficult because the candidates from Central and Eastern Europe are so much poorer than the current EU-15. This might be the case from a political point of view. However, it misses one basic tenet of economics, namely that integration between different economies should actually lead to more economic gains than integration between similar economies.

This idea is illustrated in the following model, which formalises the most basic set-up in which two separate economies with different capital–labour ratios become totally integrated. One can then compare world income before and after integration. World GDP increases, of course, with integration as capital moves from a region with relatively low marginal capital productivity (the EU-15) to a region with relatively high marginal capital productivity (the CEEC). However, this is not the main result. The main result is that the *increase* in world GDP is higher the greater the difference in capital–labour ratios prior to integration. The model also shows that the gain does not go only to the CEEC. The present EU-15 also benefit and their gain is also an increasing function of the initial difference in capital labour ratios.

An illustrative calibration suggests that the gain for the EU-15 should be modest, about 1 per cent of income, versus a 50 per cent gain for the CEEC. The calibration also shows the importance of distinguishing between GNP and GDP when assessing growth in the CEEC. The relative gains and losses are as predicted by the Stolper–Samuelson-type model.

## A standard framework

### The basic model

This section uses the simplest model one can use to provide a framework. The model is based on a standard production function with two inputs: capital and labour. The starting assumption is that the capital–labour ratio of the EU-15 exceeds that of the CEEC:

$$\frac{K_{EU-15}}{L_{EU-15}} \geq \frac{K_{CEEC}}{L_{CEEC}} = \phi \frac{K_{EU-15}}{L_{EU-15}} \tag{9A.1}$$

with $0 < \phi < 1$. The capital stock of the CEEC is assumed to be only a fraction of that of the EU-15. This fraction is denoted by the parameter $\phi$, whose value is positive and smaller than 1. It indicates the size of CEEC per capita capital stock relative to that of the EU.

The focus is initially on world income. Equation (9A.2) shows the total income (GDP = GNP) produced in the two parts of Europe, assuming they are initially totally separated, using a Cobb–Douglas production function.

$$K_{EU\text{-}15}^{\alpha} L_{EU\text{-}15}^{1-\alpha} + \left( \frac{\phi K_{EU\text{-}15}}{L_{EU\text{-}15}} \right)^{\alpha} L_{CEEC} = GDP_{before}. \tag{9A.2}$$

with $0 < \alpha < 1$.

After enlargement (or whatever brings about total integration), the GDP of the enlarged EU will be generated by a common capital stock as is shown in (9A.3). For simplicity it is assumed that $L_{CEEC} = L_{EU} = L$ (meaning that the model works on a per-capita basis). In this case, the total stock of capital $K_{EU\text{-}15} (1 + \phi)$ would then be distributed equally across EU-15 and CEEC when the areas are totally integrated. This implies that the integrated EU's income would be given by

$$2 \left( \frac{1+\phi}{2} K_{EU\text{-}15} \right)^{\alpha} L^{1-\alpha} = GDP_{after}. \tag{9A.3}$$

The gain from integration can be measured by the ratio, $R$, between world GDP after and before enlargement. It is given by:

$$R \equiv \frac{GDP_{after}}{GDP_{before}} = \frac{\left( \frac{1+\phi}{2} \right)^{\alpha} 2K_{EU\text{-}15}^{\alpha} L^{1-\alpha}}{\left[ K_{EU\text{-}15}^{\alpha} + (\phi K_{EU\text{-}15})^{\alpha} \right] L^{1-\alpha}} = \frac{2^{1-\alpha} (1+\phi)^{\alpha}}{1 + \phi^{\alpha}}. \tag{9A.4}$$

For $\phi$ going to zero this converges to $2^{1-\alpha}$.

### Comparative statics

How a change in $\phi$ affects the welfare gain from integration can be seen by taking the derivative of R with respect to $\phi$.

$$\frac{\partial R}{\partial \phi} = 2^{1-\alpha} \frac{\alpha (1+\phi)^{\alpha-1} (1+\phi^{\alpha}) - (1+\phi)^{\alpha} \alpha \phi^{\alpha-1}}{(1+\phi^{\alpha})^2}$$

$$= \frac{2^{1-\alpha} (1+\phi)^{\alpha-1} \alpha}{(1+\phi^{\alpha})^2} \left[ 1 + \phi^{\alpha} - (1+\phi) \phi^{\alpha-1} \right]$$

$$= \frac{2^{1-\alpha} (1+\phi)^{\alpha-1} \alpha}{(1+\phi^{\alpha})^2} \left[ 1 - \phi^{\alpha-1} \right] < 0. \tag{9A.5}$$

The last term in square brackets is negative as both $\alpha$ and $\phi$ are smaller than one. This means that the more resemblance there is in the capital–labour ratio, that is the higher $\phi$ is, the smaller the output gains from enlargement will be. The result in equation (9A.5) refers to the gain in world income, but how about the EU? The gain for the EU-15 can be divided into two parts: the gain for owners of capital and owners of labour.

The gain to capitalists is equal to:

$$Gain_{Capitalists} = \frac{\frac{1}{1+\phi} 2\alpha \left(\frac{1+\phi}{2}\right)^{\alpha} K^{\alpha}_{EU\text{-}15}}{\alpha K^{\alpha}_{EU\text{-}15}} = \left(\frac{1+\phi}{2}\right)^{\alpha-1} > 1, \tag{9A.6a}$$

i.e. capitalists gain.
Workers' gain is equal to

$$Gain_{Workers} = \frac{\frac{1}{2}\left[\left(\frac{1+\phi}{2}\right)^{\alpha} 2K^{\alpha}_{EU\text{-}15}\right](1-\alpha)}{K^{\alpha}_{EU\text{-}15}(1-\alpha)} = \left(\frac{1+\phi}{2}\right)^{\alpha} < 1, \tag{9A.6b}$$

which is smaller than 1, i.e. workers lose.

The (properly weighted) sum of the gain and loss for the two groups gives the overall (GNP) gain for the EU. It sums to

$$Gain_{EU\text{-}15, Total} = (1-\alpha)\left(\frac{1+\phi}{2}\right)^{\alpha} + \alpha\left(\frac{1+\phi}{2}\right)^{\alpha-1} \tag{9A.7}$$

$$\frac{\partial Gain}{\partial \phi} = \frac{(1-\alpha)\alpha}{2^{\alpha}}(1+\phi)^{\alpha-1} + \frac{\alpha(\alpha-1)}{2^{\alpha-1}}(1+\phi)^{\alpha-2}$$

$$= \frac{(1-\alpha)\alpha}{2^{\alpha}}(1+\phi)^{\alpha-2}(1+\phi-2)$$

$$= \frac{(1-\alpha)\alpha}{2^{\alpha}}(1+\phi)^{\alpha-2}(\phi-1) < 0. \tag{9A.8}$$

Equation (9A.8) confirms what was already suggested by equation (9A.5): the gain for the EU-15 and $\phi$ are negatively related. A smaller capital stock in the CEEC would thus generate a higher gain for the EU-15.

## An illustrative calibration

The general consequences of full integration between the EU-15 and the CEEC can be described quite easily: it should lead to a convergence of their respective capital–labour ratios. This would imply a fall in the capital–labour ratio of the EU-15 and a rise in that of the CEEC. The new common ratio will hence settle in between, as EU-15 capital flows into the CEEC (and labour – to the extent that it is flexible – migrates from the CEEC into the EU-15). This would involve a fall in the marginal productivity of EU-15 workers and CEEC capital, which would translate in a fall in their respective factor returns. Conversely, EU-15 capitalists and CEEC workers should gain from integration. The capital inflow into the CEEC resulting from integration would also raise their foreign debt as well as the ratio between GDP and GNP. While the direction of the effects is clear, a quantitative estimation of all these effects can be obtained by calibrating the model developed above. A key parameter will be the share of capital in production. What might be a reasonable value for the parameter $\alpha$? A by now standard value would be 0.5, if one includes human capital in the total capital stock. (But focusing on the physical capital alone, a value of 0.3 would be more appropriate for $\alpha$.) If one uses 0.5 and the observation that the (real, PPP adjusted) GDP per capita in some of the CEEC is only about one-third of that of the EU-15 average,

Table 9A.1. *Income (GNP)*

|  | EU | CEEC | Total | $K_{EU}$ | $L_{EU}$ | $K_{CEEC}$ | $L_{CEEC}$ | $K_{total}$ | $L_{total}$ |
|---|---|---|---|---|---|---|---|---|---|
| Before | 100 | 13 | 113 | 50 | 50 | 7 | 7 | 57 | 57 |
| After | 101 | 20 | 121 | 58 | 43 | 3 | 17 | 60 | 60 |
| In % gains | 1.08 | 50 | 7 | 16 | −14 | −62 | 162 | 7 | 7 |

*Notes*: GNP EU-15 before = 100; income of factors of production by nationality of ownership.

Table 9A.2. *Production (GDP)*

|  | EU | CEEC | Total | $K_{EU}$ | $L_{EU}$ | $K_{CEEC}$ | $L_{CEEC}$ | $K_{total}$ | $L_{total}$ |
|---|---|---|---|---|---|---|---|---|---|
| Before | 100 | 13 | 113 | 50 | 50 | 7 | 7 | 57 | 57 |
| After | 86 | 35 | 121 | 43 | 43 | 17 | 17 | 60 | 60 |
| % gains in | −13.66 | 162 | 7 | −14 | −14 | 162 | 162 | 7 | 7 |

*Notes*: GDP EU-15 before = 100; income of factors of production by location.

Table 9A.3. *Foreign debt of the CEEC*

| % GNP | 74.5 |
|---|---|
| % GDP | 42.7 |

*Source*: Own calculations.

the result is that the capital–labour ratio in the EU-15 should be about ten times higher than in the CEEC.

The last value to choose is the labour supply. As the population of the CEEC-10 amounts to about 40 per cent of that of the EU-15, it is natural to put $L_{CEEC} = 0.4 \, L_{EU\text{-}15}$.

All the results are listed in tables 9A.1 to 9A.3. The signs confirm the theoretical considerations. The orders of magnitude are interesting: they imply that capital imports of the CEEC could well be on a very large scale, possibly reaching over 50 per cent of GDP. A number of CEEC have run current account deficits of over 5 per cent of GDP. These simple calculations imply that this could go on for quite a while.

## Notes

1. A reminder of terminology: a *preferential trade area* (PTA) accords to its members easier access than to non-members; a *free trade area* (FTA) is a special PTA with no trade restrictions among members; a *customs union* is a FTA with common external tariffs (and hence also a PTA); a *common market* is a customs union with free movement of capital and labour; and an *economic union* is a common market supported by coordinated, joint or supranational policymaking in selected domains.

2. For a critical review see Rollo (1992) and Hughes and Hare (1992b).
3. The often-heard counter-argument that the EU is running a trade surplus with Eastern Europe cannot invalidate this finding because this is the only way in which the EU can transfer capital to the East and thus finance part of the reconstruction.
4. This is where the threat of protectionism against Central European exports is greatest.
5. The motivation for EU expansion is not completely symmetric. The optimum size of the EU is therefore treated separately in section 9.3.
6. Canada exported 78 per cent of its total exports to the USA and Mexico exported 76 per cent before NAFTA.
7. Empirical studies conclude that 'trade creation in the EC has been substantial in absolute terms and has exceeded trade diversion several times' (Balassa 1975).
8. Even without an explicit policy regional trade integration affects the terms of trade. The terms of trade gains of the initial six EC members, originating in the manufacturing sector, were estimated to represent between 0.3 and 0.5 per cent of GNP (Petith 1977).
9. This statement is true for any country evaluating its potential gains from joining an FTA. From a global perspective, a small or a large number of FTAs are welfare superior to an intermediate case (Krugman 1991b). A single FTA spanning the world is equal to global free trade; a number of FTAs equal to the number of countries in the world is the status quo. Between these extremes there are cases where welfare may be inferior to the status quo.
10. To assess the degree of overlap between imports from different sources we use the similarity index, which was first introduced by Finger and Kreinin (1979). The similarity index is used here to compare the structure of intra-EU imports, $j$, with that from country $r$ (or any other supplier of imports to the EU market):

$$S_{rj} = \sum_{l=1}^{n} \min \left( w_{rl}, w_{jl} \right) \times 100,$$

where $w_{rl}$ is the share of product $l$ in total EU imports from country $r$, and $w_{jl}$ is the share of the same product in intra-EU imports. The higher the value of the index the more similar are the two countries' export structures. On the other hand, if products that are important in one country's exports are of little significance in the other country's exports, then the value of the index will tend towards zero. An important issue is the level of disaggregation at which to apply the analysis. We compute the index of similarity at an intermediate level of disaggregation, the four-digit level of the HS, which is sufficiently detailed to capture within-industry specialisation but not highly sensitive to product-specific policy distortion.

    To check whether the results depended on the particular measure of trade similarity used here the simple correlation coefficient between national and intra-EU trade structures was also used. All the tests gave the same results as the trade similarity index used here. Across the twenty-four countries the cross-sectional correlation was over 90 per cent.
11. Repeating the same exercise at a lower level of disaggregation yielded essentially the same result. The exact number of products chosen is thus not relevant.
12. Balassa and Bauwens (1988) contains extensive tests of this view. Möbius and Schumacher (1990) provide a sectoral analysis of the trade of Eastern European countries that also confirms this general view.
13. Portugal does not have a coast on the Mediterranean Sea, but it is nevertheless usually counted as an honorary member of Club Med.
14. Formally defined as administrative units at the 'NUTS II' level. This corresponds to *Länder* in Germany and *regioni* in Italy.
15. The threshold for the Cohesion Funds at the national level is 90 per cent of the EU average, but spending under this fund amounts only to 2.5 per cent of the EU budget, a fraction of spending under Objective 1.

16. For example, if the EU population were to increase by 10 per cent and the average of the new members was only 50 per cent of the EU-15, the EU-20 plus average would be 5 percentage points lower.

17. Some regions above the threshold in richer member countries have also been classified as Objective 1 for political reasons, but they receive only a small part of the total spending. Ireland, whose GDP per capita is now above the EU average, is being phased out. In future, increased competition for funds may lead to the desirable result that support stops when the right to it vanishes.

18. It has never been clarified why Ireland, although substantially richer than Greece and Portugal, received substantially more per capita under Objective 1. The main factors might be that Ireland was more efficient at taking up available funds than other recipient countries, and at political bargaining.

19. Only in Romania is the average holding, at four hectares per farmer, even smaller than in Poland; but given the fact that Romanian soil and climate are better adapted to fruits and vegetables that can be efficiently produced on smaller plots this is not a relevant comparison.

20. Poland would then have to deal with its 3 million inefficient and poor farmers on its own. But this is a problem that it would have to face even outside the EU. Membership should strengthen growth and provide at least some of them with a decent alternative job.

21. Baldwin et al. (1997) use an explicit model of how 'power politics' determines EU expenditure and predict that the distribution of votes in the Council of Ministers will favour heavy spending on the Central European countries.

22. Membership will also force the Central and Eastern European countries to reduce their tariffs on imports from the rest of the world. But since these imports are small compared with their imports from the EU, this effect is not important for the size of the welfare benefits.

23. Taking exports and imports of goods and services at 25 per cent of GDP plus 5 per cent for other current account transactions yields 30 per cent on both the export and import side. Transaction cost savings of 2.5 per cent on 60 per cent of GDP yields the gain of 1.5 per cent of GDP.

24. Since agriculture accounts for only a minor fraction (6–10 per cent) of GDP, the gains from freeing trade in this sector cannot be large in relation to GDP.

25. Four to five times the amount found by Baldwin et al. (1997). Moreover, a large part of the gains in real income found by these authors do not correspond to welfare gains since they result from increased capital accumulation, which does not come for free (like the transaction costs savings from a common currency) but require households to postpone consumption.

# 10   Saving the Balkans

GABLE
*GLOBE AND MAIL*
Toronto
CANADA

Cartoonists & Writers Syndicate

W e described in chapter 4 how the transition to a market economy is almost completed in those countries that are to become full members of the EU in 2004. But there are other parts of Europe where the transition is less advanced, and where the prospect of EU membership seems so far away that it does not provide a guide for political action today. This raises the question to what extent countries that have a 'European vocation' could benefit from the EU anchor even if membership is only a distant dream. This is the key policy issue for the countries in South-East Europe today.

We will concentrate on the particular case of the countries that emerged from the dissolution of Yugoslavia, avoiding a definition of the Balkans explicitly, as membership of this region is not considered a badge of honour. Moreover, each case in this region has specific problems. For our purposes the Balkans (or SEE – South-East Europe) is that part of Europe that is not included in the next wave of accession to the EU, but that is on the path towards EU membership in the long run. This implies that Slovenia is definitely not part of the Balkans and Croatia might leave this region if it can convince the EU that it has left its authoritarian regime behind. But a country like Romania, which is an official candidate for membership in 2007, risks slipping back into the Balkans if its regime does not start real reforms. The approach proposed here could also be applied to countries that feel a 'European vocation', but are further away from this region: for example Moldova, Ukraine, perhaps even Armenia and Georgia.

Despite the fact that EU membership is years away, the starting point of any economic order for the entire SEE region must be a clear orientation towards Europe. It is often assumed that the international financial institutions (IFIs, i.e. IMF, World Bank, EBRD, EIB) play a key role in the reconstruction of the Balkans. This is the case to some extent, but the effectiveness of the IFIs is limited in two crucial aspects.

The first difference between the EU and the IFIs is that the latter can provide only credits. The EU is the only source for substantial transfers (although politicians in some countries in the region might not appreciate the difference between credits and grants). The natural division of tasks is therefore that the EU provides income support whereas the IFIs provide credits for reconstruction. Given that most of the countries in the region already have a large foreign debt, they would be ill-advised to use further balance-of-payments assistance. This applies in particular to Serbia, which on paper owes over $10 bn to Western creditors. While some debt forgiveness might be forthcoming, a long-term recovery in Serbia would become even more difficult if the country were to burden itself with large additional debt.

The second difference is more important: only the EU can offer a long-run economic (and political) framework that is attractive for all the countries in the region and that can constitute the basis for a sustained recovery. This will be the main theme of this chapter.

A basic point that must be kept in mind is that a large part of the economic activity that survived the decade of turbulence resulting from the break-up of Yugoslavia (or the civil war in Moldova) is not viable in open markets. Most of the industrial plant had been installed under the old regime and was kept going for political reasons during the wars. In terms of economic hardware, one starts thus essentially with a tabula rasa.

The end of the wars and fall of the authoritarian regimes in Croatia and Serbia in 1999–2000 opened a window of opportunity for a radical reform; to establish the basic

Table 10.1. *Balkan GDP per capita ($ 000)*

|  | 1991 | 2000 | 2000 as % of 1991 | |
|---|---|---|---|---|
|  |  |  | current $ | at PPP |
| Croatia | 4.0 | 4.2 | 105 | 166 |
| Macedonia, FYR | 2.1 | 1.8 | 86 | 164 |
| Poland | 2.0 | 4.1 | 205 | 212 |
| Russian Federation | 5.4 | 1.8 | 33 | 75 |
| Yugoslavia FRY | 2.5 | 1.0 | 39 | 78 |
| US | 23.5 | 34.9 | 149 | |

*Source*: Wiener Institut Für International Wirtschaftsvergleiche.

elements of a new order immediately, before special interest groups and political rivalries came into play. The basic elements of a new economic order (multilateral free trade and euroisation) could thus have been established rapidly. Unfortunately, the occasion offered by the fall of the dictators was not used for radical reforms, but some gradual steps in the right direction were undertaken. The economic performance has mirrored the timidity in the reforms: growth has generally been unsatisfactory. With close to stagnant economies, political progress has also been slow. Parts of the region thus risk drifting into a sort of limbo in which there is little progress, but at the same time the danger of an explosion of popular discontent remains low because the region is still under a soft international protectorate.

This chapter treats all of SEE in the same way. However, this does not mean we propose a regional approach, for example for trade within SEE. For most of the countries in SEE, trade within the region is only one-tenth of their trade with the EU, and the dominance of the EU in trade terms is not likely to diminish over time. Gravity equations that simulate the trade pattern that the countries in the region would have in a free trade environment (and after a reasonable recovery), indicate that the EU market would take 70–80 per cent of their exports (see also Gros and Steinherr 1995).

This chapter is organised as follows: Sections 1 and 2 discuss the proposed trade and currency regimes. Section 3 draws the lessons from the experience of Montenegro and section 4 concludes. Appendices provide a comparison with the dollarisation experience of Ecuador and Panama.

A word of caution: there are no reliable long-term data for this part of Europe, partly because some of the countries did not exist ten years ago, and partly because some of them were involved in wars. But even given this data limitation there can be little doubt that the region had a rough time during the 1990s. Table 10.1 shows some of the available data.

The first two columns of table 10.1 concentrate on GDP per capita in current US dollars, for some of the countries from the region, plus Poland and Russia as comparators. This table compares 1991 (already not exactly the best year for Yugoslavia, as disintegration had already started) to 2000. It is apparent that by 2000 the income per capita in both Macedonia and Yugoslavia (today mainly Serbia minus Kosovo) was even lower than in Russia, about half of that in Poland and less than that in Croatia, which managed to stabilise

Table 10.2. *The Balkans – basic data (2000)*

| Country | Population (m) | GDP (US$bn) | GDP per capita |
|---|---|---|---|
| Albania | 3.4 | 3.7 | 1100 |
| Bosnia-Herzegovina | 4.0 | 4.4 | 1105 |
| Croatia | 4.4 | 19.0 | 4345 |
| FR Yugoslavia | 10.6 | 8.5 | 794 |
| Macedonia | 2.0 | 3.6 | 1759 |
| Memo: Greece | 10.6 | 112.6 | 10667 |
| Luxembourg | 0.4 | 18.9 | 43093 |

*Source*: World Bank, *World Development Report* (2000).

and open its economy soon after war ended in 1995. This might be compared to Poland, which started at a much lower level in 1991, but ended up with four times the Yugoslav level in 2000.

Measuring income in current dollars has the well-known drawback of neglecting differences in price levels: a dollar might buy much less (or more) in some countries than in others. The last column in table 10.1 therefore gives a measure based on GDP per capita adjusted for differences in purchasing power parity (PPP), which confirms the differences in progress between the Central European countries (typified again by Poland), Russia and the Balkans. Poland's income per capita is now twice as high as a decade earlier (if measured in constant PPP dollars). Croatia, the best performer in the region, is also up by two-thirds. By contrast it seems that Serbia is following more the pattern of Russia, remaining clearly below the starting level (which was already depressed).

The population of the region has clearly not been able to reap the benefits of transition. It is thus crucial that the changes take place quickly to prevent the re-emergence of populist/nationalistic policies that typically result from frustrated aspirations for better living standards.

## 10.1   The importance of free trade

A key fact that must determine any approach to the economic problems of this region is that all of the states and territories of SEE are so small in economic terms that they can develop only if they have access to the EU market. For example, the GDP of Serbia, the largest country in the region, is at present of the same order of magnitude as that of Luxembourg and the GDP of Macedonia or Albania is similar to that of tiny Liechtenstein. The entire SEE region represents a market of only around $100 bn, smaller than Greece and its combined exports are smaller than those of Luxembourg. Table 10.2 provides some basic data.[1]

We showed in chapter 9 that trade between the EU and the candidate countries has reflected a liberal regime by growing strongly over the last decade (tripling in value in many cases). By contrast, trade between the EU and SEE countries has stagnated at best (Croatia), or actually fallen. For example, official trade between the EU and Serbia collapsed over the

Table 10.3. *Merchandise trade as a percentage of GDP (2000)*

|                    | Exports | Imports |
|--------------------|---------|---------|
| Albania            | 7.4     | 32.3    |
| Bosnia-Herzegovina | 22.1    | 58.8    |
| Croatia            | 24.1    | 44.4    |
| FRY                | 18.4    | 44.4    |
| FYROM              | 33.7    | 45.1    |
| Bulgaria           | 37.6    | 49.1    |

*Source*: EBRD *Transition Report* (2001).

last decade: exports from Serbia have fallen by 75 per cent, from about $6 bn in 1990 to close to $1.5 bn in 2001.[2]

## *The starting point*

The EU has emerged as the crucial trading partner of the countries in the western Balkans. The latter's share in the EU market is negligible – 0.6 per cent of total extra EU imports. Bilateral trade is far from being balanced. Exports to the EU are only half the value of imports in the case of Croatia and FR Yugoslavia, only a quarter in the case of Albania and a fifth in the case of Bosnia and Herzegovina; only for Macedonia do exports to the EU approach the value of imports. (See also table 10.4). For most of the countries in the region the current account is heavily influenced by other items – tourism for Croatia, remittances for Albania – which cover at least part of the deficit in goods.

Trade is important for all Balkan countries, but there are two important qualifications:

(1) One has to distinguish between exports and imports (see table 10.3). For most of the Balkans, exports constitute a rather small share of GDP. Albania is the most conspicuous case, with a ratio of exports to GDP of only 7 per cent whereas imports account for over 30 per cent of GDP. But Bosnia-Herzegovina shows an even larger absolute difference between imports (58.8 per cent of GDP) and exports (22.1 per cent).

(2) Even if one looks at the import numbers only, the Balkan countries do not appear to be open for their size. EU members, or other transition countries in Central Europe of similar size, have trade-to-GDP ratios of 70 per cent and higher, compared to less than 50 per cent for most Balkan countries.

The countries in SEE differ substantially in their relationship with the EU. Bulgaria and Romania, for example, signed an Association Agreement with the EU ten years ago (see chapter 9) and are scheduled to join the EU in 2007. The countries of the 'western' Balkans are generally far behind in this process. Some of them (e.g. Croatia and Macedonia) have signed a so-called Stabilisation and Association Agreement (SAA) which is supposed to prepare them for the stage when they can actually submit a realistic application for EU membership and start negotiations to that end.

While waiting for the nirvana of EU membership, most SEE countries enjoy some EU trade preferences. There already exists a high degree of duty-free access to the EU market

Table 10.4. *Structure of Balkan trade with the EU (1999)*

| Country | Trade/GDP ratio (%) | Share of exports to EU (%) | Share of imports from EU (%) | EU trade preferences[1] | Export share covered by 'managed' trade measures of EU | Nominal average import tariff (%) |
|---|---|---|---|---|---|---|
| Albania | 35 | 92 | 82 | GSP[2] | 61 | 15.9 |
| Bosnia-Herzegovina | 60 | 49 | 40 | ATP | 2–44 | 7–8 |
| Croatia | 60 | 38 | 39 | SAA | 2–44 | 12 |
| Macedonia | 90 | 44 | 36 | TCA | 58 | 15 |
| FR Yugoslavia | >40 | 85 | 76 | ATP[3] | N/A | 13.5 |

[1] GSP = Generalised System of Preferences; ATP = Autonomous Trade Preferences; SAA = Stabilisation and Association Agreements; TCA = Trade and Cooperation Agreement.
[2] To be replaced by ATP.
[3] These preferences have been suspended.
*Source:* Adapted from study on Trade Policy in South East Europe, Trade Development Institute of Ireland (September 1999).

Table 10.5. *Structure of exports from the Balkans to the EU, 1998 (% of total)*

|  | Albania | Bosnia-Herzegovina | Croatia | FR Yugoslavia | Macedonia |
|---|---|---|---|---|---|
| Agriculture | 9.9 | 2.1 | 3.2 | 13.5 | 9.4 |
| Textile | 35.2 | 33.7 | 27.9 | 17.5 | 39.3 |
| Footwear | 29.6 | 16.3 | 8.5 | 4.0 | 3.7 |
| Iron and steel | 5.6 | 3.7 | 0.7 | 19.2 | 23.5 |
| Wood | 3.5 | 16.4 | 9.1 | 4.2 | 1.5 |
| Total of the above | 83.8 | 72.2 | 49.3 | 58.4 | 77.4 |
| Other | 16.2 | 27.8 | 50.7 | 41.6 | 22.6 |

*Source*: Adapted from 'The road to stability and prosperity in South-Eastern Europe – a regional strategy paper', World Bank, Washington, DC, March 2000.

(around 80 per cent officially) but SEE exporters are often unable to use EU trade preferences because they lack the technical knowledge to get the necessary paperwork done. Moreover, tariff ceilings and quotas (measures falling under the category of 'managed trade') still govern some industrial products, such as textiles, steel and chemicals. Agricultural exports are subject to a number of restrictions. Table 10.5 provides information on the structure of exports from the western Balkans to the EU.

Intraregional trade is relatively insignificant, on average 12 to 14 per cent of the total. This average, however, conceals some disparities – trade between Croatia and some parts of Bosnia-Herzegovina can be substantial, and Macedonia trades extensively with almost all countries in SEE.

The trade regimes of the countries of the Western Balkans are generally protective. Trade protection is relatively high, in terms of both tariffs and non-tariff measures (NTMs). The nominal average tariff is over 10 per cent (with the exception of Bosnia-Herzegovina). Over the last few years the countries in the region concluded a complete matrix of free trade agreements (FTAs) to liberalise bilateral trade flows.

The small size of the home markets and the big differences between imports and exports suggest that trade policy in SEE should be geared even less than elsewhere to the protection of domestic producers. The only justification for keeping border taxes in the Balkans is the public finance argument. Tariffs act essentially like a sales tax, given that there is usually no competing domestic production. Therefore non-tariff protection does not make sense in the region. The public finance argument should be openly acknowledged and there is a way to accommodate it, as suggested below.

On the EU side there is a tendency to be liberal for all the products that the Balkan countries do not generally export and maintain protective measures for the rest, which hit de facto a large proportion of regional exports to the EU. This suggests that liberalisation should be across the board so as to blunt the power of EU interest groups to stop imports of competing items from the countries concerned. The difficulties of some Balkan countries are compounded by the fact that they are not yet members of the World Trade Organisation (WTO) or the Central European Free Trade Area (CEFTA).

## The way forward

The data presented so far suggest that a sustained recovery of the region depends on rapid growth of exports to the EU. The natural conclusion is that the EU should recognise this and eliminate all barriers to imports from all the countries of this region. Given that the combined exports of all SEE to the EU amount to less than 1 per cent of overall EU imports, this would have no appreciable impact on the EU market.

Some progress has already been made since the end of the Kosovo war and the fall of Milošević. Since 2000–1, the EU has been offering Stabilisation and Association Agreements (SAA), which foresee some further liberalisation and should culminate in the establishment of bilateral free trade after a ten-year transition period.[3] This appears excessively timid, given the fall in living standards suffered by the populations of the region over the past decade.

Moreover, the SAAs limit free trade to industrial products. This is sure to delay recovery because the only sector in the region that still works is agriculture. The Common Agricultural Policy (CAP) could not and should not be exported to the Balkans. However, the EU should grant generous tariff-free quotas. In order to illustrate to politicians and the farmers' lobby that the imports from countries like SEE do not represent a serious threat to farming in the EU, the duty-free import quota could be set at 1 per cent of EU production. As the combined imports from all SEE countries amounted to about 0.01 per cent of EU production in 1997 (see Gros et al. 1999) such a quota would allow for a very substantial expansion of SEE exports to the EU with no appreciable impact on the EU market. But this could be particularly important for countries with little industry left. It would also be easier to jump-start agricultural production. Most countries in SEE would anyway specialise in products that are the least problematic for the CAP (e.g. fruit and vegetables).[4]

The standard bureaucratic argument against throwing the EU market open for the countries in the region is that the EU would then be obliged to offer the same treatment to everybody (all LDCs, or at a minimum North Africa?). However, this is not the case. The countries in SEE have been recognised as having a European bent. This is not the case for North Africa or other LDCs. Moreover, the SEE countries are in a critical economic situation because of the political turmoil of the last decade. Their actual exports are only a fraction of their long-term potential (and their pre-war level). If the European vocation is not considered sufficient to warrant free access to the EU market because it might still lead to demands for similar treatment by other countries, one could simply grant countries from the region a duty-free quota equal to the level of EU imports from them in 1990 (or 1995). This would be several times the level of exports today.[5]

But access to the EU market is not enough. It is also imperative that governments in the region do not have the power to protect inefficient domestic industries against external competition and that the potential for corruption at the border be reduced. The countries in SEE should thus also abolish tariffs on imports from the EU and apply the (low) common external tariff of the EU to third-country imports. This might be politically sensitive at a time when what little industry survived a decade of neglect, sanctions and wars is in difficulty. However, it is imperative to seize this occasion and ensure that a 'new economy' develops. Keeping the remaining large industrial plants alive would place a heavy burden on the budget and would lead to further prolonged stagnation. The industrial structure of the region was frozen at the level of the late 1980s. Keeping it there would be a disaster. The political honeymoon should be used to let enterprises fail if they cannot be competitive in open markets.

How can one lock in free trade? The best way to do so would be for the EU to invite countries from the region to join a bilateral customs union with the EU, thus cementing commitment on both sides. Having differentiated tariffs against the rest of the world would anyway not be significant for the small economies of the region and it would maintain the temptation to use tariff policy in particular sectors.

One practical advantage of a customs union (over a free trade agreement) is that only the former renders rules of origin superfluous. How important are these rules of origin? Regarding trade among highly developed economies with large firms which have considerable experience in the documentary requirements for foreign trade, it has been found that firms often actually prefer to pay the tariff (as long as it is not too high, e.g. below 10 per cent) rather than incur the costs of proving origin. This indicates that even in the best of cases rules of origin can represent a considerable obstacle to trade. For the much smaller and less experienced firms in SEE, proving origin remains even more difficult. Part of the problem is intrinsic (to determine where a particular merchandise comes from). But part of the problem is that the particular rules that the EU applies in its free trade agreements to determine eligibility for duty-free access to the EU are often very restrictive, with the effect that a substantial proportion of exports from the region to the EU in reality does not receive preferential access under free trade agreements.[6] These rules of origin are particularly restrictive for clothing products, which are a principal export from many of the countries in the region. One way of avoiding the costs associated with these restrictive rules of origin is the establishment of outward processing relationships with EU firms. However, this has the cost that the supplier of the raw materials must be an EU firm (and not the lowest-cost supplier anywhere).

The fact that rules of origin are not needed in a customs union (which implies a common external tariff) is thus important. A concrete illustration of this proposition is the case of Turkey, which has a customs union agreement with the EU. It provides an example of clothing and other sectors developing in a framework where duty-free access to the EU is guaranteed and the sourcing of materials can be made from the cheapest locations to enhance competitiveness in the EU market.

The decisive argument against a regional free trade zone in the Balkans is that it would in reality lead to welfare losses. As documented above, most of the countries in the region maintain rather high levels of external protection, usually with spikes in those sectors in which there is some industry left from the old times (steel, textiles) and agriculture. This implies that the potential for trade diversion must be high. Trade diversion occurs when a domestic consumer buys a product from an FTA partner. For the consumer this product (e.g. Serbian steel for use in Croatia) might become cheaper than imports from a non-partner country after the FTA because imports from the FTA partner enter duty free. However, from a general equilibrium standpoint, the tariff that is levied on a product from elsewhere is just a transfer from the consumer to the government. As a concrete example, assume that the world market price of a certain type of steel is 1,000 euros per tonne and that the import tariff in both Croatia and Serbia is 20 per cent. If Serbian suppliers can produce this type of steel only at a higher cost, say 1,150 euros per tonne, they have no chance on the Croatian market before the FTA. Once an FTA has been concluded between Croatia and Serbia, however, Croatian consumers will switch to Serbian suppliers because for Croatian consumers the price of steel from the rest of the world will remain at 1,200 euros whereas Serbian steel will cost a bit less. This process of switching to suppliers from FTA partners is called 'trade diversion'. Its net cost to the Croatian economy is 150 euros per tone (200 less in tariff revenue for the government less the 50 euros gain for the consumers).

How important could this trade diversion be in the Balkans? Unfortunately, the answer must be very important, because imports are a rather high percentage of GDP (much higher than exports as documented above).

In a customs union with the EU this problem of trade diversion would not arise because the common external tariff of the EU is much lower and because the EU (especially the expanded EU-25) is likely to contain anyway the lowest-cost supplier for most products. Moreover, in a customs union with the EU, the Balkan countries would automatically also be in a customs union with Turkey, which is an important consideration given the large transit trade that crosses the Balkans between the EU and Turkey. On top of this the Balkan countries would also become party to the large number of preferential or free trade agreements that the EU is negotiating or has already negotiated, thus increasing market access all over the world.

Inviting SEE countries to join the EU customs union might seem to imply a bilateral approach. But in reality, this would also constitute the quickest way to establish free trade within the region because all the countries that join the EU customs union will automatically have free trade among themselves.

Moreover, as more and more SEE countries accede to the EU customs union they would no longer need customs controls among themselves. This would be an important advantage, given that the customs administrations in the region are notoriously corrupt, and that border controls constitute costly obstacles for trade.

Taking SEE into the EU customs union territory would thus be a far more effective way to liberate trade within the region than the official approach, which has been to invite the countries concerned to complete a matrix of bilateral free trade agreements. Given the high external rates of protection in some key sectors, most countries maintain this costly trade diversion as argued above. But even if this were not the case, many practical problems would persist. There will still be a need for customs controls and the customs administrations in the region will have great practical difficulties in coping with dozens of different rules resulting from dozens of slightly different bilateral free trade agreements (which can differ in terms of the list of products exempted from free trade, the transition periods, etc.).

---

### Box 10.1    The loss of tariff revenues from free trade

In states with weak fiscal structures taxes on trade constitute an important source of revenues, and the new democratic governments will need all the revenues they can get since, with the onset of economic reforms, fiscal revenues typically fall. However, in the Balkans, frontier controls are also a major source of corruption and harassment so that in reality trade barriers are much higher than the official tariff rates. Making borders easy to pass is thus very important. But the EU should also recognise the fiscal need for trade taxes and compensate the countries that choose to follow this approach for the loss of tariff revenues that arises through the customs union regime.

The loss of tariff revenue from entering a customs union with the EU might be substantial, as tariff revenue on trade with the EU will disappear completely. The external tariffs of the EU are very low, hence very little tariff revenue can be obtained from duties on third-country imports.

How high would that loss be? Table 10.6 provides some preliminary calculations, based on 2001 data, which suggest that the annual loss of tariff revenues for the entire region should be around 600–700 million euros. Part of this loss can be recovered by the countries themselves through fiscal measures. A modest increase in VAT would be appropriate in this context. However, for a few years, financial support from the EU would be essential to soften the transition to a different regime. This support should be transitory with a sliding scale: e.g. almost full compensation for one year, two-thirds during year two and one-third during year three. This might amount to 600, 400 and 200 million euros in EU transfers to the region during three years.

Payment of compensation for tariff revenue would be subject to strict monitoring of the effective implementation of honest and efficient external border controls (still necessary for third-country trade and excise).

---

The one drawback of a customs union is that SEE countries would no longer receive tariff revenues on their imports from the EU. Box 10.1 estimates the loss of tariff revenues from free trade with the EU. The amounts would be substantial, but they must be seen against the important economic benefits. Moreover, most of this loss will occur anyway in the context of the SAAs mentioned above, which also bind the SEE countries to eliminate over time their tariffs on imports from the EU (but without offering the same degree of trade integration a customs union would imply).

Even with open borders some sectors might still not become fully competitive. Application of strong competition policy rules (i.e. those of the EU) would thus also be necessary. The general purpose of opening the economies in SEE as much as possible to competition could be furthered in a next step by extending the opening to sectors whose products became tradable in the EU only through the internal market programme. The most important examples here are utilities, which in weak states dominated by party politics are usually organised as local monopolies. It would therefore be important, for example, to link Serbia to the electricity grid of the EU and then to liberalise and privatise this sector. Experience has

Table 10.6. *Loss of tariff revenue from an EU–SEE customs union*

|  | Tariff revenues lost (million euros) | Tariff revenues lost (% of GDP) | Nominal average import tariff % |
|---|---|---|---|
| Croatia | 248 | 1.1 | 12.0 |
| Bosnia-Herzegovina | 92 | 2.3 | 8.0 |
| Yugoslavia | 250 | 1.8 | 13.5 |
| Macedonia | 43 | 1.4 | 15.0 |
| Albania | 70 | 2.3 | 15.9 |
| SEE | 703 | 1.8 | 12.9 |

shown that privatisation that preserves local monopolies (e.g. in telecommunications and other network industries) does not eliminate the influence of political structures. Countries in SEE should thus take over step-by-step the *acquis communautaire* of the internal market. The logical final step in this process would be that they could de facto participate in a sort of European Economic Area mark II long before they become full EU members.

Going beyond free trade and the customs union will, of course, be much more demanding in terms of implementation, and therefore time. The *acquis* of the internal market involves basically the entire administration of a country. Proper implementation thus requires a minimum degree of efficiency (and honesty) throughout a large number of ministries, regulatory agencies, local administrations, etc. Implementation of the customs unions requires 'only' disciplining the customs administration so that it conducts the necessary controls at the EU border, delivers certificates of origin and applies the common external tariff at the external border, with a minimum cost for traders. Even in the larger countries of the region this would involve less than a thousand civil servants, which could be put under the supervision of EU personnel where needed. However, it is not possible to do the same with the entire public administration of a country, which runs in the tens, if not hundreds, of thousands. The EU–Turkey customs union provides an example of how deeply a customs union can transform the economy of a country that had hitherto been rather protectionist.

## 10.2   Monetary regime: adopt the euro!

All the new (democratic) governments in SEE had to choose a monetary regime. The advice from 'competent' bodies such as the IMF was predictable: get the budget under control, liberalise carefully and try to stabilise the currency step-by-step. This conventional approach can work, but it risks disappointing the expectations of the population, and the case of Turkey (and many other emerging-market economies) shows that such a process can be quite arduous, especially when the external environment deteriorates. The Turkish adjustment programme, which was proceeding well and had the blessing of the IMF, was suddenly made much more difficult as the turbulence on US stock markets in late 2000 led to a sudden increase in the risk premium for emerging markets, causing an increase in domestic interest rates of over ten percentage points and, as a result, a banking and foreign exchange crisis!

## *What to do?*

The former regimes, especially in Serbia, used the central bank to finance high-profile public expenditure, including wars. This blatant abuse of the printing press stopped with their overthrow. But a credible low-inflation regime cannot be created overnight by conventional means. This is why in times of crisis one has to resort to unconventional measures. Examples are the currency board of Bulgaria, introduced in the wake of hyperinflation, the currency board of Bosnia-Herzegovina and the full Dinarkisation/euroisation chosen by Montenegro. We would argue that this last approach is the most promising.

Why go for the full adoption of a foreign currency? Monetary stability is one key consideration. But for countries under tight IMF control hyperinflation is not really a danger, as the IMF usually intervenes whenever there is a threat that the country may deviate from its agreed programme. An even more important advantage of euroisation would be its systemic impact, in transforming the political economy inside the country and thus creating the chances of healthy economic growth. The banking system was especially corrupt in SEE because it was a key conduit for large-scale money laundering and political intervention in the economy. The new democratic leaderships want to stop this. They will face obstacles in doing so because it will remain difficult to stop supporting loss-making state- (or privately) owned enterprises or politically well-connected 'businessmen'. But this will be easier to achieve by throwing away the key to the central bank.

Introducing foreign notes and coins is not enough. To reap the political economy benefits it is imperative also to liberalise and privatise the banking system, which at present offers little more than primitive transfer services. Allowing competition from EU banks and establishing and implementing an appropriate regulatory and supervisory framework will be essential. The entire Yugoslav banking system is blocked by enormous amounts of de facto frozen foreign exchange assets and liabilities which were accumulated over the last ten years and which are essentially dead wood. They date from a previous attempt to introduce a hard dinar in the distant past, when Yugoslavia was an open economy. Disentangling these claims (inter alia the deposits of an entire generation of savers) is a Herculean task which will take a long time. But until it is accomplished the banking system will remain in limbo, unable to provide financial services. At present even basic banking functions like withdrawals of cash from deposits are not routine. Moreover, the confidence of the population cannot be gained quickly. It is thus essential that clean foreign banks be allowed to operate immediately in Serbia.

The main economic argument usually advanced against currency boards (or full dollarisation/euroisation schemes) is that they might make it more difficult to adjust the real exchange rate. This argument is based on the observation that in well-established economies nominal wages and prices are usually rigid. However, this argument does not apply to SEE. In Serbia, as in many of the countries of the region, wages are not set in national agreements and can thus adjust much more easily to market conditions. Rigid nominal wages have also not been the key problem in the two real-world examples (Panama and Ecuador) of countries adopting another currency (the dollar) discussed in appendixes 10.1 and 10.2.

Any attempt to have national monetary policies would, at any rate, face considerable problems since the euro is already playing an important role throughout the region. See IMF (1999) for a discussion of monetary policy in dollarised economies.

Bosnia-Herzegovina, Montenegro and Bulgaria chose to anchor their currencies to the DM as the unit of account because DM banknotes were widely used in the region (and replaced by the euro since early 2002).

Euroisation can be achieved simply by declaring the euro legal tender, like the dollar in Ecuador or Panama. Such a law is not strictly necessary; encouraging the use of the euro would be sufficient. The example of Montenegro shows that it is enough that the government pays out salaries and pensions in euros. This puts a large amount of euro in circulation and encourages shops to start pricing in euro as well.

On the monetary side the 'European choice' would also have a desirable regional dimension. Serbia could thus soon be part of a 'euroised' Balkans, including:

* Montenegro (already fully euroised)
* Kosovo (also euroised)
* Bosnia-Herzegovina (euro-based currency board)
* Bulgaria (euro-based currency board)
* Croatia (80 per cent of banking system operates using the euro, the central bank has enough reserves to euroise after the devaluation required to establish external equilibrium).

### *What will it cost?*

Euroisation is technically straightforward in an economy in which financial markets do not exist and the banking system performs only a rudimentary transactions service. But it has one disadvantage: Serbia (or any other country undertaking this step) would have to borrow its currency from the eurosystem, and seigniorage would thus revert to the ECB. It seems unfair that the rich EU should benefit from poor countries in a difficult transition process. But how can it be avoided? The solution is simple: the euro cash needed for the currency exchange in Serbia (for example) should be provided through an interest-free loan by the EU. In this way Serbia does not lose its seigniorage (its central bank keeps the assets it had and can place the funds on the money market). The loan would have to be repaid upon accession as a full EMU member, or if Serbia were to abandon the euro. The cost to the EU budget would consist of the debt servicing, but as the eurosystem would earn more monetary income the net cost for the EU (or at least eurozone member countries) would be zero.

A country that wants to euroise needs to have enough foreign currency reserves to convert its monetary base, essentially cash, into euros. How much would this be? The foreign exchange required for euroisation would not be very large, given that the SEE economies have shrunk so much. In Montenegro DM 25 million (12.5 million euros) were sufficient to start Dmarkisation. The Serbian economy is perhaps twenty times larger, requiring about 250 million euros as starting capital for euroisation, less than the available reserves. This approximate calculation is confirmed by the actual data on the stock of dinars in circulation, which amounted to less than 150 million euros at the exchange rate of 60 dinars per euro prevailing at the end of 2000.

In countries with moderate inflation, and at least a rudimentary banking system, the ratio of currency in circulation to GDP is generally between 5 and 10 per cent. Given that the states of the region are all very poor, the euro value of their currency in circulation is actually quite low (e.g. 500 million euros for Albania – which has a very high cash ratio because it has no proper banking system). With interest rates around 5 per cent, the cost to the EU budget for these amounts would be minuscule. less than 25 million euros annually for Albania and 15 million euros for Romania. The parts of ex-Yugoslavia most involved in wars (Serbia, Bosnia-Herzegovina, Montenegro, Kosovo) would perhaps together need 3 bn euros in cash (for comparison, the total for the euro area is over 300 bn), which would mean interest costs of around 150 million euros p.a. (two-thirds of which would be accounted for by Serbia). These sums would thus definitely be below 1 per cent of the overall EU budget of around 100 bn euros.

In this way the EU would effectively lend its currency (and hence its monetary stability) to the countries concerned. The countries would not lose their seigniorage because they could keep the assets accumulated by their central banks through the issuance of their defunct national currency. Of course, this leaves them only with the small amount of seigniorage that is compatible with price stability. But this is entirely appropriate, as argued.

The national monetary authorities would have no seat on the Governing Council of the ECB, which would thus not be affected, but it would still be preferable to have an explicit agreement on the details of euroisation. For example, there should be an undertaking to radically liberalise the domestic banking system (in particular, allowing EU banks to acquire local ones), and to institute deposit insurance and proper banking supervision. EU authorities, including the national central banks in the eurosystem, should be able to provide the required technical assistance.

IMF monitoring (reduced to fiscal policy and, to some extent, the banking system) should continue. Normal IMF credit lines should still be available subject to conditionality, which would, however, have to be adapted. Full euroisation would only make apparent what has de facto already been happening in many instances: IMF credits are not motivated by and used for a balance-of-payment deficit, but are used to finance a fiscal deficit.

The EU institutions (European Commission, European Council and the ECB) strongly oppose euroisation anywhere. The official reasons given vary. They range from a concern for monetary control in the eurozone to fears for the external value of the euro. These concerns seem to be overblown. Euroisation would not affect materially monetary policy since the money supply in Serbia would amount to less than 0.1 per cent of the euro money supply, and even all of SEE together would not reach 1 per cent. There has never been any suggestion that the dollar might have been weak because it was used in Panama, and the full-scale adoption of the dollar in Ecuador (which is of a similar economic size to Serbia) during the summer of 2000 did not dent its strength. The real reason why EU institutions oppose euroisation is simply the feeling 'Keep your hands away, this is our toy!'.

Given this opposition of the EU institutions it is unlikely that direct EU support will be forthcoming for euroisation. However, this should not deter countries in SEE to adopt this policy. The currency boards of Estonia and Bulgaria were initially also viewed with suspicion. But their success transformed this approach into orthodoxy. The same would happen to euroisation: once it proves successful, the opposition of the EU is likely to disappear.

Euroisation would have one important additional advantage: recent research shows that sharing a common currency can foster trade considerably. For example, Glick and Rose (2002) find that if two countries have the same currency, trade between them could double. These results have been criticised on the ground that they are based on data for the trade flows of small economies, such as the Caribbean islands or countries taking part in an African monetary union. One could thus argue that results based on such 'exotic' economies should not be used as a benchmark for EMU. But the SEE economies are not much larger than the countries that drive the results in Glick and Rose (2002), so it is not unreasonable to expect that adoption of the euro should indeed lead to a big expansion of trade.

## 10.3   Lessons from the experience of Montenegro (and Bosnia-Herzegovina)

The experience of Montenegro is instructive. Montenegro long remained one of the two republics that comprised the Federal Republic of Yugoslavia (the other being Serbia), now reconstituted under EU pressure as the state of Serbia and Montenegro.

The most visible element of the reform strategy of the Montenegrin government, which in 1997–8 ceased to follow orders from Belgrade, consisted of the substitution of the highly unstable Yugoslav dinar with the DM in order to provide the population with a stable currency. The introduction of the DM began in November 1999 and was a success. After a few months the DM had already become the main transaction currency and most taxes were also paid in DM. The introduction of the DM consisted of only two acts: first, the government of Montenegro legalised its use; second, then it started to pay out salaries and pensions in DM.

Paying out approximately DM 25 million in November 1999 was enough to get the economy operating on DM. The workers and pensioners spent their money in local shops and these DM flowed back to the government in tax payments. The private sector followed quickly by providing prices in DM and also using the DM for salaries etc. After a few months the deposit balances in DM at the central payment system had risen to about DM 100 million, implying that about DM 75 million had been attracted from the underground and cash economy.

The experience of Bosnia-Herzegovina provides another example, this time of what should be avoided. Despite massive inflows of foreign aid (amounting to over $5 billion since the end of the war), and a stable currency provided by a currency board, the local economy has not developed any sustainable independent productive capacity. One of the reasons for this is that, in the absence of economic reforms, local political elites have maintained a stranglehold on the economy. This applies in particular to the housing market and the payments system. These two elements are key to the political power of the old elite and thus acquire particular importance in the case of Yugoslavia. In a socialist system housing in cities is usually not private, but linked to the workplace. This implies that local officials who can influence employment decisions (for example in the public sector or large state-owned enterprises) wield immense power. Privatising housing must thus be one priority.

The payment system is even more important as a source of power and corruption. In the socialist Yugoslav economy payments among enterprises were channelled through a central system (ZPP), which gave bureaucrats the power to interfere with all transfers of funds. This system still exists in Yugoslavia (also in Bosnia-Herzegovina, making a mockery of the official currency board), and survives partially even in Croatia. The experience of Bosnia-Herzegovina shows that to give local politicians the ability to interfere with the payments system is a recipe for disaster, especially in a situation in which the legal system does not really function and lines of political responsibility are unclear. In Montenegro the payments system was not a disaster, but its existence still stifled the development of a real banking system.

Structural economic reforms (including rapid privatisation) in Serbia are thus not only a condition sine qua non that foreign assistance can initiate sustained economic growth, but also a key element to assure the survival of political reforms.

## 10.4   Conclusions

Experience in Central Europe has shown that the prospect of eventual integration into Europe constitutes the most powerful stimulus for economic reform (and acceptable political behaviour). In the Balkans an additional concern is speed. The population must be able to see tangible signs of their European future quickly, otherwise there could be a return to nationalist politics.

We propose two elements that might lead to a jump-start of the region: establishing a customs union with the EU and full euroisation. Our prescription is not based on deep pessimism concerning the region. On the contrary, most of the Balkan countries have a better basis on which to establish a functioning market economy than many other formerly socialist countries had at the beginning of the 1990s. The ex-Yugoslav republics, in particular, inherited an acceptable administrative apparatus, a history of openness to international trade, and a legislative framework that was not ideal but that left a lot of room for the market. The last element means that in this region there is no need to start from scratch. The functioning administration means that it is possible to collect enough taxes to keep fiscal policy under control and to implement reforms. The experience of Macedonia confirms this. Under strict IMF and World Bank guidance the currency has been stabilised and the budget actually shows a surplus. The usual problems with loss-making large SOE were kept in check through a combination of privatisation and downsizing, so that modest growth could start from solid bases. But this experience also shows that merely avoiding an economic disaster is not enough to stabilise the region. Progress towards further liberalisation has been slow and the political system remains deeply involved with the economy in a variety of ways. A more radical approach is thus needed, both to create clean political systems and to allow the economy to make up for the loss of an entire decade.

Creating a new economic order for the area will be more important than the size of the sums allocated to reconstruction. In Germany industrial production continued to decline for three years after the Second World War had ended, although during this period some of the basic infrastructure was repaired. Growth started only after the radical changes that came with the currency reform of 1948. The EU has a tendency to emphasise the sums of aid it is disbursing (or promising to disburse) in the region. Its main contribution could, however, be much more important and turn out to be less costly. We argue that a resolute European policy, based on the two pillars of a customs union with the EU and adoption of the euro as a replacement for national currency, can sow the seeds for a quick recovery of the region.

## Appendix 10.1 Lessons from Ecuador?

Ecuador went through a series of crises in 1999, during which the exchange rate doubled, inflation shot up, foreign debt could not be serviced and there was a run on banks. When conventional measures failed, the government adopted, with support from the IMF and the international community, a broadly based reform programme which included dollarisation of the economy, i.e. making the US dollar legal tender in Ecuador, thus completely substituting the national currency (the sucre). We do not wish to hold up Ecuador as an example for Serbia, but the two economies do have certain similarities which suggest that the initial results from euroisation might also be similar.

Is the experience of Ecuador relevant for SEE, and especially a country that perceives itself to be large, like Serbia? It should be since the economic data for Ecuador are in many respects very similar to that of Serbia. Ecuador has a population of about 12 million (versus about 10 for Serbia). Ecuador had a pre-crisis GDP of about $20 bn, now down to about $10 bn. Estimates for this are again similar to the values for Serbia, which vary even more depending on the year chosen.

### *Ecuador and Serbia compared*

Ecuador is much larger in terms of its international trade. Exports run at about $4 bn p.a., versus less than about $1.5 bn recorded for Serbia.

Total foreign debt of pre-crisis Ecuador was about 60–80 per cent of GDP or $13 bn. Again the numbers are very similar for both countries (see table 10A.1). After the crisis this rose to over 100 per cent of GDP for both countries as the real exchange rate fell considerably. The ratio of debt to exports, which is less affected by gyrations in the real exchange rate, and which measures the capacity of the country to earn hard currency for debt service, differs, however, considerably: for Ecuador it is about 230–250 per cent versus over 500 per cent for Serbia (or rather the FRY). However, negotiations on debt forgiveness are likely to reduce the outstanding debt for FRY. Hence Serbia might end up with a similar level of indebtedness.

Currency in circulation at the outset of the dollarisation programme amounted to about $500–600 million in Ecuador. This is somewhat more than in Serbia, with only about $350 million when Milošović fell. But the partial re-monetisation of the economy has since increased the value for Serbia.

One major difference is in the banking system. Ecuador had a hyperactive banking system that lent too much to the private sector. The IMF notes that 'The worsened macroeconomic

Table 10A.1. *Ecuador and Serbia compared*

|  | Ecuador | | Serbia (FRY) | |
|---|---|---|---|---|
|  | 1998 | 2000 | 1998 | 2000 |
| GDP (bn $) | 19.7 | 13.6 | 18.2 | 8.1 |
| Exports (bn $) | 4.9 | 5.0 | 2.9 | 1.9 |
| External debt (% GDP) | 80 | 97 | 84 | 145 |
| External debt (% exports) | 360 | 264 | 380 | 396 |

*Source*: Own calculations from IMF, Deutsche Bank and EBRD.

conditions accentuated the problems in the banking system stemming from connected lending practices, the growth of foreign currency credit to borrowers that did not generate earnings in foreign currency, and lax oversight, particularly of offshore operations.'

By contrast, in Serbia banks were just serving the regime to get around sanctions. Banks in Serbia have also massive amounts of dead wood on the balance sheets, namely the foreign currency transactions that were frozen almost a decade ago. If these assets and liabilities are simply cancelled, as they probably should be, the banking system in Serbia will turn out to be rather small. By contrast, in Ecuador the fiscal cost of saving banks (to avoid a total liquidity crunch for industry) is estimated by the IMF at around 25 per cent of GDP.

## Appendix 10.2    Euroisation: any lessons from the Panamanian experience?

Until recently the only example of a country that had adopted a foreign currency was Panama.[7] A brief review of the experience of that country is therefore instructive. Panama uses the US dollar, has no central bank and no official foreign exchange reserves (they are not needed). This arrangement has by now worked without technical problems for almost a century. The 'balboa' is mainly used for accounting purposes and exists only as silver coins. (Guatemala had, until the mid-1980s, a similar fixed-rate regime against the dollar, but this ended with its civil war, in which over 10 per cent of the population were killed.)

In the following we will address three key issues that arise when discussing euroisation for South-East Europe. Is Panama a useful example? Are perfect labour markets a prerequisite for the adoption of a foreign currency? Can euroisation protect against financial shocks? The answers, in short, are: yes, no and yes.

### Is Panama a useful example for South-East Europe?

Panama is often perceived as a special case that has no relevance for other situations. Even a superficial examination reveals, however, that in three key areas there are close parallels to the countries in SEE.

First, *size*. Panama has a population of about 2.7 million, larger than Kosovo or Macedonia and only a little less than Albania. Its total GDP, around $9 bn, is much larger than that of these countries, and in the same order of magnitude as that of Bulgaria.

Second, *weakness of institutions*. Panama also resembles the countries of SEE in that it has rather weak administrative structures and democratic institutions (as can be seen from the coup d'état of the 1980s).

Third, the *importance of transfers from abroad*. Panama is often perceived as an artificial country that lives off the Canal, but has no significant economic activities of its own. But this impression is wrong. The country does have a sizeable industry. Exports of goods are at the same level, per capita, as in its larger neighbour, Colombia, and agriculture occupies a similar share of the population.

Moreover, the transit fees from the Canal make Panama actually more comparable to the countries in SEE for which the 'euroisation' option should be considered because these countries will also receive substantial transfers from abroad. These transfers will be reduced sooner or later, which will require substantial changes in relative prices. However, these problems are not insurmountable; Panama had to deal with large swings in the revenues from the Canal, but there was never any argument that the country would need a flexible exchange rate to deal with them. The importance of the revenues from the Canal should also not be exaggerated. In 1998 total revenues from it amounted to about $650 million, equivalent to about 7 per cent of GDP. The Canal is not a free lunch, however – operating costs were of a similar magnitude (with about one half for labour). The (net) rent the country receives from the Canal is thus probably only around 3 per cent of GDP, which is less than the countries in SEE can expect over next few years (and much less than Bosnia–Herzegovina receives at present).

The Canal is more important for public finances: the Canal authorities and users contributed about $150 million to an overall budget of about $1.1 bn. It is interesting to note that, even after a reduction in rates, import tariffs still amount to about $250 million, or slightly less than the 3 per cent of GDP used as a benchmark.

### Are perfect labour markets a prerequisite for the adoption of a foreign currency?

It is often argued that a national currency is needed as a safety valve in case domestic price and wage pressures mount. Many opponents to EMU implicitly argue that this is especially the case in poorer countries with weak institutions. This concern seems unwarranted in the case of Panama. There has been no long-term price pressure on the dollar/balboa link. On the contrary, over the last thirty years prices have actually increased less in Panama than in the USA, on average by 1.7 per cent less each year. Over the entire period (between 1967 and 1997) the US CPI increased by about 370 per cent, whereas in Panama the increase was only 170 per cent. There is also absolutely no indication that Panamanian labour priced itself out of the market. Unemployment in Panama hovers presently at around 13 per cent, but this compares well with other Latin American countries, and is much below the current 20–40 per cent unemployment rates of some of the countries in SEE. The data from overall employment are even stronger. Despite its young population, the overall employment rate (employment/population) is 33 per cent which is much higher than in its Latin American neighbours (Colombia 15 per cent, Guatemala 8 per cent) and the countries in SEE with their much older population (Macedonia 17 per cent, Bulgaria 22 per cent).

This is not to say that the labour market in Panama is perfect. On the contrary, it was actually the model for the Harris-Todaro model of a dual labour market in which there are two sectors: an international and modern one and a traditional rural one. The first sector pays above-market clearing wages to reduce the incentive to shirk. (High transactions costs make it impossible to enforce contractual behaviour by labour.) The second, traditional, sector absorbs surplus labour at a wage rate that is determined informally through household and other non-market activities (subsistence agriculture, small-scale commerce, etc.). In equilibrium there is substantial unemployment in cities until the cost of moving there just equals the expected wage differential (which in turn depends on the probability of finding a job, i.e. the unemployment rate). This is exactly what is likely to happen in SEE (and was already the norm in pre-war Kosovo). A different monetary regime does not change the fundamental reasons for this dual economic structure, which characterises many Central American countries. But the experience of Panama shows that a stable currency regime does not increase the problems that result from such a dual labour market. On the contrary, each time Panama had to face a major political or economic crisis (e.g. US embargo, oil price increase) the informal sector was able to absorb the surplus labour liberated by the formal sector without excessive unemployment problems in the cities.

The countries in SEE are likely to have imperfect labour markets whether or not they adopt the euro quickly. Their problems are likely to be similar to the ones faced by other countries, like Panama, with a similar income per capita (and weak institutions), but different from the ones facing EU members with their highly developed social systems.

## Can euroisation protect against financial shocks?

The clear answer here is yes. Adopting the dollar has protected Panama against most financial problems and allowed it to survive the recent global financial crisis much better than other countries in the region. A recent IMF report notes that its economy was affected by the fall in demand in the rest of the region, but there were no signs of financial instability in Panama itself. Deposit and lending rates remained essentially at the average of the five preceding years (around 7 and 10 per cent, respectively) whereas dollar equivalent rates in other Latin American countries were often 20 percentage points above Libor. Dollarisation thus protects the domestic economy against external financial shocks.

A key issue for many countries with large external debts is to what extent euroisation could lower the risk premium paid on foreign debt. For a country with an external debt-to-GDP ratio of 80 per cent (e.g. Bulgaria in 2000) a risk premium of 10 per cent (not unreasonable in current circumstances) implies an additional annual transfer of 8 per cent of GDP to foreign creditors. The experience of Panama shows that euroisation could be a big help in this area as well. The public external debt of Panama is also substantial, now around 60 per cent of GDP (after a peak of 75 per cent in 1995), but the government never had to pay a large risk premium on its indebtedness. Why should dollarisation lead to radically lower risk premia also on external debt? Per se, the monetary regime in countries with weak institutions does not cure the chronic difficulties of the public sector to raise tax revenues (and limit pressure for more expenditure). But euroisation has several consequences.

First of all, it eliminates the difference between external and internal debt. This in turn has two consequences: the government cannot discriminate against foreign creditors, and it cannot rely on a captive domestic market to finance deficits.

Secondly, it eliminates a key source of uncertainty about the capacity of the government to service external debt. With euroisation, the large swings in the real exchange rate that result from the large, sudden depreciations which often arise during currency crises are no longer possible. Russia is a case in point, as discussed in chapter 8. When the exchange rate of the rouble quadrupled in 1998 (going from 6 to 24 roubles per dollar), the capacity of the Russian government to service its foreign debt was cut to one-fourth (and the price of Russian eurobonds went to 25 per cent of their face value, implying a risk premium of over 30 per cent). After a year domestic prices had doubled, so the real devaluation was 'only' 50 per cent, but this still implies that the dollar value of Russian tax revenues had been halved (and the price of Russian eurobonds went back to 50 per cent). With euroisation swings of the real exchange rate – and the price of foreign debt – of this order of magnitude will not happen.

Euroisation thus improves debt service capacity in a number of ways. A much lower country risk premium is therefore entirely appropriate.

## Notes

1. The following material draws extensively on Daskalov et al. (2000).
2. The sanctions imposed during the wars might have played a part in this, but the economic mis-management of Serbia was probably even more important. Moreover, during the wars a large part of the 'cross-border' economic activity between Serbia and its neighbouring countries consisted of sanctions busting and smuggling.
3. Daskalov et al. (2000) present a detailed and comprehensive trade policy plan for the western Balkans, which describes how free trade could be reached more quickly, but still step-by-step.
4. If the EU continues to subsidise its own agricultural exports to the countries in the region, which are anyway twenty times as large as EU imports (see Gros et al. 1999) the importing countries should impose countervailing duties of the amount of the EU subsidies. The impact of any EU subsidies would thus be neutralised and their effect would simply be to provide revenues for SEE governments. EU subsidies for exports of agricultural products would thus result merely in transfers. One is tempted to argue that these EU subsidies should be as high as possible in order to help government budgets in the region.
5. This approach could be 'safely' extended to non-European countries because, except for countries with major political or civil disorders, EU imports from LDCs have tended to grow rapidly.
6. See Brenton and Manchin (2002).
7. This section is based on information from IMF (1999) and Moreno-Villalaz (1999).

# 11 The outlook

Reforms: what about the navy?

In this volume we have analysed the economic transformation of the Central and Eastern European countries, their struggle for economic (and indeed political) renaissance, their successes and their failures.

We started with an overview of the communist system, both as a theoretical construct ('just an idea' of Karl Marx) and the performance of the Soviet Union, once a serious challenger to the United States in superpower rivalry. We found that socialism was successful in producing certain basic goods that can be measured in physical units: tonnes of steel, kilowatt-hours of electricity, gold medals at Olympic games, etc. But since this system never grasped the importance of opportunity cost it turned out that a lot of this production was economically useless (or worse). The industries most cherished by social planners were usually the ones that had the greatest adjustment difficulties once market forces were allowed to work and economies were opened to international competition.

The extent to which socialism failed to deliver can best be seen in two real-world examples. Before Poland fell under communism its level of development was comparable to that of Spain. After forty years of communism Poland emerged in 1990 with a GDP almost ten times lower than Spain, which had also endured forty years of dictatorship, but one that left market mechanisms broadly intact. A similar situation can be found in the former Austro-Hungarian empire, where up to the Second World War Austria and Czechoslovakia were at a broadly similar level of development, with Austria slightly worse off because industry was concentrated in Czechoslovakia. After forty years of communism Austria's GDP per capita was vastly higher than that of its neighbour. And even now, after a decade of transition, it is still almost four times as high if evaluated at PPP.

What is the outlook for transition countries ten years after their economic and political liberalisation?

Our analysis of the initial conditions and the reform efforts during the first ten years have led us to treat transition countries in three groups. We are convinced that this grouping remains pertinent for their future development.

The first group is composed of the Central European and Baltic countries. They have implemented reforms successfully and will receive a significant institutional strengthening from EU membership. Their future is assured even if convergence to EU living standards will take longer than initially hoped. Elsewhere the future is more uncertain and convergence will take much longer, if it happens at all.

The second group is composed of the Balkan countries with less favourable starting positions, a longer queue for EU membership and much greater uncertainty about their capacity to create efficient institutions.

The greatest question marks surround the third group: Russia and the other successor states of the former Soviet Union. They will not benefit from EU membership, but may be able to enjoy special relationships. The 1990s have been bad for all of them because neither market nor democratic institutions were familiar and trustworthy concepts. Russia has to cope with its new status as an economically 'small' and a geopolitically 'medium-to-large' country. All other CIS countries had to set up political and administrative structures to assume their independence. In so doing they often became bogged down in internal power struggles and in fights over territorial definitions. As noted by Shleifer (1998), most of the political leadership in Poland consists of new politicians. In contrast, the Russian political elite is composed of former communist bosses. In other countries of the FSU the old bosses and their old methods are even less challenged. The near future does not look particularly bright, notwithstanding the dissipation of the gloom and doom of the late 1990s in the wake of Russia's recent recovery enlarged upon in chapter 9.

In section 1 we assess the outlook in terms of three criteria, which for us are the most important conditions for success. As this book has made clear all along, these are: institutions, openness and geography. In section 2 we again apply these criteria in a gravity index to arrive at a future map of Europe.

## 11.1   Conditions for success

### *The role of institutions*

There is now a consensus among economists that the quality of institutions has a determining influence on economic prospects. Institutions refer here to the political and legal systems and the administration that enforces policy and the laws.

Quality is, of course, difficult to measure, but there are a number of indicators collected by respected international institutions (both official and NGOs) that allow for cross-country comparisons. These indicators have been used widely in the economic literature, which has found that they help to explain development and growth in GDP per capita. Chapters 4 and 5 in particular used these indicators.

There are two issues here: what is the starting point for the CEEC and what can one say about the likely long-term evolution?

The starting point correlates well with our grouping into three classes: Central Europe with Slovenia, perhaps Croatia, and the Baltic states are all well advanced in institution-building; the Balkan states are a mixed bag, with Romania and Bulgaria somewhat more advanced than Albania and Yugoslavia (Serbia). Russia and the CIS countries also still have to deliver most of the job. How likely is delivery? This is hard to say. In this book we have encountered, on several occasions, the risk of multiple equilibria, usually one desirable and the other a bad one. Unfortunately this is also the case here.

Some authors (see e.g. Gallup et al. 1997) find that poor countries might end up in a self-made poverty trap in which an inefficient political system does not dare to reform the economy because it is feared that this will have unacceptable social consequences. As long as bad policies are not reformed, the country does not grow and might even get poorer. Over time it will remain very difficult to implement reforms, so this situation might persist. Ukraine, Belarus, Moldova, the Caucasian republics and others may already be in such a bad equilibrium, although the years since 1998 have seen progress even there.

## *Openness*

Openness is, of course, essential to any but the largest countries. Openness is partly a natural consequence of being small (as most CEEC are), but it can be greatly fostered, or hindered, by policy. Openness can be fostered by the right policy choices in two key areas: trade policy and money. In both areas the outlook seems to be excellent for the EU candidates, but less so for the CIS, with the Balkans as usual in between.

In trade policy all transition economies moved in the right direction, adopting in general relatively liberal trade regimes. The next challenge was to turn liberal trade laws into reality. In the CEEC that are candidates for EU membership constant supervision by the EU ensures that this is the case. But Russia, and most of the CIS, are in a different category and require a lot of strengthening of their customs services. In this case, strengthening does not mean giving customs officers more power, but providing them with the appropriate training and introducing procedures that are straightforward and transparent, thus minimising the potential for abuse and corruption. WTO membership would also help. Russia has taken almost a decade to negotiate this, mostly because it was not perceived as a high priority in Moscow.

Recent research (see Frankel and Rose 2000) suggests that every 1 per cent increase in trade (relative to GDP) raises income per capita by roughly 0.33 per cent over twenty years. Increasing the trade-to-GDP ratio by 30–60 percentage points could thus increase income per capita by 10–20 per cent. This might be seen as a modest gain, but it would come in addition to other factors, such as overall productivity gains. It would considerably speed up the catching-up process in which the CEEC must engage if they are not to miss the gravy train called the EU.

The new EU members are all candidates for euro area membership once they join the EU. As discussed in chapters 9 and 10, this will bring large economic benefits. Direct benefits materialise through lower transactions costs, which are important for small open economies, often with trade-to-GDP ratios in excess of 50 per cent. But the indirect benefits through deeper market integration and access to the EU capital market without an 'emerging market' risk premium should be even larger. Gros et al. (2002) suggest that euro area membership could come almost immediately after EU membership because most CEEC are closer to satisfying the Maastricht criteria for participation in the euro area than is widely realised.

The Balkan countries have the same long-term goal. However, they are much further from EU membership, which will require years of painstaking reforms of the administrative apparatus. We argued in chapter 10 that they should not wait that long, but just adopt the euro unilaterally. This would allow them to reap most of the benefits of euro-area membership. The only difference would be that they would not have a governor from their own country sitting in the Governing Council of the ECB. But this cannot be regarded as an economic cost since all members of the Governing Council of the ECB are supposed to look after the interests of the entire euro area, and not their home country.

Russia and the other CIS countries have a more difficult monetary future. Under strict IMF surveillance they have achieved some macroeconomic stability, but their currency regimes limit their integration in world markets.

## *The role of geography*

Finally, let us turn to geography, the one immutable factor in European history. It might be useful to stress that we do not give much importance to natural resources. An abundant endowment of coal, or oil does not guarantee high growth. On the contrary, it might hinder growth. Academic research has shown that countries with abundant natural resources grow in general more slowly.[1] The reason for this result is quite simple. The distribution of property rights over natural resources almost always involves the government. This implies that the best way to get rich in a resource-rich country is to lobby the government. Rent-seeking thus dominates entrepreneurship.

Even the best policies cannot produce high growth in a small country that is isolated from the major world markets (e.g. Kyrgyzstan). Gallup et al. (1997) find that distance from markets has a decisive influence on economic development as measured by GDP per capita. Most CEEC are situated rather close to the EU market, closer than Russia and closer than some EU members such as Greece, Portugal or Finland. Distance from markets is thus not a negative factor for most CEEC, but is a serious handicap for many CIS countries. Gallup et al. (1997) also find that access to maritime transport is very important. Their estimates would suggest that even the Balkan countries have a hope because most of their population lives close to a coast.

Most of the states in CEEC are small. Including the Baltics and the Balkan countries there are fifteen states with a population of 10 million or less in this region. This might pose problems for the complicated decisionmaking mechanisms within the EU as discussed in chapter 9. But otherwise there is no presumption in economics that small states do less well.

The experience of Switzerland is instructive in this regard. Until the middle of the nineteenth century this country was extremely poor; and since it had neither coal nor iron, nor a strong agricultural base, it was generally assumed that the Swiss were condemned to remain underdeveloped. However they are now among the richest Europeans. They were able to grow out of poverty because they made the most of their favourable geographical position in the heart of Europe by opening their economy and offering investors a stable political environment plus an efficient administration. Recent economic research confirms that this is not just an isolated experience but a general rule.

Size plays even less of a role for the CEEC that are on the road to membership because they will join the largest integrated market in the world.

Table 11.1 presents a synthetic view of all three arguments combined. The emerging classification is unambiguous. Central Europe receives close to top marks in all three domains; the Balkans perform moderately and the CIS countries are consistently bad. We now combine the constraints of geography, namely size of the country and distance to major markets, with income and trade arrangements to look into the crystal ball.

## 11.2   The new Europe

By 2010 the EU will have its eastern borders from along the Visegrad countries to the Black Sea, including Romania, Bulgaria and possibly some successor states of former Yugoslavia.

Table 11.1. *Factors that condition the future*

|              | Central European countries | South-East Europe | CIS |
|--------------|----------------------------|-------------------|-----|
| Institutions | ++                         | +/−               | −   |
| Openness     | +++/++                     | +                 | −   |
| Geography    | +++/++                     | ++/+              | +/− |
| **Overall**  | ++                         | +                 | −   |

*Note*: maximum +++; minimum −.

To test whether this size of EU makes sense we concentrate on the geographical position of Eastern European countries by using again the gravity model. We develop a gravity index (see box 11.1) that measures the trade potential of a given country by taking the sum of the country's supply potential (its GDP) adjusted for the size of the internal market and the trade demand it can expect given its geographical position. A country that is rich and close to other rich countries will have a high index and countries that are poor or far from the centres of economic activity will have a low index (will be 'peripheral'). This gravity (or periphery) index is attractive for several reasons. International trade structures were never as amorphous as suggested by standard trade theory. Geographic proximity, size of markets, trade arrangements and cultural affinities are part of the index and matter, as demonstrated by the estimation of gravity models. The time-dependent ingredients are relatively straightforward to forecast (GDP and population growth) and the unchanging geography is easy to measure.[2]

Figure 11.1 depicts the trade flows and shows that Europe's centre of gravity is the geographic heart of Europe, that is, the six founding countries of the European Community, plus Switzerland. The question is: what is the role of geography?

Table 11.3 lists the periphery index for various regional groupings. The value of the index reveals the density of economic activity resulting from the sum of domestic production plus trade potential with the countries in the regional groupings. The trade potential is essentially determined by the size of the other economies in the group considered and distances. The columns of table 11.3 thus represent different hypothetical trading blocs. As the absolute values are meaningless, we normalised the values on the basis of the results for the EU-25 grouping (we assume that this will be reality by about 2010).

Column 2 sets the benchmark, the expected EU-27 for 2010 (i.e. with all ten current CEEC applicants in – we neglect Malta, Cyprus, Croatia and other successor states of former Yugoslavia, which might have joined by then). Column 2 shows, not surprisingly, that Germany is most central in such a grouping, with the outlying areas (Estonia, Ireland, Portugal and Greece) the most peripheral (having the lowest values). Column 1 shows the value for the present EU-15. It is apparent from a comparison of these two columns that for the present EU-15 opening to the CEEC is not a big deal. Comparing, for example, the values of Germany across columns 1 and 2 shows that opening trade with the CEEC lifts the German index by only one point, from 631 to 632.

---

**Box 11.1   A gravity index**

We define the gravity or periphery index for country $j$ as:

$$R_j = \sum_i Y_i X_i u_{ij}/d_{ij} + bY_j X_j/d_{jj} = R_j{}^1 + bR_j{}^2, \tag{11.1}$$

where $Y_i$ is GDP in US dollars of country $i$; $X_i$ is GDP per capita deflated by the highest GDP per capita among all countries so that $0 < X_i \leq 1$; $d_{ij} = (D_{ij})^{1/2}$, where $D_{ij}$ is the distance between the capitals of countries $i$ and $j$ (in km); $d_{jj} = 1/3(S_j/\pi)^{1/2}$, where $S_j$ is the surface in km$^2$. $u_{ij}$ is a dummy variable for closeness either in an historical, cultural sense or due to trade treaties. $u_{ij}$ is 1.21 for trade among the six regions of Russia, to reflect the fact that they form an integrated country; 1.1 for various regional groupings and 1.0 for all other bilateral relations.

To calibrate the two factors in definition (11.1) the weight $b$ (identical for all $j$) is used. Weight $b$ is defined as:

$$b = \sum_j R_j{}^1 \bigg/ \sum_j R_j{}^2 \tag{11.2}$$

and forces globally the weight of the $R_j{}^1$ and $R_j{}^2$ to be equal.

The data used are listed in table 11.2, except for bilateral distances to save space. The index $R_j$ is a measure of the trade potential of country $j$ within a given set of countries. The ranking established is specific to this set and can be changed by adding or subtracting countries. For this reason computations for a variety of country groupings were carried out.

Population is assumed to be constant; GDP growth is projected at an average of 3 per cent p.a. for Japan, 5 per cent for the CIS and Central Europe to reflect catching up; all other countries are assumed to grow at 3 per cent p.a. Experimentation with different assumptions about GDP growth showed that the general thrust of the results reported below is robust. Russia is too large and heterogeneous to be treated as a single region with a well-defined centre. For this reason Russia is split up into six regions. The fact that these regions are part of one state is reflected by a dummy variable.

---

The CIS is then considered separately as a potential bloc in column 3. The values are so low, compared to those for the EU-15 (or EU-25), that it is clear that the CIS has no economic future as a regional bloc. This judgement is also valid if one considers the entire former Soviet bloc in column 4 (CIS plus CEEC plus SEE). Comparing columns 3 and 4 shows that free trade with Central Europe increases the trading potential of the former Soviet republics, but the values remain essentially of the same order of magnitude: a fraction of the EU potential.

Poor countries like Armenia or Moldova would gain most, but a jump from 1 to 3 or 4 can only be characterised as from dismal to extremely bad.

Free trade of the EU with all of Eastern Europe changes the picture dramatically, as can be seen from column 5. Comparing column 4 with column 5 indicates that this leads to a

**Figure 11.1** Trade flows in Europe east and west

twenty- to forty-fold jump in the trading potential of all East European countries. For Central Europe separately the effect is visible in the difference between columns 2 and 4: trade with the EU is all-decisive; adding the CIS and SEE is irrelevant.

The results in column 5 are used to design, in figure 11.2, the future economic map of Europe. The more central a country is according to the index of column 5, the darker is its surface.[3] Siberia (not shown) would have the purest white as the most peripheral area, followed by the Central Asian republics. The area or republics closer to Western Europe gain light grey tones and black is achieved in the epicentre represented by Germany.

Finally, column 6 reveals that adding the rest of the world (mainly the United States and Japan) increases the trading potential of Central European countries and most Western former Soviet republics substantially, by similar absolute amounts. For Germany this would imply an increase in the index of about 10 per cent, whereas for Estonia the same amount, starting from a smaller basis, would mean a doubling. This is substantial, and explains why the smaller 'fringe' members of the EU perform with their political clout the useful service of ensuring that the EU remains a promoter of free trade. But a doubling of the trading potential to be gained by CEEC from free trade with the rest of world is still small if compared to the over twentyfold jump implied by free trade with the EU. This result confirms once more that for the European transition countries free trade with the EU economic space

Table 11.2. *Raw data used in gravity index**

| | 2000 | | 2000 | | 2010 | |
|---|---|---|---|---|---|---|
| | Area (000 km$^2$) | Population (000) | GDP ($ mn) | Per head ($) | GDP ($ mn) | Per head ($) |
| St Petersburg | 529 | 11128 | 33384 | 3000 | 54379 | 4887 |
| Moscow | 1530 | 47339 | 142017 | 3000 | 231331 | 4887 |
| Volgograd | 589 | 20810 | 67430 | 3000 | 101692 | 4887 |
| Sverdlovsk | 3097 | 39489 | 118467 | 3000 | 192970 | 4887 |
| Novosibirsk | 3564 | 15886 | 47658 | 3000 | 77630 | 4887 |
| Vladivostok | 7767 | 13289 | 39867 | 3000 | 64939 | 4887 |
| Ukraine | 604 | 51000 | 49677 | 974 | 80919 | 1587 |
| Belarus | 207 | 10000 | 22629 | 2263 | 36860 | 3686 |
| Estonia | 45 | 1000 | 4682 | 4682 | 7626 | 7626 |
| Latvia | 64 | 2000 | 5527 | 2764 | 9003 | 4501 |
| Lithuania | 65 | 4000 | 9585 | 2396 | 15613 | 3903 |
| Moldova | 34 | 4000 | 1872 | 468 | 3049 | 762 |
| Armenia | 30 | 4000 | 1628 | 407 | 2652 | 663 |
| Azerbaijan | 87 | 8000 | 4399 | 550 | 7166 | 896 |
| Georgia | 70 | 5000 | 5244 | 1049 | 8542 | 1708 |
| Kazakhstan | 2717 | 16000 | 22165 | 1385 | 36104 | 2257 |
| Kyrgyzstan | 198 | 5000 | 1764 | 353 | 2873 | 575 |
| Uzebekistan | 447 | 24000 | 25047 | 1044 | 40799 | 1700 |
| Tajikistan | 143 | 6000 | 1990 | 332 | 3242 | 540 |
| Turkmenistan | 488 | 5000 | 4397 | 879 | 7162 | 1432 |
| Poland | 313 | 39000 | 135659 | 3478 | 266862 | 6843 |
| Czech Republic | 128 | 10000 | 52035 | 5204 | 102361 | 10236 |
| Hungary | 93 | 10000 | 45725 | 4573 | 89948 | 8995 |
| Slovenia | 238 | 2000 | 18201 | 9101 | 35804 | 17902 |
| Bulgaria | 111 | 8000 | 10085 | 1261 | 19839 | 2480 |
| Romania | 238 | 23000 | 34843 | 1515 | 68541 | 2980 |
| Slovakia | 49 | 5000 | 19461 | 3892 | 38283 | 7657 |
| Croatia | 57 | 5000 | 19081 | 3816 | 37535 | 7507 |
| Bosnia-Herz. | 51 | 4200 | 4082 | 972 | 8030 | 1912 |
| Macedonia | 26 | 2000 | 2201 | 1101 | 4330 | 2165 |
| Serbia | 102 | 11000 | 17400 | 1582 | 34228 | 3112 |
| France | 547 | 59000 | 1392501 | 21182 | 1871405 | 31719 |
| Germany | 357 | 82000 | 2092320 | 19086 | 2811903 | 34292 |
| Italy | 301 | 58000 | 1145560 | 18856 | 1539537 | 26544 |
| United Kingdom | 245 | 59000 | 1286488 | 17243 | 1728932 | 29304 |
| Spain | 506 | 39000 | 532034 | 13642 | 715009 | 18334 |
| Portugal | 92 | 10000 | 112006 | 11201 | 150527 | 15053 |
| Scandinavia | 831 | 19000 | 517510 | 27237 | 695490 | 36605 |
| Benelux | 74 | 26000 | 602801 | 23185 | 810114 | 31158 |
| Austria | 84 | 8000 | 206232 | 25779 | 277159 | 34645 |
| Greece | 132 | 11000 | 122946 | 11177 | 165229 | 15021 |
| Ireland | 70 | 4000 | 75030 | 18758 | 100834 | 25209 |
| Norway | 324 | 4000 | 153363 | 38341 | 206107 | 51527 |
| Switzerland | 41 | 7000 | 255265 | 36466 | 343055 | 49008 |
| United States | 9373 | 268000 | 7834036 | 29231 | 10528289 | 39285 |
| Japan | 378 | 126000 | 4190233 | 33256 | 5631323 | 44693 |
| Pakistan | 804 | 128000 | 61667 | 482 | 100449 | 785 |
| Turkey | 781 | 64000 | 189878 | 2967 | 309291 | 4833 |

*Note*: *Data are for 1998 and 2008, but for simplicity we use 2000 and 2010.

Table 11.3. *Periphery indexes (2010)*

| | (1) EU | (2) EU + CEEC | (3) CIS | (4) CEEC + CIS + SEE | (5) EU + CEEC + CIS + SEE | (6) EU + CEEC + CIS + SEE + RoW |
|---|---|---|---|---|---|---|
| France | 378 | 379 | | | 380 | 464 |
| Germany | 631 | 633 | | | 634 | 717 |
| Italy | 338 | 340 | | | 341 | 420 |
| UK | 452 | 453 | | | 454 | 537 |
| Spain | 153 | 155 | | | 155 | 235 |
| Portugal | 109 | 110 | | | 111 | 191 |
| Scandinavia | 178 | 180 | | | 181 | 262 |
| Benelux | 446 | 448 | | | 448 | 521 |
| Austria | 225 | 228 | | | 229 | 309 |
| Greece | 102 | 103 | | | 104 | 177 |
| Ireland | 146 | 147 | | | 147 | 248 |
| Estonia | | 85 | | 4 | 86 | 165 |
| Latvia | | 88 | | 3 | 89 | 167 |
| Lithuania | | 88 | | 4 | 89 | 166 |
| Poland | | 106 | | 3 | 79 | 154 |
| Czech Republic | | 135 | | 2 | 58 | 128 |
| Hungary | | 111 | | 2 | 55 | 126 |
| Slovenia | | 130 | | 2 | 59 | 130 |
| Bulgaria | | 84 | | 2 | 45 | 117 |
| Romania | | 80 | | 2 | 45 | 117 |
| Slovakia | | 119 | | 2 | 47 | 118 |
| St Petersburg | | | 2 | 4 | 77 | 154 |
| Moscow | | | 4 | 5 | 73 | 149 |
| Volgograd | | | 3 | 4 | 64 | 136 |
| Sverdlovsk | | | 3 | 4 | 56 | 129 |
| Novosibirsk | | | 1 | 2 | 45 | 120 |
| Vladivostok | | | 1 | 1 | 33 | 157 |
| Ukraine | | | 2 | 3 | 79 | 154 |
| Belarus | | | 2 | 4 | 86 | 162 |
| Moldova | | | 1 | 4 | 86 | 165 |
| Armenia | | | 1 | 3 | 89 | 167 |
| Azerbaijan | | | 1 | 4 | 89 | 166 |
| Georgia | | | 1 | 3 | 79 | 154 |
| Kazakhstan | | | 1 | 2 | 58 | 128 |
| Kyrgyzstan | | | 1 | 2 | 55 | 126 |
| Uzebekistan | | | 1 | 2 | 59 | 130 |
| Tajikistan | | | 1 | 2 | 45 | 117 |
| Turkmenistan | | | 1 | 2 | 45 | 117 |
| Croatia | | | | 7 | 114 | 192 |
| Bosnia-Herz. | | | | 3 | 98 | 175 |
| Macedonia | | | | 3 | 87 | 162 |
| Serbia | | | | 4 | 95 | 171 |

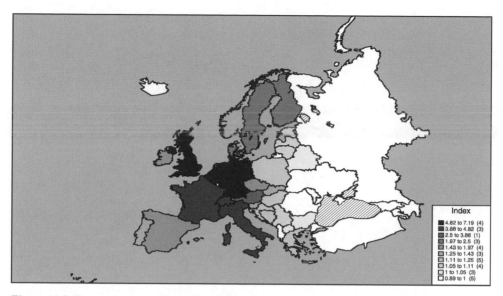

**Figure 11.2** Economic centres in Europe, 2010

is the key to future growth. Opening to globally free trade might in theory be superior, but in reality it would not add a lot to the potential for trade because the EU market is so much closer than the United States or Japan.

As for the core of Western Europe, the main trade potential is within the EU, but the United States adds another 10–20 per cent to the already very high level reached with intra-EU trade.

The map in figure 11.2 reveals a pronounced core–periphery pattern. What does this imply for the future development of Central and Eastern Europe? Krugman (1991a) argues that there might be a 'U'-shaped relationship between transportation costs and the probability of the emergence of a link between a manufacturing core and its agricultural periphery. At zero transportation costs location does not matter, and at very high transportation costs each region will produce its own mix of food and manufacturing products and will thus gain some of the economies of scale in manufacturing. At the extremes of the 'U' no core–periphery pattern should therefore develop. However, there is an intermediate region where transportation costs are positive, but just low enough to make it worthwhile to produce manufacturing goods at the core (which thus gets all the economies of scale) and export them to the periphery, which specialises in agriculture.

Liberally interpreted, this view suggests the following: within the EU there is a core around Germany which encompasses France, the UK and the Benelux countries and which may be extending into Southern Europe. The Central European countries which are very close to the core might benefit from the proximity of the core and may ultimately become part of it. However, the countries further away might fall into the category where transportation costs are just high enough to induce manufacturing firms to locate in the core rather than in the

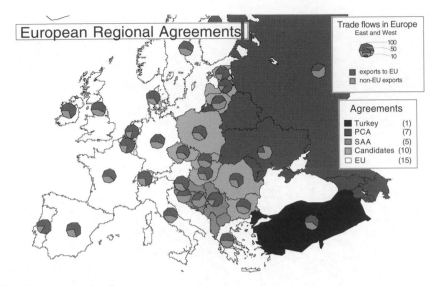

**Figure 11.3** European regional agreements

periphery. Only the Asian regions of Russia (not shown on the map) might be sufficiently far away to make it worthwhile to locate some manufacturing activities there because transportation costs are too high.

We showed in chapter 9 that the radical shift in trade patterns predicted by gravity models has already taken place in the case of the Central European countries. This is not the case for CIS and SEE countries. But, even if they fully seized their structural potential by 2010, they would still represent Europe's periphery. This core–periphery pattern is likely to become a long-run equilibrium.

Figure 11.3 shows the different trade arrangements of the EU and the trade flows. It is important that the European trade policy should not be limited to membership. Free trade arrangements are a boost for CIS and Balkan countries and should be on the EU political agenda.

Free trade from the Atlantic to the Pacific would make the EU the hub of attraction for a much larger area. For the countries of the former Soviet Union it will take longer to close the gap with the Union and most likely this will never happen. But the continental geographical arrangements would be such as to provide the most favourable environment.

The gravity index has been used so far for foreign trade relations. Inspection of its definition in box 11.1 suggests another interpretation: countries close to each other, with comparable incomes, are likely to share the same history and culture (closeness) and operate similar economies (income). Indeed, all rich industrial countries trust in private property, market-based decisions and an efficient public sector. GDP is thus highly correlated with the institutional build-up of a market economy. Therefore, countries in, or close to, the core on the basis of the gravity indicator are the obvious candidates for EU membership. Membership itself, of course, biases the index upwards. Inspection of figure 11.2 from this perspective paints a clear picture. Switzerland would be a perfect EU member. The

FSU countries are too poor and too far away. The CEEC-10 have many more 'membership qualities', which is what allowed them to be the first to graduate from transition.

## Notes

1. See, for example, Sachs and Warner (1995) and, for an application to transition countries, Gylfason (2000).
2. Bismarck already emphasised the importance of geography 'as the only stable factor in external relations'. Of course, measurement is a different matter. Transport costs are not always strongly correlated with distances: transport from Tokyo to San Francisco is much cheaper than from one side of the Himalayas to the other. Nevertheless it is preferable to use an imperfect proxy variable than to neglect geography.
3. Gravity indexes were computed for all European countries, even for those not shown in table 11.3. Indexes were regrouped into six classes (the five groups of table 11.3 plus the rest of the world), to which correspond six colour shades.

# References

Aganbegian, A.G. (1989) *Inside Perestroïka*, Harper and Row, New York

Aitken, N.D. (1973) The Effect of EEC and EFTA on European trade: a temporal cross-section analysis, *American Economic Review*, 63 (5), pp. 881–92

Akerlof, G., Rose, A., Yellen, J. and Hessenius, H. (1991) East Germany in from the cold: the economic aftermath of currency union, *Brookings Papers on Economic Activity*, 1, pp. 1–87

Alesina, A. and Drazen, A. (1991) Why are stabilizations delayed?, *American Economic Review*, 81 (5), pp. 1170–88

Amalrik, A. (1970) *Will the Soviet Union Survive until 1984?*, Harper and Row, New York

Aoki, M. (ed.) (1984) *The Economic Analysis of the Japanese Firm*, North-Holland, New York

Arrow, K.J. (1987) Rationality of self and others in an economic system, in Hogarth, R.M. and Rider, M.W. (eds.), *Rational Choice: The Contrast Between Economics and Psychology*, University of Chicago Press, Chicago, pp. 201–15

Artus, P. (1991) Réunification allemande, dynamique et contraintes: un cadre d'analyse, Caisse des dépôts et consignation, Paris, January

Aslund, A. (ed.) (1994) *Economic Transformation in Russia*, Pinter, London

Balassa, B. (1975) Trade creation and diversion in the European Common Market, in Balassa, B. (ed.) *European Economic Integration*, North-Holland, Amsterdam, pp. 79–118

Balassa, B. and Bauwens, L. (1988) *Changing Trade Patterns in Manufactured Goods: An Econometric Investigation*, North-Holland, Amsterdam

Baldwin, R.E. (1994) *Towards an Integrated Europe*, Centre for Economic Policy Research, London

Baldwin, R.E., François, J. and Portes, R. (1997) The costs and benefits of eastern enlargement: the impact on the EU and Central Europe, *Economic Policy*, 24, pp. 127–76

Barbone, L. and Zalduendo, J. (1996) EU accession and economic growth: the challenge for Central and Eastern European countries, World Bank Policy Research Working Paper No. 1721

Barro, R.J. (1996) Democracy and Growth, *Journal of Economic Growth* 1 (1), pp. 1–27

Begg, D. and Portes, R. (1992) Eastern Germany since unification: wage subsidies remain a better way, CEPR Discussion Paper No. 730

— (1993) Enterprise debt and economic transformation: financial restructuring in Central and Eastern Europe, *European Economic Review*, 37, pp. 396–407

Bennett, J. and Dixon, H.D. (1993) Macroeconomic equilibrium and reform in a transitional economy, CEPR Discussion Paper No. 758

Berg, A. and Blanchard, O. (1994) Stabilisation and transition in Poland 1990–1991, in Blanchard, O., Froot, K. and Sachs, J. (eds.), *The Transition in Eastern Europe*, Chicago: National Bureau for Economic Research and University of Chicago Press, pp. 51–92

Bergson, A. (1961) *The Real National Income of Soviet Russia Since 1928*, Harvard University Press, Cambridge, MA

(1984) Income inequality under Soviet socialism, *Journal of Economic Literature*, 22 (3), pp. 1052–99

(1991) The USSR before the fall: how poor and why? *Economic Perspectives*, 5 (4), pp. 29–44

Berliner, J.S. (1966) The economics of overtaking and surpassing, in Rosovsky, H. (ed.), *Industrialization in Two Systems: Essays in Honor of Alexander Gerschenkron*, Wiley, New York, pp. 159–85

Bernstein, E. (1899) *Die Voraussetzungen des Sozialismus und die Aufgaben der Sozialdemokratie*, J.H.W. Dietz, Stuttgart

Blanchard, O., Dornbusch, R., Krugman, P., Layard, R. and Summers, L. (1990) *Reform in Eastern Europe*, Report of the WIDER World Economy Group, MIT Press, Cambridge, MA

Bofinger, P. and Gros, D. (1992) A multilateral payments union for the Commonwealth of Independent States: why and how? CEPR Discussion Paper No. 654

Boltho, A., Carlin, W. and Scramozzino, P. (1996) Will East Germany become a new Mezzogiorno? CEPR Discussion Paper No. 1256

Boycko, M., Shleifer, A. and Vishny, R. (1996) *Privatising Russia*, MIT Press, Cambridge, MA

Brada, J.C. and Graves, R.L. (1988) Slowdown in Soviet defence expenditures, *Southern Economic Journal*, 54, pp. 969–84

Braguinsky, S. and Yavlinsky, G. (2000) *Incentives and Institutions*, Princeton University Press, Princeton, NJ

Breach, A. (2000) Russia: an anatomy of adolescent capitalism, Global Economics Paper No. 54, Goldman Sachs, October

Brenton, P. (1999) *Trade and Investment in Europe: The Impact of the Next Enlargement*, Centre for European Policy Studies (CEPS), Brussels

Brenton, P. and Kendall, T. (1994) *Back to Earth with the Gravity Model: Further Estimates for Eastern European Countries*, Centre for European Policy Studies (CEPS), Brussels

Brenton, P. and Manchin, M. (2002) 'Making EU trade agreements work: the role of rules of origin', CEPS Working Document No. 183

Brunetti, A., Kisunko, G. and Weder, B. (1998) How businesses see government: responses from private sector surveys in 69 countries, World Bank IFC Discussion Paper No. 33

Calvo, G. (1999) On Dollarization, draft, University of Maryland

Calvo, G.A. and Coricelli, F. (1993) Output collapse in Eastern Europe, *IMF Staff Papers*, 40 (1), pp. 32–52

Calvo, G.A. and Frenkel, J.A. (1991) Credit markets, credibility and economic transformation, *Journal of Economic Perspectives*, 5 (4), pp. 139–48

Canning, D. (1999) Infrastructure's contribution to aggregate output, World Bank Policy Research Paper No. 2246

Carrère d'Encausse, H. (1991) *La gloire des nations ou la fin de l'Empire soviétique*, Fayard, Paris

Chenery, H.B. (1960) Patterns of industrial growth, *American Economic Review*, 50, pp. 624–41

CIA (various years) *Handbook of Economic Statistics*, US Government Printing Office, Washington, DC

Coase, R.H. (1937) The nature of the firm, *Economica*, 4 (16), pp. 386–405

Cohen, B. (1998) *The Geography of Money*, Cornell University Press, Ithaca

Collins, S.M. and Rodrik, D. (1991) *Eastern Europe and the Soviet Union in the World Economy*, Institute for International Economics, Washington, DC

Commander, S. and Mumsen, C. (1999) Understanding barter in Russia, EBRD Working Paper No. 37

Commission of the European Communities (1988) The economies of 1992: an assessment of the potential economic effects of completing the internal market of the European economy, *European Economy*, 35

(1990a) One market, one money. An evaluation of the potential benefits and costs of forming an economic and monetary union, *European Economy*, 44, p. 347

(1990b) Stabilisation, liberalisation and devolution: assessment of the economic situation and reform process in the Soviet Union, *European Economy*, 45, p. 187

Cottarelli, C. and Blejer, M.I. (1992) Forced saving and repressed inflation in the Soviet Union, 1986–90, *IMF Staff Papers*, 39 (2), pp. 256–86

Courtois, S. et al. (1997) *Le livre noir du communisme*, Paris: Ed. Robert Laffont

Dabla-Norris, E. and S. Freeman (1999) The enforcement of property rights and underdevelopment, IMF Working Paper No. WP/99/127

Daskalov, S. and Nicholay, M. with Gros, D., Brenton, P., Emerson, M. and Whyte, N. (2000) A comprehensive trade policy plan for the western Balkans, Centre for European Policy Studies and European Institute (Sofia), CEPS Working Document No. 146

Davis, J., Ossowski, R., Richardson, T. and Barnett, S. (2000) *Fiscal and Macroeconomic Impact of Privatization*, IMF Occasional Paper No. 194

De Benedictis, L. and Padoan, P.L. (1994) The integration of Eastern Europe into the EC: a club-theory interest groups approach, in Lombardini, S. and Padoan, P.L. (eds.), *Europe between East and South*, Kluwer Academic, Dordrecht, pp. 9–35

De Melo, M., Denizer, C. and Gelb, A. (1996) Patterns of transition from plan to market, *World Bank Economic Review*, 10 (3), pp. 397–424

De Melo, M., Denizer, C., Gelb, A. and Tenev, S. (1997) Circumstances and choice: the role of initial conditions and policies in transition economies, World Bank Research Paper

De Melo, J. and Panagariya, A. (eds.) (1993) *New Dimensions in Regional Integration*, Cambridge University Press, Cambridge

De Nicola, C. and Gros, D. (1994) The Efficiency of Emerging Foreign Exchange Markets: The Case of the Rouble/Dollar Rate, Centre for European Policy Studies (CEPS), Brussels

Decaluwe, B. and Steinherr, A. (1976) A portfolio balance model for the two-tier exchange market, *Economica*, 43, pp. 111–25

Denizer, C. (1997) Stabilization, adjustment and growth prospects in transition economies, World Bank Policy Research Working Paper No. 1855

Desai, P. (1986) *The Soviet Economy: Efficiency, Technical Change and Growth Retardation*, Blackwell, Oxford

Dewatripont, M. and Tirole, J. (1993) Efficient governance structure: implications for banking regulation, in Mayer, C. and Vives, X. (eds.), *Capital Markets and Financial Intermediation*, Cambridge University Press, Cambridge, pp. 12–35

Dixit, A. (1989) Entry and exit decisions under fluctuating exchange rates, *Journal of Political Economy*, 97 (3), pp. 620–38

Dobb, M.H. (1939) *Political Economy and Capitalism*, International Publishers, New York

(1966) *Soviet Economic Development since 1917*, Routledge and Kegan Paul, London

Döhrn, R. and Heilemann, U. (1991) Sectoral change in Eastern Europe: the Chenery hypothesis reconsidered, Rheinisch-Westfälisches Institut für Wirtschaftsforschung, Essen, RWI Paper No. 25

Dooley, M. (2000) A model of crises in emerging markets, *Economic Journal*, 110, pp. 256–72

Dornbusch, R. (1980) Employment, the trade balance and relative prices, in Dornbusch R., *Open Economy Macroeconomics*, Basic Books, New York, pp. 33–56

Dornbusch, R. and Fischer, S. (1981) *Macroeconomics*, McGraw-Hill, Singapore

Dornbusch, R. and Wolf, H. (1990) Monetary overhang and reforms in the 1940s, NBER Working Paper No. 3456

(1992) Economic transition in eastern Germany, *Brookings Papers on Economic Activity*, 1, pp. 235–72

Duchene, G. and Gros, D. (1994) *Cases of Output Decline in Reforming Economies*, Centre for European Policy Studies (CEPS), Brussels

Easterly, W. (1993) How much do distortions affect growth? *Journal of Monetary Economics*, 32 (2), pp. 187–212

(1999) Life during growth: international evidence on quality of life and per capita income, World Bank Policy Research Working Paper No. 2110

Easterly, W. and Fischer, S. (1994) The Soviet economic decline: historical and republican data, NBER Working Paper No. 4735

EBRD (various issues) *Transition Report*, European Bank for Reconstruction and Development, London

Eckaus, R.S. (1990) Some lessons for development economics for Southern and Eastern Europe, draft, MIT

Eichengreen, B. (1993) A payments mechanism for the former Soviet Union: is the EPU a relevant precedent?, CEPR Discussion Paper No. 824

Emerson, M., Gros, D., Italianer, A., Pisani-Ferry, J. and Reichenbach, H. (1992) *One Market, One Money. An Evaluation of the Potential Benefits and Costs of Forming an Economic and Monetary Union*, Oxford University Press, Oxford

Ericson, R.E. and Ickes, B.W. (2000) A model of Russia's 'virtual economy', Bank of Finland, BOFIT Discussion Paper No. 10/2000

*European Economy* (1996) Economic Evaluation of the Internal Market, *European Economy*, 4

Fama, E.F. (1990) Banking in the theory of finance, in Mayer, T. (ed.), *Monetary Theory*, Gower, Aldershot

Feshbach, M. and Friendly, A. (1992) *Ecocide in the USSR*, Basic Books, New York

Fidrmuc, J. (2001) Democracy in transition economies: grease or sand in the wheels of growth?, *EIB Papers*, 6 (2), pp. 24–40

Finger, J.M. and Kreinin, M.E. (1979) A measure of 'export similarity' and its possible uses, *Economic Journal*, 89, pp. 905–12

Fischer, S. (1982) Seigniorage and the case for a national money, *Journal of Political Economy*, 90 (2), pp. 295–313

Fischer, S. and Gelb, A. (1991) The process of socialist economic transformation, *Journal of Economic Perspectives*, 5 (4), pp. 91–105

Fischer, S. and Sahay, R. (2000) Macroeconomic performance in transition economies, Paper presented at the AEA conference, New York

Fischer, S., Sahay, R. and Vegh, C.A. (1997) From transition to market: evidence and growth prospects, in Zecchini, S. (ed.), *Lessons from the Economic Transition: Central and Eastern Europe in the 1990s*, Kluwer Academic, Dordrecht, pp. 79–101

(1998) How far is Eastern Europe from Brussels?, IMF Working Paper No. 98/53

Frankel, J. and Rose, A.K. (2000) Estimate of the effect of currency unions on trade and output, CEPR Discussion Paper, No. 2631

Frydman, R. and Rapaczynski, A. (1991) Markets and institutions in large-scale privatisation: an approach to economic and social transformation in eastern Europe, in Corbo, V., Coricelli, F. and Bossak, J. (eds.), *Reforming Central and Eastern European Economies*, World Bank, Washington, DC, pp, 253–74

Gaddy, C. and Ickes, B. (1999) A simple four-sector model of Russia's 'virtual' economy, *Post-Soviet Geography and Economics*, 40 (2), pp. 79–97

Gaidar, Y. (1999) Lessons of the Russian crisis for transition economics, *Finance and Development*, 36 (2), pp. 6–8

Gallup, J.L., Sachs, J. and Mellinger, A. (1997) Geography and economic development: some empirical findings, *International Science Review*, 22 (2), pp. 179–232

Gerschenkron, A. (1962) *Economic Backwardness in Historical Perspective*, Harvard University Press, Cambridge, MA

Glick, R. and Rose, A. (2002) Does a currency union affect trade? The time-series evidence, *European Economic Review*, 46 (6), pp. 1125–51

Goldman, M. (1983) *USSR in Crisis. The Failure of an Economic System*, Norton, New York
(1991) *What Went Wrong with Perestroika?*, Norton, New York

Gomulka, S. (1986) *Growth, Innovation and Reform in Eastern Europe*, University of Wisconsin Press, Madison

Gray, D. (1995) Reforming the energy sector in transition economies: selected experiences and lessons, World Bank Discussion Paper No. 296
(1998) Evaluation of taxes and revenues from the energy sector in the Baltics, Russia, and other former Soviet Union countries, IMF Working Paper No. WP/98/34

Gregory, P.R. and Stuart, R.C. (1986) *Soviet Economic Structure and Performance*, Harper and Row, New York
(1989) *Comparative Economic Systems*, 3rd edn, Houghton Mifflin, Boston

Griffith, K. and Gurley, J. (1985) Radical analyses of imperialism, the Third World and the transition to socialism, *Journal of Economic Literature*, 23 (3), pp. 1089–143

Gros, D. (1988) Dual exchange rates in the presence of incomplete market separation: long run ineffectiveness and implications for monetary policy, *IMF Staff Papers*, 535 (3), pp. 437–60
(1991) A Soviet payments union?, CEPS Working Document No. 58
(1993) Bilateralism versus multilateralism in the FSU: What is the potential gain from the ISB?, manuscript, CEPS, May
(1996) Self-fulfilling public debt crises, CEPS Working Document No. 102

Gros, D., Castelli, M., Jimeno, J., Mayer, T. and Thygesen, N. (2002) *The Euro at 25*, Special Report of the CEPS Macroeconomic Policy Group, CEPS, Brussels

Gros, D. and Dautrebande, B. (1992a) Did Soviet planners follow the rules of the market after all?, manuscript, CEPS, March
(1992b) International trade of former republics in the long run: an analysis based on the 'gravity' approach, CEPS Working Document No. 71

Gros, D. with Duchene, G., Hager, W., Najman, B. and Schobert, F. (1999) Notes on the economy of Montenegro, CEPS Working Document No. 142

Gros, D. and Gonciarz, G. (1994) A note on the trade potential of Central and Eastern Europe, manuscript, CEPS, November

Gros, D. and Jones, E. (1991) Price reform and energy markets in the Soviet Union and central Europe, CEPS Working Document No. 57

Gros, D. and Steinherr, A. (1990) Currency union and economic reform in the GDR: a comprehensive one-step approach, CEPS Working Document No. 49
(1991a) Economic reform in the Soviet Union: pas-de-deux between disintegration and macroeconomic destabilisation, *Princeton Studies in International Finance*, 71, pp. 1–73
(1991b) Einigkeit macht stark – the Deutsche mark also?, in O'Brien, R. (ed.), *Finance and the International Economy: 5*, Oxford University Press, Oxford, pp. 52–67
(1992) *Redesigning Economic Geography after the Fall of the Soviet Empire*, Centre for European Policy Studies (CEPS), Brussels
(1995) *Winds of Change: Economic Transition in Central and Eastern Europe*, Addison Wesley Longman, London

Gros, D. and Thygesen, N. (1999) *European Monetary Integration*, Addison Wesley Longman, London

Gros, D. and Vandille, G. (1994) Seigniorage in economies in transition, draft, CEPS, July
(1997) Output decline and recovery in the transition economies: causes and social consequences, *Economics of Transition*, 5 (1), pp. 113–30

Grossmann, H. (1929) Die Änderung des ursprünglichen Aufbauplans des Marxschen 'Kapital' und ihre Ursachen, *Archiv für die Geschichte des Sozialismus und der Arbeiterbewegung*, 14 (2), pp. 305–8

Gylfason, T. (2000) Resources, agriculture and economic growth in economies in transition, CESifo Working Paper No. 313

Hamilton, C.B. and Winters, L.A. (1992) Opening up international trade with Eastern Europe, *Economic Policy*, 14, pp. 77–116

Havrylyshyn, O., Izvorski, I. and van Rooden, R. (1998) Recovery and growth in transition economies 1990–97: a stylized regression analysis, IMF Working Paper No. WP/98/141

Havrylyshyn, O. and Pritchett, L. (1991) European trade patterns after the transition, World Bank Working Paper No. 748

Havrylyshyn, O. and Wolf, T. (1999) 'Determinants of growth in transition countries', *Finance and Development*, 36 (2), pp. 12–15

Helpman, E. and Krugman, P. (1985) *Market Structure and Foreign Trade: Increasing Returns, Imperfect Competition, and the International Economy*, MIT Press, Cambridge, MA

Hirschman, A.O. (1958) *The Strategy of Economic Development*, Yale University Press, New Haven

Hoffmann, L., Bofinger, P., Flassbeck, H. and Steinherr, A. (2000) *Independent Advisers and the IMF: Kazakstan 1993–2000*, Physica Verlag, Berlin

Hughes, G. and Hare, P. (1992a) Industrial policy and restructuring in Eastern Europe, CEPR Discussion Paper No. 653

(1992b) Trade policy and restructuring in Eastern Europe, in Fleming, J. and Rollo, J. (eds.), *Trade, Payments and Adjustment in Central and Eastern Europe*, Royal Institute of International Affairs, London

Hughes Hallett, A.J. and Ma, Y. (1994) Real adjustment in a union of incompletely converged economies: an example from East and West Germany, *European Economic Review*, 38, pp. 1731–61

Ingram, G.K. and Li, Z. (1997) Motorization and road provision in countries and cities, World Bank Policy Research Paper No. 1842

International Monetary Fund (1990) German unification: economic issues, IMF Occasional Paper No. 75

(1999) Monetary policy in dollarized economies, IMF Occasional Paper No. 171

(various years) *International Financial Statistics*, IMF, Washington, DC

International Monetary Fund, World Bank, Organisation for Economic Cooperation and Development and European Bank for Reconstruction and Development (1991) *A Study of the Soviet Economy*, Organisation for Economic Cooperation and Development, Paris

Jensen, M.C. (1988) Takeovers: their cause and consequences, *Journal of Economic Perspectives*, 2 (1), pp. 21–48

Johnson, S., McMillan, J. and Woodruff, C. (1999) Property rights, finance and enterpreneurship, mimeo, MIT

Judy, R. and Clough, R. (1989) Soviet computer software and applications in the 1980s, Hudson Institute Working Paper No. H1-4090-P

Kaplan, J.J. and Schleiminger, G. (1989) *The European Payments Union: Financial Diplomacy in the 1950s*, Clarendon Press, Oxford

Kautsky, K. (1902) *Krisentheorien*, Berlin; also in *Die Neue Zeit*, 20 (2) (1901–2), ss. 37–47, 76–81, 110–18, 133–43

Kellogg, R.L. (1989) Inflation in Soviet investment and capital stock data and its impact on measurement of total factor productivity, CIA Office of Soviet Analysis, Washington, DC

Keynes, J.M. (1975) A short view of Russia, in *Essays in Persuasion, The Collected Writings of John Maynard Keynes*, vol. 9, Macmillan, London

Klodt, H.P. (1999) Industrial Policy and the East German Productivity Puzzle, CESifo, November

Knack, S. and Keefer, P. (1995) Institutions and economic performance: cross-country tests using alternative institutional measures, *Economics and Politics*, 7, pp. 207–27

Knaster, B. (1997) European agricultural policy: between enlargement and reform, CEPS Working Party Report

Koen, V. and Phillips, S. (1993) Price liberalisation in Russia, IMF Occasional Paper No. 104

Komulainen, T. (1999) Currency crisis theories – some explanations for the Russian case, Discussion Paper No. 58, University of Potsdam

Konovalov, V. (1994) Russian trade policy, in Tarr, D. (ed.), *Trade in New Independent States*, World Bank, Washington, DC

Kornai, J. (1992) *The Socialist System – The Political Economy of Communism*, Princeton University Press, Princeton, NJ

Krkoska, L. (1999) A neoclassical growth model applied to transition in central Europe, *Journal of Comparative Economics*, 27, pp. 259–80

Krugman, P. (1991a) Increasing returns and economic geography, *Journal of Political Economy*, 99 (3), pp. 483–99

(1991b) The move to free trade zones, *Federal Reserve Bank of Kansas City Economic Review*, 76 (6), pp. 5–25

(1993) Regionalism versus multilateralism: analytical notes, in De Melo and Panangariya, pp. 58–78

Lawrence, R.Z. (1991) Emerging regional arrangements: building blocks or stumbling blocks?, in O'Brien, R. (ed.), *Finance and the International Economy: 5*, Oxford University Press, Oxford, pp. 23–35

Layard, R. and Parker, J. (1996) *The Coming Russian Boom*, Free Press, New York

Leite, C. and Weidmann, J. (1999) Does Mother Nature corrupt? Natural resources, corruption and economic growth, IMF Working Paper No. WP/99/85

Lerner, A.P. (1936) The symmetry between import and export taxes, *Economica*, 3, pp. 306–13

Levine, R. (1997) Financial development and economic growth: views and agenda, *Journal of Economic Literature*, 35, pp. 688–726

Levine, R. and Renelt, D. (1992) A sensitivity analysis of cross-country growth regressions, *American Economic Review*, 82, pp. 924–63

Lipton, D. (1990) Privatization in Eastern Europe: the case of Poland, *Brookings Papers on Economic Activity*, 2, pp. 293–333

Lipton, D. and Sachs, J. (1990) Creating a market economy in Eastern Europe: the case of Poland, *Brooking Papers on Economic Activity*, 1, pp. 75–133

(1992) Prospects for Russia's economic reforms, *Brookings Papers on Economic Activity*, 2, pp. 213–65

Lopez-Claros, A. and Alexashenko, S.V. (1998) Fiscal policy issues during the transition in Russia, IMF Occasional Paper No. 155

Luxemburg, R. (1922) *Die Akkumulation des Kapitals. Ein Beitrag zur ökonomischen Erklärung des Imperialismus*, Vereinigung Internationaler Verlags-Anstalten, Berlin

MacKibbin, W. (1990) Some global macroeconomic implications of German unification, Brookings Discussion Papers in International Economics No. 81

Marx, K. (1933 [1867–1905]) *Capital*, 3 vols., Charles Kerr, Chicago

Marx, K. and Engels, F. (1930 [1848]) *The Communist Manifesto*, M. Lawrence, London

Mayhew, A. (1998) *Recreating Europe*, Cambridge University Press, Cambridge

McKinnon, R.I. (1991) *The Order of Economic Liberalisation: Financial Control in the Transition to a Market Economy*, Johns Hopkins University Press, Baltimore

Mendoza, E. (2000) On the benefits of dollarization when stabilization policy is not credible and financial markets are imperfect, NBER Working Paper No. 7824

Möbius, U. and Schumacher, D. (1990) Eastern Europe and the European Community: trade relations and trade policy with regard to industrial products, paper prepared for the Joint Canada Germany Symposium, Toronto, November

Moreno-Villalaz, J.-L. (1999) Lessons from the monetary experience of Panama: a dollar economy with financial integration, *Cato Journal*, 18 (3), pp. 421–39

Newbery, D.M. (1991) Reform in Hungary: sequencing and privatisation, *European Economic Review* 35, pp. 571–80

North, D.C. (1990) *Institution, Institutional Change and Economic Performance*, Cambridge University Press, Cambridge

(1993) The paradox of the West, Economics Working Paper Archive, Washington University-St. Louis, MO

Nove, A. (1969) *An Economic History of the USSR*, Penguin, London

Nuti, M.D. (1986) Hidden and repressed inflation in Soviet-type economies: definitions, measurements and stabilization, *Contributions to Political Economy*, 5, pp. 37–82

OECD (1997) Russian Federation, OECD Economic Survey

(2000) Russian Federation, OECD Economic Survey

Ofer, G. (1987) Soviet economic growth: 1928–1985, *Journal of Economic Literature*, 25 (4), pp. 1767–833

Perotti, E. (1999) Banking regulation under extreme legal underdevelopment: lessons from the Russian meltdown, mimeo, University of Amsterdam

Petith, H. (1977) European integration and the terms of trade, *Economic Journal*, 87, pp. 262–72

Pinto, B., Belka, M. and Krajewski, S. (1993) Transforming state enterprises in Poland: evidence on adjustment by manufacturing firms, *Brookings Papers on Economic Activity*, 1, pp. 213–62

Powell, R.P. (1968) The Soviet capital stock and related statistical series for the war years, The Economic Growth Centre, Yale University, New Haven

Pritchett, L. and Summers, L. (1996) Healthier is wealthier, Journal of Human Resources, 31 (4), pp. 841–68

Qian, Y. and Roland, G. (1994) Regional decentralisation and the soft budget constraint: the case of China, CEPR Discussion Paper No. 1013

Quehenberger, M. (2000) Ten years after: East Germany's convergence, unpublished manuscript, European Investment Bank

Querioz, C. and Gautman, S. (1992) Road infrastructure and economic development: some diagnostic indicators, World Bank Policy Research Working Paper No. 921

Rautava, J. (2002) The role of oil prices and the real exchange rate in Russia's economy, Bank Of Finland, BOFIT Discussion Paper No. 3/2002

Ricardo, D. (1887) *Principles of Political Economy and Taxation*, G. Bell and Sons, London

Riphahn, R.T., Snower, D.J. and Zimmermann, K.F. (2000) *Employment Policy in Transition*, Springer Verlag, Berlin

Roland, G. (2000) *Transition and Economics: Policies, Markets and Firms*, MIT Press, Cambridge, MA

Rollo, J. (1992) *Association Agreements Between the EC and CSFR, Hungary and Poland: a Half Empty Glass?*, Royal Institute of International Affairs, London

Rosati, D. (1994) Output decline during transition from plan to market, *Economies of Transition*, 2 (4), pp. 419–42

Rostow, W.W. (1960) *The Stages of Economic Growth*, Cambridge University Press, Cambridge

Rostowski, J. (1993) The inter-enterprise debt explosion in the former Soviet Union: causes, consequences, cures, CEPR Discussion Paper No. 142

*Russian Economic Trends* (various years) Centre for Economic Reform, Government of the Russian Federation, Whurr Publishers, London

Sachs, J. (1993) *Poland's Jump to the Market Economy*, MIT Press, Cambridge, MA
   (1994) Russia's struggle with stabilization: conceptual issues and evidence, Paper presented at the Annual World Bank Conference on Development Economics, Washington, DC, 28 April
Sachs, J. and Warner, A. (1995) Natural resources abundance and economic growth, NBER Working Paper No. 5398
Sah, R. and Stiglitz, J.E. (1992) *Peasants versus City-dwellers*, Clarendon Press, Oxford
Sapir, A. (1992) Regional integration in Europe, Economic Papers of the Commission of the EC, No. 94, Brussels
   (2000) Trade regionalism in Europe: towards an integrated approach, *Journal of Common Market Studies*, 38, pp. 151–62
Seitz, H. (1999) Where have all the flowers gone? Die öffentlichen Finanzen in den neuen Ländernen, *IFO Schnelldienst*, 32–3, pp. 26–34
Shleifer, A. (1998) Government in transition, *European Economic Review*, 41 (3–5), pp. 385–410
Shleifer, A. and Treisman, D. (2000) *Without a Map*, MIT Press, Cambridge, MA
Shleifer, A. and Vishny, R. (1986) Large shareholders and corporate control, *Journal of Political Economy*, 94 (3), pp. 461–88
Sinn, G. and Sinn, H.-W. (1991) *Kaltstart*, J.C.B. Mohr (Paul Siebeck), Tübingen
Sinn, H.-W. (2000) Germany's economic unification: an assessment after ten years, CESifo Working Paper No. 247
Smith, R.C. and Walter, I. (1993) Banking industry linkages: models for Eastern European economic restructuring, in Fair, D. and Raymond, A.J. (eds.), *The New Europe: Evolving Economic and Financial Systems in East and West*, Kluwer Academic, Dordrecht, pp. 41–60
Snoy, B. (2000) The Russian financial crisis and the pitfalls in the Transition Process, mimeo, EBRD
Sommariva, A. and Tullio, G. (1987) *German Macroeconomic History 1880–1979: A Study of the Effects of Economic Policy on Inflation, Currency Depreciation and Growth*, Macmillan, London
Steinberg, D. (1987) Estimating total Soviet military expenditures: an alternative approach based on reconstructed Soviet national accounts, in Jacobsen, C.G. (ed.), *The Soviet Defence Enigma: Estimating Costs and Burdens*, Oxford University Press, New York, pp. 27–57
Steinherr, A. (2000a) Which reforms will be necessary following eastern enlargement?, Working Paper No. 6, Free University of Bozen-Bolzano
   (2000b) *Derivatives: The Wild Beast of Finance*, Wiley, London
Steinherr, A. and Huveneers, C. (1992) Universal banking in the integrated European market place, in Steinherr, A. (ed.), *The New European Financial Market Place*, Longman, London, pp. 49–67
   (1993) On the performance of differently regulated financial institutions: some empirical evidence, *Journal of Banking and Finance*, 18, pp. 271–306
Stiglitz, J.E. (1987) The causes and consequences of the dependence of quality on price, *Journal of Economic Literature*, 25 (1), pp. 1–48
Streeten, P. (1959) Unbalanced growth, *Oxford Economic Papers*, new series, 11 (2), pp. 167–90
Suhrcke, M. (1999) Economic growth in the transition economies of Central and Eastern Europe, PhD thesis, Hamburg University
Sweezy, P.M. (1942) *The Theory of Capitalist Development*, Modern Reader, New York
Tugan-Baranowsky, M. (1901) *Studien zur Theorie und Geschichte der Handelskrisen in England*, G. Fischer, Jena
Tullio, G., Steinherr, A. and Buscher, H. (1994) German wage and price inflation after unification, in De Grauwe, P., Micossi, S. and Tullio, G. (eds.), *Inflation and Wage Behaviour in the EMS*, Oxford University Press, Oxford, pp. 13–29
United Nations (1990) *Economic Survey of Europe 1969–1990*, UN, New York
US Department of the Treasury (1991) Modernizing the financial system: recommendations for safer, more competitive banks, Washington, DC, 5 February
Vickers, J. and Yarrow, G. (1988) *Privatisation – An Economic Analysis*, MIT Press, Cambridge, MA

Wang, Z.K. and Winters, A. (1991) The trading potential of Eastern Europe, CEPR Discussion Paper No. 610

Werth, N. (1990) *Histoire de L'Union Soviétique*, PuF, Paris

(1993) Goulag, les vrais chiffres, *L'Histoire*, 169, pp. 38–51

World Bank (various issues) *World Development Report*, Oxford University Press, Oxford

Wyplosz, C. (1991) On the real exchange rate effect of German unification, *Weltwirtschaftliches Archiv*, 127, pp. 1–17

Zveteremich, P. (1988) *Il grande Parvus*, Garzanti, Milan

# Index